HOW DEVELOPING COUNTRIES TRADE

The Institutional Constraints

Sheila Page

London and New York

First published 1994
by Routledge
11 New Fetter Lane, London EC4P 4EE

Simultaneously published in the USA and Canada
by Routledge
29 West 35th Street, New York, NY 10001

© 1994 Overseas Development Institute

Typeset in Garamond by
Florencetype Ltd, Stoodleigh, Devon

Printed and bound in Great Britain by
Mackays of Chatham PLC, Chatham, Kent

British Library Cataloguing in Publication Data
A catalogue record for this book is available from the British Library

Library of Congress Cataloging in Publication Data
A catalogue record for this book has been requested

ISBN 0–415–11777–1
0–415–11778–X (pbk)

HOW DEVELOPING COUNTRIES TRADE

During the last two decades there have been major changes in the world trading system, many of which have had a dramatic impact on developing countries. Non-tariff barriers, intra-firm trade, regional blocs, tied and trade-related aid: these with other changes in the way private and public institutions intervene in market-based trade have joined the traditional concerns; commodity cartels, tariffs, agricultural policy, and exchange rate policy. In the last fifteen years increases in both private and public forms of intervention in trade have been large and persistent enough to have had an effect on total development performance and on individual sectors. In contrast, the trading system among industrial countries is now one of low tariffs and few controls.

This book brings together what is known about each type of intervention to understand better the nature of the trading system facing developing countries, in general and for particular countries and sectors. It considers how changes in the countries which are their markets have an effect on the domestic economies of developing countries and how they might alter the pace and nature of their development in the long run. Do they undermine the potential trade benefits? What is the appropriate policy response?

The book shows that the changes have had a profound effect not only on countries' trade strategies, but also on their choice between industry and raw materials, among industries, and between a broad and more concentrated pattern of development. Case studies of countries in Africa, Asia and Latin America show that there have been sharp differences among countries affected by these changes with the poorest and least powerful most dis-advantaged. But there are also differences which depend on how actively the countries have attempted to manage their response to these external constraints. The increasing roles of government policy and of large private firms in international trade have meant a corresponding increase in the potential for an active trade and investment policy in countries facing markets in which intervention and bargaining are reducing the role for markets and economic choices.

CONTENTS

CONTENTS

TABLES

THE RISK OF DISTORTED DEVELOPMENT

TARIFFS AND PREFERENCES

NON-TARIFF BARRIERS

COUNTERTRADE

OTHER OFFICIAL CONTROLS AFFECTING DEVELOPING COUNTRY TRADE

FOREIGN INVESTMENT

THE WORLD TRADING SYSTEM VIEWED FROM DEVELOPING COUNTRIES

MALAYSIA

THAILAND

COLOMBIA

ZIMBABWE

MAURITIUS

JAMAICA

BANGLADESH

ACKNOWLEDGEMENTS

During the research for this I have had advice and comments from too many individuals in academic research, governments, international organisations and industry for me to be able to include all of them, and in many cases they would be unwilling to be named. I hope that I have thanked all individually, and I am particularly grateful to the exporters and trade officials in the countries which are the subject of the case studies for their information about how they traded, and also for their comments on the more general issues raised. The discussions which I had with them contributed greatly to the conclusions.

UNCTAD were generous in supplying data from their Data Base on Trade Control Measures, and advice on how this could be used. In many cases the governments of the countries included and industry associations gave me additional unpublished data, and I have indicated these in the country chapters, but many other officials and researchers also supplied background reports.

I am grateful for financial support for the research to the Economic and Social Research Committee of the Overseas Development Administration. Margaret Cornell edited the text and compiled the index with her customary care and insights.

None of these is responsible for any of the views expressed here.

1

THE RISK OF
DISTORTED DEVELOPMENT
Trade, industrialisation and other countries' policies

Begin history this way

DOES POLICY MATTER?

Analyses of the progress of developing countries and their trade in the 1980s frequently rested on an odd dichotomy of views. Each country's own trade policy, and in particular 'trade liberalisation', took central importance, while the policies of its trading partners were treated as, at worst, secondary problems. This approach was part of a more general shift towards treating developing countries as responsible for their own success or failure. In the 1950s and 1960s, it was argued that they depended on the nature of the advanced industrial economies, perhaps on active policies on their part, but certainly on their economic performance. In the 1970s, while the policy interpretations started to change, aggregate international models, both formal and implicit, preserved this dependency. Frequently, their growth was directly constrained by imports, which in turn depended entirely on exogenously determined exports and capital inflows. A more historical approach suggested that there might be times when there were insuperable natural or social or other obstacles to their development. This last interpretation can be reconciled with the 1980s emphasis on how countries themselves act if the way in which they respond to external conditions, whether by policy or by economic changes, is brought into the central focus, and if external conditions are analysed in more detail.

The question of the role of the policy (or policies) towards trade in developing countries themselves has been extensively investigated, and this is not the place to review the literature or conclusions. Some of the elements of the debate, however, offer lessons for a study of the effects of other countries' trade policies. Early assertions that good export performance could be taken as a sufficient indication that the policy was one of export promotion are paralleled by the first reactions to complaints about protection in the industrial countries which are developing countries' markets: that their imports were increasing, therefore the policy could not be protectionist. Serious analysis of both questions has moved beyond this (although

1

examples can still be found), and since the early 1980s studies have repeatedly shown that exports by developing countries facing new non-tariff barriers have grown more slowly than before, or than exports to similar markets, or than similar goods to the same market. (These were summarised in Page, 1987.) There remain, however, serious methodological problems in measuring the degree of protection from the supplier's point of view as well as the universal problem in economics of defining the alternative: how would we expect the exports of countries, which are (or want to be) rapidly growing and which are changing their industrial structure, improving their inputs and thus altering their advantages relative to other traders, to behave in the absence of policy? To this must be added estimates of the effects of all other policies and economic conditions and changes taking place in them at the international level. Finally, there is interaction directly between the trade policies of a country and those of its trading partners, and between different perceptions of these. If developing countries' performance does improve or falter relative to whatever normal path or alternative international system is assumed, is this because of (in spite of) their own policies or those of their trading partners? Too frequently the answer seems to be: it depends on which is being analysed.

Two conclusions would seem to emerge from the studies of developing country trade policy, which have relevance to looking at the effect of others' actions: first, that the policies can matter to trade, but second that the way in which they affect trade, and through trade the rest of the economy, depends strongly on how exporters and potential exporters respond to them, not simply on the legal details of the policies. A third conclusion from trade liberalisation studies is also relevant, however: that the ways in which policies work through beyond exports to the rest of the economy, and how changes within the economy interact with the policies and affect exports, depend on a variety of conditions in each country. Any general results about the nature of growth, the importance of competition, and the roles of intervention or market signals therefore need to be placed in the particular context of each country.

The first of these conclusions, that policies matter, helps to justify the present study, although the second will prove as significant here as in the other studies, and the third will again be relevant. Changes can be identified in the general level of protection and the relative levels facing different types of country (or exporters of different products). In particular, it is possible to show a change from reducing to increasing protection in the industrial countries, traditionally the principal market of most developing countries, and more recently the beginning of a process of reducing protection in some developing countries which are potential and in some cases actual markets. There are identifiable differences in the distribution of protection as it affects different countries, arising from the nature and extent of preference arrangements, or from variations among different industrial country markets, as well as differences for different products or for different stages of production. All these could affect the total value or the composition of a developing country's exports, and the changes and differences provide potential ways of analysing the nature and the size of the effects. The effects of the policies and of the changes in policies in the last 10–15 years are sufficiently large to have influenced long-term decisions about investment and development strategy which can be identified, if not quantified, at country, and even international, level.

Analysing the impact of these trade policy-induced effects beyond trade on the rest of a developing economy can follow at least two routes. The level, rates of change, and changes in composition of trade can have the same effects, both macro- and microeconomic, as changes induced by home country government policies or by market effects. These are direct economic responses to policies which change market sizes or relative prices. But the fact that the external influences are the result of policy decisions, and that these are taken outside national control, may itself affect those reactions which lead to long-term decisions about sales and production. These responses will be influenced by whether the results of policy interventions appear more or less permanent, or more or less easily reversible by intervention through negotiation or other non-economic forms of action. Such decisions may perhaps even change the type of producer company which is seen as successful, to those able to anticipate, influence, and respond to policy rather than those which take a narrower production or industrial approach.

Many conditions outside the market or industry will be important for external trade policy effects. These include the nature of the productive structure and alternatives, the political and social situation and history, and relations between the economic and political decision-makers, as well as the traditional factors in policy analysis like the country's own development strategy, size, and the immediacy of non-economic problems.

The purpose of this study is to examine how the external policies facing a developing country can affect its industrial structure and thus its development by their total effect and their nature, and therefore how far such conditions need to be taken into account in a country's own development strategy. But it will need to look beyond this to suggest the range of possible responses. This means looking at the scale and nature of each of the possible policy interventions, and then examining how they have acted in combination. The emphasis is on the last 10–15 years when there appear to have been major changes in their nature.

This first chapter will survey the types of intervention which seem important (and general and identifiable) enough to be worth examining, and will indicate the types of effects which can be expected from changes in trade policy. The following five chapters will then examine each in turn, to measure its importance, and changes in it, and suggest how this has affected different countries or types of trade, and Chapter 7 discusses their effects taken together. The country chapters in the second half of the book examine the results in the context of different conditions.

HOW POLICIES ACT ON TRADE

The effects which can be expected are on the size, type, and direction of trade flows. Stemming from these would be more general and fundamental changes in the observed pattern of sectoral development and in the type of development policy which is available to decision-makers in industry or trade, or to the government. Not only countries' trade, but also their choice of development path, between industry and raw material development, and between a broad or a more concentrated pattern of development, can be affected. This in turn could have effects on other economic objectives, including the distribution of income among the population and between major sectors or different regions, but these go beyond the scope of this study. If the policy decisions of the importing countries have a significant effect on the pattern of exports, this may also affect a country's approach to economic development. It may encourage an emphasis on finding and exploiting policy-based opportunities or alternatively lead to more emphasis on avoiding policy obstacles, while concentrating on more nationally determined criteria for choice (whether these are market-based or determined by a national economic strategy). The reverse may also be true: an interventionist approach to development at the national level may affect attitudes to trading partners' policies. The final chapter will look particularly at these interactions.

In analysing the reasons for long-term changes, a major problem is the difficulty of moving from recording apparent correlations between policy changes and responses to reasonable confidence about causation, particularly in developing countries which would be expected to be changing their trading and industrial structure. Some changes may be induced by changed expectations about 'normal' trading policy in trading partners, as well as actual changes. If the development strategy itself changes to fit the changed external situation, the nature of the problem becomes even more complex. There is also a more practical problem of measurement. After fifteen years of a shift to greater protection, any structural adaptations in an economy should be large enough to measure, but the more completely and successfully a country has adjusted, the more difficult it will be to find surface indicators. It may be continuing to grow, and to increase its exports, and to develop its industrial structure, and there may be no obvious excess capacity or immediate ability to respond to a reduction in a barrier.

The examination in detail of seven countries, therefore, explores the history of individual industries or firms or country policies, and how the decision-makers interpret what has happened. Such evidence must, however, be treated with as much caution about direction of causation as the more quantitative correlations. There is the inevitable problem that the producers and policy-makers who are available to give opinions are largely those who have succeeded in the actual conditions observed, and these are not necessarily those who would have been there in other circumstances. On questions like the effectiveness of preferences or of barriers to trade it is tempting to believe that at least a *prima facie* assumption of their effectiveness can be made because presumably well-informed companies or countries lobby for them. But even this common-sense approach may not be valid. What may be beneficial for an individual company at a particular point in time may not be so at an aggregate level or in the long run. Companies, and countries, have objectives other than maximising returns or growth, in particular security of markets or of supply. In the case of international 'lobbying' by governments rather than companies, there is a further possibility of divergent objectives between the government and industries or between the 'national interest' and the sum of individual interests.[1]

The case-study countries were chosen to give a network of pair (at least) comparisons between countries which have similar products, similar locations or size, similar levels of industrialisation or general development, or similar access arrangements to market countries, combined with differences on at least some of these points with others in the group. The combination of comparisons and interview evidence provides a test of the aggregate conclusions from the first half of the book.

The principal objective of the study is to understand how strongly and in what ways countries are influenced by their trading partners' (or potential partners') economic policies, and to offer evidence of what this has meant for the current development and development policies in developing countries. The principal emphasis, therefore, is on recent experience and evidence. But the important changes in the direction of industrial country policy occurred in the second half of the 1970s, and it was in the late 1970s or early 1980s that their effects on developing country trade were first identified. Restricting an examination of the evidence to too recent a period risks starting from a base which already incorporates the effects to be studied. The period to be examined must therefore vary between types of influence and types of country.

This frequently means going back to 1974. This is the year which marks a clear turning point in trade policy, as well as in the growth of trade, its composition and the importance of different trading groups (Table 1.1). It was the end of the last commodity price boom, and it could also be held to mark the end of the development optimism and enthusiasm of the 1960s. Barriers to trade had fallen during the 1950s and 1960s. The war-induced controls were eliminated, and average tariffs also fell with a series of worldwide rounds of negotiations under GATT and regional agreements on further preferences. For developing countries, the commodity exports which

5

Table 1.1 Growth of exports (annual average percentages)

	All goods					Manufacturers			
	1960–8	1968–73	1973–81	1980–5	1985–90	1968–73	1973–81	1980–5	1985–90
World	7.3	9.7	3.3	2.3	4.5	10.2	5.7	4.1	6.0
Non-oil developing countries	4.6	9.0	4.8	7.7	9.9	–	8.8	9.4	15.8
Asia	5.5	14.3	4.0	7.9	18.0	19.9	11.9	10.1	19.3
Latin America	2.2	4.4	0.7	3.5	−0.6	15.9	4.8	8.6	5.5
Africa	−1.0	22.7	−6.4	−3.9	−1.1	9.8	−6.9	0.7	12.9

Sources: UN, *Monthly Bulletin of Statistics*; UNCTAD, *Handbook of International Trade and Development Statistics*; IMF, *International Financial Statistics*; IMF, *IFS Supplement on Trade Statistics*; Author's estimates

they were then exporting in exchange for manufactures imports revived first, in the 1950s. Although tariffs were higher on more processed products and 'tariff escalation' from one stage of production to the next was identified, this was a problem only for the most advanced, and was not increasing during this period. The economies of most industrial countries, most of the time, were expanding rapidly. This reduced general pressures for protection. Although some of the old special access arrangements for the emerging independent ex-colonies were reduced or eliminated, by the end of the period the industrial countries as a group had been persuaded to introduce the Generalised System of Preferences. As with trade barriers, it is difficult to demonstrate convincingly whether preference schemes have long-term effects on industrialisation, or the structure of the recipients' economies. The evidence on tariffs and preference areas, on has been available, what appears to have been used, and what the reactions to the preferences are, is given in Chapter 2.

Trade in manufactures was rising among the industrial countries, with increasing importance for specialisation and intra-industry trade, and thus a growing share of trade in total output. It was only towards the end of this period, in the early 1970s, that manufactures started to become a significant export (and target for export policy) even for the advanced developing countries (Table 1.2). Development throughout the 1960s (and earlier in most countries) had always meant industrialisation, but the primary focus had been on replacing imports in national markets, certainly as the first step, and there was little thought beyond that. The debates were between those who wanted to give special policy assistance to this, and those who thought promoting production, and implicitly exports of primary commodities, was a more reliable way to permit industrialisation by initially accumulating the

Table 1.2 Share of manufactured exports in total exports (percentages)

Region	1970	1981	1985	1990
Non-oil developing countries	34	44	53	69
Asia	46	64	65	78
Latin America	22	21	28	37
Africa	7	4	9	18
Africa, non-oil exporters	35	22	29	45

Sources: IMF, *International Financial Statistics Supplement on Trade Statistics*; UNCTAD, *Handbook of International Trade and Development Statistics*; UN, *Monthly Bulletin of Statistics*

savings necessary for development. Promoting production of manufactures for export rather than import substitution was not perceived as a serious option, because the principal objection even to replacing imported manufactures was the low quality and high cost of the substitute. The question of obstacles to exports was therefore basically confined to the special cases of those commodities which competed with production in developed countries (sugar, cereals, fertilisers, some metals), or which had special terms of access to traditional ex-colonial buyers. The first manufactured exports to see such barriers rise, starting in the mid-1960s, were textiles and clothing.

In the 1970s the decline in the growth in demand for commodities and in their relative prices was a severe shock after the boom of 1970–3. It was accelerated by the increase in the cost of energy, both directly and through the recession which high oil prices induced in the industrial countries. This lowered the attraction of the traditional commodity path of development. At the same time, the progress of those countries which were able to increase their exports of simple manufactures, and the effect on the exporting aspirations of other countries from observing their success (and the apparent sequence from Japan's previous success to that of other Asian Newly Industrialising Countries) led to a much greater emphasis in development policy on promoting exports of manufactures, even in the most traditional import-substituting countries. Mexico introduced its export processing zones, the *maquiladoras*, as early as 1966.

What then would the trade trends of the early 1970s have implied in the absence of the policy responses which promoted exports in some developing countries and restricted imports by the industrial countries from the developing countries? The question is perhaps meaningless, because it treats policy as exogenous. The increase in export promotion itself followed the effect of the recession on the prospects for primary commodities. The restriction by developed countries of imports from developing countries followed both the recession and the early export successes of the NICs. It is difficult to believe that the policies were unrelated to these events. If the trends induced the policy changes, it is difficult to construct a credible alternative scenario, with the trends but without the policies, except by imposing the rationality (from an economist's point of view) of an economist's response to the trend as an alternative to the political or industrial interest group rationality which in fact prevailed.

Up to 1973, what had been commonly assumed would happen next was that increasing specialisation would continue, because of continuing reduction in trade barriers (implicitly this meant among the industrial countries because they were at that time the only significant industrial producers or exporters), permitting the exploitation of economies of scale, and therefore an increasing share of trade in output. As worries about the persistence of technological advantages under conditions of economies of scale had not yet passed from 'ill-informed' advocates of the protection of infant industries in developing countries into 'advanced strategic economic theory', this was accepted as beneficial to all except declining industry pressure groups in the industrial countries. Bringing in developing countries, with much lower labour costs and access to all the other required production inputs apart from trained and therefore high productivity labour, would have brought these trends under question even without two further factors. One was the recession and the consequent normal increase in protectionism, against all outside suppliers. Given the network of special arrangements some industrial countries had with others (notably the European Community and European Free Trade Association; formally on cars, less formally by habit, the US and Canada), this brought an abnormal relative growth in protection against the easier targets, the developing countries. The second was the great success, especially in the second half of the 1970s, of developing countries (although in practice it was only a small number of them) in increasing their share of markets: from 7 per cent share in world exports of manufactures in 1970 and 7.4 per cent in 1975 to 10 per cent by 1980, 13 per cent by 1985, and 17 per cent by 1990 (Table 1.3). This could be attributed either to their deliberate policies or to natural changes in competitiveness.

NEW INTERVENTIONS IN TRADE

Faced with growing unemployment because of the recession induced by their response to the oil price rise and to the preceding general economic boom, and increased low-cost imports from new suppliers, the industrial countries reversed the post-war decline in their protection. The detailed discussion of this is given in Chapters 2 and 3. It was principally implemented through non-tariff barriers, but the end of tariff reduction was also important. In outline, the reduction in tariffs in the end-1970s (Tokyo Round) of GATT negotiations was (necessarily) smaller than in earlier Rounds, because the starting level was lower (and this was true, for the same

Table 1.3 Shares of developing countries in exports of manufactures (percentages)

	1970	1975	1980	1985	1990
Shares in total exports of manufactures by developing countries					
Asia	52.4	62.8	71.8	71.2	82.7
Latin America	26.2	23.4	20.3	18.5	11.6
Africa	19.5	9.3	5.8	3.2	2.8
Shares in world exports of manufactures					
LDCs	7.0	7.4	10.0	13.3	17.1
Asia	3.7	4.7	7.2	9.5	14.1
Latin America	1.8	1.7	2.0	2.5	2.0
Africa	1.4	0.7	0.6	0.4	0.5

Sources: UN, *Monthly Bulletin of Statistics*; UNCTAD, *Handbook of International Trade and Development Statistics*; IMF, *International Financial Statistics*

reason, of the Uruguay Round in 1993). The peaks on tariffs against the most sensitive goods were not significantly lowered. Tariff escalation remained unchanged or rose. There were no significant extensions of trade liberalisation into developing country commodities (as were achieved in the Uruguay Round in agriculture and textiles and clothing). What did happen, starting in 1974 immediately after the first major rise in oil prices, was an increase in the use of quotas, demands for constraints on exports, and other non-tariff barriers. Tariffs and some other barriers among the industrial countries continued to fall in the 1970s through regional groupings (the extension of the EC and EC–EFTA arrangements), but even here non-tariff barriers appeared more frequently.

Other non-market influences on trade also increased. In the 1970s, some commodity agreements were established. In the mid 1980s, barter and other forms of countertrade, designed to provide a simple balance between exports and imports, temporarily increased (these are discussed in Chapter 4). Other traditional interventions in trade acquired new importance (Chapter 5). The tying of aid to use in the donor country rose in economic significance with the growing share of aid-financed trade in the poorest countries in the 1980s. The security restrictions on trade with the East European countries and the Soviet Union were increasingly seen as a barrier to trade in the late 1980s as these countries became (temporarily) important markets and minor security threats, and as the 'high technology' goods on the traditional security lists came to be seen as normal office equipment.

There was another type of trade which was widely believed to be increasing and which could indicate another trend towards external intervention. Concentration within industries was growing at both national and international level, with large companies thought to be gaining importance. Against this, there were changes from the innovations in industrial processes which permitted smaller-scale production by using the type of automation previously only available with large companies exploiting economies of scale. Combined with the continuing fall in the use of country-specific commodities (through the absolute savings characteristic of the 1970s, on top of the substitution of synthetics which has been evident in the whole post-war period), these trends suggested that trade might become less important than internationally directed, but dispersed, production. Local production could replace trade flows, in spite of any reduction in barriers to trade, whether economic, transport and communications costs, or policy-created like tariffs.

But while the importance of technology, and of large companies in creating and exploiting it, might make trade in physical inputs and outputs less necessary, this implies not greater national economic independence but a substitution of foreign investment for trade. This could mean a (measurable) increase in the share of intra-company trade and of total trade by multi-national companies in world trade. Where economies of scale in production remain important, a company will combine producing some of its products near their markets with 'world' factories producing all of a particular component in a limited number of sites.

Three questions about the role of foreign investment are discussed in Chapter 6. Is there evidence of an increase in intra-company trade for developing countries? Does it have effects which are different from arm's-length trade which need to be considered by a country looking at its trade and industrial structure? If a multinational company is exploiting, perhaps more efficiently, the same opportunities which a smaller or local firm would otherwise be taking, this need not be considered as an important change in the nature of a country's trade. But if it is encouraging a different type of industrialisation because of the type of component or assembly operation which it may have located in the country, or removed from it to some other country, then this is arguably another external policy-induced effect on its trade. This conclusion could be reinforced by evidence on the third question: is the growth in foreign investment, worldwide, in developing countries, or in industrial countries by developing countries, itself induced by the industrial countries' trade policies? The debate on whether more protectionist or less protectionist policies induce foreign investment in developing countries continues; clearly the conclusions are also relevant for investment in the newly protecting industrial countries.

Each of these changes in how world trade is organised has had effects on the value, composition, and direction of trade (and potentially on foreign investment, leading to a second tier of effects). These may have had corresponding effects on industrial structure. But it is not sufficient to look at them individually. Even the summary here of what the changes were has

10

shown that in some cases the introductions of new policy measures were related to each other, or to changes resulting from other policies in either the importing or the exporting countries. The effects can interact and reinforce (or offset) each other. Therefore, it is necessary to look at the combined effects in the context of individual regions, countries, or commodities. They affected not just the preferences or obstacles to a particular flow, but the relative preference offered, compared with other suppliers or with other possible exports from a particular supplier. Chapter 2 identifies an apparent contrast between areas which have seen large regional changes in trade and those where there have been regional tariff reductions. Another apparent contradiction in the 1980s is between the rise in industrial country protection and the accelerated growth of developing countries' exports relative to those of industrial countries; especially of manufactures from Asia, the area most targeted by protection (Table 1.1). This illustrates the need to go beyond testing for the effects of any one change in trade conditions. Regrouping these effects into those that directly affect all developing countries, or particular regions or countries, how has the total nature of such changes altered the conditions facing them, and therefore their own development policies, designed to fit the international system as it is? Have changes among other countries, for example regional or preference arrangements, had effects on non-participating countries?

A second, more general question is whether the changes taken together have created an international system which is more subject than in the past to policy intervention, and whether this has effects on attitudes and strategies. In particular, have the restrictions and interventions (including here the role of major companies) shifted towards the goods which are of future (and therefore strategic) interest to developing countries? Some types of intervention may have diminished (commodity agreements, for example), and the reduction in primary commodities' share in total world trade has reduced the weight of all the agriculture interventions by the industrial countries. But intervention in new industries or those in which developing countries are or will be newly competitive may be more important in its effects than might appear from a quantitative measurement of the exports currently affected. On the policy-effect side, a similar caution is necessary. Some developing countries are themselves less interventionist in trade policy than in the past, and therefore perhaps less well equipped to deal with intervening trading partners.

NOTE

1 The classic example is a (small) country each of whose inhabitants could increase his income by emigrating.

2

TARIFFS AND PREFERENCES
Traditional diversions

TARIFFS

The principal change in the global role of tariffs since the early 1970s is that there have been no major reductions to stimulate trade. Those negotiated in the Tokyo Round of GATT trade negotiations (it ended in 1979, and the staged cuts were made in the early 1980s) were from an average of about 7% to under 5%. There was little difference in the size of industrial countries' cuts, but Japanese levels were slightly below average, falling from 5.5 to 2.3%. There were no general cuts during the Uruguay Round (from 1986 to 1993); countries would not agree an interim implementation of cuts already agreed by 1988. Table 2.1 summarises the tariffs of the major industrial areas. Differences between the Most Favoured Nation averages and the tariffs applied indicate the effects of special arrangements between each of the countries and various free or preferential trade areas.

For developing countries, and especially for their most rapidly growing exports, the changes in the 1970s and 1980s were more unfavourable than this: in the Tokyo Round, cuts for their exports were smaller, and tariff escalation actually worsened. On the individual products which have the highest share in their trade, they continue to face some of the peak tariffs. Average rates for food (5%), textiles (8%), footwear (9%), and clothing (12%) are all above the average for all products. Weighting by their composition of exports further raises the effective average. While only 7% of imports by industrial countries from industrial countries face tariffs above 7% (even excluding intra-EC trade), 20% of imports from developing countries do. These differences apply to all three major industrial areas: the United States, the European Community and Japan (Table 2.2).

The expected effect of these changes would be (increasing) diversion of industrial country imports from developing to other industrial country suppliers, and encouragement of developing countries to specialise in basic raw materials. In addition there is a risk of a general slowing in trade growth.

Table 2.1 Post-Tokyo Round, applied, and GSP tariffs in selected industrial countries (percentages)

Product group	MFN tariffs				Average applied				GSP tariffs			
	EC	Japan	US	All developed	EC	Japan	US	All developed	EC	Japan	US	All developed
All food items	3.7	9.7	4.1	6.4	4.4	9.4	3.5	5.3	5.0	11.1	3.6	5.5
Food and live animals	3.2	10.0	3.8	6.5	4.8	9.7	3.2	5.3	5.1	11.7	3.4	5.6
Oilseeds and nuts	10.3	5.6	1.4	5.3	4.9	4.8	1.0	4.0	6.2	5.0	0.3	4.5
Animal and vegetable oils	0.1	0.3	0.9	0.1	0.0	0.3	1.0	0.2	0.0	1.2	0.1	0.4
Agricultural raw materials	3.4	0.7	0.3	0.8	0.4	0.3	0.3	0.5	0.5	0.5	0.1	0.5
Ores and metals	2.8	2.5	1.9	2.3	0.7	1.8	2.2	1.5	0.5	1.3	1.1	0.9
Iron and steel	5.5	5.0	4.3	5.1	2.3	2.9	5.0	3.4	3.3	2.0	3.5	3.0
Nonferrous metals	3.2	5.5	0.7	2.3	0.5	4.3	0.7	1.3	0.5	3.1	0.3	1.1
Fuels	0.1	1.5	0.4	1.1	0.3	1.2	0.4	0.6	0.2	1.3	0.3	0.6
Chemicals	8.4	5.5	3.7	5.8	3.4	4.8	3.9	3.1	4.1	5.1	1.0	3.7
Manufactures excl. chemicals	8.1	5.7	5.6	7.0	4.6	4.6	4.9	4.7	6.4	4.2	6.6	6.7
Leather	10.2	11.9	4.2	5.1	2.1	10.7	2.7	3.1	2.8	8.4	1.4	3.2
Textile yarn and fabrics	17.3	8.6	10.6	11.7	5.3	7.1	12.1	7.9	7.6	6.1	9.0	8.4
Clothing	19.9	15.0	20.3	17.5	7.3	10.0	13.1	11.9	9.3	8.6	17.8	14.6
Footwear	22.5	14.2	11.7	13.4	6.5	12.5	9.5	9.0	9.1	7.9	9.4	10.1
Other items	4.8	2.3	n.a.	n.a.	0.1	0.7	3.6	3.3	0.1	1.0	0.4	3.8
All products	4.2	3.5	3.9	4.7	2.5	3.1	3.8	3.0	2.1	2.3	3.6	2.7
Developing country weights	3.2	3.0	4.9	n.a.	2.1	2.4	4.5	n.a.	2.1	2.3	3.6	2.7

Source: Finger and Olechowski, 1987

Table 2.2 Distribution of 'high tariff' and other imports in EC, Japan and US, from world and developing countries, 1984

Post-Tokyo MFN tariff rates	Percentage of all tariff lines[a]	Percentage of total imports from world[a]	Percentage of total imports from developing countries[a]	Percentage share of developing countries in total imports
EC				
'High tariff' items (above 10%)	21.5	9.3	10.7	45.9
Lower tariff items (10% or less)	66.9	88.3	86.9	39.4
All[b]	100.0	100.0	100.0	40.0
Japan				
'High tariff' items (above 10%)	17.1	6.6	5.0	44.4
Lower tariff items (10% or less)	82.8	92.7	94.4	59.4
All[b]	100.0	100.0	100.0	58.3
US				
'High tariff' items (above 10%)	16.0	7.9	11.4	53.5
Lower tariff items (10% or less)	83.1	89.7	87.0	35.8
All[b]	100.0	100.0	100.0	36.9

Notes:
[a] Owing to tariff-lines with no post-Tokyo MFN rates available the shares do not add to 100%
[b] All items include also those tariff-lines for which no post-Tokyo MFN rates were available

Source: UNCTAD, 1988

Table 2.3 indicates how serious tariff escalation remains, in all markets for all commodities. Rates for raw materials were reduced after the Tokyo Round to under 1% on average; semi-manufactures averaged 4% and finished goods 6.5%. The extent of escalation varies among the different industrial countries, but like high tariffs it is particularly serious for food, textiles, and tobacco. The escalation applied to developing countries is worse than that for industrial countries.[1] This is partly because some important manufactured products are excluded from the Generalised System of Preferences by some of the industrial countries which grant this (see next section) or face strict limits on the quantities that come in on GSP terms, and partly because there are more preference areas which include manufactures among the industrial countries. The effect of this would tend to be to divert the processing stages either to the importing country or to other industrial

14

Table 2.3 The escalation of trade barriers

Processing chain	Average tariffs				
	Developed[a]	Developing[b]	EC	Japan	US
Meat products					
Fresh and frozen meat	6.2	6.6	6.6	10.1	1.6
Prepared meat	8.4	21.9	17.9	22.5	2.3
Fish					
Fresh and frozen fish	4.3	10.9	6.3	5.3	0.5
Fish preparations	4.1	30.1	12.4	10.7	1.1
Vegetables					
Fresh vegetables	6.9	16.6	6.7	9.0	7.6
Vegetable preparations	13.2	26.9	15.1	17.5	11.0
Fruit					
Fresh fruit	7.4	17.0	7.7	21.5	1.1
Prepared fruit	17.1	11.1	16.6	21.8	20.3
Coffee					
Green or roasted beans			3.8	0.0	0.0
Coffee extracts			13.8	17.4	0.0
Vegetable oils					
Vegetable oilseed	0.0	18.1	0.0	0.3	1.0
Vegetable oils	4.4	26.5	6.1	6.2	0.7
Sugar					
Raw sugar	1.0	23.5	0.0	3.3	0.6
Refined sugar	20.0	24.3	0.0	82.5	9.9
Chocolate					
Cocoa beans	1.0	11.6	1.9	0.0	0.0
Powder and butter			9.0	2.9	0.1
Chocolate	3.0	29.7	0.1	24.3	0.1
Tobacco					
Raw tobacco	1.2	126.0	0.0	0.0	8.8
Tobacco products	18.1	662.1	61.8	82.1	9.1
Rubber					
Natural rubber	0.0	7.2	0.0	0.0	0.0
Unvulcanised rubber			2.2	5.5	6.4
Rubber products	3.9	19.4	3.0	3.8	3.9
Leather					
Hides and skins	0.1	4.8	0.0	0.0	0.8
Leather	2.9	17.5	2.4	8.5	3.7
Leather products	7.2	33.9	5.5	12.4	9.2
Wood					
Rough wood	0.0	8.0	0.0	0.0	0.0
Shaped wood	0.2	13.1	0.1	1.1	0.1
Wood manufactured	3.5	27.6	4.2	1.2	4.7
Paper					
Pulpwood			0.0	0.0	0.0
Paper and board			2.3	5.7	0.3
Paper manufactures			6.0	3.6	3.8
Wool					
Not carded or combed			0.0	0.0	5.2
Carded or combed			2.4	0.0	11.1
Wool yarn			1.4	3.9	12.9
Wool fabrics			2.7	11.0	37.3

Table 2.3 Continued

Processing chain	Average tariffs				
	Developed[a]	Developing[b]	EC	Japan	US
Cotton					
Not carded or combed	0.0	3.2	0.0	0.0	0.5
Carded or combed			0.2	0.0	5.0
Cotton yarn	3.0	29.7	2.3	3.8	8.7
Cotton fabrics	5.8	32.1	5.6	5.9	10.4
Iron					
Iron bars and ingots	2.2	12.1	2.3	3.7	1.6
Iron plates and shapes	3.4	19.9	2.2	2.3	5.3
All non-ferrous[c]					
Ores	0.0	4.1			
Metals	2.4	18.2			
Copper					
Unwrought copper			0.0	1.5	0.8
Refined copper			1.8	5.9	1.8
Aluminium					
Unwrought aluminium			0.8	6.6	0.6
Refined aluminium			2.1	9.0	3.2
Lead					
Unwrought lead			0.6	3.0	3.5
Refined lead			5.8	6.8	1.6
Zinc					
Unwrought zinc			0.9	3.0	1.7
Refined zinc			4.1	6.6	2.3
Tin					
Unwrought tin			0.0	0.0	0.0
Refined tin			1.8	2.0	4.4
Phosphate					
Natural phosphates	0.0	12.8	0.0	0.0	0.0
Phosphoric acid			6.1	5.2	1.7
Superphosphates			2.6	0.0	0.0
Fertilizer	3.2	9.4			
Petroleum					
Crude petroleum	0.5	5.1	0.0	1.4	0.3
Refined petroleum	1.0	12.8	1.0	2.2	1.1
Memo items					
Percentage of chains in which escalation occurs			96.0	96.0	96.0
Average tariff difference from primary to processed stage			6.7	12.5	4.7

Notes:
[a] Trade-weighted average of the MFN, GSP or special preference tariff rate actually applied
[b] MFN tariff rates for Algeria, Bangladesh, CARICOM, CEUCA, Egypt, India, Indonesia, Ivory Coast, Kenya, Rep. of Korea, Malaysia
[c] Includes aluminium, copper, tin, zinc and lead

Source: Finger and Olechowski, 1987

countries, as well as further discouraging the production of manufactured goods.

Until the mid-1980s, tariffs on imports by developing countries were much higher than those by the major industrial countries (Table 2.4), and trade among developing countries was low. Since then, there have been substantial reductions in the tariffs and rises in intra-regional trade. This gives rise to two possible questions in the context of changes in the international system. Is the change in access to other developing country markets sufficient to change the structure of trade by developing country exporters, given that even now the shares of intra-regional trade are still typically lower than those of exports to the industrial countries? Can extending the reductions of tariffs by forming regional agreements among developing countries be an important influence on future prospects for exports and output?

The reductions in tariffs that have occurred have been significant in some areas, and particularly in those where intra-regional trade was lowest and tariffs were highest in the past. Table 2.4 shows that in 1985 developing country tariffs averaged 30%, well above the average for developed countries. Although it is notable that the differences between manufactures and the average were relatively small, the combination of tariff and non-tariff barriers in some sectors of finished manufactures was prohibitive. The individual countries which were major markets for other developing countries in 1985 were Hong Kong, Singapore, Malaysia, China, and Brazil. These are still the most important, but the other countries which have become important since then are also shown in Table 2.4.

In Asia, and in particular in some of the most important market countries, tariffs were already relatively low, compared with the other developing areas (and for Hong Kong and Singapore, compared with those of the industrial countries). South Korea still had tariffs of around 20% on some processed primary goods, and Thailand's were up to 60%, with both showing a high degree of tariff escalation on these products, supplemented by NTBs (Safadi and Yeats, 1993). Since then, South Korea has implemented a programme to reduce average tariffs to 8% by 1993, and Thailand has also made major cuts. Some of the less significant importers, including Indonesia, the Philippines, and Pakistan, have also cut tariffs, all of which were previously above 30%.

In Latin America, in 1985 tariffs averaged 50–60%. By the early 1990s the average level was estimated at about 15%, with Argentina and Mexico even lower at about 10%. Mexico's liberalisation had started earlier in the 1980s. Tariffs were substantially higher in Brazil, the major importer, even as late as 1987; it now has a target of reducing them to the average industrial country level. Venezuela lowered tariffs on some products in the late 1980s.

In Africa, a large number of countries lowered tariffs because of the provisions of their structural adjustment programmes. However, as the area even as a whole is not a significant market for other countries, any effects will be small.

17

Table 2.4 Developing country tariffs, 1985: regional averages and major importers

Geographical region	Tariff rates[a]	
	Manufactures	*All sectors*
Caribbean	20	17
Central America	71	66
South America	55	51
Brazil	78.5	75.2
Argentina	41.2	38.6
Chile	19.7	20.2
Mexico[b]	16.0	13.4
Venezuela	31.0	31.4
North Africa	45	39
Sub-Saharan Africa	37	36
Middle East	6	5
Other Asia	27	25
Hong Kong	3.7	2.5
Singapore	0.0	1.2
Malaysia	18.2	15.0
China	37.1	32.1
Thailand	41.2	36.9
South Korea	25.0	22.7
All regions	32	30

Notes: [a] Ad valorem tariffs
 [b] 1988

Sources: UN, 1992; UNCTAD, 1988

Increases in regional trade in the second half of the 1980s can be seen for developing countries as a whole and for each continent (Table 2.5). The largest increase was among the Asian countries, where trade was already most open (even if the entrepôt countries, Singapore and Hong Kong, are excluded). The increase was general, across both primary and manufactured products. The share of trade to Asia, however, grew for all developing regions and for the industrial countries. This expansion, combined with the fact that Asian tariffs were lower and fell less, suggests, first that tariffs have not been responsible for the change, and secondly that the growth of trade within the region cannot be regarded as a peculiarly regional response.

There are a variety of alternative explanations. Table 2.6 suggests two. One is that the mid-1980s was a relatively depressed period, in post-war terms, for developing countries' intra-regional trade. Many areas' imports had been severely compressed by balance-of-payments adjustment to meet debt repayments and by general deflation of demand. In these circum-

Table 2.5 Intra-regional trade (percentage shares of markets in total exports)

to	Developing countries		Developing Asia		Own region	
by Region/country	1985	1990	1985	1990	1985	1990
Developing countries	30.1	33.0	10.8	21.0		
Asia	36.7	40.1	27.6	33.4	27.6	33.4
Korea	26.4	25.9	13.8	17.6	13.8	17.6
Bangladesh	46.6	24.0	14.6	10.1	14.6	10.1
China	52.5	60.9	39.2	53.5	39.2	53.5
Thailand	41.4	32.0	29.1	22.3	29.1	22.3
Malaysia	43.9	48.9	40.5	44.6	40.5	44.6
Latin America	23.5	25.2	4.3	5.0	12.7	15.9
Mexico	9.3	9.1	1.3	1.2	5.4	6.7
Brazil	31.5	30.0	6.9	10.6	9.7	11.1
Argentina	38.3	44.5	6.5	7.0	18.7	26.3
Colombia	18.5	19.3	0.9	0.7	14.0	16.9
Jamaica	14.9	12.3	0.0	0.1	11.6	9.5
Africa	14.8	15.0	3.3	4.2	4.9	5.4
Mauritius	4.5	5.9	1.5	1.4	2.9	4.1
Zimbabwe	39.9	38.0	7.7	7.8	26.4	21.0

to	Industrial countries		Asia	
by Region/country	1985	1990	1985	1990
Industrial	72.7	76.3	9.2	9.9
EC	77.8	81.7	4.2	4.5
North America	72.9	72.7	10.5	12.8
USA	61.4	63.9	13.4	15.5
Japan	58.0	58.6	26.4	31.3

Source: IMF, *Direction of Trade Statistics*; Colombian trade data

stances, the industrial countries were a more favourable market. The growth in intra-developing country trade up to 1990 may mark a return to normal rather than a change to a new trend. The other, which would explain why it is imports by Asia which have risen from all areas, is that Asian trade is becoming a larger share of total world trade. If the share of each area's intra-regional trade is normalised by dividing by its region's share in total world trade, the picture is very different (the third block of Table 2.6). There is always a tendency for trade within a region to be higher than with more distant regions. Transport costs are lower, familiarity with markets and perhaps also similarity of markets are greater. As intra-industry trade and trade in complementary products have risen at the expense of the share of simple commodities-for-manufactures trade this natural advantage may tend

Table 2.6 Trade shares and the intensity of intra-regional trade, 1928–90 (percentages)

	1928	1938	1948	1958	1968	1979	1983	1990
A Intra-regional trade share								
Western Europe	51	49	43	53	63	66	65	72
Eastern Europe	19	14	47	61	64	54	58	46
Total, Europe	61	61	52	61	71	72	72	76
North America	25	23	29	32	37	30	32	31
Latin America	11	18	20	17	19	20	18	14
Total, America	45	44	59	56	52	47	47	45
Asia	46	52	39	41	37	41	43	48
Japan	63	68	60	36	32	31	31	35
Developing Asia	27	28	37	35	22	25	27	34
Africa	10	9	8	8	9	6	4	6
Middle East	5	4	21	12	8	7	8	6
Total, World	39	37	33	40	47	46	45	52
B Share of world trade								
Western Europe	47	45	36	40	43	44	39	46
Eastern Europe	5	6	5	9	10	8	9	5
Total, Europe	52	51	42	49	53	51	48	51
North America	18	14	22	19	19	15	16	16
Latin America	9	8	12	9	5	6	5	4
Total, America	26	22	34	28	24	21	21	21
Asia	18	16	12	13	13	15	18	21
Developing Asia	12	9	11	9	6	8	10	12
Africa	4	5	7	6	5	5	4	3
Middle East	1	1	2	3	3	7	6	3
Intensity of intra-regional trade index (defined as share A/share B)								
Western Europe	1.13	1.14	1.21	1.38	1.51	1.57	1.63	1.60
Eastern Europe	4.36	2.61	10.22	7.62	7.30	7.88	7.28	10.88
Total, Europe	1.20	1.21	1.27	1.27	1.35	1.43	1.53	1.51
North America	2.59	2.91	2.39	3.07	3.57	3.63	3.63	3.50
Latin America	1.37	2.30	1.71	1.95	3.55	3.80	3.47	3.53
Total, America	1.76	2.00	1.77	2.07	2.21	2.29	2.23	2.26
Asia	2.61	3.33	2.74	3.15	2.84	2.77	2.41	2.31
Japan	4.17	4.65	4.29	3.28	3.81	3.08	2.62	2.33
Developing Asia	2.40	3.42	3.56	4.13	3.44	3.21	2.95	2.83
Africa	2.37	1.73	1.27	1.38	1.91	1.24	1.03	2.48
Middle East	7.56	3.47	9.55	4.25	3.00	1.17	1.38	2.23
Total, World	1.85	1.92	2.43	2.65	2.81	2.64	2.68	2.62

Source: Anderson and Blackhurst, 1993

to rise. The world and the industrial countries show this happening in the period since 1948, although with little change since 1979. Latin America (with a possibly recession-induced dip) shows it as well, and the increase since 1983, to a level still below that of 1979, seems rather small if it is to be seen as a response only to the massive tariff cuts. Measured in this way Asia actually shows a fall in 1990: intra-regional trade in Asia appears to have increased less than would be expected, given its growing share in total world trade.

If the response of Latin America to the massive tariff cuts of the 1980s was as small as these tables suggest, and if Asian intra-trade and the trade of other countries with Asia during its tariff cuts may be a response to the general growth in the region, expectations of large results in response to further cuts, which cannot be as large as in the past, seem difficult to justify. There are particular cases of high tariffs (those relevant to the case-study countries are discussed later), and there are also some trade flows where both tariff and non-tariff barriers may fall and produce a more important total effect, but at least on these trade-flow trends the case for expecting future major effects is not made.

GENERAL PREFERENCES

By 1983, about half of all non-oil trade, including about 55–60% of exports from developing countries were covered by some type of preference scheme (UNCTAD, 1983: 7). The Generalised System of Preferences was introduced in 1970 following the revision of the GATT agreement to permit 'differential' treatment for developing countries. This allowed industrial countries to grant concessions that were not available to all countries, as would normally be required under the Most Favoured Nation clause. (It also gave developing countries more freedom to protect sectors.) It was justified by the argument that some differential was needed to give new industries an initial advantage in export markets. The types of constraints normally included on its extent or total use were intended, therefore, to limit it to industries which were not yet competitive, whether by limiting the quantity of exports which could receive reduced tariffs or by withdrawing the preferences from products which crossed a threshold of quantity or market share, which was taken as an indication of readiness to compete. On the importing country's side, the loss of tariff protection was likely to be acceptable only for products which did not compete on a significant scale with domestic output; it therefore tends to be restricted to products not produced at all in the market country or to very small quantities. The scheme is not in fact uniform; each industrial country sets its own preferences, and can unilaterally withdraw or alter the provisions for individual products or countries. The GSP is a purely concessionary scheme on the part of the industrial countries and is in no way contractual. The products which receive preference under it are therefore not necessarily those most favoured by the exporter, but rather those which are least likely to be disruptive to the importer's producers.

Normally, agreements are for ten years. The EC and Japan introduced their schemes in 1971, the US in 1976. As with tariffs, an important unfavourable change has been (for most developing countries) the fact that since 1977, the concessions have not been increased. In 1977, the first restriction reduced the rate of expansion of tariff-free quotas (for goods where the benefits are limited by quantity). The concepts of graduating goods or countries were introduced in 1980–1 by all three major importers. For the most advanced exporters, the privileges have been removed, either from entire countries (the US graduation of the NICs) or from individual goods (by the EC).

The GSP schemes have not been revised significantly since 1986: a major review was due in 1991, but it was postponed (repeatedly) because of the Uruguay Round. If there is not a revision after the Round, the tariff reductions, some of them to zero, will erode GSP preferences. As the highest remaining tariffs are on goods (including clothing and textiles) which are excluded from the GSP, even after revision any new scheme is likely to offer a smaller margin of preference.

The European Community has restricted the quantities of individual goods covered, while some of those most important to developing countries are excluded altogether. The US excludes textiles and clothing, and the EC includes them only for countries which have accepted quotas under the Multi-Fibre Arrangement (MFA); for these the GSP cannot therefore promote additional exports by developing countries. Japan restricts the products covered, excluding all processed foods and imposing tight controls on textiles and clothing.

The general structure and relative levels of tariffs are the same as under MFN rates. The relatively small differences in most commodities between the average applied rates and the GSP rates as shown in Table 2.1 indicate how small a proportion of developing exports actually receive a worthwhile preference from GSP schemes. Many of the products covered are not exported by industrial countries, and those which are competitive with either home production in the importing countries or imports from other industrial countries tend to receive only small or restricted preferences. Middle-level developing countries have gained in relative preference from the graduation of the most advanced, but have lost it from the introduction of a special, more generous GSP for the least developed. Similar special privileges have also been extended by the US and the EC to the Andean countries (Colombia, Peru, Bolivia, Ecuador). The GSP is also eroded by the other special schemes discussed in the following section. In 1991 both the US and the EC extended their GSP schemes (with some exceptions) to the eastern European countries and in 1993 the US took the first steps towards extending it to countries of the former USSR. These changes further eroded its value to existing members.

In Japan, although the share of GSP-receiving imports in total imports from developing countries has increased, it was only 5% in the early 1970s, rising to 6% in the early 1980s, and touching 10% in 1988 (calculated from data in IDE 1990: 111). These small proportions are partly because a large share of imports from developing countries are primary products which enter without tariff. The GSP share was, however, further reduced because only about a half of eligible imports actually used the scheme (54% in 1983, up from 47% in 1976). The problem of low utilisation is not confined to Japan. The rate for the EC has been lower, about a third in 1980, rising to 44% in 1990 (IRELA, 1993). Of all its imports from developing countries, 6% were under GSP in 1980, 19% in 1990.

In contrast, the rate for the US in 1990 was 65%. This had been reduced from an even higher level by the relatively low rate in 1990 for imports from Latin America and the Caribbean; this had fallen from 70% in 1987 to 54% (Kuwayama, 1992: 27). The reduction was partly because of the increase in the share of imports eligible for better treatment under the Caribbean and later the Andean Trade Preferences (discussed below). There was also a shift from using the GSP to using the exemptions for off-shore processing because of a change in the Customs user fee. Even with these reductions, however, the differences among the three areas' schemes remain large.

There have been two limitations built in to the GSP schemes which have restricted their use from the start, and thus potentially also distorted their impact on exporting countries. All preference or free trade schemes require rules of origin in order to prevent countries from importing, then re-exporting goods from non-preferred countries. Each of the industrial countries has set its own levels of local content, and in some cases the ways of defining them have also varied. The two broad methods are requiring that processing in the developing country be sufficient to make a significant change in product classification (measured by the standard customs classification) or requiring that a (varying) percentage of the value added derive from the exporting country. In some circumstances, an import from the industrial country or from another GSP country can be 'cumulated' with value added in the final exporter; for other products or importers, it cannot. Most developing countries lack fully integrated industries, especially at the initial stages of industrialisation, and some are too small ever to find local origin rules easy to meet, except for a specialised range of products. This type of rule can therefore give an advantage to domestic resource-based industries, including, in countries with large supplies of suitable labour, labour-intensive ones. It also clearly gives an advantage to relatively large countries. These may not be the most appropriate industries or the most efficient suppliers.

For an individual exporting firm, the differences among the rules for the various schemes have tended to mean that it needs to decide which market it is seeking and produce to its rules, unless it is large enough to maintain a range of production processes or to meet all the most restrictive rules. In some cases the conditions are such as to lead to a tendency for the majority of producers in a country to specialise in one market. In others (there are examples of both in the country studies) the industry may divide informally into US-suppliers and EC-suppliers. This can leave a company, if not a country, more vulnerable to loss of demand in a single country than aggregate data would show. This has been countered by a tendency to demand short-term returns for any GSP-based production.

The other general limitation (indeed the rules of origin could be treated as an example) has been the complexity of each scheme, and even more of the system as a whole. This is a universal complaint, of every company in every country about every form of government assistance, but the low utilisation rates found for GSP schemes, especially those of the EC and Japan, and the lack of confidence in the exact rules found during interviews with even experienced firms (which offered evidence of contradictory official information) suggest that GSP schemes are worse than the average for trading arrangements. The views expressed in the interviews supported the evidence here that the EC scheme is more difficult than that of the US. Japanese analysis (IDE, 1990) suggests that the Japanese scheme has become more complicated. The growing number of products subject to quantitative limits or exclusions and the long period since full revision of all the schemes mean that there is likely to be a growing problem in all the schemes. The significance of this complaint is heightened by the relatively low benefits offered and by the fact that such schemes are explicitly targeted at encouraging new production for new markets. Thus the cost of full information may be high relative to the benefit, and may fall on the firms least able to bear it: new or inexperienced exporters. Such a bias would tend to favour large firms, or those with access to a well-resourced official advice office. It encourages specialisation in a limited number of markets or product lines, to minimise the average cost of acquiring information, with potentially adverse effects on diversification and vulnerability.

Table 2.7 shows the countries which have had the largest shares in the EC scheme. Of the countries studied here, only Malaysia and, in 1988, Thailand appear on the list; for the others trade with the EC is low either because they export to other areas or takes place under other preferential schemes. The characteristics of the major beneficiaries, aside from size, include lack of access under other schemes and being exporters of manufactures.

Latin America does not have other special access to the EC, so its usage of GSP is higher than average – 53% of elegible exports in 1990 – but its trade is still concentrated in primary goods more than other areas' exports to the EC. The result is that only 16% of its total exports to the EC are covered (IRELA, 1993). Brazil, Peru, and Venezuela are the only major countries

Table 2.7 Share of top ten beneficiaries in total EC GSP trade 1981, 1985, 1988 (percentages)

	1981			*1985*			*1988*	
Country	Share in covered trade	Share in GSP benefits	Country	Share in covered trade	Share in GSP benefits	Country	Share in covered trade	Share in GSP benefits
Brazil	7.9	9.2	Kuwait	5.1	10.6	China	13.1	13.8
Romania	6.9	9.0	Brazil	8.7	9.3	Brazil	10.0	13.8
Venezuela	3.4	7.6	Romania	5.9	8.4	India	6.8	9.3
Hong Kong	17.2	7.3	India	5.3	6.7	Thailand	4.8	6.3
China	5.9	7.3	Venezuela	3.0	6.4	Hong Kong	13.2	5.6
India	6.4	7.2	South Korea	9.2	6.0	Romania	3.6	4.6
South Korea	10.7	7.0	China	6.7	6.0	Indonesia	3.4	4.3
Saudi Arabia	4.0	4.7	Hong Kong	13.1	5.3	Kuwait	2.7	4.1
Malaysia	3.9	4.6	Saudi Arabia	3.9	4.5	Singapore	7.0	3.9
Philippines	3.1	4.3	Malaysia	4.1	4.4	Malaysia	3.8	3.9

Source: EC Commission, 1990

with shares above this, but still only at 20%, although all have usage rates of 55–65%.

For Japan, the major users have been South Korea, Taiwan, and China.

In 1988 only about 10% of all US imports from developing countries were under GSP schemes, lower than the EC figure. Even if the Asian countries which had by then been graduated from the scheme are subtracted, the figure was still only 13%; the figure for Latin America alone was also 10%. In the US, as for areas other than Latin America, in the EC scheme, the usage of GSP is greatly reduced by other schemes (notably the special provisions for Caribbean countries), and, recently, by the number of goods which have been graduated as competitive.

The major apparent recorded gainers under all the schemes are thus the Asian and Latin American countries. They are the relatively advanced and large countries identified as most likely to gain.

The potential erosion of benefits from various directions implies a very limited range of countries or goods for which the GSP could increase exports, and a limited period for each country (or commodity). The goods must be neither so unprocessed that they enter on zero or negligible tariffs on MFN terms nor so advanced that they compete with industrial country products and are excluded. Similarly the countries are neither very low-income (and therefore included in more preferential schemes) nor high-income (and graduated). They are also, for any individual industrial country which operates the GSP, the countries with which it does not have a special trading relationship, since the GSP tends to be the least that is offered to developing country trading partners. The schemes offer only limited trade creation with the industrial country partner because competitive products tend to be excluded. They could allow developing countries to benefit from trade diversion to them from other industrial countries which do not have special trading relationships with the country offering GSP. This is likely to be more important for trade with the US (with Canada the only industrial country receiving special access) or with Japan than with the EC, which has free trade with the EFTA countries and now special arrangements with eastern Europe. GSP schemes limit the trade diversion from the less favoured developing countries to the developing countries which receive even more preferential treatment (discussed in the next section).

It is not surprising therefore that aggregate studies have found only small effects for preference schemes. Nevertheless, rather than looking for a prolonged effect on an individual export, and therefore industry, it is useful to ask whether the GSP has been used as a way of permitting the development and first entry into industrial country markets of new exports, by middle-income countries. This can be done only in the country-level studies. But the GSP cannot help a traditional first source of manufactured exports – textiles and clothing – and it is probably not generous enough (see Table 2.1) to counter the tariff escalation on processed foods. Any effect would in any case now be diminishing because of the reduction in its benefits.

On the policy side, the GSP has offered developing countries a concessionary scheme to implement the GATT special treatment clause, and to provide an offset to the normally contractual trading agreements made among industrial countries. This means that developing countries have been placed in an inferior position in terms of bargaining at multilateral level (at most they could use renouncing GSP privileges in exchange for smaller, but contractual, gains). Combined with their *de facto* disadvantage from lack of access to the preference arrangements among industrial countries and from the persistence of high tariff (and, as we shall see in Chapter 3, non-tariff) barriers, this could be a disincentive for them to consider trade as a predictable and non-discriminatory way of promoting development or trade bargaining as a two-way process, and an incentive to seek trading advantages by exploiting preferences on a short-term basis. As a concessionary scheme the GSP may be withdrawn for non-trade reasons. This has been done on occasion by the US to support either other economic objectives (it has been threatened against countries unwilling to offer patent protection) or non-economic objectives (it has been removed from countries judged to have unacceptable social or political policies). In July 1993, the new US Administration announced a stepping-up of such uses, and Thailand was among those warned.

SPECIAL PREFERENCE SCHEMES

Preference schemes (or free trade areas, customs unions, etc.) among developing countries have not been significant for most of them during most of this period. There are a few exceptions, which will be discussed with regard to the case-study countries for which they are relevant (among the Caribbean countries, for Jamaica; with South Africa and the Preferential Trading Area which includes several southern and eastern African countries, for Zimbabwe; with Venezuela, for Colombia). These and the Central American Common Market and Mercosur in southern Latin America and the Southern African Customs Union between South Africa and its smallest neighbours have had some effect on their members, but they are not (perhaps not yet for Mercosur) large or successful enough to have effects on the world trading system or on the trade prospects of their neighbours. South Korea offers a few preferences to other Asian countries and there are small reductions on a few products within ASEAN (de Rosa, 1986), but these are not significant in size or effect, even on the countries directly affected.

Some of the schemes between developing and industrial countries are old and large enough to exert long-term effects on trade and industrialisation. These are the various EC schemes for its associated countries in North

Africa (the Maghreb) and in Sub-Saharan Africa, the Caribbean and the Pacific (the ACP countries), and the US preferences for Caribbean producers, under the Caribbean Basin Initiative (CBI). There are smaller or more recent US and EC arrangements with the Andean countries and among the US, Canada and Mexico in the North American Free Trade Area (NAFTA).

The EC gives special access to the ACP countries under the Lomé Conventions, with the current agreement, Lomé IV, running for ten years until 2000. Many agricultural goods are excluded (entirely or in their Northern Hemisphere season) because of the Community's Common Agricultural Policy, or are subject to special quotas (these include sugar and beef). Many primary goods enter duty-free from all developing countries. The principal Lomé benefits are thus intended to go to manufactures. For the goods included, there are, at least formally, no quota limits on total imports or those receiving special treatment, but warnings or surveillance have been used to indicate when imports are reaching a 'sensitive' level. Countries have not been excluded since the Lomé Conventions were first signed, but the arrangement included none of the countries whose success has led to their exclusion from GSP arrangements, for example the South-East Asian countries, or large countries like India.[2]

Both the Lomé Convention's rules for local content and the administration of them are stricter than for the GSP. Cumulation is allowed with other ACP countries or the EC, and this might be expected to be important for an association of mainly rather small countries, but it has not in fact been much used.

The African countries form the majority of members, so that a measure of the advantage which they receive is a reasonable indication of the advantage which all the members get, but many are also 'least developed countries', and therefore eligible for more favourable than average treatment under the GSP. Finding an appropriate measure indicates the uncertainties surrounding the concept. Table 2.8 shows the difference between the average duty paid on imports from African countries in each of the industrial country markets and that which would be paid on the same set of goods, but weighted by the average composition for all developing country exports and at the average rates for all developing countries. Although the average duty paid is lowest in the EC, the apparent difference is smaller for trade with the EC than with the US. This measure, however, means that differences in composition can affect the comparison. While all the industrial countries have a relatively high weight for (non-tariff-paying) primary goods in their imports from Africa, the EC has this also for other areas of developing countries, which lowers its 'all developing' average. But some real differences are highlighted by this method. The high US figures for all developing countries probably show a large effect from excluding the 'graduated' countries (which now pay MFN rates) from all preferences. The high figures for some African countries (e.g. Mauritius) show the importance of the exclusion of some products (clothing) from the GSP. More generally, the much larger variation among different countries for the US shows the effect of its more varied tariff structure. The low EC figure for all developing countries indicates how its range of schemes for various developing groups limits the advantage given by any one of them, even to the ACP, at least on tariffs.

At an aggregate level, it is difficult to find evidence of a large increase in the volume of trade with the EC or a shift into manufactures because of Lomé. This could be not only because of the small aggregate advantages shown in Table 2.8 but also because of the limitation of membership to countries which in general are not as developed or suited to take advantage of preferences as those which have benefited from the GSP. Some individual countries and companies have used ACP access intensively (Mauritius, Zimbabwe, and Jamaica among the case-study countries offer examples of users, non-users and mixed), but the other, non-tariff, advantages of Lomé membership may also be part of the explanation for their good trade performance. There are not enough success stories among total ACP membership to justify a presumption that Lomé access is helpful. There are, as with the differing GSP schemes, examples of countries or companies dividing into EC and non-EC suppliers because of the differing (and potentially conflicting) conditions on local content or other characteristics, and thus some intra- or inter-country distortion.

The Lomé arrangement is contractual, rather than concessional. This should provide a check on erosion of benefits from other preferences. By the terms of the agreement, the members (including the EC) may not negotiate preferences with other countries without consultation. In the past, the renegotiations have roughly coincided with GSP agreements, offering an opportunity to balance concessions. These provisions have not, however, fully protected the value of the agreement to the ACP countries. Changes negotiated under the GATT do not require consultation (although in practice the ACP countries have lobbied the EC), and the tariff reductions and agricultural changes of the Uruguay Round affect the Lomé countries as they do the GSP arrangements. The gradual phasing out of MFA textile and clothing quotas (from which the ACP countries have been exempt) could divert trade from them. More correctly, but not more palatably, this is a removal of the trade diversion to them which the preference brought. The granting of new preferences to the Eastern European and Andean countries could have affected them, but initially was too short-term. The eastern European preferences have already been replaced by Association agreements and modified by barriers to some commodities and threats of anti-dumping action. The Andean preferences were for only four years, with no guarantee of renewal (see the Colombia case study). The eastern European countries were also too unready to use them to any significant effect. But even this (abridged) list of other trade arrangements made by the EC during only the

29

Table 2.8 Weighted tariff averages on Sub-Saharan African countries' exports to the EC, Japan and the US[a]

Exporter	EC		Japan		US[a]	
	Facing the exporter	Facing all developing	Facing the exporter	Facing all developing	Facing the exporter	Facing all developing
Total	0.01	1.75	1.64	1.71	0.48	6.63
Angola	0.0	0.7	0.0	0.0	0.7	0.8
Benin*	0.0	0.5	4.1	0.5	0.7	4.0
Botswana	0.0	1.7	0.8	0.1	1.8	15.3
Burkina Faso*	0.0	1.3	0.6	1.3	8.6	11.1
Burundi*	0.0	1.9	0.0	0.0	0.2	1.7
Cameroon	0.0	0.9	1.1	3.2	0.8	3.5
Cape Verde	0.0	2.1	–	–	0.0	0.0
C.A.R.*	0.0	1.6	0.0	0.0	0.4	5.0
Chad*	0.0	1.6	0.0	0.0	29.9	32.0
Comoros*	0.0	2.2	0.2	0.1	0.7	7.5
Congo	0.0	0.6	0.0	0.0	0.6	0.7
Djibouti*	0.0	1.9	1.9	5.0	2.2	6.0
Ethiopia*	0.0	1.7	0.2	0.1	0.3	3.5
Equatorial Guinea*	0.0	1.5			17.0	27.7
Gabon	0.0	0.9	0.0	0.0	0.7	3.5
Gambia*	0.0	1.9	0.5	4.0	0.0	1.2
Ghana	0.0	1.4	0.4	1.2	0.0	1.8
Guinea*	0.0	1.6	0.8	4.3	0.0	4.0
Guinea-Bissau	0.0	1.1	0.5	4.0	0.7	4.3
Ivory Coast	0.0	1.2	0.2	0.1	0.1	4.1
Kenya	0.0	1.7	3.1	1.7	0.6	7.1
Lesotho*	0.0	1.8	0.0	5.6	13.6	18.6
Liberia	0.0	1.2	0.0	0.0	0.0	6.1

Table 2.8 Continued

Exporter	EC		Japan		US[a]	
	Facing the exporter	Facing all developing	Facing the exporter	Facing all developing	Facing the exporter	Facing all developing
Madagascar	0.0	1.4	1.6	1.9	0.0	2.4
Malawi*	0.0	1.7	0.0	0.0	11.1	3.7
Mali*	0.0	1.3	4.3	3.4	1.9	7.9
Mauritania*	0.0	1.3	0.7	4.1	4.3	11.5
Mauritius	0.0	2.1	2.6	5.1	14.4	8.7
Mozambique*	0.0	1.0	2.9	2.6	0.2	2.5
Namibia	–	–	–	–	0.4	1.4
Niger*	0.0	0.6	0.0	0.0	0.9	4.4
Nigeria	0.0	0.8	2.6	3.1	0.7	2.0
Réunion	–	–	–	–	–	–
Rwanda*	0.0	1.8	0.0	0.0	0.3	5.9
Sao Tome*	0.0	2.3	–	–	1.9	3.5
Senegal	0.0	1.4	3.4	2.3	2.6	9.2
Seychelles	0.0	2.1	3.5	4.6	3.3	6.7
Sierra Leone*	0.0	1.2	3.0	3.0	0.7	5.8
Somalia*	0.0	2.2	0.0	0.0	6.1	8.7
Sudan*	0.0	1.2	0.0	0.1	1.1	18.5
Swaziland	0.0	2.4	0.0	0.0	2.2	7.9
Tanzania	0.0	1.6	0.2	1.3	0.4	1.0
Togo*	0.0	1.3	0.0	0.0	0.0	3.8
Uganda*	0.0	1.6	0.0	0.0	0.0	1.6
Zaire	0.0	0.8	0.0	0.1	0.5	1.0
Zambia	0.0	2.1	0.0	0.1	0.7	2.0
Zimbabwe	0.0	2.0	1.2	0.1	3.2	8.1

Notes: [a] Trade weighted actual average tariffs in 1986, including preferences. The average for the individual S-SA country is based on its own trade weights in the market concerned. The corresponding average for 'all developing' is restricted to the same products – however it uses aggregate trade weights of all developing countries

  * Least developed countries (LDCs) according to the UN. Mozambique was added to the list in 1988

Source: Erzan and Svedberg, 1989

first third of the current Lomé period clearly indicates that exporters (and researchers) cannot assume that even a negotiated, long-duration trade preference will have a constant or predictable value.

A possible test of how important different Lomé elements are for exporters who have increased their exports to the EC may come from other schemes which the Community is now introducing. The EC agreement with the Andean countries is superficially like the trade side of Lomé. It offers similar basic privileges on import duties, but without the quota or special access arrangements for individual products like sugar and bananas, and it is only for four years (not ten like the GSP, Lomé, or the US Andean arrangements). It thus does not offer the same long-term security of access, and the costs of the complications of adjusting to its provisions need to be recovered over a shorter period. As it was introduced in full only in 1992, there is no statistical evidence yet on its success. Interview and survey evidence in Colombia does not suggest that it is widely used.

The US arrangements under the CBI (the Caribbean Basin Initiative which includes most Caribbean and Central American countries) were introduced in 1984, initially for twelve years. This was already longer than the normal ten years for most other preference programmes, and it was designated a permanent programme in 1990. Unlike Lomé it does not include even a limited guarantee of not altering the preferences, so that the effective value of the 'permanent' arrangement can alter. It has already been reduced by the US agreement with the Andean countries, the Uruguay Round agreement and, what the Caribbean countries see as the major threat, the North American Free Trade Agreement.

The CBI excludes textiles and clothing, shoes and some other leather products, canned tuna and (the largest item) oil. As with Lomé, sugar is subject to separate quotas. Immediately following its introduction, dutiable imports by the US from the members had fallen from 84% to 57%. Excluding oil, the share of other imports entering duty-free had risen from about a third to over half (31% to 57%). Its effects interact with the GSP and the special provisions for processing and assembly known as 806/7.[3] At least some of the apparent impact of the CBI was diversion of existing exports from the GSP, and the choice between CBI and 806/7 depends partly on the amount of local content compared with US content.

Kuwayama (1992: 29) estimates that of the 14% of US imports from the CBI countries which were recorded as using CBI provisions in 1989, about a third (5% of total imports) were new CBI results, with the remainder goods which had switched from using the GSP. In 1983 10% of US imports from the Caribbean were 806/7 items. Higher local content may lead to using the general CBI preference for the whole product; higher US content means that paying non-preferential tariffs on the element of processing is better; for products like clothing which are excluded from the CBI, only 806/7 is available. At the other end, from 1986 even duty-free goods entering the

32

US had to pay a 'Customs user' fee, from which the US content of 806/7 goods was exempt. This led to a recorded increase in the use of 806/7, but is unlikely to have had distorting effects, except on the recording of the two schemes.

Table 2.9 shows a rise in apparent 806/7 usage from 12% to 18% in US imports of manufactures from developing countries. In 1989, 10% of total US imports from developing countries used it. Although on average the goods using this mechanism did not pay high duties, and the share of (dutiable) processing was more than a half, so that the saving was small, in textiles and clothing it is clearly of major importance, with low processing (it is one of the few sectors with under 50%) and high duty. In 1989, although imports in this sector were only 4% of total US imports under the scheme, they accounted for more than half the total duty savings (Kuwayama, 1992). The principal countries using it have been Mexico (in all industries in the *maquiladoras*) and Brazil; the Asian countries, including Malaysia and Thailand (these two groups are the same large and relatively advanced industrialising countries which were identified as the major users of other schemes); and the countries of the Caribbean, including Central America (Table 2.10). Since 1986 they have had more favourable access under the scheme ('super 807'), effectively giving them exemption from quotas in the clothing sector if US cloth is used. Although small in the share of US trade, these flows represent major values for them (as is discussed in the study of Jamaica). For Latin America, therefore, the total utilisation is remarkably high: 44% of total US imports of manufactures from the region.

This very simplified discussion of general and special preferences illustrates only some of the potential distortions. The nature and impact of the MFA are discussed as a non-tariff barrier in Chapter 3, but this description has highlighted the tariff preferences which interact with it; by the EC for the Lomé countries, but subject to strict rules about local content, and by the US 806/7 provisions, especially those for the Caribbean under super 807, but only for products using US inputs. The EC has provision for outward processing (as does Japan), but the EC scheme has been much less used, presumably because the Lomé countries enjoy more favourable tariff and quota terms. It has been used mainly in non-Lomé countries, especially in the 1980s in the Eastern European countries.

The Caribbean countries are favoured under both the US and the EC regimes, and they give an opportunity to examine how the different provisions by two major importers act. Chapter 13 on Jamaica will be used to discuss this. NAFTA (discussed below) exempts Mexico from the MFA, but with even stricter local and/or US content restrictions.

The potential effects of the CBI and Lomé are to shift the location of new industries towards favoured countries, and of 806/7 to encourage processing-intensive products or processing stages of production. To the extent that some of these were produced using foreign investment, its

33

Table 2.9 US imports under outward processing '806/7' (HTS 9802.00.80) from developing countries

	1986	1988	1989	1990
Total from developing countries (US$m)	10,219	21,770	21,529	22,722
Share in total US under outward processing (%)	28	30	30	30
Share of processing in value (%)	55	59	56	56
Share of US manufactured imports from developing countries (%)	12	18	17	17
Rate of duty(%)	4.3	2.5	2.4	2.4
Textiles, clothing and footwear				
Total from all countries (US$m)	1,434	2,382	2,757	
Share of processing in value (%)	37	45	45	
Rate of duty (%)	20	19	15	

Source: Kuwayama, 1992

Table 2.10 Shares of principal developing countries using US outward processing (percentages)

Country	1980	Country	1986	Country	1990
Mexico	37	Mexico	62	Mexico	56
Malaysia	13	South Korea	9	South Korea	10
Singapore	13	Taiwan	4	Malaysia	6
Taiwan	8	Brazil	4	Singapore	6
Philippines	7	Singapore	3	Taiwan	4
Hong Kong	7	Dominican Rep.	2	Dominican Rep.	3
South Korea	5	Haiti	2	Brazil	3
Haiti	2	Hong Kong	2	Philippines	2
Brazil	2	Malaysia	2	Thailand	2
Dominican Rep.	2	Philippines	2	Hong Kong	1
Thailand	1	Costa Rica	1	Costa Rica	1
		Jamaica	1	Haiti	1
		Colombia	0.4	Jamaica	1
		Honduras	0.3	Colombia	1
		Thailand	0.3		

Source: Kuwayama, 1992

direction was also distorted. CBI, GSP and Lomé treatment encouraged local-content-intensive processes and possible excessive use of local suppliers.

The US extended privileges similar to those under the CBI to the Andean countries in 1990, with the difference that this was limited to ten years. It is too early to see aggregate effects, and unlikely that there will be strong effects on third countries from being excluded. The effects are discussed in the Colombia chapter. Again this area offers an example for comparing the 'best available' preferences from the US and the EC to give a guide to the importance of the various differences in their legal provisions (particularly the EC preference for short-term arrangements) and their implementation.

EFFECTS ON DEVELOPING COUNTRIES FROM THE EC'S OTHER SCHEMES

In addition to the effects on developing countries of arrangements in which they participate, they may, in traditional trade terms, suffer trade diversion because of those from which they are excluded. They may, however, gain from any dynamic, growth-creating, benefits of such schemes (what is called trade creation in analyses of the dynamic effects of the Single European Market). They may see direct or policy effects from any increase in the importance of trading groups in the international economic system. The only existing group large enough to have such effects on outsiders has been the European Community.

The major changes in the Community in recent years have been the admission of three countries which are much closer in trading and industrial structure to the middle-income developing countries than are the original six or the first new group of three to be admitted, and also the process of further integration towards a 'Single European Market' (the '1992' exercise). The admission of Spain, Portugal and Greece meant that the potential for trade diversion was increased directly (through the removal of tariffs between old and new members) and indirectly, through the greater number of products which became 'sensitive' to outside competition and therefore potentially protected. The 1992 process was intended to lead to greater internal trade, through both creation and diversion, and also to more rapid growth, with corresponding dynamic effects on the rest of the world. This latter development has been examined for potential effects on the developing countries (Davenport and Page, 1991; Page, 1992) (see also Table 2.11).

The new concern about EC changes which appeared among developing countries pre-1992 reflected the higher share of competitive exports, especially manufactures, in their trade (as discussed in Chapter 1, Table 1.2). There was also perhaps a greater awareness of, or sensitivity to, trading groups and preferences because of the proliferation of preference arrange-

Table 2.11 Estimates of '1992' and Uruguay Round effects on developing country export of goods

Region	1992 effects[a]		GATT[e] Uruguay Round
	Percentage of exports to EC	Percentage of total exports	
All developing countries[b,c]	+1.5	+0.3	2.8
ACP[c]	+2.3	+1.0	−1.3
Maghreb countries[c]	+0.9	+0.5	n.a.
South Asia and China[d]	−1.0	−0.1	5.5
Four Asian NICs[d]	−6.1	−0.9	2.0
ASEAN countries[d]	−0.3	−0.0	2.1
Western Hemisphere[c]	+1.3	+0.3	1.5
OPEC[d]	+3.8	+1.1	n.a.

Notes:
[a] The elasticities and calculations are based on those reported in Davenport and Page (1991). For primary goods, the elasticities are between 0.5 and 0.7, except for fuels, at 1.2; for manufactures, and are about 2 except for machinery and transport, at 2.4. Diversion effects are expected only for manufactures, and are highest (about 5) for chemicals and for machinery and transport, and about 2 for the others. That report gives a fuller discussion of the details and limitations of the methods, and calculations for the ACP, Maghreb and Western hemisphere. The other classifications use a simplified version of this method
[b] The areas overlap and exclude some countries, so this is not the sum of the other lines
[c] 1987 values
[d] 1988 values
[e] The calculations use methods similar to those for 1992 effects and are reported in Page, Davenport and Hewitt, (1991). These are based on estimates, not final results for the settlement

Source: Page, 1991; Page with Davenport and Hewitt, 1991

ments which occurred in the late 1980s, combined with the general concern at that time about the risks of protection, discussed in more detail with respect to non-tariff barriers in Chapter 3. Because the 1992 Single Market was an extension of existing agreements within an existing group, there was effectively no requirement for consultation, under the GATT or even for groups like the ACP countries with contractual arrangements. However, the complete disregard for all outside countries, industrial and developing, which characterised both the plans and their implementation, was unusual for such a major change. Although probably legitimate under a very limited interpretation of GATT rules, because the absolute barriers to the rest of the world were not (with some exceptions) being altered, it ignored the *de facto* change in relative protection from removing internal barriers. It also ignored the provocative effect on all the EC's trading partners of such an attitude, especially in the middle of a GATT negotiating Round.

The direct effects of trade diversion will be on products which compete with EC products. These are more numerous since the entry of the

Mediterranean countries, and are particularly common among those exported to the EC by the Latin American and the East and South-East Asian countries. Any increase in the level of EC output because of more efficient allocation of resources among the member countries or in EC growth because of dynamic effects of this type will increase their demand for exports of all countries which export to them. But even in the effects from this, the normal factors favouring high-elasticity manufactured goods over low-elasticity primary products would be reduced by the diversion effect.

The conventional estimate of the effect amounts to an extra 5% on EC output. This could be more if there are greater dynamic effects, although there would not be a proportional increase in effects on the rest of the world because the dynamism would have to come from even greater benefits from integration and therefore greater diversion. It could be less if the other changes which have actually occurred since the pre-SEM estimates were made are allowed for: slower growth, which may postpone or attenuate the effect, and greater openness to Eastern Europe. The possible effects on different areas are summarised in Table 2.11 which assumes that most countries lose slightly on exports of manufactures (i.e. diversion outweighs dynamic effects), but gain on primary products. The gains therefore come to those whose exports are mainly primary, and are largest for those with significant exports to the EC.

There may also be gains particularly for firms or countries which already trade with more than one member country of the EC, and which will therefore secure some of the gains from integration. This suggests large firms or countries. There may be gains for those able and willing to watch and adapt to the very detailed changes occurring in standards for products, trading practices, etc. This again suggests size as a determinant, but it would also favour a propensity to look for policy advantages. It also probably suggests a continued bias towards encouraging exporters to specialise in one area or country. It thus reinforces the favouring of large countries.

EFFECTS FROM OTHER US ARRANGEMENTS

Even before it was implemented, expectations about the effects of NAFTA were strong, and may have had real consequences for investment, if not yet for trade flows or production. Initial US arguments were that the other Latin American, and the Caribbean countries in particular, would have little to fear because a high share of their output already enjoys preferential or duty-free access under the arrangements already discussed. But this ignored the loss of relative preference. There are strong fears in the Caribbean countries that giving Mexico the same access as they have on textiles and clothing (the rules of origin would be as tightly drawn, effectively, as those on super

807 outward processing, so it would not be better) and better (quota-free) access on agricultural products, including sugar, will have a serious effect on their exports. (One of the modifications in late 1993 was to restrict the conditions under which Mexico would be allowed to export sugar to the US.) This is discussed in more detail in the chapter on Jamaica. Broadly speaking, the effects should be similar to, but stronger than, those from admission of the Mediterranean countries to the EC, in diverting trade in a range of goods directly competitive with exports from the more advanced developing countries.

In the long run, NAFTA creates a regional group which includes a NIC as well as industrial countries. There could, as in the EC, be trade creation effects from faster growth in the member countries. If this increases their total imports, it will offset some of the loss. The difference would be that there would be substantial diversion for some primary products as well as for manufactures, so that the contrast in effects between the two and the offset in value terms would be less. The US and Canada were already much less important importers of primary goods than the EC, so that the long-run benefits to such goods from any improvement in their growth will be less. For this reason, the aggregate effects could be greater, but there may not be the risk of the specific distorting effects of damaging prospects for manufactures relative to primary products.

EFFECTS OF THE PROLIFERATION OF PREFERENCES

These may be more important than the strictly economic diversion effects which are conventionally expected from a more regional international system. As the discussion at the beginning of this chapter indicated, real regionalisation beyond normal economies of location may not be happening, but concern about it has helped to encourage the introduction or modification of a large number of schemes during the period since the mid-1980s. This encourages exporters, both firms and countries, to look towards preferences at least for short-term advantage. On the other hand, the very proliferation has illustrated the vulnerability of any schemes to the introduction of new ones, and this may discourage reliance on preferences in the long run. This could lead to the choice suggested in Chapter 1: some countries may look for preferences while others try to live with or in spite of them.

NOTES

1 Although full details were not available by December 1993, the Uruguay Round settlement displayed the same pattern of small changes, slightly biased against developing countries, and few changes in peaks or degree of escalation (GATT, 1993).

2 The agreement includes other types of assistance as well as trade so that an assessment of its trade effects does not fully reflect the implied commitment to assist these economies.

3 This was formerly under the Customs Classifications 806.30 and 807, and is frequently referred to as 806/7; in the new Tariff Classification it is now under HTS 9802.00.60 and 9802.00.80.

3

NON-TARIFF BARRIERS
International diversion

DEFINITION, AND HOLES IN THE THEORY AND THE MEASUREMENT

Most of the increase in protection after 1974, particularly by industrial countries, was not in tariffs. The restrictions imposed by the GATT system (and in some cases regional organisations) on the permitted level of tariffs, on autonomous national changes, and on discrimination among suppliers, led to a search for substitutes.

The barriers which are normally included in NTBs include quotas, licences or other types of surveillance, price administration, restraints on purchases of foreign goods, and administration of any non-trade controls in a way intended to deter imports. The most important are quotas which exist on a formal basis: import controls, fully quantified (the best known example is in textiles and clothing) or in some cases (e.g. in some agricultural trade) subject to variation with production or prices. These account for most of the measurement of recorded barriers, partly because they are most used, and partly because some of the other recognised NTBs (limits on public purchasing, for example) cannot easily be allocated to individual import categories. Administrative barriers may be difficult to distinguish from careful observance of legitimate health or safety rules or from inefficiency. Much discussion concentrates on import quotas, but export quotas (or variants of this) are also non-tariff barriers. As the international data used here are collected by the importing country and concentrate on their limits on imports, this chapter will focus on these interventions. Individual country export controls on some products (typically primary products for reasons of either security, food or military, or to promote domestic processing) are being reduced or eliminated, and no measurement will be made. Most are no longer sufficiently important to influence the trading patterns or prospects of other countries, and are therefore not relevant. The export controls which do, at least potentially. affect the trade of other countries are the remaining commodity agreements, tied aid and controls on trade with the ex-centrally planned economies. These are discussed in Chapter 5.

There are also a variety of semi-official controls on imports which amount to non-tariff barriers: voluntary export restraints imposed through government negotiation, or industry-to-industry negotiation with or without government acknowledgement, assistance, or threats of enforcement; and even greyer areas of restraint, through surveillance backed by threats that transgressing unspoken limits will encounter the imposition of a more formal control.

On other controls, stemming from internal national politics, the line between intent and effect is difficult to draw in theory, but in practice there have been surprisingly few disagreements on major trade flows. When they were first set up, mostly around 1980, official data collections were expected to be seriously biased downwards because of constraints on their ability to accuse governments of such transgressions and reluctance to include informal measures, but they have included the major private agreements (quotas among industries) or semi-trade barriers (on procurement). Private observers also hesitate before including barriers which are in many cases closer to the accepted country-specific advantages of a local producer over imports, in terms of familiarity with markets or suitable output patterns than to intentional discrimination against imports. A rigorous interpretation could lead to virtually all trade being called 'managed', in the sense that it is subject to familiarity with existing suppliers or markets, good will, legal norms, etc. This is a valid way of stressing the general market access problem for any new supplier, one which may well be particularly important for a developing country with many new suppliers, but it does not capture the real changes which have occurred and the continuing differences among markets and products in more formal and recorded barriers.

The detailed discussion of types of quotas and other possible barriers is best treated on a country and sector basis, as the variants in type and implementation are extremely large in theory, and can give rise to extraordinarily complex classification schemes, but are considerably more manageable if individual cases are considered. What is important at the aggregate level is to indicate broad trends, differences over time among importing countries or among sectors, and the overall significance of non-tariff barriers in the context of international trade and of other types of policy intervention.

That is the principal purpose of this chapter. But there are less quantifiable questions which need to be considered in assessing their level and their potential impact. In particular, much of the literature on their effects (and the quantification used in measuring them) sees them as substitutes for tariffs (it takes for granted the first of the explanations suggested at the beginning of this chapter). But this is in some ways the least plausible reason for using them: it is true that the GATT restricts tariffs, but it forbids (or has even stronger restrictions on) quotas, discrimination among suppliers, and the use of domestic regulations or taxes to discriminate against imports.

Furthermore, many countries have national legislation as well, explicitly restricting the type of cartel which is required for intervention in trade by industrial groups (or directed at foreign sectors).

If those countries which wish to move away from the multilateral system for trading and regulating trade policy which is embodied in the GATT have chosen to do so by adopting non-tariff measures rather than tariffs, other explanations must also be present. Certainly one is that an administrative measure seems more certain in its effect (particularly to any policy-maker who lacks full confidence in economic assessments of price effects and elasticities), and may also be faster. In that sense, a quota or other administrative solution is a substitute for a tariff in the same way as price control is for relying on competition: it is seen as a more effective way of achieving the same objective.

The fact that quotas are outside the GATT system means that they are unquestionably a purely national decision (or, if desired, can be taken by a restricted group of countries). This reinforces the fast response advantage, but it also means that no international justification for the reason or instrument need be made. For some types of measure, it even means that no national accounting need be made (if they are taken outside national trading law as well).

That they can be selective among suppliers (not just among products) is definitely seen as an advantage. Introducing selectivity into the tariff or safeguard measures which are permitted under the GATT has been one of the principal objectives of the countries most active in imposing non-tariff barriers, in both the Tokyo Round of trade negotiations in the 1970s and the Uruguay Round of 1986–93, the two periods when NTBs have flourished. Almost all these countries' non-tariff measures, especially those on manufactures, have been selective. In terms of the economic or industrial self-interest motives usually considered for tariff protection, an advantage for selectivity among suppliers is difficult to understand, yet the question of why this is wanted is rarely asked. None of the traditional arguments (with their varying theoretical or empirical support) for temporary or partial protection is in terms of who the potential supplier of the imports is. A balance-of-payments problem or constraint, whether cyclical or long-term, is sensitive to the total value of imports. An industrial strategy is sensitive to imports of particular products. A strategic dependency argument also is usually in terms of product. The possible justifications in traditional terms for selectivity would be either from micro-economics (predatory pricing by a firm or export subsidies by a particular government) or from non-economic security (doubts about the military vulnerability to a particular supplier). Both of these, however, could use mechanisms of protection available under the GATT, and most cases that have occurred of non-tariff barriers are difficult to interpret in these terms.

Full discussion would require more analysis of economic decision-making in developed countries than is relevant here. However, one conclusion which can be drawn from the evidence on how NTBs are used is necessary for the analysis in this chapter. Non-tariff barriers are not seen exclusively (perhaps even principally) as substitutes for tariffs. Some of the objectives are the same, but not all. It is not therefore appropriate to measure them in terms of finding a 'tariff equivalent'. This is fortunate, because the theoretical and technical problems in defining or computing one are insuperable, even if motives other than restraining imports are excluded. The tariff which would produce the same level of imports (or reduction in imports) as a given quota or other quantitative restraint could in principle be calculated for a particular point in time if the demand and supply functions governing the trade flow were known, but this would change immediately any of these conditions changed, assuming that the NTBs were not altered. In other words, one is forced to accept that the tariff equivalent is itself a function of relative prices, costs of production, levels of income, and other determinants of the import and export function. Arithmetically, such a concept may be devised. As a behavioural assumption about why the NTB is set at a particular level or how economic agents respond to it, it is clearly untenable.

There is also an additional effect from the deterrent impact of uncertainty. Unlike tariffs under the GATT system, NTBs are variable, can be imposed rapidly, and have tended to spread from product to product and supplier to supplier within affected sectors. The imposition of a control on one product and one supplier may therefore have a much wider effect – a 'discouraged exporter' problem – than can be found by looking only at the actual flow controlled. This makes an NTB-controlled international market in some ways like a pre-GATT one, when tariffs were purely national and variable.

That the NTB gives a constant quantity is (normally) the essence of why it is imposed, and the certainty that it cannot be mitigated by greater efficiency or economic developments in demand or cost conditions has an effect which cannot be expressed as a tariff-type relationship to the value of imports. There may be partial exceptions, if the NTB is expressed in terms of market share, explicitly or implicitly (through provision for regular adjustment). Some of the NTBs which are not quotas, but barriers of inconvenience (administrative barriers, deliberately excessive documentation or health or safety requirements, differentiated national standards, etc.) could be seen as equivalent to tariffs in altering costs rather than imposing quantities, although they are rarely as strictly proportionate to quantity or price as a tariff would be. It is, also, important to distinguish here between 'traditional' NTBs and those introduced by the new protection of the 1970s. Developing and some developed, if not fully industrial, countries as late as the 1970s (Greece and New Zealand, for example) had systems of licences for all imports or quotas for all imports of particular goods (frequently consumer goods), and many still retain such systems for agricultural products. These are not necessarily selective by supplier (or, as in agricultural cases like sugar quotas, the selectivity is secondary to the overall control). While the effects of any of these (except perhaps the administrative or delaying type) will be more difficult to analyse than those of a tariff, in principle the cost of any of them can be measured, at least at a particular point of time.

While an NTB may give both national control, and apparently greater certainty from the point of view of the government imposing it, the effect on private companies or individuals (even in the protecting country) is very different. One important disadvantage of NTBs compared with tariffs is that there is no legal requirement to report them to any international organisation. This is a serious problem for traders, especially new entrants. It has also been an obstacle to measuring and analysing them. The earliest international record of NTBs was the annual IMF report on restrictions. This did not include non-governmental actions, and normally mentioned only changes. It was, however, the first publication of an international organisation to recognise the end of the decline in barriers from 1974. Until the early 1980s, all research was by occasional national governments (on their own or their trading partners' policies) or individual researchers keeping systematic records of announced and reported interventions (Walter 1971, 1972; Page, 1979). The GATT began keeping internal, and then published, records in the late 1970s, but without compiling them into systematic data. UNCTAD took these over and continued them, introducing programs to permit their analysis by country imposing them or by countries affected, as part of its programme of advising trade negotiators. These have now replaced other databases in the World Bank and OECD. Since 1990, the GATT has included some information on them in its *Trade Policy Reviews*. These regular reports on all member countries were one of the few early results of the Uruguay Round. Most of the results reported in this chapter rely on data published by UNCTAD or made available from its database, or analysis by other researchers of the UNCTAD data. GATT reports have also been used for the case-study countries.

There are four possible ways of approaching the measurement of the costs of these barriers. One is direct measurement through modelling. Three use the expected effects of the barriers: (1) if quotas are assigned to a supplier country or firm, these may have a value, equivalent to a monopoly rent; (2) relative prices will be altered, so price differentials between the importing and exporting country should indicate one effect; and (3) the relation between the quantity imported and income (or output or a particular component of this) will be distorted, so measuring actual imports against some 'normal' level may be used.

The first method, modelling, is unsatisfactory because the barrier may be imposed explicitly because markets are assumed not to work efficiently and because its presence may alter the behaviour and responses on which the model was based. It is also normally empirically impossible, especially for developing countries, or for new products in trade, or for products which have been under controls for many years (even many centuries) where the structure of demand and supply are not satisfactorily modelled and are changing. The other methods are unsatisfactory because, in the absence of any market equivalent, they effectively give evidence of the presence and apparent *effect* of a barrier, not the *level* or intensity of the control. They are also unsatisfactory in practice because they require strong assumptions about what 'normal' prices or import/income relationships would be.

They may also make unreasonable assumptions about where the effects occur, or are intended to occur. It is frequently assumed that a quota allows the constrained exporter to raise prices (to the market-clearing level, given the quantity imposed). This assumption is subject to qualifications. If the importer is able to choose among various exporters (different firms within one constrained supplying country, among constrained countries, between countries with quotas and those with free access), it is the importer who will capture the 'quota rent'. This has been particularly important for the most differentiated selective schemes, as will be seen in the case-study countries subject to the textiles and clothing controls. The existence of the quota itself is a clear disadvantage (in terms of uncertainties and costs), so that it raises the effective costs of production and/or trading, reducing the rent available for all in the exporting country, and perhaps increasing exporters' costs and prices in unconstrained markets. The measured quota rent may therefore be too small because it ignores the share going to the importer and the increased cost of trading. A quota may increase the certainty, and therefore effective return to the importer. Competition may then also appear among importers. Measurements of relative prices or quantities need to be interpreted, given these possible effects, which alter the previous model; they also need credible models.

A selectivity motive makes any of these measurements inadequate, and further complicates the practical measurement of levels and effects. If the objective of a quota is (at least partially) selective by supplier, it is not possible to transfer all the rent to the importing country.

Although giving monopoly or oligopoly access to quotas on each side may make some allocation of the quota between importer and exporter more likely, rather than having it go entirely to one or the other, the amounts will depend on bargaining. The literature on quotas frequently supports auctioning as a means of allocating them (and also as a means for researchers to measure their value and thus acquire an indirect measure of the NTB). Auctioning, however, seems more likely to introduce further uncertainties in the transmission and calculation of the effect, and certainly increases uncertainty about the size of the available market for any individual supplier. This makes it unlikely to occur in an importing country, if reducing uncertainty from free markets is one of the motives for using the quota in the first place. If lower uncertainty is considered a benefit by policy-makers, then introducing new elements of uncertainty in the market seems an odd

45

way of implementing the policy. It is possible that certainty for producers of competing local products but uncertainty for importing distributors are both policy objectives in the importer, and that creating additional uncertainty for export producers is considered acceptable in the exporting country, and that none of these uncertainties alters the costs or expected return perceived from producing or selling the product, but this seems a rather restrictive set of assumptions. The fact that free markets rarely use auctions for the products which tend to face import controls (or for any other products for which there are regular markets) suggests that they are rarely regarded as the most efficient method of allocation by private decision-makers.

The case-study countries show a variety of ways of allocating quotas, and they face a variety of types of market in their importing countries. The principal conclusion relevant to this chapter is that they are too mixed to permit any general conclusion about how relative prices measure the value of the quotas or the cost of NTBs, and conditions have changed too fast in competitiveness and demand in the clothing industry for any number to have held for more than a year. For a control which has been in place for some time, and where prices in the importer, the exporter, and (for industries where controls are widespread) also in third countries have adapted to the existence of the control and expectations about its permanence, the problem is different, but equally incalculable. In these cases, it would also be hard to find comparable controlled countries to use as a normal level.

For this reason, most serious analysis of non-tariff barriers since the first quantification in Walter 1971[1] has been based on measuring the quantity of trade subject to such barriers. Within this tradition, Walter and other early measurements (Page 1979; Jones, 1983; informal GATT estimates) used what has become known as the coverage ratio: the ratio of trade in products subject to controls to total trade (for a particular sector or for a country's total imports). The alternative strand, introduced in particular by UNCTAD when it began to keep a database of NTBs in the early 1980s, was to use the frequency ratio, the ratio of the number of products covered to the total number, now normally calculated as the ratio of tariff lines covered to total tariff lines.

The central problem of measurement was the same as for tariffs or any other control: if there is an effect on volume, the greater the control, the lower the quantity imported, and therefore the lower its weight in the measure. At the limit, a total prohibition would appear as no control under the coverage ratio. The tariff line frequency measurement was devised to solve this problem, but because of the wide differences among the sizes of the flows covered by different classifications, and the changes in tariff classifications in many major importers in the last few years, this is subject to arbitrary sizes and changes. Both systems are difficult in practice to compute for countries with controls which are more disaggregated, by product or by country, than the product classification of either trade statistics (for coverage) or customs (for tariff lines). The 1970s measurements, particularly those emphasising the change in protection post-1974 in the major industrial countries, were able initially to use pre-1974 trade weights and post-1974 barriers (cf. Page, 1979). But changes in trading pattern and innovations in products mean that this needs frequent rebasing, and it becomes progressively less helpful. The problem of differing patterns of trade across countries has also discouraged the use of other countries' import patterns as a measure of 'normal', no-barrier, trade. (There are very few countries which would qualify as open, and it is arguable that they are too exceptional to use for the same reasons which explain their relatively open trade policy.) The difficulty in finding a 'normal' comparator is also an obstacle to using the relative price or import/output approaches.

None of the principal studies attempts to measure different intensities of control.[2] While any findings of increases over time, therefore, are probably valid (but underestimates) because most existing controls have been either unchanged or tightened while new ones were added, comparisons among countries, especially with very different import composition or initial tightness, must be treated with caution. This is another point on which evidence from those facing such controls in exporting countries is an important check on an aggregate measurement.

The aggregate measures of non-tariff barriers in this chapter will use coverage as far as available, because this seems to have the fewest disadvantages in showing where barriers are important, how this varies, and how it has changed. It also permits comparison with other types of intervention discussed earlier, such as the amount of trade in regional groups or the coverage of preference schemes.

A final point may need to be made about the vocabulary of discussion of non-tariff barriers. In economic terms, they do (normally) 'distort' prices, but that is their objective. The purpose may be a relatively simple alteration of incentives, in favour of domestic over imported production, or a more complex one if they are to achieve selectivity, certainty, or other non-market ends. If it is apparent what the objective is, it may be possible to suggest that other means would be more efficient. But it is clearly absurd to assume that the objective is to minimise price distortion, and then to suggest either an alternative policy or a measurement of their effect which makes this assumption. If the barriers are introduced because the importers consider their distorting effects desirable, pointing out these distortions will not prove a sufficient argument for removing them. From the perspective of this study of the effect of other countries' policies on the economies of developing countries, they may be a distortion in both the economic and (pejorative) non-economic use of the word.

RECENT TRENDS AND LEVELS OF NTBs

The goods controlled as imports most often and earliest by all importers have been first food, and then textiles and clothing. In the last thirty years, these have been joined by steel, and most recently by cars and some electronics goods. To some extent this simply reflects the commodities which have been most important in world trade.

For most of the tables in this chapter, the focus is on imports by the EC, Japan, and the US as the major importers from the developing countries, although there are some numbers available for all industrial countries. The final section of the chapter discusses controls by developing countries which affect other developing countries. These are different from those imposed by industrial countries because they have tended to be more general, at least across all suppliers and in some cases across all products. The EC has followed the usual product pattern, with additional controls on fuels (from its first foundation as the European Coal and Steel Community to its interventionist approach to oil post-1974), ships and aircraft. The US has covered substantially the same goods, while Japan has put a much stronger weight on food imports and fewer controls on manufactures.

As most agricultural trade, and frequently production as well, in industrial and developing countries has been regulated, with trade measures reinforced by domestic price and quantity controls, throughout the last 40 years (it was largely exempted from the GATT system from the beginning), coverage measures are unlikely to show major changes and, for the same reason, probably underestimate the importance of the controls. Because it tends to be regulated simultaneously by a variety of controls – tariffs, quotas, price controls or intervention points, seasonal differentials in countries – it is likely that the intensity of control is greater than for most manufactures. The long history of control also suggests that output and behaviour have adapted to such an extent that any measurement at a single point in time of the impact must be suspect. No 'normal market conditions' comparators exist, and the fluctuations in prices and flows which are not themselves controlled will be exaggerated. During the 1970s, the effect of the controls and subsidies in the EC and the US was to increase the share of production behind their barriers, making the effects of controls on the markets in and of third countries greater, more variable, and more obvious. Controls have spread to new products as these have been developed as substitutes for those already controlled (an increasing number of animal feedstuffs in the EC, for example). In some products, there have been clear switches to stronger forms of controls (dairy products in the 1980s in the EC: and towards quotas to supplement price controls). The enlargement of the EC to the south reduced the number of fruits and vegetables regarded as non-competitive, and NAFTA could do the same for the US market.

The controls on foods and other goods, with the exception of textiles and clothing, have reflected individual national policies. Japan has restricted or forbidden most imports of food in order to secure self-sufficiency and the preservation of the farming sector (and its votes). (The Japanese virtual ban on imports of rice until the Uruguay Round settlement illustrates the weighting problem: the value of its rice imports in 1990 was only $5 million; complete control of this product therefore 'counted' as only 0.002% of Japanese imports being controlled.) It has also controlled tobacco and leather. Other barriers (not allocatable to individual goods) include those on public procurement (including by public enterprises).

The US controls sugar (through quotas on individual suppliers) and has a number of restrictions on other foods (especially fresh foods, some for health or standards reasons). It has had controls on steel and shoes during part of the period under study. The earliest steel controls date from 1967. It also manages imports of oil and ships, with some coordination with Canada.

The EC effectively controls all non-tropical food imports. Most are through the collective intervention under the Common Agricultural Policy, but there are formal quotas for sugar and beef, and other arrangements for a few other products (bananas will be discussed under the case-study countries where they are important exports). A few are formally exempt from control, but surveillance and health controls affect these as well. Collective intervention in iron and steel dates from the pre-EC European Coal and Steel Community. This has been supplemented by control through public ownership in some countries at some times, and by quotas and production allocation during this period. The ECSC also provided the legal structure and the tradition of controlling coal imports, again supplemented by public ownership and/or commitment to energy policies of self-supply. On coal and oil, the difficulty of quantifying varying policies on self-sufficiency probably makes the UNCTAD estimates for controls used in the tables too low: it is arguable that both have been completely 'controlled' by a combination of identifiable controls and the threat of formal limits, at least since 1973, and for coal, since the 1940s.

Since the first 'Arrangement on Cotton Textiles', in 1961, textile and clothing imports have been controlled by the combination of an international framework with bilateral detailed controls by commodity and supplying country. The EC, the US, and Japan have all participated (although Japan mainly on silk). The numbers of importing and exporting countries and of fibres and products covered have increased in each new agreement, with the same process as was seen in animal feedstuffs of substitutes for controlled goods themselves becoming controlled. The Cotton Arrangements were replaced by the first Multi-Fibre Arrangement in 1974, which had seven bilateral agreements. This figure rose to 15 by 1977, 33 by 1978, and 80 by 1984, while the first MFA was succeeded by the Second (1977–81), Third (1982–6) and Fourth, originally also for four years, but repeatedly renewed to await the results of the Uruguay Round of GATT negotiations; it will expire at the end of 1994, when the transition away from quotas will begin. The Second MFA covered more products, and more precise categories within them, and introduced the possibility of extending controls without renegotiation as new products reached a threshold in quantity or share of market. The Third further increased restrictions by reducing the built-in annual growth rates (from 6% to, in some cases, 2% or less). It also tightened a number of restrictions on transferring quotas from year to year, on rules of origin (which also increased administrative barriers), and even on the rate at which quota utilisation could rise. The number of exporters covered also increased (China became important). The Fourth brought in the final fibres (ramie, jute, sisal), but otherwise made little quantifiable change.

For food and textiles and clothing, the regular extensions to new products or new substitutes make it arguable that the sectors should be treated as entirely subject to the effects of NTBs. The measurements used here do not use that convention, and for this reason and because tight controls themselves reduce shares and therefore weights, they are particularly vulnerable to underestimating the level and the increases in these sectors. These effects can be discussed more usefully in the context of the individual case studies.

The initial selectivity (including early clothing controls) in manufactures frequently meant the US or the EC targeting Japanese exports. The agricultural interventions were most significant against competing producers of temperate products: Canada in the northern hemisphere; Australia, New Zealand and Argentina in the southern. Coal controls were important for East European and (some other developed) countries. Oil controls were almost entirely directed at Middle Eastern countries (and Libya), as it was only later that other developing countries, including Mexico, became major exporters. It was only the later (from the 1970s) textiles and clothing controls which made serious inroads on trade with any non-OPEC developing countries, and until the 1980s, the impact of all controls on developing countries was principally on the NICs.

Table 3.1 summarises the coverage in 1986, at the beginning of the Uruguay Round of trade negotiations, with some additional data for 1981 and 1992 to show the effects of different years' trade composition. UNCTAD data on an annual basis from 1981 to 1992 show little change (except for reasons of the composition of trade, especially the share of fuel), and other observations tend to confirm this. There are various reasons for this. One, unfortunately, is the nature of the measurement. Much of the change which has occurred has been in tightening controls on commodities already facing quotas. Some quotas have been formally reduced but, more important, they have not been increased in line with incomes or changing output patterns. For goods already counted as controlled, any tightening either does not change or reduces the recorded control. But it does appear to be true that the changes since about 1980-1 have been more in details than in

Table 3.1 Non-tariff barriers[a] by sector, against industrial and developing countries (percentages)

SITC	Product coverage	MFN tariff	NTM coverage in imports from: (1981 weights)						1981 coverage using 1984 weights			1992 coverage using 1988 weights	
			World		Developed countries		Developing countries		World	Developed countries	Developing countries	World	Developing countries
			1981	1986	1981	1985	1981	1986					
0+1+22+4	All food items	6.4	40.8	42.6	44.7	47.6	32.2	33.1	35.3	40.2	26.7	26.2[b]	20.8[b]
0	Food and live animals	6.5	47.1	49.0	56.2	59.1	35.0	36.0	41.2	50.6	30.0		
22	Oilseeds and nuts	5.3	7.5	11.0	2.4	6.9	20.8	19.7	3.2	2.2	3.7		
4	Animal/vegetable oils	0.1	9.1	12.5	7.5	17.9	7.1	7.0	7.1	9.3	3.9		
2 less (22+27+28)	Agricultural raw materials	0.8	2.8	3.4	2.3	10.2	2.8	3.9	3.0	2.4	3.1		
27+28+67+68	Ores and metals	2.3	12.7	24.7	13.1	29.4	8.6	12.8	15.0	15.5	10.3		
67	Iron and steel	5.1	29.0	64.2	26.8	65.4	24.8	54.6	36.0	34.8	30.0	50.5	40.4
68	Non-ferrous metals	2.3	3.8	6.4	1.9	6.0	6.1	6.4	3.8	2.5	4.4		
3	Fuels	1.1	42.4	15.5	57.7	20.5	40.1	12.5	40.9	60.3	37.4	17.8	13.1
5	Chemicals	5.8	13.2	12.7	13.8	12.9	11.4	12.6	12.2	13.2	9.6		
6-8 less (67+68)	Manufactures, not chemicals	7.0	18.6	20.5	15.4	17.8	31.3	31.0	18.1	14.5	29.3		
61	Leather	5.1	8.2	15.9	5.5	17.9	9.9	9.9	8.6	5.4	9.9		
65	Textile yarn and fabrics	11.7	37.3	39.6	18.6	21.2	57.6	61.4	38.1	18.4	57.3	52.2	70.7
84	Clothing	17.5	67.3	67.4	40.2	38.9	77.1	77.9	59.6	37.1	67.2		
85	Footwear	13.4	71.3	32.5	65.1	24.1	71.0	27.0	80.5	67.5	83.6	35.0	42.5
0-9 less 3	All items, excluding fuels		19.6	22.7	17.2	21.1	25.3	26.2	18.7	16.0	24.1	17.7	23.5
0-9	All items	3.7	27.3	20.3	20.9	21.0	34.7	17.5	24.2	19.6	30.5	17.7	20.9

Notes:
[a] Computations have been made at the tariff-line level and results aggregated to relevant product group levels
[b] Food (excluding fish and fish products) and agricultural raw materials

Source: UNCTAD, Database on Trade Control Measures, 1992; UNCTAD 1993a

introducing major new sectors or areas into the system of controls. The Uruguay Round period from 1986 to 1993 was in principle subject to a requirement of 'standstill' for any trade barriers. (At the beginning, countries were also encouraged to 'rollback', but there is no evidence in the numbers or elsewhere of this.) Although, given that most of the barriers were contrary to the GATT, there may appear to be no logical reason for a commitment not to increase them to be regarded as more binding than the existing one not to impose them at all, in practice the existence of the negotiations probably acted as a constraint on blatant extensions.

Even with the downward biases, NTBs cover about a fifth of total imports by the industrial countries, and a quarter of their non-oil imports from the developing countries.[3] Using 1984 or 1988 instead of 1981 import weights lowers the estimated levels of controls in total and in most of the major categories. This is particularly striking for developing countries and for some categories of special interest to them (food and clothing). It is evidence of faster growth in trade in the uncontrolled categories. The share of controlled trade in their exports of food is lower than for developed countries. This could be partly because of non-competing (tropical) foods, and partly because of tighter controls. It is in manufactures that the major contrast between developing and developed countries can be seen. The differences, like the levels, for textiles and clothing are particularly high. But it is notable that industrial country controls on these categories are extremely high even in the trade among themselves, confirming that this sector, like food, has been much more outside normal economic forces than any of the other, partially controlled sectors.

The sectors which face high NTBs are also those which face the highest tariffs (except for chemicals, also in Table 3.1). The pattern is thus that certain sectors are controlled by all available methods, against all potential imports. This underlying division of trade into controlled and uncontrolled sectors must be emphasised, as much of the rest of this chapter will discuss the variations: over time, among importers, exporters, or products.

Official statistics inevitably lag behind the appearance of new economic flows,[4] but it is unfortunate that the statistical services of the international institutions responded so slowly to the growth in use of NTBs in the 1970s. It is useful to have documentation of the high level and small adjustments in the 1980s, but the period in which the major increase occurred has only occasional estimates, by different researchers, using different databases, definitions, and methods of aggregation, and with much less sophisticated recording or quantitative analysis facilities than are now available to the international organisations.

Table 3.2 summarises the principal estimates made for all industrial countries and all products. (There have been many more special studies of particular products, especially in agriculture, but these are not fully comparable.) It includes one study using the UNCTAD data but restricted to the

Table 3.2 Managed trade by country (percentage of total imports)

| Country | Walter (1972) | Total trade % | | | | | | Manufactures | | |
| | | Page (1981)[a] (1974 weights) | | | Laird and Yeats (1990) (1981 weights) | | | Page (1981) (1974 weights) | | |
	1967	1974	1979	1980	1981	1983	1986	1974	1979	1980
UK	13	38.5	47.4	47.9	11.2	13.4	12.8	0.2	17.0	17.4
Belgium/Luxembourg	30	27.5	33.4	34.0	12.6	15.4	14.3	0.9	9.1	10.0
France	20	32.8	42.6	42.7	15.7	18.8	18.6	0.0	16.0	16.2
Germany	26	37.3	47.1	47.3	11.8	13.6	15.4	0.0	17.9	18.3
Italy	19	44.1	52.2	52.3	17.2	18.7	18.2	0.0	16.1	16.4
Netherlands	14	32.5	39.8	40.1	19.9	21.4	21.4	0.0	12.8	14.8
Denmark	7	29.5	42.8	43.2	6.7	8.0	7.9	0.0	21.1	21.7
Ireland		26.8	33.5	34.0	8.2	9.7	9.7	1.5	11.0	11.7
EC		35.8	44.5	44.8	13.4	15.6	15.8	0.1	15.7	16.1
US	39	34.2	44.4	45.8	11.4	13.7	17.3	5.6	18.4	21.0
Canada	11	22.4	18.3	18.3				11.4	5.8	5.8
Japan	32	56.1	59.4	59.4	24.4	24.5	24.3	0.0	4.3	4.3
Finland		32.9	33.6	33.6	7.9	8.0	8.0	3.1	3.5	3.5
Norway	9	16.3	33.7	33.7	15.2	14.7	14.2	0.0	24.6	24.6
Sweden	12	24.7	36.3	36.3				3.1	3.4	3.4
Austria	12	20.8	30.3	30.3				0.0	13.1	13.1
Switzerland	12	16.9	18.3	18.3	19.5	19.6	19.6	2.1	3.4	3.4
Portugal	33	23.5	27.5	27.5				10.5	11.7	11.7
Australia	4	17.9	34.8	34.8				7.8	30.0	30.0
New Zealand					46.4	46.4	32.4			
OECD	13	35.3	43.8	44.5	15.1	16.7	17.7	4.0	16.8	17.4
OECD (using UNCTAD table, see Table 3.4)					27.3	28.2	20.3			

Note: [a] Including export controls by supplying countries

Sources: Walter, 1972; Page, 1981; Laird and Yeats, 1990

most limited of the definitions used by UNCTAD ('hard core' barriers, i.e. principally quotas: the fuller definition used in the principal UNCTAD tables and for the other tables in this chapter uses the broader definition given at the beginning of this chapter). All the series use weights from the first year estimated, and they all confirm that a substantial proportion of trade was and is under NTBs.[5] All the major importing countries had a high share of controlled imports.

Some of the difference in levels between the 1974 and 1981 series will be the result of the change in the share of manufactures in world trade. Although it was there that the principal rise in NTBs occurred (Table 3.2), they remained on average much less controlled than primary products. This is particularly true if trade in oil is included as controlled. Controls on imports from the developing countries were much tighter than on total imports (Table 3.3), at over 50% for all goods and 21% for manufactures compared with 44% and 17% on average, and only 24% and 11% for other industrial countries.

The estimates for changes in controls on different areas' exports in the 1970s are much more uncertain, being constrained by limitations on the data to use much broader categories of products and definitions. As most industrial countries' trade is with other industrial countries, it changed in the same direction as the total. Largely because controls on manufactures are lower, the level of controls on industrial countries' exports is lower than on their imports. For total OECD trade, it was found that about 34% of imports and 17% of exports were controlled in 1974, rising to 41% and 28% in 1979. The estimates should be treated as very uncertain, but it is probably true that while they themselves control a large proportion of their imports, they do not face as restricted an environment in their markets and have faced smaller changes. Although a questionable benefit in terms of economic welfare, this imbalance is an advantage in terms of ability to operate an independent trading strategy. The data on developing countries are very different. In their trade with the OECD countries, controls on their exports were already 50% in 1974, rising to over 60% in 1979, while even then they controlled a much lower proportion of their own imports (at least on average).

CONTROLS ON EXPORTS OF DEVELOPING COUNTRIES

It was already being argued in early UNCTAD meetings, quoted in Walter (1971), that the actual impact of such controls is greater on developing countries because they are less likely than industrial countries to have the information or the structurally flexible economies to be able to adapt to them. There are also particular difficulties in the very detailed quotas which they face on textiles and clothing. Tariff-quotas (quotas up to a certain limit, then higher tariffs, often used for their products) also raise uncertainties because, especially near the end of the year, it cannot be known until after an

Table 3.3 Managed trade between OECD/EC and developing countries
(as a percentage of total)

Country	Total trade %					Manufactures
	Page (1981) (1974 weights)		Laird and Yeats (1990) (1981 weights)			Page (1981) (1974 weights)
	1974	1979	1981	1983	1986	1979
Switzerland			18.1		18.1	
Finland			15.3		15.9	
Japan			17.4		17.4	
Norway			46.9		41.2	
New Zealand			35.3		29.1	
USA			15.5		19.1	
OECD Imports	54	62	18.8	19.6	20.6	21
Belg/Lux			12.4		13.2	
Denmark			20.9		20.9	
F.R.Germany			24.3		28.6	
France			15.5		17.4	
Greece			12.5		12.3	
UK			25.4		24.7	
Ireland			15.6		15.8	
Italy			21.2		21.3	
Netherlands			27.0		27.1	
EC Imports	55	63	21.7		23.2	34

Sources: Page, 1987; Laird and Yeats, 1990

export has arrived at its destination what duty it will pay. As noted earlier, the developing countries affected are more likely to be new entrants or to have relatively small flows, and therefore the cost of becoming and remaining informed about quotas and standards will be higher relative to the value of the export. But there is also quantifiable discrimination.

More detailed data on the 1980s from the UNCTAD database (Table 3.1) confirm that developing countries face higher barriers. This is true because the commodities which they export face more barriers and because they face higher than average barriers on some of their major exports. Walter (1971) also showed both influences, calculating that developing countries accounted for 16% of total imports by major industrial countries, but 21% of the imports covered by NTBs. For manufactures and semi-manufactures, he also found a difference.

The structure of NTBs also shows a bias against the type of products which developing countries are most likely to export first. Table 3.4 demonstrates that on the whole it is the low-technology goods which face the highest barriers; countries beyond this stage and into higher technology goods find much lower barriers. Combined with the tariff escalation up to

Table 3.4 Import coverage ratios of selected non-tariff measures applied on high technology products by selected industrial countries against all countries in 1986 (percentages)

Product groups	USA	EC	Japan
Aerospace	0	0	3
Office machines and computers	0	0	0
Electronic components	9	22	0
Telecommunications equipment	7	22	0
Drugs and medicine	1	0	4
Scientific instruments	0	14	0
Electrical machinery	1	7	0
Non-electrical machinery	5	5	0
Chemicals	3	3	64
All high technology	2.6	7.4	13.5
Medium technology	19.7	19.5	14.9
Low technology	38.1	36.1	20.9

Source: UNCTAD, *Database on Trade Control Measures*

this low technology level found in Chapter 2, this structure gives an interesting contrast in incentives: to move out of primary products into manufactures is made more difficult (because of tariffs), and the first stage within manufactures is particularly difficult (because of NTBs). It is only later that the structure becomes increasingly favourable to more advanced countries (NTB de-escalation). It would probably be wrong, however, to assume that this cross-section difference could be applied over time: the spread of controls from textiles to clothing and from primary goods in general to manufactures shows that present exporters of low technology goods cannot assume that they can rely on open markets in higher technology goods when they reach that stage.

As well as reinforcing high tariffs by falling on the same goods, NTBs substantially modify the favourable effects of GSP (Table 3.5). A quarter of the exports eligible for GSP are subject to NTBs; more than half of EC imports under GSP face NTBs. This means that only about 10% (5% for the EC) of apparently GSP-eligible goods can in fact take full advantage of the preferences which makes the relatively limited role of GSP in EC trade, which was observed in Chapter 2 even without allowing for NTBs, even more restrictive. For the countries which receive tariff preferences from the EC (and therefore do not use the GSP), in particular the ACP countries, NTBs reinforce their special position because on most goods (competing agriculture is the major exception) they are exempt from NTBs. Japan and the US have lower shares of NTB coverage as well as higher numbers for GSP. This means that, although the final line of Table 3.5 indicates that for

Table 3.5 GSP and NTBs on imports from developing countries

	EC	Japan	US	All industrial
1986 US$m				
Total imports from lcds	72,160	40,546	100,763	265,001
Imports under GSP	7,866	7,087	13,981	33,339
GSP imports facing NTBs	4,216	439	1,636	7,656
Imports facing NTBs	21,237	5,616	19,064	46,375
Percentages				
GSP imports/total imports	10.90	17.48	13.88	12.58
Share of GSP imports under NTB	53.60	6.20	11.70	23.00
Other GSP imports/total	5.06	16.40	12.25	9.69
NTB imports/total imports	29.43	13.85	18.92	17.50
Share of NTB imports under GSP	19.85	7.82	8.58	16.51
Other NTB imports/total	23.59	12.77	17.30	14.61
Share: NTB and/or GSP imports	34.49	30.25	31.17	27.19

Sources: GSP: Clark, 1991; NTBs: UNCTAD, Database on Trade Control Measures; Trade values: UN, *Monthly Bulletin of Statistics*

all three areas about a third of imports from developing countries takes place under a regime other than simple MFN, for Japan this is principally because of preferences; for the USA, more goods are subject to NTBs, but there is also a substantial GSP element; and for the EC it is principally because of NTBs.

Table 3.6 makes it clear that the principal erosion of GSP preferences by NTBs for all three areas is in textiles and clothing. (These are not eligible at all for GSP in the US scheme.) Food is also important (most food products are excluded from the EC GSP scheme). The interaction between NTBs and GSP also modifies the actual access of the apparent major beneficiaries of GSP (cf. Table 2.7 and the discussion in Chapter 2). Table 3.7 shows that many of these, especially, among the Asian NICs, Hong Kong, Taiwan, and South Korea, some of the other Asian countries, and also the major Latin American exporters, Mexico and Brazil, face NTBs on a substantial proportion of their exports. The ratios are (consistent with Tables 3.5 and 3.6) particularly high for the EC, but the Japanese figures are also very high. This suggests that the actual benefits of GSP to major exporters of manufactures among the developing countries need to be examined in more detail. The case studies confirm that it is only in some commodities and to some markets that it can be a major benefit.

Differences in their level of competitiveness with the industrial countries,

Table 3.6 GSP and NTBs by importer and by sector (percentages, 1989)

SITC	Product coverage	EC	Japan	US
0+1+22+4	All food items	27.8	9.0	49.4
0	Food and live animals	28.7	9.7	58.0
22	Oilseeds and nuts	–	–	–
4	Animal/vegetable oils	–	–	–
2 less (22+27+28)	Agricultural raw materials	0.2	4.0	61.3
27+28+67+68	Ores and metals	81.5	–	12.0
67	Iron and steel	96.3	–	13.5
68	Non-ferrous metals	1.1	–	13.7
3	Fuels	–	–	–
5	Chemicals	3.8	17.5	2.8
6–8 less (67+68)	Manufactures, not chemicals	60.9	5.6	4.9
61	Leather	3.5	69.8	–
65	Textile yarn and fabrics	75.2	35.3	2.4
84	Clothing	89.4	–	–
85	Footwear	0.7	–	–
0–9	All items	53.6	6.2	11.7

Definition: share of imports eligible for GSP covered by NTBs

Source: Clark, 1991

Table 3.7 Major beneficiaries affected by non-tariff measures on GSP-covered products (percentages, 1989)

EC		Japan		US	
Beneficiary		Beneficiary		Beneficiary	
Hong Kong	47.8	Taiwan	33.9	Mexico	10.4
South Korea	41.7	China	63.0	Brazil	24.0
China	42.5	South Korea	27.5	Dominican Rep.	40.4
India	56.9	Hong Kong	64.5	Colombia	59.5
Romania	46.0	Saudi Arabia	99.9	Philippines	21.7
Brazil	29.3	Singapore	66.8	Venezuela	31.1
Thailand	55.0	Malaysia	72.9	Guatemala	61.8
Macao	75.7	Brazil	31.5	Thailand	6.1
Pakistan	54.4	Mexico	44.8	Peru	12.8
Philippines	39.7	Bahamas	100.0	Costa Rica	20.4

Source: Clark, 1991

Table 3.8 Non-tariff barriers by major importers or regions and case study countries (percentages excluding fuel)

Region	EC	USA	Japan	Sum of these
World	23	26	24	14
Developing countries	31	24	26	15
Asia	35	28	28	16
Bangladesh	34	35	86	26
Malaysia	7	11	6	1
Thailand	67	28	35	28
Latin America and Caribbean	22	17	18	12
Colombia	5	18	5	10
Jamaica	37	40	_[a]	23
Africa	24	6	31	16
Mauritius	71[b]	26	_[a]	63
Zimbabwe	20[b]	10	2	11

Notes:
[a] Value of trade insignificant
[b] Trade with EC is under Lomé: see country chapter

in their special relationships with individual countries, in their own composition of exports, and in their level of development all affect which developing countries and areas face the most barriers. As with the pattern of escalation followed by de-escalation shown for the interaction of tariffs and NTBs, while other industrial countries enjoy the easiest access to the industrial country markets, it is in general the most advanced developing countries which face the most barriers (Table 3.8). In Tables 3.8 and 3.9a–e, the 'total' columns measure the share of controlled exports to the three major exporters in their total exports to all markets, not the total share of all controlled exports.[6]

This measurement is used principally because of the data limitations. It does, however, also indicate how important the actions of three major markets are to the trading environment faced by developing countries. Tables 7.2a–e (pp. 128–9) show how much of each area's trade is with them, and thus indicate how much of the effect comes from their share in the total and how much from how protective they are. Using 1986 controls and 1990 weights, there is little difference between average controls in total and against developing countries, but those against developing countries are significantly higher in trade with the EC. Asia faces the highest barriers (especially into the EC). It is also clear from comparing the figures for the three major industrial importers with the total that it is only Asia's much higher trade with other countries (particularly other Asian countries, as was shown in Table 2.5) which is keeping its total down. Apart from exports to

Table 3.9a World: non-tariff barriers
(percentages 1986 weights on 1990 data)

SITC	Product coverage	EC	US	Japan	Total
0+1+22+4	All food items	36	22	59	24
0	Food+live animals	43	24	64	24
22	Oilseeds and nuts	1	3	3	1
4	Animal/vegetable oils	4	1	9	2
2 less (22+27+28)	Agricultural raw materials	4	45	5	n.a.
27+28+67+68	Ores and metals	19	40	6	13
67	Iron and steel	65	80	5	35
68	Non-ferrous	6	3	1	3
3	Fuels	26	0	15	11
5	Chemicals	3	7	35	3
6–8 less (67+68)	Manufactures, not chemicals	25	26	12	15
65	Textiles, yarn and fabric	51	53	48	25
84	Apparel and clothing	71	63	10	44
85	Footwear	100	0	9	54
(0–9) less 3	All items, excluding fuels	23	26	24	14
0–9	All items	23	23	21	14

Source: Calculated from UNCTAD database

other Asian countries, it faces much higher barriers in individual markets. Thailand, which has a high share of trade with the industrial countries, therefore faces one of the highest levels of barrier. The country figures (although subject to various qualifications discussed in the case-study chapters) indicate that it is now not just the more advanced, NIC, countries which are affected. Malaysia, the most advanced, on the other hand, appears to be the least affected, because of the composition of its trade.

Although overall Africa faces higher barriers than the rest of the world, this is partly because of its relatively high share of trade with these three groups. The African figures are also distorted by the fact that these data do not allow fully for the access arrangements to the EC under the Lomé Conventions. For this reason, the high apparent share of barriers in trade with the EC is misleading. Nevertheless, the figures for Mauritius' trade with the US confirm that even African countries can face high barriers on manufactures exports.

Latin American countries face widely varying conditions, according to their trading patterns (the contrast between Colombia and Jamaica illustrates

Table 3.9b Developing countries: non-tariff barriers
(percentages 1986 weights on 1990 data)

SITC	Product coverage	EC	US	Japan	Total
0+1+22+4	All food items	28	15	62	18
0	Food+live animals	32	16	64	n.a.
22	Oilseeds and nuts	3	89	12	5
4	Animal/vegetable oils	1	1	8	1
2 less (22+27+28)	Agricultural raw materials	6	13	9	n.a.
27+28+67+68	Ores and metals	15	30	5	5
67	Iron and steel	73	74	0	20
68	Non-ferrous	11	5	0	4
3	Fuels	27	0	2	4
5	Chemicals	2	14	19	3
6–8 less (67+68)	Manufactures, not chemicals	41	26	9	17
65	Textiles, yarn and fabric	74	76	46	19
84	Apparel and clothing	86	74	10	50
85	Footwear	100	9	2	26
(0–9) less 3	All items, excluding fuels	31	24	26	15
0–9	All items	29	19	14	13

Source: Calculated from UNCTAD database

this). Overall, their relatively high trade with the US, and growing trade with other industrial countries (and now other Latin American countries) lower the significance of the controls of the three major importers.

Some of the reasons for the variations among the different areas can be seen in Table 3.9 which gives details of the main commodities (chosen from those with the highest share in total exports by developing countries in the mid-1980s). For controls on all countries, the EC's controls seem to be spread across most products, while the US and Japanese controls are more concentrated on food and on textiles and clothing (and on metals and ores for the US). Only Japan has lower controls on manufactures than on primary goods, and this is principally because of lower controls on the more finished goods. This difference among controls appears also for commodities not shown in these summaries, such as electronic goods or cars. The de-escalation of NTBs is thus subject to qualifications.

For barriers specifically against developing countries Table 3.9b shows the contrast between Japan's relatively low controls, especially on manufactures, on developing country exports. For manufactures, they are half the level of

Table 3.9c Asia: non-tariff barriers
(percentages 1986 weights on 1990 data)

SITC	Product coverage	EC	US	Japan	Total
0+1+22+4	All food items	40	11	70	24
0	Food+live animals	49	14	73	n.a.
22	Oilseeds and nuts	0	27	15	3
4	Animal/vegetable oils	0	0	8	0
2 less (22+27+28)	Agricultural raw materials	7	4	9	n.a.
27+28+67+68	Ores and metals	12	51	4	6
67	Iron and steel	62	76	0	11
68	Non-ferrous	1	1	0	0
3	Fuels	26	0	2	1
5	Chemicals	3	17	14	3
6–8 less (67+68)	Manufactures, not chemicals	39	29	10	16
65	Textiles, yarn and fabric	71	76	46	17
84	Apparel and clothing	76	76	11	46
85	Footwear	100	7	2	n.a.
(0–9) less 3	All items, excluding fuels	35	28	28	16
0–9	All items	32	25	13	12

Source: Calculated from UNCTAD database

the total for the three markets. Japan's controls on manufactures are 9% compared to 26% for all non-oil commodities, while for the other two areas controls on manufactures are higher than for other goods. While for imports from all countries, the levels of control for manufactures by the US and the EC are similar to or slightly higher than controls on other goods (all are around a quarter), for developing countries the EC is much higher (41% for manufactures compared with 31% for all non-fuel) and the US is again slightly higher. The problem for exporters is that total Japanese imports of manufactures are much lower (and the greater competitiveness of Japanese manufactures makes the lack of formal barriers less valuable, and may help to explain it). Comparing controlled exports to the major importers with trade with all importers, however, the greater share of manufactures in trade among developing countries greatly reduces the differential between the average barriers faced by their manufactures and the total, to 17% compared with 15%. The contrast between the EC and the others can also be seen in comparing its own levels for barriers to manufactures from developing

Table 3.9d Latin America and the Caribbean: non-tariff barriers
(percentages 1986 weights on 1990 data)

SITC	Product coverage	EC	US	Japan	Total
0+1+22+4	All food items	24	17	31	13
0	Food+live animals	27	18	31	n.a.
22	Oilseeds and nuts	0	4	4	0
4	Animal/vegetable oils	0	8	2	0
2 less (22+27+28)	Agricultural raw materials	7	32	10	n.a.
27+28+67+68	Ores and metals	16	26	7	11
				0	29
67	Iron and steel	76	79		
68	Non-ferrous	16	7	0	8
3	Fuels	23	0	1	2
5	Chemicals	1	13	37	5
6–8 less (67+68)	Manufactures, not chemicals	37	15	4	13
65	Textiles, yarn and fabric	93	80	26	49
84	Apparel and clothing	56	64	20	46
85	Footwear	1	0	4	n.a.
(0–9) less 3	All items, excluding fuels	22	17	18	12
0–9	All items	22	12	15	9

Source: Calculated from UNCTAD database

countries and those against all countries (41% compared with 25%), with the differences for the others much less (and for Japan, developing countries are slightly lower). For the reasons given earlier in this chapter, it is probably comparisons within data for the same country which are less at risk of differences in intensity, definition, etc.

It is mainly foods which raise the level of all primary exports controlled, and within this, the barriers imposed by the EC and Japan. The US is the major controller of metal exports. There is again a contrast between the EC and Japan in treatment of textiles and clothing, with the EC controls on clothing higher than on textiles. This reflects the improvement in competitiveness of the EC textiles industry, with the substitution of capital-intensive processes. It is now clothing where most of the EC's controls are concentrated. The US still controls both very extensively, and more from developing countries than from others.

It is in fact the high EC controls on food which raise its controls on Asian exports above the average (Table 3.9c), and the controls by the EC and Japan

Table 3.9e   Africa: non-tariff barriers (percentages 1986 weights on 1990 data)

SITC	Product coverage	EC[a]	US	Japan	Total
0+1+22+4	All food items	22	5	62	17
0	Food+live animals	23	6	63	n.a.
22	Oilseeds and nuts	4	14	0	1
4	Animal/vegetable oils	8	0	5	7
2 less (22+27+28)	Agricultural raw materials	3	0	1	n.a.
27+28+67+68	Ores and metals	9	0	3	5
67	Iron and steel	70	0	0	26
68	Non-ferrous	9	0	0	6
3	Fuels	29	0	0	17
5	Chemicals	0	0	1	0
6–8 less (67+68)	Manufactures, not chemicals	58	18	1	40
65	Textiles, yarn and fabric	66	65	83	29
84	Apparel and clothing	67	14	0	59
85	Footwear	99	0	4	n.a.
(0–9) less 3	All items, excluding fuels	24	6	31	16
(0–9)	All items	26	1	25	16

Note: Except for food and agriculture, most African countries are exempt from most controls through Lomé Convention provisions. They are included here because they restrict the use of imported material, because informal restrictions have been imposed, and because they would otherwise be treated as controlled by a regional preference scheme

Source: Calculated from UNCTAD database

help to make food the most controlled sector for Asia. But the contrast with the other importers is greatest in manufactures. Within manufactures, the controls by the EC and the US on clothing mean that almost half of all Asian exports are controlled by these two importers (helping to explain the high number for all developing countries' exports of clothing).

Latin America (Table 3.9d) faces higher controls on food from the US than does Asia, and overall on both textiles and clothing, but the figure in total is smaller because of its still heavy weight of primary exports. For both Asia and Latin America, controls on metals by the EC and the US are severe, but these have a reduced effect on the averages because they have a lower weight in their trade with these countries than in that with the rest of the world.

The aggregate figures for Africa are difficult to interpret because they do not take account of concessions like the ACP arrangements. These do not remove 'controls' from imports, because imports need to meet stringent rules of origin and also because there have been enough cases of 'surveillance' or warning to make it clear that the right of entry is not guaranteed. But they greatly reduce the intensity for ACP countries relative to other suppliers and for the EC compared with the US or Japan as a market for Africa, if a measure of this were available. The ACP countries also have a much more concentrated pattern in trade with industrial countries, and with the EC in particular, so that the controls shown in Table 3.9e represent a much larger share of their total trade. As Japan is a minor trading partner, the most important controls for them are on the exports of manufactures, especially clothing to the EC. Subject to the above qualifications, these affect 40% of their total exports of manufactures. They are thus a much more important part of their trading environment than are such controls for the other areas. Those countries which export fuels to the EC also face more controls on these exports than do fuel exporters in Latin America and Asia to the US and Japan, while African food exports, especially to the EC, also face important barriers. Even those products and countries which receive quotas (some fruits, sugar, beef, special seasonal access for vegetables and fruits) must be considered subject to controls, because they are all vulnerable to future policy in the EC, and the quotas are themselves limits. Similarly, the entry of goods like fish is considered to be controlled here because of the regulations which affect them

The data in both Tables 3.8 and 3.9 are for one year and one set of weights only. The possibility that individual countries have followed the strategy suggested earlier of increasing exports of less controlled goods rather than controlled, whether deliberately or because exporters have followed available markets, means that the impact of the controls may be underestimated, and by an increasing amount compared with the findings in the discussion of Table 3.1. The tables nevertheless offer clear evidence that, in some goods or sectors or markets, the share of controls has been high, limiting significant segments of these areas' markets and of individual commodity markets. The very high ratios for some of the commodities (even without allowing for any intervention by other importers) make it inevitable that the whole nature of the international markets in these goods has been altered, in terms of demand and supply, but also in terms of making developing countries perceive themselves as vulnerable to policy decisions taken in a limited number of countries. The evidence that this structure of controls has remained roughly unchanged throughout the 1980s makes it reasonable to expect that countries trading or producing those commodities have adapted their trading patterns, methods of approach, and perhaps industrial structures.

NTBs IN DEVELOPING COUNTRIES

One obvious response to barriers in the three principal industrial country markets would be to shift to trading with more open markets. The data on other industrial countries and on the average for all industrial countries in Tables 3.1, 3.2, and 3.3 suggest that there may be slightly lower barriers in some of these markets, but these markets are small and diverse. In the past, barriers in the developing countries were normally higher. Table 3.10 gives the figures for 1986/7 (using a frequency, not a coverage measure). On average, the levels then were not much higher: 27% compared with 20% (or even 24% using 1984 weights for industrial countries, which are perhaps more comparable with the 1983 weights used in this table). The barriers tended to be more easily seen (because they had not been recently imposed and were not concealed in the face of GATT rules), more familiar, and more stable. All these differences make them less likely to have had the effect of deterrence across a range of uncovered goods suggested for the new barriers by the industrial countries.

There are important differences among products and among areas. The controls were highest for the Latin American countries: barriers of 45% are clearly higher than those of 17–22% facing Latin America in the major industrial markets. But for Asia (excluding the oil producers of West Asia), 30% is within the same range as the controls it faced (24–31%). De Rosa (1986) also found that the Asian barriers were restrictive in the South Asian countries, but not those of South East Asia. (Although controls were low for Africa, low income may be a greater deterrent to intra-trade there.)

Among products, the principal barriers were on primary goods: food, as usual, but also ores and metals, with manufactures lower, although within these the same manufactures that are controlled by the industrial countries (in categories 6 and 8) were the most controlled. Neighbouring countries were thus a reasonable low-barrier alternative for Asia, but less so for the others. Since then, as noted earlier, there has been a tendency for developing countries to reduce their barriers, and Latin America has substantially changed its controls. By 1990, all Latin American countries had virtually eliminated the use of NTBs.

There has been a shift in trade by developing countries, and particularly by the Asian countries, to greater trade with Asia (as shown in Tables 2.5 and 2.6). This would, arithmetically, reduce the share of their exports controlled by the EC, Japan, and the US, and the lowering of NTBs in Asian and Latin American countries suggests that this also reduced the total share of controlled trade. Again, this reduces the intervention which they apparently face, but such an interpretation disregards the fact that the need to change the direction of trade itself is an 'effect' of controlled trade. The change of direction was, of course, also for other reasons, notably the faster

Table 3.10 Frequency of non-tariff measures in 70 developing countries (1986/7) (percentage of tariff categories)

	All NTMs[b]		Of which: quantitative restrictions
Product groups and regions	General + product specific	Product specific only	
A By product groups:			
All food items (SITC 0+1+22+4)	72.0	38.6	51.3
Agricultural raw materials (SITC 2−(22+27+28))	61.4	21.6	36.5
Ores and metals (SITC 27+28+67+68)	65.9	29.4	28.2
Fuels (SITC 3)	59.5	20.0	34.0
Manufactures (SITC 5+6+7+8−(67+68))	62.6	26.7	40.0
Chemicals (SITC 5)	57.7	20.6	34.9
Machinery and transport equipment (SITC 7)	59.6	22.7	37.1
Other (SITC 6 I 8−(67+68))	65.5	31.6	43.8
Miscellaneous (SITC 9)	78.1	44.5	55.5
B By regions of developing countries:			
South America and Mexico	65.5	44.6	38.0
Central America	100.0	12.7	42.2
Caribbean	50.2	44.6	11.5
North Africa[a]	88.3	48.3	25.5
Other Africa	44.5	22.4	37.4
West Asia[b]	12.8	7.6	8.8
Other Asia	36.1	29.7	28.7
70 developing countries, simple average	57.6	26.9	34.8
Idem, trade weighted average (1983 imports)	40.2	27.0	23.5

Notes:
[a] Algeria, Egypt, Morocco, Sudan and Tunisia
[b] Bahrain, Cyprus, Jordan, Kuwait, Oman, Qatar, Saudi Arabia, Syrian Arabic Republic and United Arab Emirates

Source: UNCTAD, *Database on Trade Measures*

growth of output and imports in Asia, as argued in Chapter 2, but it was, at least, not inconsistent with an effect from relative controls.

NOTES

1 He already recognised the difficulty of quantifying an effect: 'their restrictive impact may be felt at the point of importation or at several other points in the relevant credit–distribution–marketing chain. Uncertainties created by such measures . . . bear additionally on importers and distributors as well as on foreign exporters and suppliers, and tend to reinforce the primary effects of the non-tariff obstacles themselves.' (p. 196)

2 Ray, 1981 had a simple, 1, 2, 3 scheme based on his own judgement. This worked only for a few countries and barriers. Havrylyshyn 1988 (in a frequency measure for developing countries' barriers) tried giving double (or higher) weight to items with more than one type of control. This does not solve the problem of tightening a control (reducing or altering the conditions for a quota), and in some cases a second control may be introduced because the first is not binding. It has not been available for all flows.

3 It is necessary to treat fuel separately, as far as possible. The large price changes mean that in any reweighting it can have a disproportionate effect on the total. The type of controls exercised, in the forms of a preference for national (or politically reliable) suppliers or surveillance or regulation of traders are particularly difficult to classify in terms of at what point, or in which periods, they are actual barriers.

4 Good data on international lending were not available until the late 1970s.

5 The variations on all the measures among the EC countries, which in principle have had a common external trade policy (except for the UK, Ireland, and Denmark in the 1967 data, when they had not yet joined) show how composition of trade can affect the averages even when the formal controls on most goods are the same.

6 Data on other markets are either not adequate to include in the quantitative measures or completely lacking.

4

COUNTERTRADE
An amusing diversion

In the early 1980s, barter arrangements among developing countries and between them and industrial countries began to attract attention. By the mid-1980s, the estimates of its share in world trade were escalating, with even specialists and normally careful international institutions agreeing on 10–15%, although the IMF remained more cautious at about 1%. These estimates, unlike the studies quoted later in this chapter, appear to have been based on little more than other estimates (plus a little for growth since the previous estimate), and a general feeling that if it was attracting attention, it must be large. There was little precision about whether the estimates were of new arrangements or included a large proportion of old ones, now newly given a common name. Although traditionally barter trade was a way of trading with and among the non-market, centrally planned economies, the new flows were considered to be largely by, and with, the developing countries. Any increase in barter's share in total world trade approaching these estimates would have meant a significant proportion of their trade (10% of world trade in 1985 equalled 35% of their exports). This would have been much larger than the estimates discussed in Chapters 2 and 3 for such constraints as preferences or NTBs. Even if initially any increase had come as the result of individual countries' own policies, a share as high as this in total developing country trade would have been a major alteration in the trading system for all.

It is now clear that countertrade's actual importance never approached these estimates, and it had started to fall back by 1987–8 when industrial country policy-makers were responding to its apparent importance. Governments were adjusting export credit schemes, Miami and Singapore were proposing formal Barter Exchanges, and the first books were appearing.[1] It remains necessary to examine what its role in trade strategy could be and was expected to be, and how important it was at its peak if only because it was given such importance both as a new way for developing countries to intervene in trade and as a new institutional element which they needed to understand. It is also worth examining its emergence as a useful warning of the need to find a way of measuring, however approximately, an apparent change in trade before looking for its effects. The exaggerated view of countertrade was in sharp contrast to the delay in international institutions' recognition of the quantitative significance of NTBs in the late 1970s. It was perhaps partly a reaction to that error. It would perhaps be unkind to draw any parallels with the recent discovery of intra-regional trade.

THE ROLE OF COUNTERTRADE

Countertrade was seen by observers and the countries encouraging it as a means of reducing requirements for trade finance (by effectively offering a substitute for normal trade credit) and as a marketing mechanism to increase total exports. It was a response to the balance-of-payments constraints, and specifically the prior claims of creditors on foreign exchange, following the debt crisis which began in 1982 and caused a widespread collapse of bank lending to developing countries and reduction in trade credits to the most seriously affected. Where countries made countertrade compulsory, it was as an alternative to traditional quantitative controls on imports, set to match the available foreign exchange. Using it could affect the direction and composition of trade both directly, if legal conditions were different for different types of trade, and indirectly, through favouring partners willing to barter. As a developing country policy instrument, it could also be argued that it resembled special preference schemes. It was a way of introducing new exporters to new markets, by giving them an association with (by assumption) more experienced importers or brokers. At the same time, it had the advantage over preferences of being at the initiative of the developing country. In some cases (e.g. the 1983–4 Colombia scheme) experienced trading firms (including multinationals) were encouraged to find unrelated local firms to supply the exports whose certificates they needed in order to have access to imports.

Countertrade was also, like NTBs for the industrial economies (cf. Hveem, 1989; Stewart and Singh, 1988), a possible response to a greater uncertainty in the international economy, the product of a desire to introduce some quantitatively fixed elements through policy, even at the cost of some loss of economic efficiency. Some (e.g. Hveem, 1989) argued that because intra-firm trade and other 'bilateral contracting relations' were increasing, countertrade was an additional tool that served the same purposes.

These arguments are not consistent with each other, as some stress the advantages of escaping government-imposed uncertainties and others offer governments a way of intervening to avoid commercial uncertainty. This reflects the lack of clarity over which type of countertrade was in fact acquiring a new importance. The policies which initially attracted attention were launched by governments, but the brokerage and many of the reported deals were private. Officially promoting countertrade may have reflected a correct perception that trading successfully requires learning how to enter markets as well as making a competitive product. But it did not recognise the difference in effect on exporters between using it because of a public programme and learning to use trading contacts effectively.

As with traditional preferences, it was experienced exporters who were better able to take advantage of the schemes. (Although many official schemes stressed 'additionality' and, where possible, either new products or new markets, ways of defining or ensuring this had not been developed by the time countertrade declined.) More important, learning how to engage in official organised countertrade, with limited choice of trading partner and explicitly using another company for making any trading contacts abroad, was quite different from normal trading experience.

During its brief period in public discussion, it was never entirely clear what was properly included in the term. It probably normally implied a basically trade deal, not simply exports linked to and following foreign investment. It required an initial bilateral arrangement, although resale was common, with the two sides of the bargain specified simultaneously, although shipments were not necessarily at the same time. But some much broader trade agreements, between governments for example, or mixed trade and financing deals were also included by some measurements. Some observers also extended it to cover some special arrangements, like those for arms sales with local offsets, which were neither new nor normally recorded in trade. This uncertainty over terminology was the stage NTBs went through in the late 1970s; the difference proved to be that countertrade effectively disappeared before a consensus was reached on how to define it and before official statistical measures were devised.

Related deals between imports and exports, or specific importers and exporters, are normal in some industries, and it is hard in these cases to draw a line between continuing trading relationships, perhaps associated with investment, and identifiable countertrade. Countertrade was traditional in countries with substantial government involvement in trade, in particular the centrally planned economies, for the trade among themselves and with both industrial and developing countries. Some developing countries had used what might have been called countertrade as a form of exchange control (the requirement in the 1960s on some Mexican importers to show certificates of export, normally by buying them, for example), while the formal or informal export requirements imposed on foreign investors by Latin American and Asian countries were also related types of controls.

The distinguishing feature of the trade which grew in the early 1980s was that some developing countries made prior specification of the products involved on both the import and export side, normally with some evidence that the exports were additional to a country's normal exports a legal requirement for some types of trade. The first developing country to make a direct exchange of goods a requirement in the revival of the 1980s appears to have been Indonesia (1982), followed by, among others, Malaysia (for government contracts in 1983) and Colombia (in 1984, very temporarily). Other governments then encouraged it, at a minimum by introducing legislation to make it legal, and the shortage of foreign exchange and high cost of borrowing were probably also a spur to both state-owned utilities and private traders to move towards direct arrangements. Although the industrial countries and international organisations officially discouraged it, as a primitive and inefficient form of trade, they also provided first technical assistance, and later, in some cases, credit to their exporters who wished to become involved. At least part of the increase was therefore because of government intervention, and therefore a non-tariff intervention in trade. In some cases, it was also directly tied to import controls, as an alternative to exchange controls as a way of administering the allocation of export receipts among importers.

It was also encouraged by international banks, including in particular those from which the debtor countries had borrowed, although the areas and countries with the highest proportions of countertrade were not, in general, the major debtors (Kostecki, 1987). This throws some doubt on the argument that it was used to avoid showing an increase in foreign-exchange assets which could encourage demands for repayment, and also on how far it can be considered a government strategy by the developing country rather than by foreign private banks and traders. An alternative interpretation would treat it as an instrument of international banks to reduce credit exposure to developing countries while preserving their presence in them.

HISTORY OF THE BELIEF IN COUNTERTRADE
IN THE 1980s

It is striking that although most of what was written about countertrade in the mid-1980s, by researchers, the international institutions, or industrial country policy-makers, started with an explicit or implicit assumption that most other writing had been strongly negative (claimed by, *inter alia* Hveem, 1989; Banks, 1983; Stewart and Singh, 1988), it is surprisingly difficult to find condemnations written in the mid-1980s by this hypothesised school of rigidly correct economists. In fact, the pattern of almost all the literature was to give the theoretical and practical arguments against it: it restricts choice of markets, probably therefore lowers prices and increases costs, and is administratively cumbersome. The effectively cut-price exports made under it may undercut, and thus divert, normal trade flows. Then the authors point out that in the special circumstances of the 1980s (debt, lack of liquidity) there were strong arguments for it. This was normally accompanied by remarkably high estimates of its value and share in the total trade of the world or of developing countries, and an assumption that the rise of the early 1980s would prove permanent. The analysis (cf. Hveem, 1989; Stewart and Singh, 1988) assumed that the conditions which explained the rise in countertrade, the uncertainties and costly or restrictive credit, would continue, especially as legal and commercial systems had been set up to arrange deals. Countertrade was expected to continue, although probably on a plateau rather than the rapid rise estimated for the early 1980s.

But barter has always been a response to temporary or unfamiliar economic difficulties (the post-World War II dollar shortage was the most recent before the countertrade fashion (Hammond, 1990); the very short-lived, 1991–2, proposals for a ruble area in the ex-USSR), and the particular problems of shortage of liquidity and high interest rates of the early 1980s were not permanent. Nor were the institutions: the symbolic end of the countertrade era may perhaps have been the closure of Lloyds Bank's countertrade office in 1991, as it had been one of the most enthusiastic of the banks which switched from sovereign lending to countertrade brokerage. By 1992, all the countries which had introduced it as a legal requirement had rescinded their legislation. It is probably true that the extensive discussion and commercial promotion of it had led to its being considered more widely than in the 1970s as a possible strategy, but clearly this did not provide a foundation for a permanent change in trading policies.

Traditional countertrade, used by the centrally planned economies, had also increased strongly in the 1980s, as some of these countries grew (temporarily) at rapid rates, and started to turn outward; this impulse to total use, from their example and their share of markets, ended with the decline and reorganisation of their economies from 1990. Trade fell more than output and relative to world trade, and all were trying to convert their remaining trade to a currency, instead of an exchange, basis. This could have led to the reappraisal of countertrade by developing countries, but in fact the decline there appears to have preceded the changes in Eastern Europe. There was also the special case of South Africa which set up a barter bureau in 1985, when sanctions began to be effective, and which also needed it less by the end of the decade. The two commodities where arrangements which could be renamed countertrade had always been important were arms and oil (where exchanges among producers and between producers and refiners have notoriously always made defining international prices or precise destinations impractical). Both were at high levels in the 1980s (oil because of its relative price), and both declined thereafter.

HOW MUCH COUNTERTRADE WAS THERE?

As with NTBs, there was no official requirement to report countertrade deals to any international agency, and for those not under a government scheme, none to report them to an official agency even in the countries involved. As it completed its rise and fall as an item of interest for newspapers, researchers and brokers before a system like that of UNCTAD for

NTBs appeared, all measurements derive from individuals' or agencies' collections of reported deals. These were supplemented by hints of unrecorded deals which were more numerous and more valuable, and unrecorded for that reason. For developing countries, the two reports by Jones (Jones, 1984; Jones and Jagoe, 1988) provide the most comprehensive summary. These data are supplemented here by information from the UK Department of Trade and Industry files, and a report using the Oslo CT Database (Hveem, 1989) and surveys by the USITC. Among the case-study countries, three, Malaysia, Colombia and Zimbabwe, are in the top ten countries for recorded deals, and Zimbabwe in particular kept what were intended to be comprehensive data. The recorded rapid build-up in 1980–3 is uncertain because until it was recognised as an event, there was little incentive to report it, or to keep files of the reports, and there is certain to be a bias from increased reporting.

Using the Jones and Jagoe data, the total number of deals involving developing countries increased from 18 in 1980 to 304 in 1985, falling back to about 270 in 1986–7, a total of 1,358 deals over 8 years (Table 4.1). Although a total of 96 countries were involved, only five (Indonesia, China, India, Brazil and Iran) carried out more than 100 deals each, and the tenth largest (Colombia) had only 49. For Brazil's imports and Iran's exports, the principal commodity included was oil, and China as a centrally planned economy is a traditional countertrader. The value for the 55% of deals for which information is available was a total of $107 billion. It is probable that it is the largest deals which are most likely to be recorded properly, but if the value of known deals is simply extrapolated without allowance for this, it suggests a total value of just under $200 billion – 4% of total developing country exports during 1980–7. In 1985, the number of deals was roughly twice the yearly average over the period, so it is possible that countertrade affected 8–9% of their exports in that year. Excluding all deals which did not involve developing countries, this would be 2–3% of total world trade in that year.

The reasons given in the analysis, here and elsewhere, for an increase in countertrade in the 1980s were intended to explain more interest in it for industrial country–developing country trade or (in the case of liquidity shortage) trade with other developing countries. In fact, about 40% of developing country deals were with industrial countries and 35% with other developing countries, with about a quarter with the centrally planned economies. The recorded increase occurred for all of these directions (Table 4.2).

It has been conventional to assume that countertrade was more important for developing countries than for industrial countries. A Norwegian survey including the US (for which arms deals of various types may influence the data) found that a higher share of its exports than its imports came under countertrade (5% compared with 2%) (Hveem, 1989: 43). This could cast doubt on the relative importance of developing countries, but given the

Table 4.1 Reported countertrade deals involving developing countries, by partner 1980–7 (number of deals by year deal signed)

	Total	1980	1981	1982	1983	1984	1985	1986	1987	Year not known
Total	1,358	18	32	48	123	160	304	270	272	131
of which with:										
OECD countries	610	9	7	56	67	84	136	104	110	77
Eastern bloc countries	286	3	12	14	15	32	63	61	64	22
Developing countries	462	6	13	18	41	44	105	105	98	32
Number of developing countries	56	13	23	27	35	44	60	72	65	

Source: Jones and Jagoe, 1988

Table 4.2 Regional summary of reported third world countertrade deals, 1980–7 (number of deals by period in which deal signed)

Region	Total	1980–3	1984–7	Year not known	Shares to: Industrial countries	Developing countries	Centrally planned countries
North Africa	128	10	104	14	40	45	16
Middle East	215	27	170	18	36	54	11
Sub-Sabaran Africa	209	22	162	25	23	50	27
South Asia	213	38	157	18	31	48	21
East Asia	466	117	323	26	50	38	12
Latin America	352	42	265	45	32	45	23
Caribbean Islands	51	8	38	5	45	43	12
Total of table[a]	1,634	264	1,219	151			
Total deals	1,358	221	1,006	131	40	35	25

Note: [a] Total of table does not sum to the total number of deals because South/South deals between developing countries in different regions are counted in each region. However, deals between two developing countries in the same region are counted only once. Therefore, the total figure for each region represents the total number of deals that region has been involved in

Source: Jones and Jagoe, 1988

double-sided nature of countertrade, this divergence between imports and exports is inherently implausible (and is a useful reminder of the unreliability of informal surveys). The Oslo data in general found average values for countertrade by country which, when compared with export data, gave at most 2% for the major participants. (If US military exports and exports tied to investment rather than imports are excluded from the data, the figure for US exports could also have been about 2%.) If trade among the centrally planned economies is excluded, this suggests a share in total world trade of 1.5%, giving a total for industrial and developing country countertrade in its peak year, on generous estimates, of about 4%. The number of deals was perceptibly declining by 1987–8, and inevitably the attention of analyses and data banks faded, but the total by the early 1990s is unlikely to be more than the average for the mid-1980s of about 2%, and was probably less. The centrally planned economies (including China) started to end their arrangements in 1990, and except for a few special cases of long-term contracts (Cuba, India) had probably done so by 1993.

At the time when data suggested it was important, it was principally used for primary products (although promoted by governments to encourage manufactures and other products), with oil accounting for almost a quarter of the deals (Table 4.3). The breakdown of individual products by sector gives a questionable weighting (because there can be several products in each deal), but in general it confirms the importance of primary products.

The small numbers involved, the high concentration on a few countries, and probably major recording differences between important and less important countries, make more disaggregated analysis increasingly questionable, but Tables 4.2 and 4.3 give the available numbers by area and similar tables are presented for the three major countertrading case-study countries, Malaysia, Colombia and Zimbabwe, in the country chapters. The Asian countries account for almost half the total deals. For South Asia, they are mainly used in trade with other developing countries, while East Asia has used them in trade with industrial countries. Even for these (manufactures-exporting) countries, primary products are most important, but for both South and South-East Asia clothing and textiles have also had high recorded shares in exports. The construction and other capital equipment among South-East Asia's imports probably come from the government contracts which were required to use countertrade. None of the major products listed here could be considered a non-traditional export.

In Latin America, however, there is an apparent intra-industry trade in cars and parts, reflecting the region's increasing competitiveness as a part of international production in this industry during the period. This was the area where there are most examples of explicit requirement of additionality in the form of new products or destinations: this seems at least to have affected the way in which these commodities were traded, if not the total

Table 4.3 Total deals by product (percentages)

Sectors	Developing countries		E and SE Asia		South Asia		Latin America		Caribbean		Africa	
	Exports	Imports	Exports	Imports	Exports	Imports	Exports	Imports	Exports	Imports	Exports	Imports
Agricultural, forestry and food products	40.5	24.9	49.4	22.2	37.8	18.1	44.2	22.1	33.3	28.6	53.2	19.7
Ores, minerals and metals	13.6	10.4	11.8	11.8	10.5	22.0	15.5	6.1	24.4	7.1	13.2	7.1
Crude oil, gas and related products	10.6	6.9	4.2	4.5	2.1	9.3	6.0	15.3	10.2	5.9	6.8	3.0
Vehicles, transport equipment and military equipment	5.9	13.6	5.2	12.0	6.5	7.6	8.4	20.4	1.3	13.1	3.0	15.8
Manufacturing/ processing equipment and construction projects	5.3	16.3	5.2	20.3	9.9	16.2	5.8	13.1	5.1	15.5	2.5	14.9
Miscellaneous manufactured products	22.1	24.0	22.3	25.5	29.5	24.1	18.3	18.8	23.1	27.4	20.3	36.4
Service and miscellaneous	1.9	4.0	1.9	3.7	3.6	2.6	1.8	4.2	2.6	2.4	1.0	3.0
Total (rounded)	100.0	100.0	100.0	100.0	100.0	100.0	100.0	100.0	100.0	100.0	100.0	100.0

Table 4.3 Continued

Products	Developing countries		E and SE Asia		South Asia		Latin America		Caribbean		Africa	
	Exports	Imports	Exports	Imports	Exports	Imports	Exports	Imports	Exports	Imports	Exports	Imports
Crude oil	23.9			3.3		7.6		11.2			6.5	
Tobacco											6.2	
Cereals	16.0		7.2				6.6	4.2			5.8	3.7
Road vehicles and parts	6.5				7.8		4.1	9.0		8.3		7.1
Agricultural machinery (excl. tractors)											4.1	
Clothing and textiles	15.2		6.1	8.6			3.9					3.9
Sugar and products							11.5		15.4			
Bauxite and alumina								4.3				
Coffee and products	6.3											
Timber and plywood	8.7		7.5									
Rubber	8.1		3.6									
Fruits and vegetables	6.4											
Vegetable oils			4.0									
Fertilisers				6.4		5.5						
Construction projects				4.1								
Iron and steel				3.7		4.5						
Electricity supply equipment				3.4								
Tea						5.3						
Cotton						4.6						

Source: Jones and Jagoe, 1988

value of the trade flows. Except by the Caribbean countries, it was mainly used for trade with other developing countries.

African trade was predominantly in primary exports in exchange for manufactured exports (and imports of cereals). This product composition is surprising, given the direction of African countries' countertrade which is more to other developing countries.

COUNTERTRADE AS A STRATEGY OR RESPONSE

The explanations offered *a priori* for countries to consider countertrade, as indicated earlier in this chapter, were a mixture of explanations for governments to adopt it as a policy and for traders to use it as a response to policies or economic constraints. As such, it can be interpreted as simply the equivalent of any other financial tool to be adopted in particular liquidity and interest conditions.[2] The large number of banks and economic consultancies which established countertrading arms would support this interpretation. But if it was only this, it was an unusual financial instrument, since it was being advocated, simultaneously, by interventionist developing country policy-makers (and their academic supporters) as a way of taking an initiative on their own exports, or at least of evading controls by others. It shared this dual interpretation with bank lending to developing countries in the 1970s, perhaps strengthening the case for regarding it as a substitute for that lending.

The idea that it was a response to, or a part of, a more managed, less arm's-length-trading international economy could be consistent with these financial explanations, but its rise and subsequent fall in the 1980s still need to be explained by defining the circumstances which made such a tool first needed, then less needed. In fact, part of the explanation of the rise and fall of recorded non-government deals could simply be that normal arrangements between companies were attracting unusual attention and reporting because more people had become aware of them. International trade studies had been moving into increasing recognition of structural and institutional elements which have always been present in trade.

There were some market problems of the early 1980s which might have encouraged countertrade as a temporary financial tool, but which then diminished. These include high interest rates, large fluctuations in exchange rates and prices (even the 1992 changes were substantially less than the earlier 40% move for the dollar within a year or the rise and fall in the oil price), and the temporary removal of even basic government cover for export credits to the most heavily indebted countries. The shift from primary products to manufactures in developing country exports reduces the demand for countertrade as an insurance against instability in commodity markets, both absolutely and because they are a less important part of most developing countries' trade.

Most of the top twelve countries in countertrade (which means those with a recorded total of at least 44 deals in eight years) were among the major developing country traders. The exceptions are India, Zimbabwe, Colombia, and Pakistan, which are major users of countertrade but not major traders, while the major traders which do not appear to have been major counter-traders are Hong Kong and Singapore. The absence of the latter two is consistent with their normal lack of direct government intervention in trade, but it also suggests that private companies in those more financially secure countries saw no reason to use countertrade, either to gain new access to markets or to avoid foreign-exchange restraints or other constraints on trade. For India, a high share of trade with the ex-USSR is probably responsible for its familiarity with this type of trade. It was natural for it to expand its use during the 1980s to trade with other developing countries (Jones and Jagoe, 1988: 74), when it became an accepted instrument, and using it was consistent with a still administered economy.

Some countries saw it as as a national policy initiative, and it is probably possible to see it as part of the general shift of developing country policy towards looking at active export promotion, rather than import-substitution policies, which followed the success of exports by the NICs in the 1970s, although they had not used countertrade as a tool. It also followed the explosion of advocacy outside developing countries of the export-led model of development. Initially, at least, this interpretation of the NICs' success put insufficient emphasis on how an increase in exports was to be achieved; thus a method which appeared to encourage an increase in exports but to shift the difficulties of achieving it to specific actors, whether public or private companies, had an obvious attraction for governments. Heavy indebtedness or liquidity problems and high interest rates could have increased the attraction.

If export promotion was an important part of the explanation, at least for government involvement in countertrade, then the more thorough examination of how the NICs achieved their success and the general retreat from policy intervention, which has been seen in Chapters 2 and 3 on the use of tariffs and NTBs, may have contributed to explaining its decline in the second half of the 1980s.

The case-study countries were not chosen with countertrade as a criterion but five of them were in the top fourteen identified countertraders; Jamaica was relatively important for its size (it had fourteen deals) and only Mauritius appears to have shown little interest.[3] For, at least, Malaysia, Thailand, Colombia, and Zimbabwe, countertrade was definitely regarded as part of an export promotion policy. But among these, the Asian countries did not see it as particularly directed at new or manufactured exports, and therefore in their case it appears to have been more an attempt to avoid increasing debts. Zimbabwe saw it principally as a way of promoting primary exports, although with some emphasis on finding new markets in other developing countries to supplement trade with the industrial countries. Only Colombia used it as an instrument of promoting the non-traditional goods implicitly assumed in export-led strategies.

The explanations for countertrade in individual countries and the *a priori* suggestions which appear consistent with the aggregate data are principally found in the international economic circumstances of the early and mid-1980s, of uncertainty, fluctuating prices, and inadequate and expensive credit. Contrary to views at the time, there does not appear to have been a general move to barter or other forms of bilateral trading deal, for either the industrial or the developing country policy reasons which were advanced. Although it reached significant shares of individual countries' trade flows in a few years, this can be explained in terms of their own policies in a particular situation. It does not appear to have reached an international level which required other developing countries to alter their own trading or policy responses.

NOTES

1 Specialist conferences, an earlier indicator, had already peaked.
2 'It is a modern management technique, used in much the same way as a sophisticated trade financing package is used, to win an important export contract,' (Hammond, 1990: 42).
3 The only example found in any of the files was of 250 Mauritian teachers sent to Zimbabwe and paid for in beef.

5

OTHER OFFICIAL CONTROLS AFFECTING DEVELOPING COUNTRY TRADE

A variety of other policies can have major effects on the trade of individual developing countries, although their impact on total world trade is limited. Tied aid, export credits and security-inspired restrictions on types and directions of some exports impose constraints on their imports from industrial countries. The few remaining commodity agreements can affect both importers and exporters of the relevant products. For most small countries (or small exporters of a commodity) they are effectively external interventions, even if there is formal participation in decisions. Finally there is a range of other policies accepted, for example by their inclusion in GATT negotiations, as potentially related to trade. These have effects which are difficult to measure or to quantify on a product and market basis, but which are potentially important constraints on a country's own trade strategy. They include regulations on the protection of health, the environment, and intellectual property.

OFFICIAL DEVELOPMENT ASSISTANCE

All aid is tied to some extent because its use is restricted formally or informally to the objectives of the donor. It is sometimes argued that any capital inflows can be used to replace a country's own spending and the equivalent amount spent on other imports, but this is true only if the aid is for purposes within a country's own programme and budget. It need not be true, at least for a whole aid programme, or it may be true only over a period of years. Donors have their own view on what types of structural change are desirable and of priorities among these. The more important aid is in total to a country's total external flows and in its economy generally the more likely it is that some part of it should be considered an effective constraint on how external resources are used.

In addition, some aid is formally tied to procurement in the donor country or in a restricted choice of countries: EC countries' bilateral aid can in principle be spent in any member state or, normally, in other ACP countries; Japanese aid normally in any OECD or developing country.

Actual donor-tied aid may in fact be larger than is formally recorded because of informal pressure, backed by the desire of the recipients to ensure future flows. Aid that is constrained by supplier can perhaps be considered analogous to an external tariff on imports, while aid constrained by purpose is more analogous to a quantitative control. Given that all donors prefer their own suppliers, the reason for formal tying is likely to be that the donor is not the most competitive supplier; there is also direct evidence that goods obtained in this way cost more than others available (see the Bangladesh study, in particular).

The tables in this chapter measure the potential effect of aid in diverting trade by looking at the ratio of aid flows to the value of imports (Tables 5.1 to 5.3). Imports of goods data are used, although some of the aid is tied to imports of services, in particular technical assistance (Table 5.4). As imports of services data are unreliable for all countries, and particularly so for developing countries and for all regional aggregates, there is little choice, and using goods as the base makes possible comparisons with other trade constraints. Technical assistance can be formally tied or untied. On average it amounts to about a fifth of the total, but it is particularly high for the EC countries, and low for Japan.

The decline in the role of official assistance in capital flows to most developing countries in the 1970s led to a fall in the proportion of imports dependent on donors' priorities (Table 5.1). The share had been around 10% in 1970; it fell to about 6% in the mid 1970s, and reached its lowest point at the end of the decade. From about 1980 there were two major changes. The first was the rise in the ratio for all developing countries, back to 8% by 1990. As this took place not because of a strong rise in aid inflows, but because of a fall in private inflows, it is likely to indicate more constraints on the composition as well as the level of imports. The second change was the increasing concentration of aid on the poorest countries and on Africa in particular. In 1970, Asia was as important a recipient as Africa, and Latin America still had a significant share of its imports financed by aid (over 6%). The fall in share for Asia was much larger because the decline in relative flow for Latin America was moderated by an even sharper fall for private inflows. But both are now under 5%, so that it is reasonable to assume that for many countries the allocation could be managed to minimise any constraint on the composition of trade or output.

For Africa, in contrast, aid now finances more than a third of its imports. The potential effect of this on imports, and through them on the domestic economy, is very different from the ratios of 10–15% of the early 1970s. Table 5.2 also gives the 1990 share of aid flows in total output. This makes the difference between Africa and the other developing countries even more striking (10% in contrast to 1% or less), and also indicates that there is a clear polarisation between major aid recipients and other countries which receive quite small amounts (data for countries not shown here support this).

Table 5.1 Aid and imports

Region/country	1970	1975	1979	1980	1985	1990
Aid: Official development assistance ($ m)						
Developing countries	6,950	12,135	18,642	22,186	32,260	57,986
Asia	3,103	5,877	11,520	13,318	11,649	17,933
Latin America	1,181	1,784	2,542	3,055	3,427	5,388
Africa	1,245	3,174	6,734	8,078	9,533	17,884
Bangladesh	n.a.	956	1,161	1,262	1,131	2,100
Malaysia	27	97	125	135	229	469
Thailand	74	90	393	418	459	797
Colombia	160	86	54	90	62	96
Jamaica	11	53	98	131	169	273
Mauritius	6	26	32	33	27	89
Zimbabwe	1	4	12	164	237	340
Ratio of aid to imports of goods (%)						
Developing countries	10.33	6.26	5.53	5.09	7.74	7.83
Asia	12.78	8.81	8.32	7.36	5.21	3.81
Latin America	6.48	3.31	2.91	2.64	4.67	4.77
Africa	14.29	13.41	18.73	17.54	25.81	35.25
Bangladesh	n.a.	72.37	60.85	48.56	40.81	58.37
Malaysia	1.91	2.72	1.59	1.25	1.86	1.60
Thailand	5.70	5.75	5.49	4.54	4.97	2.39
Colombia	18.98	4.72	1.67	1.93	1.50	1.72
Jamaica	2.11	7.88	9.86	11.96	15.21	14.69
Mauritius	8.00	0.43	5.66	5.42	5.18	5.50
Zimbabwe	0.26		1.29	11.33	22.99	16.01

Sources: OECD, *Development Co-operation* and *Geographical Distribution of Financial Flows to Developing Countries*, annual issues

Among the countries to be examined in detail, only two were minor recipients in 1970 (Bangladesh and Zimbabwe were not then independent countries). Thailand, Malaysia, and Colombia (which was erratically high in 1970) are now low, with Mauritius also low, but Bangladesh, Zimbabwe, and Jamaica all have high shares. The persistent figure of around 50–60% for Bangladesh suggests a very strong role for aid flows and donors in the economy.

Table 5.2 shows that about a third of aid is tied to donors' exports. This share has been falling, partly because more aid is going through multilateral institutions and partly because the share of bilateral aid which is untied rose in the 1980s compared with the 1970s. For Africa, however, even tied aid alone is now a very substantial share of its total imports (14% in 1990), as it

Table 5.2 Aid and tied aid ratios 1990 (percentages)

Region/country	All aid/ imports	Tied aid/ imports	Aid/ GNP
Developing countries	7.83	3.89	n.a.
Asia	3.81	1.23	1.0
Latin America	4.77	1.66	0.5
Africa	35.25	13.87	10.8
Bangladesh	58.37	14.98	11.4
Malaysia	1.60	0.68	1.4
Thailand	2.39	0.99	1.2
Colombia	1.72	0.79	0.3
Jamaica	14.69	6.41	7.9
Mauritius	5.50	2.65	n.a.
Zimbabwe	16.01	7.15	6.3

Sources: OECD, *Development Co-operation* and *Geographical Distribution of Financial Flows to Developing Countries*, annual issues

is also for Bangladesh. For both, this is in spite of the high share of their aid inflows from multinational institutions.

Except for joint EC aid, which is tied to EC and ACP suppliers, most aid from multinational institutions is effectively without restraint by supplier, and in the case of the World Bank, an increasing proportion has been used in other developing countries. This change in source by the international institutions and efforts by bilateral donors to introduce constraints on the change by setting up bilateral/multilateral projects with a tying element suggest that supplier constraints in bilateral aid should now be considered a constraint in potentially limiting exports by developing countries, as well as a constraint on the imports of the recipients of tied aid. This is particularly important for the more advanced countries in Latin America and Asia which have tended to receive the aid contracts. But even the less advanced can supply some aid projects. ACP countries obtained about a quarter of European Development Fund projects in 1985–90, some complained of informal preference shown to EC suppliers over ACP suppliers. The diversion effect from developing country exports cannot be calculated. It is probably still quantitatively small. (The ratio of all tied aid to developing country exports is 2%.)

EXPORT CREDITS

There are two reasons to include the use of export credits as a potentially distorting influence on trade. The first is that few developing countries have schemes comparable to those of the industrial countries, and industrial

Table 5.3 Multilateral and untied aid ($ m or percentages)

Regions	1970	1975	1980	1985	1990
All developing countries					
Multilateral	1,277	4,046	9,177	6,111	15,979
A Multi exc. EC	1,119	3,371	7,219	5,770	12,421
Bilateral aid	5,672	9,801	13,009	24,460	56,684
B Bilateral untied	(1,615 est.)	2,790	6,966	10,595	31,446
Total untied = A + B	2,734	6,161	14,185	16,365	43,867
Tied/imports	(6.26% est.)	3.97%	1.84%	3.41%	3.89%
Asia multilateral		2,423	3,713	3,242	4,868
Asia bilateral		9,097	9,605	8,407	13,065
Asia bilateral untied			5,143	2,900	7,248
Asia total untied			8,856	6,142	12,116
Asia tied/imports			2.47%	2.46%	1.23%
Latin America multi-					
lateral		668	920	799	1,171
Latin America bilateral		1,874	2,135	2,628	4,217
Latin America bilateral					
untied			1,143	907	2,339
Latin America untied			2,063	1,706	3,510
Latin America tied/					
imports			0.86%	2.35%	1.66%
Africa multilateral		1,971	2,409	2,844	6,066
Africa bilateral		4,763	5,669	6,689	11,453
Africa bilateral untied			3,035	2,308	6,354
Africa untied			5,444	5,152	10,847
Africa tied/imports			5.72%	11.86%	13.87%

Note: The average tied ratio for all bilateral aid is assumed for all areas

Sources: OECD, *Development Co-operation* and *Geographical Distribution of Financial Flows to Developing Countries*, annual issues

countries offer lower interest rates on credits to developing than to other industrial countries. There could be distortion on both the demand and the supply side, i.e. favouring increasing the share of imports from industrial countries in developing country trade, and of exports to developing countries in industrial country trade. In its impact on developing countries, this is effectively a distorting (relative) constraint away from trade with other developing countries. It is probable that any effect has been small because the value of export credits has not been high relative to total trade (Table 5.5, but data are very unreliable and probably not comparable from country to country). The role of official credits and official guarantees declined in the mid-1980s as many major debtors (or potential debt problem countries) were removed from the lists of eligible countries. As their circum-

Table 5.4   Relative importance of technical co-operation, 1989–90 average
(percentages)

| | Share of T.C. in: | |
	Bilateral ODA	Total ODA
Belgium	38.7	22.6
Denmark	16.3	10.0
France	35.4	29.7
Germany	31.2	28.9
Ireland	53.8	21.3
Italy	16.6	10.7
Netherlands	39.1	31.0
Portugal	47.5	37.0
Spain	26.8	16.4
UK	40.8	25.2
Japan	15.4	13.7
US	28.5	25.6
Total DAC	25.8	21.0

Source: OECD, *Development Co-operation*, annual issues

stances improved, the demand for the relative security of official inter-vention became more important for some exporters than in the past, and there was considerable pressure in 1990–1 to reach agreement on the use of official credits and guarantees. As banks have been more ready to re-enter more markets, the symbolic role of official credit may have declined again, helped, until the late 1992 currency realignments, by reduced competition among lending countries with varying currency prospects.

The other source of influence is when the credits are used with tied aid, to provide financing which, on average, is on softer than average interest terms, and with a strong tie to the donor's country, and to a particular firm. This can be important in particular projects in particular countries, but the aggregate values of aid plus credits to the relatively high-income countries which tend to receive such packages strongly suggest that they do not have an effect on the degree of control facing other developing countries in general. As they are frequently available from more than one supplier in competition, they are more likely to influence the choice of supplier for an already chosen project, without external effects on other trade. Colombia, Malaysia, and Thailand have attracted such finance.

Both the use of tied aid and the proportion of aid specifically tied to trade credits are higher among the EC countries than for the US. Both are very low for Japan (data are inadequate, and informal tying occurs as well as recorded, but both industrial studies and the limited OECD data support this). The distortions on the import side are therefore most likely for

Table 5.5　Export credits as share of imports (percentages)

Region/country	1980	1990
Developing	1.23	0.67
Asia	0.00	0.00
Latin America	0.00	0.00
Africa	0.00	1.25
Bangladesh	0.00	0.00
Malaysia	0.08	0.06
Thailand	0.98	0.89
Colombia	2.36	0.25
Jamaica	1.46	2.26
Mauritius	0.00	0.00
Zimbabwe	0.00	0.00

Sources: OECD, *Development Co-operation* and *Geographical Distribution of Financial Flows to Developing Countries*, annual issues

countries with a high share of trade with the EC. The US has, however, been shifting since 1991 towards more use of tying. As Table 5.6 indicates, there are significant and persistent differences among donors in the regional distribution of their aid. In US aid, apart from that going to the Middle East, there has been a sharp shift from Asia to Latin America. Asia remains the most important for Japan. EC aid, except from Germany and the Netherlands, goes predominantly to sub-Saharan Africa, so that any effects on import or export diversion are likely to be strongest on Africa, reinforcing the effect of the large quantity of aid, although African countries also have a high share of their aid from multilateral institutions. Table 5.7 for 1990 confirms these differences for the principal recipients.

COMMODITY AGREEMENTS

The only remaining agreements which might be affecting exports are those for oil and coffee. These would principally affect Colombia among the case-country studies. Agreements in other, mainly agricultural, commodities were nominally in force at some points in the 1980s, but not with enforceable effects on prices or volumes. For other commodities, therefore, it seems unlikely that countries' trade or output intentions are now being influenced by pacts or the expectations or recent history of pacts. This does not mean that commodities do not face intervention, but it is more likely to be either on the importer side (quotas such as those for sugar or bananas) or the exporter's own policies. There is no separate influence from commodity agreements. Even for the two which remain, it has always been uncertain how strong their long-term influence on maintaining market shares or prices has been. The disappearance of the other commodity agreements may have

Table 5.6 Regional distribution of ODA by individual DAC donors and multilateral agencies (percentage of gross disbursements)

Country/institution	Sub-Saharan Africa			South Asia			Other Asia and Oceania			Middle East and North Africa[b]			Latin America and Caribbean		
	80/81	85/86	90/91	80/81	85/86	90/91	80/81	85/86	90/91	80/81	85/86	90/91	80/81	85/86	90/91
DAC countries, bilateral															
US	15.8	14.9	11.8	12.8	8.7	6.7	9.2	7.8	3.6	50.2	48.2	58.1	12.2	20.3	19.8
Japan	10.0	10.4	11.5	25.8	25.0	15.3	49.1	48.0	53.2	8.3	8.3	11.7	6.9	8.3	8.3
France	49.2	52.6	57.9	4.4	4.7	3.0	19.9	18.6	18.3	19.3	16.7	15.4	7.3	7.4	5.3
Germany	29.2	31.1	43.0	20.4	18.7	10.4	9.3	14.2	11.9	29.5	22.9	24.6	11.7	13.1	10.0
Nordic countries, total	52.6	60.6	59.6	24.9	22.6	15.4	13.9	8.4	8.0	4.8	2.8	6.9	3.8	5.5	10.1
of which: Denmark	51.6	60.1	58.8	31.1	26.3	22.4	8.9	6.8	4.9	6.2	4.7	7.5	2.2	2.2	6.4
Finland	60.6	63.8	56.4	7.5	14.9	12.0	21.0	8.7	11.5	6.6	5.5	12.0	4.1	7.2	8.0
Norway	54.1	64.0	63.8	30.0	25.7	19.8	6.1	3.8	4.0	6.7	1.1	1.2	3.1	5.4	11.0
Sweden	51.5	58.1	59.0	22.2	20.2	10.9	18.4	12.4	10.2	3.2	2.1	7.4	4.7	7.3	12.4
Italy	55.2	68.2	45.0	1.7	6.1	2.4	6.5	4.0	4.2	28.5	11.8	19.6	8.1	10.0	21.1
Netherlands	31.2	39.4	35.8	24.8	20.2	18.6	10.6	12.6	16.5	5.4	6.1	5.9	27.9	21.8	23.1
UK	37.0	39.4	48.1	40.0	33.2	26.1	8.5	11.1	10.4	8.3	8.7	7.1	6.2	7.5	8.2
Canada	38.6	40.3	51.7	34.8	27.5	14.8	5.8	11.5	12.5	8.0	2.8	7.8	12.8	17.8	13.2
Australia	5.7	6.0	8.6	10.8	4.8	7.2	81.4	87.8	81.8	2.0	1.0	2.4	0.1	0.4	0.1
New Zealand	2.5	1.2	1.9	2.1	0.7	0.9	94.2	97.7	96.3	–	–	0.3	1.2	0.5	0.8

Table 5.6 Continued

Country/institution	Sub-Saharan Africa			South Asia			Other Asia and Oceania			Middle East and North Africa[b]			Latin America and Caribbean		
	80/81	85/86	90/91	80/81	85/86	90/91	80/81	85/86	90/91	80/81	85/86	90/91	80/81	85/86	90/91
Other DAC, total	45.7	54.9	40.9	8.8	7.6	7.4	15.6	6.8	18.6	23.5	21.5	16.9	6.3	9.2	16.1
of which: Austria	7.3	9.1	15.8	5.1	2.8	5.1	29.5	6.7	37.9	53.9	77.0	35.6	3.7	4.4	4.8
Belgium	66.0	76.3	63.2	5.0	3.8	4.5	11.9	7.7	9.9	12.2	6.1	12.3	4.9	6.1	10.2
Ireland	95.9	96.5	93.8	1.4	1.9	1.9	0.7	1.6	0.6	–	–	3.1	1.4	0.8	1.2
Portugal	–	–	100.0	–	–	–	–	–	–	–	–	–	–	–	–
Spain	–	–	22.5	–	–	4.6	–	–	22.7	–	–	16.8	–	–	33.5
Switzerland	59.8	57.1	45.7	26.7	15.2	17.1	6.5	6.1	10.9	12.0	3.5	10.4	14.9	17.2	15.9
Total DAC	28.5	29.3	31.3	18.7	14.7	10.0	18.9	18.5	18.9	23.7	24.1	25.6	10.1	13.3	13.0
Multilateral institutions															
EEC	50.4	65.2	58.2	17.2	9.3	7.2	5.0	5.5	4.9	12.0	12.6	19.7	5.4	7.4	10.1
IFIs[c]	21.5	32.4	43.6	44.2	42.1	34.9	11.0	8.9	11.7	4.8	3.2	1.1	18.5	13.4	8.6
UN agencies[d]	32.5	41.5	40.3	18.2	19.5	16.9	19.3	14.2	12.1	18.7	11.9	17.8	11.3	12.9	12.9
Non-DAC flows, total[e]	11.2	15.9	9.0	9.9	10.4	7.4	17.4	32.5	15.8	52.9	29.0	66.2	8.6	12.3	1.6
Overall total	24.2	28.8	31.6	19.0	17.3	11.6	17.2	19.5	17.2	29.1	21.5	27.9	10.5	12.9	11.4

Notes:
a Excluding non-specified amounts by region
b For the purpose of this analysis, includes small amounts to Southern Europe
c International financial institutions. Includes IDA, regional banks' soft windows and IFAD
d Includes UNDP, UNICEF, UNWRA, WFP, UNHCR and UNFPA
e Arab donors, ex-CEECs and China

Source: OECD, Development Co-operation, 1992

Table 5.7 Sources of aid 1990 ($m)

	All LDCs	Africa	Bangla-desh	Jamaica	Mauri-tius	Zim-babwe
Total DAC + multilateral	57,986	17,884	2,100	273	89	340
Multilateral	15,979	6,006	1,008	21	12	24
Bilateral	42,007	11,878	1,092	252	77	316
EC (bilateral + EC)	24,354	8,889	412	60	66	147
US	20,446	1,002	169	104	1	15
Japan	9,928	830	374	26	6	26

Sources: OECD, *Development Co-operation* and *Geographical Distribution of Financial Flows to Developing Countries*, annual issues

affected expectations about the future success of OPEC and the Coffee Agreement.

The long-term effects of continuing intervention, whether by importers or through commodity agreements, may be more indirect, however. On many, there is a history of intervention in both industrial and developing countries which has in turn contributed to a tradition of joint political counter-action by governments and producers in other countries, both industrial and developing. The justifications, if not always the reasons, include as arguments (other than protection of producers' interests) security of food, energy or military supplies. There is thus a tradition of politicisation of production and trading decisions in these markets. This attitude and its results are difficult to document or quantify at any level, but they have affected how some of the case-study countries have reacted to more identifiable controls on commodities, especially food and fuels. The view that commodity markets are subject to risks from intervention or manipulation, whether or not there was current evidence of this, strengthened the more general economic case, on grounds of climatic or systematic risk and declining relative demand, for treating industrialisation as an essential element in development. An alternative reaction was to assume that intervention is inherent in all trading relationships, and then adjust to this by either minimising exposure to risk (through autarky) or exploiting the negotiating possibilities (preference-seeking). The attempt to bring agriculture back into the international trading system, by including it in the Uruguay Round of trade negotiations (and also to bring in some of the sectors like textiles and clothing and services which showed signs of joining it in a non-market limbo), was for some participants a deliberate attempt to avoid validating the second view.

At the world level, the measure of the vulnerability to these biases in commodity trade is the share of the relevant commodities in international trade, and in the exports of different areas. Food and fuel exports are still more important to developing countries than to the industrial countries or to the world as a whole (Table 5.8), but the difference has declined sharply in the last twenty years, especially for food, and has disappeared for the Asian countries. There is very little difference on the import side. Most developing countries are now no more exposed to risks from management of trade in these commodities than are industrial countries, and neither group, on average, has more than about 20% of trade, imports or exports, in these groups. Coffee is only about 1% of developing country trade. Even the African countries have come down on the share of food in exports to below 15%, the average international level at the beginning of the period. Oil producers in all areas remain exposed. Latin America remains very dependent on food exports (a useful reminder of why it took a strong position on agriculture in the Uruguay Round negotiations), because it includes exporters of both temperate products, in the south, and tropical, in the north. With these and the oil producers, it is now the most generally exposed area to managed areas of trade. (The overall figure for Africa is higher, but this is because of a few oil exporters.)

The individual countries in Table 5.8 show the expected differences between the more and less developed, and therefore more and less industrialised, but even the poorest with high dependence on food markets have changed sharply from the position of the 1970s, with the three with over 50% exports of food at that time now all at about 30%. The two for whom food was a major import twenty years ago have also changed, partly because of domestic production, but more because development has increased the range of economic activity and therefore imports. On both sides of the trade account, therefore, these countries and developing countries in general face markets which on average are now less concentrated in the traditional areas of politicised and policy-driven trade. Only Zimbabwe and Colombia are exceptions to this. In Colombia, high dependence on food has been replaced by coal and oil (with exports expected to continue to rise). Oil and coffee, the two commodity-agreement commodities, together account for about half its exports. Although its total dependence on food and fuels is lower, Zimbabwe has also increased its dependence on food (including some coffee).

If dependence on primary commodities leads to a different view of how politicised the international economy is, it might be thought that most developing countries should now have moved away from such an interpretation. But this ignores why they have changed their trading pattern. The extent of the move suggests that it is itself a product of distrust of trade in commodities as a stable and predictable market. Therefore, the attitudes remain, and the change in domestic output structure is in part because of the perceived nature of these markets.

Table 5.8 Share of widely controlled primary commodities (percentages)

Region/country	Food			Fuels			Crude petroleum			Coffee	
	1970	1980	1990	1970	1980	1990	1970	1980	1990	1980	1990
Shares in exports											
World	14.7	11.1	9.4	9.2	24.0	10.1		16.2	5.7	0.6	0.3
All developing	26.3	11.3	11.6	32.4	61.3	26.1		51.3	10.4	1.9	1.2
Non-oil developing	35.6	23.0	14.1	7.4	21.8	9.5					
South and South East Asia	21.2	12.5	7.9	7.1	21.3	8.2					
Latin America & Caribbean	40.9	29.1	27.0	24.7	42.4	26.5					
Africa[d]	29.1	10.6	13.2	33.7	75.6	60.1					
Shares in imports											
World	14.7	11.1	9.4	9.2	24.0	10.1					
Non-oil developing	13.5	11.7	9.4	7.8	18.8	9.2					
South and South East Asia	13.6	11.1	8.6	9.0	24.0	10.2					
Latin America and Caribbean	16.2	10.3	6.7	7.3	23.6	9.2					
Africa[d]	11.0	10.5	10.4	11.7	25.7	8.3					
	14.4	15.8	15.2	4.7	9.3	9.3					

Table 5.8 Continued

Region/country	Food			Fuels			Crude petroleum			Coffee	
	1970	1980	1990	1970	1980	1990	1970	1980	1990	1980	1990
Bangladesh											
Exports	9.8[a]	12.5	12.5	0.0[a]	0.0	3.9	0.0[a]	0.0	0.0		0.0
Imports	52.6[a]	23.6	22.6	7.6[a]	9.5	12.8	1.2[a]	3.1	11.3		
Malaysia											
Exports	12.6	15.0	11.7	7.3	24.7	17.8	3.9	23.8	13.4		0.0
Imports	21.5	11.9	7.3	12.1	15.2	5.3	8.9	8.1	0.6		
Thailand											
Exports	52.3	47.0	28.8	0.3	0.1	0.8	0.0	0.0	0.0		0.0
Imports	5.4	5.2	5.0	8.7	30.4	9.3	3.2	20.7	6.0		
Colombia											
Exports	75.0	71.8	32.8	10.1	2.8	36.9	8.1	0.0	22.8		24.4
Imports	7.7	11.7	7.1	4.4	2.8	3.5	0.0	3.2	0.0		
Jamaica											
Exports	23.0	13.7	19.3	2.6	1.9	1.5	0.0	0.0	0.0		1.0
Imports	18.0	20.3	15.1	6.4	37.8	19.8	4.4	22.2	0.0		
Mauritius											
Exports	98.1	72.5	31.1	0.0	0.0	0.0	0.0	0.0	0.0		0.0
Imports	36.4	26.3	12.7[c]	7.1	14.1	7.4[c]	0	0.1	0.0[c]		
Zimbabwe											
Exports	36.2[b]	29.3	44.1	1.2[b]	1.5	0.7	0.0[b]	0.0	0.0		3.1
Imports	2.7[b]	3.0	3.7	19.9[b]	1.4	15.6	0.0[b]	0.0	0.0		

Notes: [a] 1975; [b] 1976; [c] 1987; [d] Including Nigeria

Source: UNCTAD, Handbook of International Trade and Development Statistics

OTHER CONSTRAINTS

There are still controls in force on exports of security-sensitive goods to the formerly centrally planned economies, now extended to Iraq, and including some developing countries: China, Mongolia and Vietnam. As well as national controls, there are controls under the Coordinating Committee for Multilateral Export Control (COCOM). Some goods require licences from their governments for export to any country (because it might re-export). The trade flows involved are small on an aggregate basis, but important in some industries, not only the obvious ones of arms and atomic energy, but also computing, telecommunications, power generation, machine tools, and some chemicals (DTI, COCOM 1990). The restrictions have been relaxed since 1989–90, both in coverage of goods and in how they are applied to some of the countries. A further reform was under negotiation in early 1994. This would not only further relax the coverage but admit Russia to the group of countries administering the system.

The COCOM system, and the proposed admission of its former target, raises issues of whether developing countries are (or can believe that they are) full participants in policy-making in multilateral trading policies. The COCOM rules were set and administered by seventeen industrial countries (NATO members plus Japan and Australia, but minus Iceland) (DTI, COCOM 1990), with a preponderant role for the US. As interpreted by the US, the system included regulation of re-export of goods imported from the US to another COCOM country. These are now seen as arbitrary interventions by industries (and in some circumstances governments) in industrial countries which consider that the US in particular, is using them to promote its own exports and to restrain those of its competitors. (US exporters, on the other hand, complain of more restraints.) This issue has become more acute since the ending of US technological superiority, which was implicitly assumed when the system was set up. The new system would give a more equal role to other industrial countries and modify the present ability of any one to veto a transaction, but it would not alter the basic division between members and outsiders.

The problem of which countries are full participants in the international system was also raised by some of the 'new issues' in the Uruguay Round of GATT negotiations. These were included because some industrial countries felt a need for more external supervision of the internal enforcement in developing countries of rules such as those protecting intellectual property. These interventions have potential implications as barriers to trade.

One is clearly similar to that of COCOM: to suggest that a self-chosen group of countries has the right to make regulations which apply to all trading countries. If the result of the new patent and copyright regulations is to impose trading constraints on the products of countries which do not accept (or do not enforce) any newly agreed protection for intellectual property, these will be additional constraints on exports from the non-conforming countries. There is little evidence that lack of protection in the past has acted as a barrier to either trade or foreign investment. The countries which are most often accused of violations, South Korea, Brazil, Singapore, Taiwan, and, among the case-study countries, Malaysia, Thailand and Colombia, have enjoyed not only rapidly growing imports, but in most cases high foreign investment. A formal control would not, therefore, merely reinforce the alleged informal reluctance to trade with such countries. If lack of enforcement is, or becomes, an important restriction on trade, it would discourage moves into exports of the most advanced products.

A further institutional effect is the extension of what is considered within the competence of the international trading regime, by bringing in these 'Trade Related Intellectual Property' issues. As such an extension is clearly more to the advantage of net exporters of new technology (almost by definition, advanced industrial countries) than to net importers, it alters the balance between them, and in a way that did not affect previous new entrants to advanced production and trade. Traditionally, developing countries have had a choice between offering immediate legal protection to, and buying, technology and minimising current costs and the costs of setting up new industries by direct copying or hiring informed external advisers. Extending regulation thus raises the initial costs of entering technology-based production and trade and tends to support a view that trade is an area in which the rules are made by other countries.

It also suggests another, even more unfavourable, alteration in the international trading system facing developing countries. Until the GATT settlement was reached, the interim solution adopted by the US was unilateral intervention. Like the unilateral NTBs discussed in Chapter 3, this may indicate to developing countries that international trade in general is more controllable by, and therefore inherently more favourable to, the industrial countries. Such fears are strengthened by other intervention based on domestic legislation. When developing countries challenge such measures through the normal channels, directly and through the GATT, it has been difficult to secure compliance with GATT rulings. The United States and the European Community issue annual lists of challenges to other countries' trading practices, backed by the threat of direct intervention. The ASEAN countries have tried a similar approach, listing complaints against the US, but the responses were not encouraging. For example on the general issue of whether the USA has the right to take unilateral action, the US reply was 'There is no article in the GATT that prohibits GATT-inconsistent laws, neither is there a requirement that GATT rules be incorporated into domestic laws'.

It is interesting that in the case of threats to Thailand on intellectual property protection, with withdrawal of GSP threatened as a sanction (in

97

1989), one result was that Thailand questioned the value of a concession like GSP which could be withdrawn unilaterally. This demonstrates how perceptions of the way international trade works link experiences of different types of barriers, but it also suggests a growing distrust of any trade advantage based on concessions or bargaining rather than more long-term conditions.

The existence of the G–7 (the US, Japan, Germany, the UK, France, Italy and Canada) economic meetings supports a view that the international system is biased against developing countries because some countries can take initiatives in international economic policy which bind others. In initial contrast, the Uruguay Round saw an unusual participation by developing countries. This was partly because of their greater importance in the world economy, but also because of their intellectual shift towards support for more liberalised trade. This was modified but not ended by the importance of EC–US negotiations in the final stages of the Round.

If the various unquantifiable influences outlined in this chapter have the effect of reviving the earlier, 1950s, views of development – that the international system was inherently unequal if not actively hostile to developing countries – then the effect of the policies discussed here will be to discourage trade as effectively as many of the more specific measures discussed in earlier chapters.

6

FOREIGN INVESTMENT
Creating and channelling
trading opportunities

Chapters 2–5 have considered external constraints imposed by public sector action. Foreign investment is not an external intervention of the same kind. But it has traditionally been asserted (the cliché that the output of company A is greater than the GDP of country B) that the economic and political power of large private firms removes trade from national control, and that this is an increasingly important influence on the nature of the international system. It is therefore relevant to look at the evidence for the importance of such organisations in trade, at any changes in this, and at differences between different types of countries or products. We must also ask how an international system in which multinational companies have a significant role would be different from a less oligopolistic one. A final section of this chapter examines how foreign investment has been changing and can be expected to change in the medium term.

WHY MULTINATIONAL COMPANIES ARE DIFFERENT

To have a high share of trade controlled by multinationals could be significant simply because of their size. They are more likely to be able to exert market power. They are more likely to have experience in trading in markets outside the host country (at a minimum, in their own home country), and therefore to be potentially interested in international trade. If one of their products made in a developing country is competitive on international markets, they may recognise this and move to trading more readily and more quickly than a new domestic producer. In some cases they will have invested with the intention of exporting because they have identified a trading advantage in the host country. Most foreign investment, however, is still undertaken as an alternative to exports (see Table 6.1), to satisfy the market in the host country, and in such cases it is more likely to replace imports than to stimulate exports, at least initially.

More generally a foreign company is more likely to be aware of, and experienced in exploiting, the advantages of moving between exporting and investing abroad, and therefore more likely to respond to new opportunities,

Table 6.1   Share of exports in US and Japanese affiliates' sales (percentages)

Region/country	US	Japan
All developing countries		
1982	22.0	32.8
1989	33.1	39.2
Africa		
1982	–	8.2
1989	–	15.2
Asia and the Pacific		
1982	60.3	33.6
1989	56.2	40.2
Latin America and the Caribbean		
1982	11.9	18.6
1989	21.4	23.9

Source: UNCTC, 1992b

whether economic or resulting from government inducements. The descriptions of the experiences of the case-study countries which acquired or lost preferences or incurred quotas on their exports support a view that foreign companies were often the first to respond.

Large and foreign companies also have different opportunities in the politics of trade. Some developing country governments believe they are able to influence their own home country government, and therefore to avoid or alleviate barriers to entry there. Evidence here is more uncertain. There are examples (for instance, the special provisions for offshore processing of clothing discussed in Chapter 2) where they can exploit this power, but this will not necessarily preserve access for other suppliers. In the short term a foreign company may be more vulnerable to pressure on the part of the host government because it is less likely to have traditional bargaining power in a foreign country, but in the long term, if it is producing for export, it is more likely to be able to move its activities elsewhere (or to threaten to do so). Surveys of foreign investors and government regulators show that they share a perception that foreign investors for the local market are more susceptible to local pressure than those for export. If foreign companies account for a high share of exports, therefore, the export sector may be less responsive to domestic political pressure, although more so to changes in market conditions. Once established, traditionally they have behaved like other large companies in developing countries, in using their bargaining power to restrict new entrants, in particular through encouraging protection against imports.

They may, in summary, be likely to encourage exports and limit imports, on both economic grounds (as competent traders or market-seeking import substitutors) and political grounds (by demanding protection from imports in the host country and opposing such protection in the home country). These are all interventions which increase trade, apart from the encouragement of local protection, and on this they may be no more distorting than a large local firm.

In the case of large firms with many foreign subsidiaries acting as alternative suppliers, they may respond less to temporary advantages for any one of them, because they would be competing within themselves. If a substantial proportion of their trade is intra-company trade, in different stages of a process, rather than alternative sources of the same components, there may be more stability in trading relationships in the case of temporary losses of competitiveness. This gives the stability from long-term relationships which was suggested in Chapter 4 as one of the motives of countertrade. But the fact that 'normal' trade is subject to other types of long-term inter-company arrangements or understandings increases the difficulty of identifying a special role for foreign investment.

In the past, it has frequently been argued (cf. van den Bulcke, 1985) that multinationals use their discretion over trading decisions to restrict the trade of their subsidiaries. This view makes three implicit assumptions which are open to question: that the home country, not the local management, makes such decisions; that the decision made is different from the one which would be made by a local manager of a locally-owned company; and that such a local company would exist and have the opportunity of trading. There seems no reason in terms of profit-seeking why the decision for the medium term should be different for a wholly-owned subsidiary, wherever the decision is made. For the short term, for the reasons listed above, a foreign company may respond more slowly if other branches are concerned or more rapidly if they are not. It is possible that in the case of a partially-owned company, in which the multinational nevertheless has decision-making control, 100% of the return on trade by an alternative, wholly-owned subsidiary, even if a less competitive one, would be greater than a smaller percentage of a higher return, and thus the decision would be different from a local decision.

In practice, it is difficult to find any evidence of such trading restrictions in a form peculiar to subsidiaries of a foreign company. There are restrictions on the sales policies of all goods bearing a company name, on competing in the same market, using company inputs or methods, etc., but these effects are those arising from dealing with a large company rather than a foreign one.[1]

The question of size also suggests another difficulty. Even for countries and companies not directly involved in high foreign investment or intra-firm trade, if some trade flows among other countries tend to be dominated by such companies, access to these markets may be made difficult, particularly if the companies are highly vertically integrated, so that there is no easy point for a small company to enter the process.

A large company may be better able to divide its production processes, putting each stage in the location most appropriate for it, rather than all stages in a location appropriate on average for the product. This may alter its mix of locations, benefiting or hurting individual countries. Because it will produce a more specialised type of production in each, this may provide a less evenly distributed benefit of increased output in each location, and these pieces of the total production chain may offer a poorer base for domestic industry based on individual smaller producers. But such splitting is part of a general world move towards more specialised production, and thus a good foundation for a new style of production.

The overall direction of the trade effect is difficult to predict from these divergent potential differences. The benefits or costs of even the identifiable effects are not certain. But together these arguments offer some reason to believe that the ways in which production decisions are made and the nature of the responses to different market or policy decisions can differ between trade by multinational companies and other trade, and particularly so for intra-firm trade. Foreign investors will respond to different policies, at different rates; they are likely to see advantages in different industries, or parts of industries, especially in those where either the market is particularly like that of their home country (production for a new market or for the global market of what it previously exported) or the local production conditions are particularly different from those of the home country (production for export of a product or part, because of the host country's comparative advantage). This can be summed up as a greater awareness of, and susceptibility to, external constraints or opportunities, combined with some constraints on seizing very short-term advantages.

TRADE BY MULTINATIONAL COMPANIES

Concern about the impact of multinationals on developing countries has always been high, but has been stimulated in recent years by claims that foreign investment and sales by foreign subsidiaries are becoming more important relative to other trade (a notable example was UNCTC, 1992b). But there is little evidence to support this.

The first difficulty in assessing these claims is that there is little evidence on trade by multinationals, and particularly poor data on intra-firm trade. The only country which regularly publishes such data is the United States. Until 1980, the US was the major foreign investor, and it remains one of the most important (Table 6.2), though its share has fallen sharply. Until the late 1970s it could perhaps be assumed that the activities of multinational companies could be approximately understood by looking at US data. This is no longer true, and it would never have been correct to regard US companies' behaviour as typical. The US was atypical in having such a high amount of foreign investment relative to its economy or to its other international activities, and comparison of its multinationals with those of other countries shows significant differences in trading practice. It is now no longer possible to ignore other countries.

Table 6.3 gives the basic data over the period 1977–90 for US trade with subsidiaries abroad of US firms (MOFAs are majority-owned foreign affiliates). The first large number to attract attention is the share of US exports accounted for by multinational companies: 85% in 1977. It has fallen since then, although it is still over 60%. On the import side (which is the US contribution to other countries' exports) the share was 59% in 1977, and fell to around 40%. However, most of this trade, in both directions, was not between the US companies and their affiliates. It simply reflects the unusual dominance of large companies in US trade. The proportion of intra-firm trade has changed little on the export side, at about a quarter of total exports, while on the import side it was also a quarter in 1977, but fell below 20% at the beginning of the 1980s, and has remained at around 18%.

Table 6.4 shows the pattern for multinationals' trade with developing countries over the period 1977–89. For Latin America (the developing region which has received the highest share of US investment during most of the period), the pattern is similar to that in Table 6.3, although the fall in total MNC-related exports is even greater (from 88% to just over 50%) Intra-firm trade is more like the average. It declined from a quarter to 22% of exports, and 18% of imports. Asia, which has become an increasingly important recipient of US investment, is no longer well below the average on total MNC trade, although it remains so on intra-firm exports (14% of US exports to the region). On imports, i.e. Asian exports, it is 22%. Neither the total nor the regional data support the view that such trade is becoming more important, although it is clearly a significant component of both areas' trade with the US.

Table 6.5 interprets the implications of these trade data for the exports of the regions concerned and the case-study countries, excluding Bangladesh for which US investment is not large. (1989 is the most recent 'benchmark' study of US investment.) For the world as a whole, the share of exports to the United States which is internal to US multinationals is 3%. It is higher for developing countries, at 5%, principally because of the high share for Latin America. This is due to that region's abnormally high total trade with the US, not, as can be seen in the other tables, to a particularly high share of intra-firm trade in total Latin America–US trade. Asia is about average for all countries, with Africa (where data are particularly uncertain) slightly above average. Two of the case-study countries, Malaysia and Jamaica, have a high share of foreign investment, and therefore an above-average share of intra-firm exports in total trade, but only in Jamaica is it of major importance measured against total Jamaican exports.

Most of the speculation about the potential effects of intra-firm trade implicitly assumes trade in manufactures. Table 6.6 indicates that, for Latin

Table 6.2 Principal investment flows 1975–91 (US$ bn)

	1975	1980	1985	1986	1987	1988	1989	1990	1991	1992
Outflows of investment by investor										
Developing countries	0.2	0.6	2.7	3.2	5.1	7.6	11.0	10	11.1	11.4
Asia	0.1	0.2	2.6	2.6	4.9	7.4	10.7	11.4	9.5	10.4
Latin America	0.1	0.3	0.1	0.6	0.2	0.2	0.7	1.0	0.8	1.0
Developed countries	27.0	57.0	59.0	86.0	132.0	162.0	203.0	213.0	171.1	147.1
US	14.0	22.0	15.0	14.0	28.0	14.0	29.0	32.7	27.1	35.3
Japan	2.0	3.0	6.0	15.0	20.0	34.0	44.0	48.0	30.7	17.2
EC	9.3	26.1	23.9	42.0	64.0	77.0	89.0	99.4	90.9	82.5
Total	27.2	57.6	61.7	89.2	140.1	168.6	212	223	182.2	158.5
Inflows of investment by destination										
Developing countries	6.3	10.1	11.5	14.0	25.0	30.0	30.0	29.8	41.5	41.0
Asia	1.6	3.2	4.5	6.7	11.6	15.0	16.2	18.6	24.0	28.0
Latin America	3.3	6.2	4.5	5.4	10.8	11.4	8.4	7.3	12.0	13.0
Developed countries	15.2	42.1	37.8	64.1	107.9	128.6	165.4	156.2	101.8	83.9
US	2.6	16.9	19.2	34.1	58.1	59.4	70.6	45.1	11.5	−3.9
Japan	0.2	0.3	0.6	0.2	1.2	−0.5	−1.1	1.8	1.4	2.7
EC	9.7	21.0	14.7	20.0	36.4	54.3	75.5	86.0	68.6	70.3
Total	21.5	52.2	49.3	78.1	132.9	158.6	195.4	186.0	143.3	124.0

Note: Total investment by developing countries in developed countries (estimates from country data) in 1992 = 4

Sources: BIS, 1993; UNCTAD, 1993b; UNCTC, 1988; IMF, 1990

America and Asia at least, the results for manufactures are not very different in aggregate, although the contrast between the two regions is even greater. The high numbers here are, however, the result of outward-processing arrangements between the US and Mexico, and imports of parts from Brazil, the two major US investment destinations. Colombia was also important in this trade in the early 1980s, but its share had declined sharply by the mid-1980s. What is interesting for both areas is that the relatively constant shares for the continents and the total conceal large changes for individual countries. In Asia, these include falls for Singapore, Malaysia and the Philippines, while Thailand's share has doubled. Supported by evidence in the country studies, this suggests that such trade is vulnerable to changes in competitiveness over the medium term, although it is not possible to judge on the basis of these data whether it is more or less vulnerable than other trade, or whether it is in US or the Asian countries' competitiveness that changes are more important.

The other major industrial investor in developing countries is Japan, for which more limited data are available (summarised in Tables 6.7 and 6.8). Japan has become as important a source of foreign investment (Table 6.2), and therefore potentially of trade effects, as the USA in the Asian countries, including some of those studied here. Table 6.7 shows, however, that intra-firm exports back to Japan were extremely small for Japanese subsidiaries, although they began to increase after the yen rose in the mid-1980s, and some evidence from individual countries suggests that they rose further by the 1990s. Most Japanese investment for export in developing countries had been to supply third-country markets.

The inadequate data for intra-firm trade for all areas other than the USA and Japan (and the confusion in data sources between intra-firm and all MNC trade) make any world estimates difficult. It is difficult in any case to avoid double counting (even if we ignore the differences of definition of foreign investment, foreign subsidiary, and intra-firm trade). Table 6.8 gives UNCTC data for the three major investors for intra-firm trade (although the estimates for Japan seem higher than those from Japanese sources, even allowing for the fact that the table includes primary goods). If we look only at export data, in order to avoid double counting, about 30% of these countries' trade is intra-firm. The data for imports are slightly higher. Most other countries do not have foreign subsidiaries on the scale of these three countries, so that their share of such trade (excluding trade with the US or Japan) will be small.

Because of the relative importance of trade and investment flows among the industrial countries (Table 6.2), intra-firm trade is likely to be more important in these flows, where there are possibilities of trade by and with subsidiaries, than in trade among developing countries or between them and industrial countries. The intra-firm trade accounted for by exports from the US, the UK, and Japan, on these estimates, amounts to about 8% of total

Table 6.3 US merchandise exports and imports associated with US TNCs 1977–90 (US$m current)

	1977	1982	1983	1984	1985	1986	1987	1988	1989	1990
TNC-associated US exports, total (1) = (2) + (7)	101,846	163,383	154,360	168,713	171,904	171,125	178,898	215,392	236,371	248,483
Shipped to affiliates, as reported on affiliates' forms (2)	40,787	56,718	57,545	66,240	69,618	71,065	78,887	95,027	102,558	108,390
To MOFAs (3)	35,813	52,753	54,468	63,408	66,510	67,749	74,904	90,916	97,488	101,661
By US parents (4)	29,275	46,559	45,107	52,533	57,567	58,916	65,248	78,336	86,050	89,649
By unaffiliated US persons (5)	6,539	10,159	9,361	10,875	8,943	8,833	9,659	12,579	11,437	12,012
To other affiliates (6)	4,974	3,965	3,077	2,832	3,108	3,316	3,980	4,112	5,070	6,729
Shipped to unaffiliated foreigners by US parents (7)	61,059	106,666	96,815	102,473	102,286	100,060	100,011	120,365	133,813	140,093
Total US merchandise exports (8)	120,163	212,276	200,538	223,976	218,815	227,158	254,122	322,427	363,820	392,923
Intra-firm exports (4) = (6)	34,249	50,524	48,148	55,365	60,675	62,232	69,228	82,448	91,120	96,378
Share of TNC-associated exports in total exports (1)/(8)	84.8%	77.0%	77.0%	75.3%	78.6%	75.3%	70.4%	66.8%	65%	63%
Share of intra-firm in total exports [(4) + (6)]/(8)	28.5%	23.8%	24.0%	24.7%	27.7%	27.4%	27.2%	25.6%	25.0%	24.5%

Table 5.3 Continued

	1977	1982	1983	1984	1985	1986	1987	1988	1989	1990
TNC-associated US imports, total (1)	86,759	120,768	124,740	140,997	153,570	147,285	166,423	179,543	201,182	214,388
Shipped by affiliates, as reported on affiliates' forms (2)	41,525	51,406	53,237	62,529	68,181	65,468	75,937	87,156	97,394	102,484
By MOFAs (3)	38,000	46,101	48,328	57,162	60,301	57,268	65,542	76,042	84,298	83,607
To US parents (4)	30,880	38,533	41,551	48,919	51,751	49,961	55,867	65,881	71,283	75,364
To unaffiliated US persons (5)	7,120	7,567	6,777	8,243	8,551	7,307	9,675	10,161	13,015	13,243
By other affiliates (6)	3,525	5,305	4,909	5,367	7,879	8,200	10,395	11,114	13,096	13,877
Shipped by unaffiliated foreigners to US parents (7)	45,234	69,363	71,503	78,468	85,852	81,817	90,486	92,387	103,788	111,904
Total US merchandise imports (8)	147,847	254,884	269,878	346,364	352,463	382,295	424,442	459,542	473,647	495,200
Intra-firm imports (4) + (6)	34,405	43,838	46,460	54,286	59,630	58,161	66,262	76,995	84,379	89,241
Share of TNC-associated imports in total imports (1)/(8)	58.7%	47.4%	46.2%	40.7%	43.6%	38.5%	39.2%	39.1%	42%	43%
Share of intra-firm in total imports [(4) + (6)]/(8)	23.3%	17.2%	17.2%	15.7%	16.9%	15.2%	15.6%	16.8%	17.8%	18.0%
Balance in TNC-associated trade (1)	15,087	42,615	29,260	27,716	18,334	23,840	12,475	35,849	35,189	34,000
Balance in intra-firm trade [(4) + (6)]	−156	5,868	1,724	1,079	1,045	4,071	2,966	5,453	6,741	7,137

Sources: Kuwayama, 1992; US Survey of Current Business, August 1992

Table 6.4 US trade associated with US parents and their MOFAs, in developing regions 1977–89 (US$m current)

	Latin America			Developing Asia		
	1977	1982	1989	1977	1982	1989
TNC-associated US exports to the region (1)	13,005	20,864	25,520	7,535	18,918	31,342
Shipped to affiliates, as reported on affiliates' forms (2)	4,730	7,339	12,452	1,882	4,769	8,659
To MOFAs (3)	3,700	6,479	11,095	1,528	4,494	8,110
By US parents (4)	2,908	5,120	9,322	1,289	4,073	7,510
By unaffiliated US persons (5)	791	1,360	1,773	238	421	601
To other affiliates (6)	1,030	860	1,358	354	275	548
Shipped to unaffiliated foreigners by US parents (7)	8,276	13,526	13,068	5,650	14,150	22,687
US merchandise exports to the region (8)	14,799	33,591	49,055	10,697	27,452	57,403
Intra-firm exports (4) + (6)	3,938	5,980	10,680	1,643	4,348	8,058
Share of TNC-associated exports in total exports (1)/(8)	87.88%	62.11%	52.02%	70.44%	68.91%	54.60%
Share of intra-firm in total exports [(4)+(6)]/(8)	26.61%	17.80%	21.77%	15.36%	15.84%	14.04%

Table 6.4 Continued

	Latin America			Developing Asia		
	1977	1982	1989	1977	1982	1989
TNC-associated US imports from the region (1)	n.a.	n.a.	n.a.	n.a.	n.a.	n.a.
Shipped by affiliates, as reported on affiliates' forms (2)	5,834	7,500	11,886	5,928	6,948	15,955
By MOFAs (3)	5,240	7,035	10,400	5,680	6,391	13,935
To US parents (4)	4,596	6,252	9,591	5,330	6,878	12,593
To unaffiliated US persons (5)	643	783	809	350	6,343	1,341
By other affiliates (6)	594	465	1,486	248	536	681
Shipped by unaffiliated foreigners to US parents (7)	n.a.	n.a.	n.a.	n.a.	n.a.	n.a.
US merchandise imports from the region (8)	20,940	39,602	60,100	17,790	31,022	60,774
Intra-firm imports (4) + (6)	5,190	6,7?6	11,077	5,578	7,414	13,274
Share of intra-firm in total imports [(4)+(6)]/(8)	24.79%	16.96%	18.43%	31.35%	23.90%	21.84%
Balance in intra-firm trade	−1,252	−736	−397	−3,935	−3,066	−5,216

Source: Kuwayama, 1992

Table 6.5 US imports from affiliates, by area, 1989 (US$m and percentages)

Region/country	Total US imports	US imports from affiliates by area	Share of US intra-firm trade in exports to US (%)	Total exports by area[a]	Share of US intra-firm in total trade (%)
All US MOFAs	492,922	84,379	17.1	2,544,800	3.3
Latin America + Asia + Africa	176,192	27,551	15.6	587,800	4.7
Latin America	60,100	11,077	18.4	117,720	9.4
Colombia	2,760	369	13.3	5,717	6.5
Jamaica	568	192	33.8	967	19.9
Asia	101,368	13,274	13.1	405,980	3.3
Malaysia	4,927	1,316	26.7	25,053	5.3
Thailand	4,635	823	17.8	20,078	4.1
Africa	14,724	3,200	21.7	64,100	5.0

Note: [a] World excludes USA

Sources: US, *Survey of Current Business*, 1991; Kuwayama, 1992; IMF, *Direction of Trade Statistics*

world trade (using 1990 data). As the share of multinationals' trade is exceptionally high for the USA, and these three are all atypical countries in that they do have major foreign investments, it is probably wrong to assume that the average relationship between exports and investment for them is typical. Using this may therefore be taken as an upper limit; this would be 18%. Other assumptions using the import shares can give a range of numbers from 10% (using only imports from own country subsidiaries) to 25% (assuming that the US without the other investors is typical). The range of possible estimates is therefore 8–25%, and 10–15% is probably the plausible range.

Whatever the number, it is falling and, for most developing countries, probably nearer the types of numbers associated with trade with foreign MNCs (the second column of Table 6.8) only. It is noteworthy that, even in the 1970s (Helleiner and Lavergne, 1979), it was found that (except for petroleum) the proportions of intra-firm trade were higher for OECD countries than for developing countries: for finished manufactures, 61% and 37%; for semi-manufactures, 43% and 17%; for primary products, 36% and 14%. For the total: 54% and 28%, excluding petroleum, or 43% including it.

It is possible (cf. Tambunlertchai, 1993) that much of the Japanese intra-firm trade consists in fact of exports of investment equipment to subsidiaries, and therefore that, while there would be high numbers on the Japanese export and the Asian import side, these would reflect a type of trade peculiar to the highly integrated Japanese firms, which produce their

Table 6.6 Share of manufactured imports shipped by manufacturing MOFAs in total US manufactured imports, by developing areas
(US$m current and percentages)

Country	1982			1989		
	Imports by mfg MOFAs (A)	Total mfd imports[b] (B)	A/B %	Imports by mfg MOFAs (A)	Total mfd imports[b] (B)	A/B %
Developing countries[a]	6,436	34,961	18.4	17,874	104,253	17.8
Latin America	2,267	8,287	27.4	8,221	28,152	29.5
Argentina	151	506	29.8	93	935	12.0
Brazil	454	1,928	23.5	1,794	5,978	32.1
Chile		402		73	659	10.0
Colombia	82	174	47.1	28	545	5.4
Mexico	1,564	5,165	30.3	6,211	19,590	31.7
Venezuela	16	112	14.3	22	545	3.1
Developing Asia	4,169	26,674	15.6	9,653	76,101	13.3
Hong Kong	584	5,808	10.1	1,421	10,081	14.8
Indonesia		312		6	1,430	0.5
South Korea	277	5,818	4.8	613	20,292	3.1
Malaysia	1,036	1,503	68.9	1,316	4,173	32.5
Philippines	281	1,305	21.5	178	2,632	7.2
Singapore	1,223	2,104	58.1	4,032	8,833	46.7
Taiwan	717	9,256	7.7	1,416	25,161	5.9
Thailand	51	568	9.0	671	3,499	20.1

Notes:
[a] The developing countries in this case consist of the listed countries only, for which data are available or whose data are not suppressed to avoid disclosure of information about individual companies
[b] Manufactured products include commodity sections 5–9 SITC Rev.1

Source: Kuwayama, 1992

own capital equipment, and to a stage when investment is increasing. It does not, therefore, have the types of effect which were discussed earlier. If the equipment were not the most suitable, but were being chosen because it was from an integrated company, this would be a consequence of dealing with large firms.

Data on the total shares of multinationals' trade in the exports of developing countries are more readily available than intra-firm trade data, but they are measuring a different type of external influence – a propensity to trade or an external constraint on breaking into existing trade flows. The figures for the US (Table 6.3) were high. Table 6.9 summarises data available for some developing countries and Table 6.10 compares these with the data for

Table 6.7 Share of Japanese intra-firm trade and other imports from overseas affiliates (manufactured products) 1980–6 (percentages)

	Share of sales to Japan in total sales of affiliates			Share of intra-firm imports in total sales of affiliates to Japan			Intra-firm share in total Japanese imports			Japanese intra-firm share in area's exports		
	1980	1983	1986	1980	1983	1986	1980	1983	1986	1980	1983	1986
World	10.9	11.6	7.8	67.5	83.3	75.9	1.44	1.81	2.69	0.11	0.15	0.21
Asia	9.8	10.8	15.8	89.2	74.4	76.5	2.78	2.54	6.37	0.59	0.43	1.01
ASEAN	–	6.5	10.0	–	63.7	78.5	0.00	1.12	3.63	0.00	0.31	0.90
Latin America	9.4	7.7	4.1	96.3	77.1	8.9	7.48	6.97	0.21	0.40	0.45	0.02
Middle East	72.3	73.0	79.1[a]	0.0	95.5	94.7	0.00	1.69	2.69	0.00	0.42	0.46

Note: [a] 79.1% is the value of the share given in the source but the computation from corresponding exports and sales figures gives 51.7%

Intra-firm is only for manufactures
World exports' excludes Japan

Sources: Ministry of International Trade and Industry, *Kaigai Toshi Tokei Soran* (A Comprehensive Survey of Foreign Investment Statistics) nos 1,2,3, taken from IDE, 1990; IMF, *Direction of Trade Statistics, International Financial Statistics*

Table 6.8 Share of intra-firm transactions in the international trade of the United States, Japan and the United Kingdom 1977–89 (percentages)

Country	Trade associated with home country TNCs	Trade associated with TNCs of other home countries	Trade associated with all TNCs
US			
Exports			
1977	28.5	2.6	31.1
1982	23.8	1.1	24.9
1985	27.7	2.0	29.7
1989	25.0		
Imports			
1977	23.3	20.5	43.8
1982	17.2	21.3	38.5
1985	16.9	24.0	40.9
1989	17.1		
Japan			
Exports			
1980	24.1	1.7	25.8
1983	30.6	1.2	31.8
Imports			
1980	31.5	10.6	42.1
1983	18.4	11.9	30.3
UK			
Exports			
1981	16.0	14.0	30.0

Sources: UNCTC, 1988; Table 6.3.

intra-firm trade. The much greater importance of the latter in US multi-nationals' activities is obvious. For all developing countries the US share rose, until about 1982, to 7% for their manufactures, and then stabilised and perhaps fell thereafter. The Japanese share also fell during the 1980s, so even on this measure the role of such trade in developing countries' exports is limited. For both, and on all measures, the shares are highest for Asia, and for Malaysia, in particular.

In spite of the rise in total Japanese investment and in the late 1980s also in investment specifically for export to Japan, in all areas exports by Japanese multinationals are a falling proportion of the total. It is difficult therefore to conclude, with the UNCTC (1992b: 203), that 'their activities have accelerated the pace at which shifts in competitive advantage have led to a changing pattern of exports', although there may have been effects on the composition by technology level. If exports by Japanese affiliates are added to the exports by US affiliates, Latin America and Africa do show rises in share, but these areas are not those normally identified as the dynamic exporters.

Table 6.9 Shares of United States majority-owned and Japanese foreign affiliates in exports of developing countries (percentages)

	United States affiliates	Japanese affiliates[a]	US and Japanese share	All firms
A Manufactures Total				
All Developing Countries				
1957	3.0			
1966	3.9			
1977	6.2			
1982	6.7	4.8	11.5	
1986	7.1			
1989	5.7	2.9	8.6	
Africa				
1982	1.6[b]	0.2	1.8	
1989	3.4	0.2	3.6	
Asia and the Pacific				
1982	6.3[b]	6.3	12.6	
1989	4.2	3.5	7.7	
Latin America and the Caribbean				
1982	10.5	2.2	12.7	
1989	14.3	1.1	15.4	
Thailand				
1984	1.0			7.0
1986	5.0			15.0
Malaysia				
1986	21.0			

	US affiliates	Japanese affiliates	US and Japanese share	All foreign
B Total Exports				
Malaysia				
1977	11.6			
1986	20.9	7.9	28.8	
1989	18.2	9.8	28.0	45.7[c]
Thailand				
1977		4.2		11.3
1986	6.3	5.3	11.6	15.9
1989	5.4	7.0	12.0	27.3

Notes:
[a] Figures cover April 1982–March 1983 and April 1988–March 1989, and represent only a sample of affiliates in developing countries and hence may understate total exports by all Japanese affiliates
[b] Part of the data are suppressed by the source to avoid disclosure
[c] 1988

Sources: UNCTC, 1992 a, b; Ramstetter, 1991, 1992

Table 6.10 Comparison of intra-firm trade and all exports of manufactures coming from US and Japanese affiliates in developing countries (shares of total exports of manufactures) (percentages)

Region	US intra-firm	Japan intra-firm[a]	Total	US affiliates	Japan affiliates	Total
All developing countries						
1982				6.7	4.8	13.5
1989	4.7			5.7	2.9	8.6
Asia						
1982		0.6		6.3	6.3	12.6
1989	3.3	1.0	4.3	4.2	3.5	7.7
Latin America and Caribbean						
1982		0.4		10.5	2.2	12.7
1989	9.4	0.0	9.4	14.3	1.1	15.4
Africa						
1982		0.0		1.6	0.2	1.8
1989	5.0	0.0	5.0	3.4	0.2	3.6

Note: [a] 1980 and 1986

Source: Tables 6.5, 6.7 and 6.9

Tambunlertchai (1993) emphasises the dominance of Japanese investment in the electrical and electronic sectors.

The shares for some sectors in Thailand and Malaysia are quite high, especially electrical machinery (50–60% for Malaysia, 44% for Thailand, in the mid 1980s, Ramstetter, 1991), and in the 1970s for clothing in Thailand. For Malaysia, this was principally US firms.

All these numbers suggest that, even on this broader measure, trade shares are not as high as the over 50% often assumed (without stating a source). Both the intra-firm and the all-MNC trade figures are clearly large but not dominant and not rising. The shares are highest for the US, the country with the best data (not unusual for economic data[a]), and this has tended to colour discussions of multinationals' influence. As a potential external influence and, more specifically, a constraint on breaking into trade flows, it is significant.

There are some countries and some sectors where foreign investment and the operations of multinationals are particularly large and therefore likely, through economic or political influence, to have the direct effects which were discussed at the beginning of this chapter. Most notable in this respect are Malaysia and Thailand, and electrical and electronic goods, although these may be difficult to disentangle in practice from the effects foreign investment has in its other aspects on those economies (Table 6.11 shows its share in gross domestic investment).

Tables 6.1, 6.12 and 6.13 give other measures of the importance of and changes in, trade by multinationals. Most foreign investment is still for markets in the host country, not for export (Table 6.12). Of the major flows, only the US to Asia, and possibly some of the Asian to Asian, investments, are mainly for export. But the importance of export sales in manufactures (Table 6.1) is rising, so that interest in exporting conditions in the host countries, and therefore perhaps the exertion of economic or policy pressure, may be becoming more likely. Exports have been more important in the Asian countries, although Latin American exports may be growing in importance. Table 6.12 (all goods) also re-emphasises the importance for US firms of intra-firm trade, even in sales to third countries and local sales.

The argument that foreign investment is becoming a more important way of supplying foreign markets than direct exports is tested by Table 6.13, which compares total sales by foreign affiliates with total exports. A rising ratio would support the view that foreign investment is becoming a more important way of selling. For the US, the ratio has been falling, with minor rises in periods when the dollar was rising. Germany shows little change in recent years. Japan's figures could be interpreted as fluctuations or a rise; the data in Table 6.2 would suggest that a continuation of the data into more recent years would show a fall.

In recent years, developing countries themselves have also become important as investors, particularly in the South-East Asian countries. Brazil has started to invest, but mainly in the US. In Asia, the first investments by Asian companies were within the region, in textiles and clothing by Hong Kong in the 1960s because of controls on its own exports, and in raw materials by South Korea. India has also been involved in textiles and clothing production in other countries because of the quotas on its exports, although this seems usually to be by means of subcontracting rather than investment. These countries are now also investing in developed countries, so probably only $4–5 billion of the outflows detailed in Table 6.2 remain within the region. Some of this will involve intra-firm trade (Hong Kong, for one, supplies textiles to clothing firms), but in most of the cases discussed in the case-study countries, the role of foreign investment by developing countries is more on the side of providing capital and market access to industrial countries, not to the home country. The cause is probably the existence and operation of quotas rather than the inherent properties of multinationals, and any trade resulting will have been included in the country measures of trade in these commodities and is not, therefore, an addition to the share of controlled trade.

While it is logical to assume that the more advanced developing countries will follow the general pattern of undertaking some foreign investment and overseas production, the fact that the US is exceptional among the present

Table 6.11 The share of foreign direct investment inflows in gross domestic capital formation (percentages)

Region/Economy	1971–5	1976–80	1981–5	1986–91
Developed countries				
EC				
Belgium/Luxembourg	7.1	5.8	7.6	16.0
Denmark	3.0	0.3	0.9	3.7
Germany, Federal Republic of	2.1	0.8	0.6	1.8
France	1.8	1.9	2.0	4.4
Greece	1.0	5.4	6.0	8.0
Ireland	3.8	6.7	4.0	1.0
Italy	1.8	0.8	1.1	2.0
Netherlands	6.1	4.5	6.1	12.3
Portugal	3.1	1.5	3.0	10.7
Spain	1.9	2.8	5.3	9.2
UK	7.3	8.4	5.4	14.4
US	0.9	2.0	3.0	5.6
Japan	0.1	0.05	0.1	0.1
Developing countries				
Asia and the Pacific				
Bangladesh	0.0	0.0	0.0	0.1
Malaysia	15.2	11.9	10.8	9.7
Thailand	3.0	1.5	3.1	6.3
Hong Kong	5.9	4.2	6.9	12.1
India	0.3	0.1	0.1	0.3
South Korea	1.9	0.4	0.5	1.1
Philippines	1.0	0.9	0.7	3.7
Singapore	15.0	16.6	17.4	29.4
Taiwan	1.4	1.2	1.5	3.5
Latin America and the Caribbean				
Colombia	1.7	2.2	7.7	6.1
Jamaica	12.9	−1.6	−1.4	6.6
Mexico	3.5	3.6	2.7	7.0
Argentina	0.1	2.1	5.0	14.5
Brazil	4.2	3.9	4.3	1.7
Chile	−7.3	4.2	6.3	5.7
Africa				
Mauritius	1.1	1.2	1.8	4.0
Zimbabwe	–	0.02	0.02	−0.8
Botswana	−24.3	24.1	16.1	15.9
Egypt	–	7.1	6.9	7.8

Source: UNCTAD, 1993b

Table 6.12 Sales by US affiliates by destination (US$m current and per cent)

Sales destination	1977		1982		1989	
	US$m	%	US$m	%	US$m	%
World						
Sales to all destinations	507,019	100.0	730,235	100.0	1,015,263	100.0
To affiliated persons	168,024	33.1	159,875	21.9	241,839	23.8
To unaffiliated persons	338,995	66.9	570,361	78.1	773,424	76.2
Local sales	313,307	61.8	477,961	65.5	697,711	68.7
To affiliated persons	34,115	6.7	28,127	3.9	40,670	4.0
To unaffiliated persons	279,192	55.1	449,834	61.6	657,041	64.7
Sales to the US	93,573	18.5	76,780	10.5	111,338	11.0
To affiliated persons	84,154	16.6	63,572	8.7	91,831	9.0
To unaffiliated persons	9,419	1.9	13,208	1.8	19,507	1.9
Sales to other countries	100,138	19.8	175,494	24.0	206,214	20.3
To affiliated persons	49,754	9.8	68,176	9.3	109,339	10.8
To unaffiliated persons	50,384	9.9	107,318	14.7	96,876	9.5
Latin America						
Sales to all destinations	58,208	100.0	103,857	100.0	87,523	100.0
To affiliated persons	15,929	27.4	24,448	23.5	24,049	27.5
To unaffiliated persons	42,279	72.6	78,370	75.5	63,474	72.5
Local sales	36,766	63.2	61,919	59.6	56,631	64.7
To affiliated persons	1,707	2.9	2,396	2.3	2,799	3.2
To unaffiliated persons	35,079	60.3	59,523	57.3	53,833	61.5
Sales to the US	11,091	19.1	16,432	15.8	18,266	20.9
To affiliated persons	9,327	16.0	13,212	12.7	15,014	17.2
To unaffiliated persons	1,765	3.0	3,219	3.1	3,253	3.7
Sales to other countries	10,330	17.7	25,507	24.6	12,626	14.4
To affiliated persons	4,895	8.4	8,879	8.5	6,237	7.1
To unaffiliated persons	5,435	9.3	16,628	16.0	6,389	7.3
Developing Asia						
Sales to all destinations	18,720	100.0	48,903	100.0	65,070	100.0
To affiliated persons	8,929	47.7	15,307	31.3	22,342	34.3
To unaffiliated persons	9,797	52.3	33,597	68.7	42,728	65.7
Local sales	7,312	39.1	20,198	41.3	35,072	53.9
To affiliated persons	727	3.9	2,035	4.2	3,524	5.4
To unaffiliated persons	6,585	35.2	18,163	37.1	31,548	48.5
Sales to the US	6,449	34.4	11,030	22.6	13,967	21.5
To affiliated persons	5,969	31.9	10,166	20.8	12,313	18.9
To unaffiliated persons	480	2.6	864	1.8	1,654	2.5
Sales to other countries	4,960	26.5	17,675	36.1	16,030	24.6
To affiliated persons	2,227	11.9	3,105	6.3	6,504	10.0
To unaffiliated persons	2,733	14.6	14,570	29.8	9,526	14.6

Source: Kuwayama, 1992

Table 6.13 Ratio of sales of foreign affiliates to total exports for selected home countries, 1982–9, and average annual growth rates, 1982–4 and 1985–9

Year	US	Japan	Federal Republic of Germany
1982	5.5	1.8	1.3
1983	6.0	1.9	1.4
1984	5.3	2.5	1.5
1985	5.6	1.8	1.5
1986	5.1	1.8	1.3
1987	4.8	2.2	1.3
1988	4.3	2.6	1.4
1989	4.1		1.5

Average annual growth rates	Sales	Exports	Sales	Exports	Sales	Exports
1982–4	−2.0	−0.3	23.0	−0.3	3.0	−5.0
1985–9	9.0	18.0	36.0[a]	20.0[a]	18.0	19.0

Note: [a] 1985–8

Source: UNCTC, 1992b

industrial countries in its combination of investment with overseas trading activities suggests that it would be wrong to assume that they will follow its extreme pattern of multinational-controlled trade. Up to the present, as far as the limited data and the studies of Mauritius, Malaysia, and Thailand suggest, they have followed varying strategies, according to the country in which they are investing.

EXPECTATIONS FOR FOREIGN INVESTMENT

Following the debt crisis of the early 1980s, foreign investment was advocated as the most suitable form of foreign capital to promote in developing countries because of its advantages in terms of low financial costs and as a source of high technology.[3] At the same time, there was a growing awareness among economists and policy-makers of the 'globalisation' of production, and the possibilities of spreading different stages of production among more than one country in order to take advantage of different factor endowments, and supplying the same product to a variety of markets. Like the 'discovery' of countertrade, this was a recognition of what some firms had been doing for some years, if not centuries,[4] although clearly improved transport and communications contributed to an increase in its importance. Flows of foreign investment, and the relative growth of investment both foreign and domestic, have therefore been as carefully watched as investment-related trade.

119

There were large rises in the second half of the 1980s, but on recent data and estimates (Table 6.2) there has been a pause, and probably a substantial fall in foreign investment, since 1989–90. This can in part be explained by the recession in most industrial countries. Inflows to developing countries have held up rather better, although in total they have done little more than regain their share of the total after the swing to developed countries of the late 1970s and early 1980s. Several of the case-study countries are experiencing falls or stagnation for reasons both of their own recessions and of those in the industrial countries (Table 6.14). Movements in foreign investment are always more dramatic than those in trade (as they are in investment within economies). The overall picture from Table 6.11 is of the developed countries becoming rather more dependent on foreign investment (a little of which now comes from the most advanced developing countries) and the developing countries becoming rather less dependent.

Colombia remains overwhelmingly dependent on the US, and Jamaica and Bangladesh also receive most from the US. Japan is still most important for Thailand, although now only marginally ahead of the NICs. Mauritius and Malaysia are already becoming mainly dependent on Asian investors. Although Europe is becoming more important as a source for Latin America, this is restricted to a few countries.

While Japan's share in total investment flows has risen (Table 6.2), much of this increase went to the US and the EC, and the shares of Japanese investment going to Latin America and Asia fell sharply in the early 1980s. There was some recovery, in Asia at least, in the second half of the decade (Tambunlertchai, 1993). In contrast to the world as a whole, therefore, Japan may have had a declining share of foreign investment in developing countries, with both European and Asian investors becoming more important. The revival in Japanese investment in the late 1980s is attributed by Japanese analysts (cf. Tran van Tho, 1989) to the rise in the value of the yen. This was the period in which Japanese firms followed US firms into full-scale globalisation of production. It became normal for products and processes to be transferred in full from Japan to the low-cost Asian producers. This was in contrast to the 1970s when only production for export and relatively unsophisticated processes were transferred (cf. Page, 1986). The shift should not, therefore, be expected to be a continuing process, and the data discussed in the Malaysian and Thailand studies, both countries which benefited strongly in investment and exports from this expansion, suggest that by 1991–2 the flows were beginning to fall. Taniuchi (1992), reviewing the evidence on what caused the surge in the 1980s, suggests that 'Japan is likely to remain a major investor' but not on the scale of the late 1980s.

If it is true that there has been little substitution between trade and investment, except for the upward shift in Japanese investment in the late 1980s, there seems little reason to expect a major increase in the role of multinationals in the future. Therefore, any changes will be dependent on

Table 6.14 Inflows of foreign investment by region and country, 1975, 1980 and 1985–92

Country	1975	1980	1985	1986	1987	1988	1989	1990	1991	1992
US$ billion										
Developing countries	6.3	10.1	11.5	14.0	25.0	30.0	30.0	30.0	41.0	41.0
Asia	1.6	3.2	4.5	6.7	11.6	15.0	16.2	18.6	24.0	28.0
America	3.3	6.2	4.5	5.4	10.8	11.4	8.4	7.3	12.0	13.0
Africa	–	1.0	1.5	1.728	2.344	2.795	4.814	2.085	2.514	–
US$ million										
Malaysia	350	934	695	489	423	719	1,668	2,332	4,073	4,118
Thailand	187	162	261	352	-,105	1,775	2,444	2,014	2,000	n.a.
Colombia	51	1016	642	253	159	547	484	433	740	n.a.
Jamaica	-2	28	-9	-5	53	12	57	138	127	86
Mauritius	6	1	8	7	17	24	36	40	8	-29
Zimbabwe	n.a.	2	3	7	-30	4	-10	-12	3	n.a.
Bangladesh	0	0	0	2	3	2	0	3	1	4

Sources: BIS, 1993; UNCTAD, 1993b; Tambunlertchai, 1993; Chirathivat, 1992; Bank of Thailand, data supplied; IMF, International Financial Statistics

the same conditions in host and home countries as for trade, and not a subject for this book. A series of projections using the relationships of the 1970s and 1980s (UNCTAD, 1993b: 106; the division which was formerly the UNCTC is one of the strongest supporters of the view that transnational corporations are becoming an increasingly important force in world investment and output) suggests growth rates of about 11–12 % in the first half of the 1990s for Asia, and between 12 and 18% for Latin America and 6–16% for Africa. These compare with figures for the second half of the 1980s (before the 1990 slowing) of 20%, 15%, and 5%. With world inflation at about 4%, these are equivalent to growth rates at constant prices of 7.5%, 7–13% and 2–12%. Current trade forecasts are similar for the Asian and Latin American countries. The African figure would therefore imply a substantial recovery, relative to its past record and to standard trade projections, although in practice such a change would probably also be reflected in trade performance. The projections for Asia and Latin America are in line with past investment and projected trade. These forecasts, therefore, do not suggest any transformation in the relationship between investment inflows and trade.

What does appear to be changing is the declining role of the US in the total and the increase in importance of investment by Asian multinationals, especially within Asia. The first, on past relationships, would imply that multinational company-related trade will grow less relative to total foreign investment than in the past. The second is too recent for there to be firm evidence about their trading propensity. The case-study evidence indicates that in some cases (Mauritius, Jamaica, Bangladesh) Asian activities are heavily trade-related, but these are countries where all foreign investment has tended to be more trade-related than in the larger or richer countries. Malaysia and Thailand (Table 6.13) also appear to have substantial sales by foreign affiliates of firms other than US and Japanese, some of which could be Asian.

An important difference between much of the new non-Japanese Asian investment and traditional foreign investment by the US, Europe, and Japan is the strong role of small and medium-sized enterprises, although large companies are also involved. The small companies are particularly important in shifting production in labour-cost sensitive industries abroad, and therefore will be among those most influential in generating exports (the clothing firms found in several of the case-study countries are examples). Many are Chinese, particularly from Hong Kong. This type of investment may therefore be the result of the changing pattern specifically of the clothing industry, itself the result partly of cost changes and partly of the NTBs discussed earlier, rather than a separate foreign investment effect. It is also possible that the reduction in trade barriers (in these countries), the increase in the share of trade, and the growing familiarity of all sizes of company with the potential for trade, have reduced the advantages of large

MNCs in foreign investment. The trend is appearing in industrial countries and also in Latin America, but Asia, and the Chinese companies there, probably have the best conditions to begin the process.

The limited expectations suggested here for future growth in foreign investment are particularly important, because foreign investment itself has always raised questions of vulnerability to external control and limitations on national action similar to those which this study suggests may be imposed by the trading regime. If foreign investment were therefore changing greatly in importance, this would have implications not just for its direct effects on trade, but for countries' feelings of vulnerability to these other external controls.

NOTES

1 A traditional concern about multinationals is their misuse of transfer prices (the recorded prices for goods traded within the company) to move tax liabilities from high to low tax countries or to avoid capital controls, or for other purposes. There is very little evidence, except for pharmaceutical firms, that this is a serious problem, and pricing decisions appear to be kept separate from actual production and sales decisions, and therefore are irrelevant to this study (for a summary see van den Bulcke, 1985; Rugman and Eden, 1985). If it occurs, it can be regarded as another example of large firms' ability to evade government policies. It affects national income, and its distribution between the government and the private sector, but normally not national output.

2 It could even be argued that the total confusion and inconsistency of both national data and all attempts by international organisations or researchers to present consistent estimates (including this chapter) should themselves be an indication that trade by multinationals is not yet considered a critical issue by most countries. (See even the Malaysian chapter.)

3 As Turner (1990) points out, quoting a League of Nations document based on experience of the 1930s debt crisis, 'Foreign direct investment has always seemed more attractive when other forms of international lending to developing countries run into difficulties.' A Latin American employers' federation briefing of 1966 could have been written in 1986: 'In the present situation, where the state of international trade makes it difficult for developing countries to grow, debt-capacity is restricted, and official aid is inadequate, the flow of direct foreign investment should revive as a means of external financing' (statement of the Reunión del Consejo Interamericano de Comercio y Producción, 3 June 1966).

4 Asian painting and engraving on a sub-contracting basis for the European market dates back at least to the eighteenth century.

7

THE WORLD TRADING SYSTEM VIEWED FROM DEVELOPING COUNTRIES

The purpose of the first part of this book has been to describe how regulated or controlled the world trading system is, as seen from developing countries. The types of intervention examined here cover a substantial amount of their trade: there are a significant number of types of trade and sectors where the nature of the market facing developing countries is measurably different from that faced by most industrial countries. By the early 1980s, there were major differences from the 1970s and earlier periods in which now-advanced countries developed, and the countries examined here faced a more complex and more controlled system. The nature of the output and trade of these countries is now bringing some of these interventions into greater prominence. The total picture includes both government interventions and the role of multinational companies or agreements among firms. The question that arises is how these differ from the point of view of an individual developing country and its exporters.

THE TRADING SYSTEM: OPEN OR CLOSED

The international system as a whole is now one of low tariffs and few controls, except in a few commodities. Only a minor part of the trade of two of the three major trading areas, the US and Japan, is helped or hindered by regional trading areas or preferences, and even for the EC countries the tariffs and restrictions which they face on most of their exports to non-EC countries are normally unimportant; the commitments they have made to the EC and its own preferences are a matter of their own policies, not those imposed by external groups of countries. The external constraints which the industrial nations face are imposed by official or unofficial international groups (or by private companies) in which they have a voice. The commodities on which they face high tariffs (notably, clothing exports to the US) or controls (agricultural products) are not major exports for most of them. If they wish to move from low to higher technology exports, they will benefit from lower non-tariff barriers on the latter. A few export products are controlled because of security policies, but their governments are on the

124

panel controlling these. The USA has a high share of trade controlled by multinational companies but this is mainly by US-owned companies; it therefore raises questions of national economic policy and regulation, not international.

The developing countries have a higher share of their exports in the remaining high-tariff sectors, and in almost all cases their exports face escalating tariffs if they wish to move from raw materials or semi-processed exports to processed. Most are able to claim access to the Generalised System of Preferences, if they are exporting to one of the industrial countries and can meet the appropriate national content and documentation requirements of that country. Many have access in addition to one or more of the special preferences by an individual importer for certain regions or groups, with different conditions of local content or production. The corollary of this is that in each of the industrial country markets they are competing with other developing countries, with more or less favourable preference arrangements, any of which may change or be extended to others or withdrawn. On some trade they face both preferences and controls which can produce different effective levels of ease of access during the year, as a quota becomes used up and reverts to a less favourable condition or tariff or to prohibition, or as an agricultural season changes.

The principal controlled commodities – food, fuels, and textiles and clothing – are a higher share of developing countries' output and trade, and on primary commodities and textiles and clothing, they face more controls, from commodity agreements and from the imposed MFA, than do industrial country exporters. Some have lowered their dependence on such exports as a deliberate response to the problems caused by controls. For many, official assistance finances a significant share of their imports, imposing constraints on how they can be used, and also implying that their effective freedom to vary imports, if they wish to adjust their external balance, operates on a smaller number than the total recorded value of trade and therefore may require larger percentage movements. On some of these imports they face an implicit extra charge from the cost of tying. The direct role of intra-MNC trade in their total trade is small for most, but high for a few. The overall impact of multinational companies, measured by the total trade of their subsidiaries or share in investment, is potentially large, although it is difficult to assess how far this is amenable to national policy or how far it is itself a result of other trading policies. Unlike the high share of MNCs in US trade, these are mainly externally, not nationally, owned companies.

Because of their high share of trade with a few industrial countries, developing countries tend to be particularly vulnerable to changes in those countries' policies, even those toward third countries, for example changes in the internal trade of the EC post-1992 or new concessions to Eastern Europe. The international organisations of which they are members are ignored and their rules are broken routinely by their trading partners. They are excluded from others which may affect their trade intentionally (G–7, COCOM) or as an uncompensated side-effect (EC, NAFTA). Their major commodity exports (food and clothing) are considered exceptions to the rules of the market internationally and in even the most non-interventionist countries. The 1993 GATT settlement is only the first step towards mitigating these exclusions.

Table 7.1 summarises the types of quantifiable intervention found. It is not possible to add the numbers in each column because there are too many cases in which the same commodity may fall under different controls or trading regimes, and the types and extent of overlap vary among the developing countries in each group and among similar commodities, and are different according to their different markets. Moreover, this variation of trading regime within country or commodity flows should not be disguised by aggregation because it is part of the complication of trading for developing countries.

Although it does not show effects such as those from different preference areas or tariff escalation (these are described in the individual case studies), even on this simplified presentation it is obvious, first, that there are significant numbers for many of the entries: a potential exporter must take into account a range of possible constraints and be familiar with their implications. Secondly, there are some countries and types of countries for which an aggregate share of trade under at least one category will be extremely large. Low levels of development inevitably bring a high vulnerability to external policy because of dependence on aid and a high share of commodity exports, and there is an additional effect from such countries' tendency to have a high share of their trade with the industrial countries. In countries like Malaysia and Thailand, and the Asian countries in general, regional trade offers an alternative to the protection imposed by the industrial countries.

One effect which cannot be quantified is the overall perception by developing countries that trade is normally policy-driven, in contrast to the implicit assumption in industrial countries and in international institutions that it is market-driven, although with identifiable exceptions. The developing country view is derived from numbers like those displayed here (and exaggerated beliefs about some of them, notably the amount of trade controlled by multinationals), and is understandable in this context. But in the last twenty years it has been reinforced by the ways in which the industrial countries have responded to changes in market conditions.

In the 1950s and 1960s, the regulation and reduction of tariffs under the GATT failed to lead to an acceptance by all interests in industrial countries that the existence of common rules on these made further intervention unnecessary. Instead, the establishment of limits on tariffs was followed by a substitution of other forms of intervention, not simply to limit total external competition but to regulate from which suppliers that competition could come, by means of selective quotas, regional preferences, and other types of selective intervention. These are not only doubly illegal under the GATT system (they are unilaterally introduced controls and they violate Most Favoured Nation treatment); they are difficult to explain even on the grounds of national or producer advantage normally suggested in analyses of why countries protect. It is understandable, if not (on a broad economic view) in the national or international interest, for a threatened producer to want to prevent competition and this is at least semi-predictable for a potential supplier. But why should it matter to such a firm whether the competition comes from one country or another? Although within preferences and within NTBs there is some evidence of discrimination in favour of developing countries, the interaction of the two and the choice of sectors have meant effective discrimination against them. Such action is not therefore a rational attempt to make higher-income competitors bear a greater part of the burden imposed by protection.

Various explanations can be suggested in particular cases of why some suppliers or some types of trade are perceived to be more damaging or unfair or unwanted. But they all depend on recognition that relationships and considerations other than those of the market are being used; as a result the policy must be implemented by non-market means, explicitly or implicitly by government intervention.

This type of intervention can make it plausible to any trading partners, particularly if they also have certain sectors or types of economic activity which they want to promote as matters of policy, to assume both that intervention is inherent in all trading relationships and that uncertainty about future intervention is an inevitable risk. The response can vary, but is unlikely to be easily measured in trade flows (except that these will be lower than the efficient level, in addition to any diversion). At an international level, the response was the Uruguay Round of GATT negotiations, an attempt to plug as many as possible of the remaining gaps in regulating what can be done, and to find more effective enforcement mechanisms. In particular, the two least market-regulated sectors, agriculture and clothing, were brought in, and the ways in which countries are operating their trade policies were made more open through regular reports by GATT. But individual countries must also respond to their trading partners' actions.

PUBLIC AND PRIVATE INTERVENTION

This perception of a growing role for policy, or, more pejoratively, the politicisation of international economic relations, is an important reason to keep official and company-based intervention distinct in the analysis, for developing countries in general and also in the range of responses that have been made by the individual countries studied. It is important to distinguish between the recognition that almost all trade involves something more than a

Table 7.1 Summary of constraints (percentages unless marked)

	World	Industrial countries	Non-oil developing countries	Asia	Latin America and Caribbean	Sub-Saharan Africa	Bangla-desh	Malaysia	Thailand	Colombia	Jamaica	Mauri-tius	Zim-babwe
GDP/capita ($US)							250	2800	1812	1400	1500	2600	700
Population (million)							116	18	58	33	2	1	9
Growth of exports 85–90	4.5		9.9	18.0	-0.6	-1.1							
Growth of exports of mfrs 85–90	6.0		15.8	19.3	5.5	12.9							
Share in world exports of manufactures 1990			17.1	14.1	2.0	0.5		0.7	0.6	0.1			
Share of manufactures exports 1990			69	78	37	45	75.5	54.2	63.1	25.1	15.0	65.6	34.0
Share of exports to developing 1990	22.8	21.5	33.0	40.1	25.2	15.0	24.0	48.9	32.0	19.3	12.3	5.9	38.0
Share of exports to Asia 1990	12.6	9.9	21.0	33.4	5.0	4.2	22.3	44.6	22.3	0.7	0.1	1.4	7.8
MFN tariffs by industrial countries	4.7		4.7										
GSP tariffs by industrial countries			2.7			<0.5							
Share of GSP exports/total exports to industrial			12.6						24.0				
Share of NTB exports/total to industrial			17.5										
Share of NTB and/or GSP			27.2										
NTBs imposed by EC	23		31	35	22	24[a]	34	7	67	6	37[a]	71[a]	20[a]
NTBs imposed by US	26		24	28	17	6	35	11	28	12	40	26	10
NTBs imposed by Japan	24		26	28	18	31	86	4	35	8	0	0	2
EC + US + Japan: 1986 weights, 1990 totals	14		15	16[b]	12[b]	16[b]	26	4	28	8	23	63	11
Sums of commodities							31	4	22	10	17	58	11
1986 weights and values	13		15	16	11	16	25	4	25	6	25	57	10

Table 7.1 Continued

	World	Industrial countries	Non-oil developing countries	Asia	Latin America and Caribbean	Sub-Saharan Africa	Bangla-desh	Malaysia	Thailand	Colombia	Jamaica	Mauri-tius	Zim-babwe
Share of trade under countertrade (c.1986, est.)							14	10		6	6	0.0	13.0
Ratio of aid to imports (1990)			7.8	3.8	4.8	25.2	58.4	1.6	2.4	1.7	14.7	5.5	16.0
Share of controlled primary exports food and fuels (1990)	19.5		23.6	16.1	53.5	73.3	16.4	29.5	29.6	69.7	20.8	31.1	44.8
Share of intra-firm trade in US subsidiaries' imports (1989): to US	17.1		15.6	13.1	18.4	21.7		26.7	17.8	13.3	33.8		
to world	3.3		4.7	3.3	9.4	5.0		5.3	4.1	6.5	19.9		
Share of intra-firm trade of Japanese subsidiaries (1986): to Japan	2.9			6.4	0.2	0.0							
to world	0.2			1.0	0.0	0.0							
Share in area's mfrs exports of: US & Japanese intra-firm				4.3	9.4	5.0							
US & Japanese affiliates			8.6	7.7	15.4	3.6							
Share of all trade by foreign affiliates in exports								45.7	27.3				
Share of foreign investment in gross domestic investment							0.1	9.7	6.3	6.1	6.6	4.0	0.0

Notes: [a] This includes goods exempted under Lomé [b] Excluding fuel

Source: Tables in Chapters 1–6, supplemented by country data in Chapters 8–14

single, simple transaction between buyer and seller and the view that public sector intervention is so prevalent that an economic approach cannot succeed, even if firms learn the institutional lessons of how to sell.

The line is not a rigid one: it is affected in particular cases by the role of public sector companies and legal systems in restricting or permitting various types of cartel or monopolistic arrangement. However, most of the interventions discussed so far are classifiable. Most are public: quotas, tariffs, preferences, official regional trading areas, tied aid, officially sponsored commodity agreements, countertrade required by law (as some was briefly in the mid-1980s). Some clearly are not: trading by multinational companies (any official limits or encouragement for this are likely to be by the host, not the home country), private company-to-company countertrade (as has always occurred and now continues without official requirement); the network of contacts and long-term relationships, even ethnic ones, which characterises the clothing industry, within all countries and between countries.

RESPONSES AND STRATEGIES FOR DEVELOPING COUNTRIES

This does not mean that a country's development strategy can be independent of the private constraints. The appropriate responses will be different. They may be through government or private decisions, but there are characteristics of the organisation of particular industries which go beyond the inputs of capital, labour, and skills which they require, and at what cost, and which have implications both for whether a developing (or other new entrant) country can be competitive in them, and whether they are appropriate for the country's policy towards the international economy in general.

The three response strategies outlined here will provide a framework for examining whether the case-study countries have recognised both the public and the private institutional constraints on trade, and how they have responded. One reaction in the past has been autarky, but the changes in developing countries' own trade barriers in the 1980s show a shift away from this. Other strategies which will be discussed in more detail in some of the individual country studies have been:

The next step from autarky: to treat the external market as less favourable because of these difficulties, and to concentrate on the local market, seizing any opportunities that arise in the external market but not relying on it (Colombia offers examples).

The reverse of this: to use the opportunities created by the system, to seek the preferences and to negotiate to obtain trading advantages (Mauritius, Bangladesh).

The most self-confident: to assume that, even given the preferences, lower costs or other advantages will prevail, even if the margin must be greater than in a free market (Malaysia, Thailand, the old NICs), although even here adjustments because of barriers are made.

Zimbabwe seems to be in transition from the first to the third (with some thought for the second); Jamaica, from the second to the third.

But the effects of intervention go further than current trade policy. There are the well-known limitations of any tariff or non-tariff average measure based on weighting the post-control flows. To these must be added the flows which have been induced in reaction to the controls. A belief in politicisation can explain why developing countries have altered their own exports, either to move away from controlled exports or to specialise in preferred flows or markets. This implies that a higher proportion of their present exports than can be measured by a spot measurement is effectively the result of industrial country interventions in markets. Specific actions of this type will be discussed in the country chapters, but one is of major importance for developing countries' understanding of what constitutes development. The view that commodity markets are subject to risks from manipulation and control, private or public, by the major countries or their companies, has for at least forty years strengthened the more general economic case, on grounds of climatic or systemic risk and declining relative demand, for treating moving away from food production and into industrialisation as an essential element in development.

The most obvious common characteristic of new exporters or exporters trying to expand in any of these countries, that they are new entrants to at least some of their markets, and perhaps to the industry as a whole, should not be neglected. If external conditions are particularly favourable to new (small) entrants – an intention of preference schemes (although not characteristic of those which are themselves so complicated that they offer a high return to prior experience) – or particularly unfavourable – perhaps industries which rely on long-term relationships within or between companies – this could influence a choice between diversification and specialisation. A country-based quota system may disperse an industry if it brings in new, less competitive suppliers, whose principal comparative advantage is being not (yet) restricted.

There is also the overriding question of the importance of the external sector itself to a country or to a firm, and this will influence the amount of analysis which is efficient in terms of its own total returns.

MEASURING THE RESPONSE

The interrelationships among different constraints, and the range of possible implications for a country, put the emphasis on how a country chooses to respond, rather than a mechanistic interpretation of how the direct implications of external constraints determine a response. The problems of *ex post* measurement of protection effects make it necessary to look beyond the numbers in Table 7.1, but these do suggest some differences. The response to fast-growing and relatively unprotected markets in Asia for Asian exporters was noted in Chapter 2 (Table 2.5). Their trade within their own region is higher and has increased more than Latin American trade within Latin America, and both are ahead of Africa with only 5% trade within the region.

The more aggregate responses, for example to the policies favouring primary or relatively unprocessed goods over manufactures, offset by higher policy uncertainty, cannot be measured at this level. This is also true of diversification among commodities. Industrialisation and diversification are essential parts of development. That changes in structure have been greater among developing countries than industrial is not in aggregate evidence of any distortions or barrier-induced shifts. But the evidence from individual countries indicates clearly some types of diversification which were motivated in part by avoiding barriers or seeking preferences. Analysis of the trade of the most successful NICs in the 1970s showed (Page, 1989) that diversifying into goods like machinery and transport equipment which were rapidly growing was a successful strategy, and that these countries also increased the share of their exports to the major industrial countries. As these goods are also the least constrained (at least by official intervention), the same types of response would be even more appropriate under more constrained conditions for other goods. The new pressures, however, may accelerate this diversification, with consequent divergence from the most efficient development path.

Table 7.1 summarises NTBs faced by the individual countries. Malaysia's exports have faced relatively limited controls, and there is no evidence from these numbers that it has changed the distribution of its exports towards more or less protected commodities or countries. In contrast, 25% of Bangladesh's exports, with the 1986 composition by commodity and importer, faced barriers from the US, the EC, or Japan. In 1990, if this is adjusted only for changes in markets (i.e. the country averages for import protection in each of the three markets are applied to Bangladeshi total exports to each market), this number rises slightly, and if the individual commodity exports at their 1990 values are used to weight the barriers (assumed to cover the same share of each commodity), the share rises to more than 30%. Bangladesh thus appears to have specialised in the most controlled commodities. The other countries show more mixed responses which combine diversification of exports, even if into apparently more protectionist markets. What both these rough measures and the country studies will indicate is that the way countries respond to opportunities and barriers is important as well as the constraints which each faces.

Comparing the results for different years' weighting of the NTB protection results (Table 7.1) with Tables 7.2 a–e shows how the regions' exports are allocated between the markets in which the barriers are found and other markets. The world as a whole has had a fairly regular pattern across all

Table 7.2 Shares of exports of major commodities to principal regions (percentages)

Table 7.2a World

SITC	Commodity	1985			1990		
		US+EC+ Japan	All developing	Asia	US+EC+ Japan	All developing	Asia
Total		53.28	22.34	8.56	59.68	22.82	12.62
0+1	Food and tobacco	55.37	23.55	6.26	64.29	21.68	8.60
3	Fuels	59.02	21.21	10.04	61.78	20.25	11.21
2+4	Other raw materials	55.20	22.24	12.69	62.38	24.36	14.73
0 to 4	Primary	57.35	22.03	9.49	62.81	21.65	11.02
5	Chemicals	51.07	24.96	9.54	57.27	25.37	14.17
7	Machinery and transport	49.60	22.69	8.05	58.17	23.88	13.37
6+8	Other manufactures	55.68	20.71	7.67	61.62	21.40	12.62
5 to 8	Manufactures	52.12	22.21	8.09	59.41	23.09	13.17
26	Textile fibres	44.02	27.22	16.47	48.11	37.74	26.38
65	Textiles	47.62	28.30	13.15	49.79	35.50	23.34
84	Clothing	68.55	9.72	1.89	70.84	12.97	6.86
67	Iron and steel	42.72	26.02	9.05	55.66	28.26	15.80
Total−3	Total excluding fuels	51.97	22.60	8.22	59.44	23.12	12.79

Table 7.2b Non-oil developing countries

SITC	Commodity	1985 US+EC+ Japan	1985 All developing	1985 Asia	1990 US+EC+ Japan	1990 All developing	1990 Asia
Total		55.16	26.09	12.72	54.36	35.17	25.40
0 + 1	Food and tobacco	52.42	21.68	6.74	56.04	28.79	14.87
3	Fuels	57.95	27.12	15.75	57.69	35.90	25.96
2 + 4	Other raw materials	48.24	28.90	21.60	52.84	35.22	23.69
0 to 4	Primary	53.76	25.54	13.79	55.79	32.79	20.81
5	Chemicals	33.51	45.95	23.69	34.47	54.43	39.86
7	Machinery and transport	54.66	27.06	14.56	53.64	37.98	30.06
6 + 8	Other manufactures	59.85	23.26	10.06	56.47	33.29	24.47
5 to 8	Manufactures	55.98	26.37	12.65	53.88	36.47	27.55
26	Textile fibres	39.34	33.42	21.09	39.07	44.86	33.91
65	Textiles	34.49	39.37	22.82	28.20	60.66	47.52
84	Clothing	76.42	10.26	1.48	71.73	16.09	10.67
67	Iron and steel	39.98	41.19	15.31	44.64	46.96	31.13
Total−3	Total excluding fuels	54.50	25.85	12.01	53.98	35.09	25.34

Table 7.2c Asia

SITC	Commodity	1985 US+EC+ Japan	1985 All developing	1985 Asia	1990 US+EC+ Japan	1990 All developing	1990 Asia
Total		56.41	28.83	20.56	51.69	39.30	33.19
0 + 1	Food and tobacco	49.56	34.58	19.81	49.72	39.54	30.60
3	Fuels	59.60	33.34	29.41	52.22	41.95	38.46
2 + 4	Other raw materials	49.39	38.59	41.25	47.23	43.76	37.24
0 to 4	Primary	54.55	34.92	29.78	50.05	41.55	35.34
5	Chemicals	27.12	50.90	45.19	28.78	62.95	58.45
7	Machinery and transport	55.26	27.28	19.36	51.88	40.34	34.53
6 + 8	Other manufactures	61.54	22.48	13.66	54.81	35.59	29.09
5 to 8	Manufactures	57.85	25.40	17.03	52.25	38.90	32.77
26	Textile fibres	33.12	47.29	42.85	35.17	50.17	45.12
65	Textiles	30.28	43.20	29.43	25.05	66.08	54.37
84	Clothing	78.12	9.09	1.73	71.13	17.70	12.43
67	Iron and steel	47.35	36.67	23.97	43.45	47.37	41.29
Total–3	Total excluding fuels	55.78	27.93	18.80	51.64	39.07	32.72

Table 7.2d Latin America and the Caribbean

SITC	Commodity	1985			1990		
		US+EC+ Japan	All developing	Asia	US+EC+ Japan	All developing	Asia
Total		61.39	19.29	2.82	58.99	21.38	4.52
0 + 1	Food and tobacco	53.84	13.34	1.14	61.07	19.53	3.41
3[a]	Fuels	69.54	14.71	1.81	48.74	9.41	0.58
2 + 4	Other raw materials	52.48	25.61	8.92	60.77	27.09	9.16
0 to 4	Primary	61.57	15.75	2.57	55.78	16.67	3.30
5	Chemicals	45.88	41.11	4.97	51.59	42.80	5.84
7	Machinery and transport	68.50	26.56	1.42	72.86	22.88	1.87
6 + 8	Other manufactures	61.68	26.49	5.61	63.98	30.24	9.34
5 to 8	Manufactures	61.40	28.66	4.26	64.87	29.81	6.69
26	Textile fibres	46.44	28.24	9.87	45.19	45.60	19.29
65	Textiles	53.68	24.52	2.79	59.14	28.20	3.14
84	Clothing	74.33	21.08	0.00	74.60	20.25	0.09
67	Iron and steel	42.16	33.69	14.18	45.34	49.99	26.06
Total–3	Total excluding fuels	56.74	21.90	3.39	62.69	25.70	5.94

Note: [a] Data for 1990 inconsistent in source

Table 7.2e Africa

SITC	Commodity	1935 US+EC+ Japan	1935 All developing	1935 Asia	1990 US+EC+ Japan	1990 All developing	1990 Asia
Total		67.46	14.02	1.67	79.52	13.17	2.87
0 + 1	Food and tobacco	63.25	20.19	2.81	72.08	17.38	2.25
3	Fuels	70.92	10.22	0.36	86.50	7.38	0.71
2 + 4	Other raw materials	56.63	18.88	6.26	64.09	23.46	10.90
0 to 4	Primary	68.57	12.39	1.23	81.91	10.62	1.95
5	Chemicals	32.44	51.00	18.91	44.66	46.81	18.08
7	Machinery and transport	45.53	47.43	0.54	60.86	33.74	7.55
6 + 8	Other manufactures	66.40	21.76	3.26	76.69	17.21	3.84
5 to 8	Manufactures	57.44	30.02	6.52	68.71	24.75	7.09
26	Textile fibres	40.24	25.71	14.19	43.47	36.50	28.05
65	Textiles	46.15	26.60	0.64	43.33	28.69	1.82
84	Clothing	n.a.	n.a.	n.a.	92.89	2.26	0.23
67	Iron and steel	n.a.	n.a.	n.a.	55.69	37.62	5.69
Total-3	Total excluding fuels	59.42	22.86	4.73	68.95	21.94	6.14

Source: UN, Monthly Bulletin of Statistics

commodities, slightly increasing the share of trade going to the three principal markets, the US, EC and Japan, and also that going to Asia, at the expense of both other industrial countries and the former centrally planned economies. Developing countries have not increased their trade with the major industrial economies and have doubled the share going to Asia. This has not been uniform across commodities. It is manufactures, particularly the less sophisticated, where the reductions in export share to the industrial countries have been largest, with massive increases in intra-developing country trade in textiles and some shift in clothing. It would be difficult to explain this as the result of a transformation of competitive conditions or demand over a five-year period. In particular, there is a clear contrast between these commodities and the behaviour of machinery and transport equipment. For the latter, exports to the major industrial markets held up in spite of the rise to Asia; it was exports to other developing countries and the rest of the world which fell. This provides quantitative evidence of reallocation, in particular of clothing away from the traditional producers, which will be confirmed in the country responses to the MFA quotas.

For Asian countries, whose mix of exports has faced the highest barriers, the shifts are largest and most general. Again, exports of machinery and transport equipment and also of chemicals provide the contrast: here their exports to Asia rose, but those to the US, the EC, and Japan were also strong. It was in the protected sectors that there was a clear shift away from the industrial countries. Latin America, with lower protection for its exports, especially in its major market, did not move out of it, in general or in the protected goods. Africa, which faces lower barriers or exemption from them in the industrial countries, has had no incentive to move away from them, and has increased its exports to the major developed markets.

8

MALAYSIA

BACKGROUND

Malaysia is the most developed country covered in this study, both in the composition of its industrial output and in the level of its income. Its growth first became rapid in the 1970s, rising to about 8%. It fell back temporarily in the early 1980s, but by the end of the decade was again growing by over 8% a year and this continued into the 1990s (although 1992 and 1993 were slower than the recent average, at about 8%). Its GDP per capita is about US$3,000. It is (and is very conscious of being) a small country by the standards of many of its Asian neighbours (18 million population), although not compared with many developing countries in other continents.

The principal changes in the structure of Malaysia's economy took place during the 1970s. This is when agriculture fell from a third to 23% of the economy (by 1990 it was about 18%), and manufacturing rose from 14% to 20% (in 1990: 28%). It was also the decade in which exports of manufactures started to rise, from 6% of exports to 19%; this has risen faster since, to over 50% by 1990. The structure is expected to continue to change, but at a declining rate with manufacturing reaching 37% of output by 2000 (Malaysia, Bank Negara, 1992). The growth target is 7% until 2020. In the 1980s, the particular target for manufacturing development was diversification into new products, many for export and many with foreign investment. The actual and planned performance of the economy was thus changing and growing rapidly by industrial country standards, but developing more slowly than in the past, and with more attention to the nature of the structure.

Malaysia has been a successful manufactures exporter since the late 1970s, and there has been an explicit policy of export-led growth, which remains in force (Mahathir, 1992). But unlike the first-round NICs, Malaysia and Thailand are still also major exporters of primary goods, including those identified in Chapter 5 as most vulnerable to barriers. Table 8.1 shows that, even in 1990, primary goods were still 45% of the total, compared with an average for all developing countries of about 30% and for Asia of 20%. The average share of manufactured exports in total exports for developing countries had reached 50% by the mid-1980s. Of Malaysia's primary exports, food and fuels accounted for 30%, about twice the Asian average (see Table 5.8). Manufactures have increased their share during two periods: in the second half of the 1970s, and again, from a quarter to a half, in the late 1980s, continuing into the 1990s (Table 8.2). The latter rise was helped by the fall in the share of petroleum, but both this and food remain among the top 10 exports. On the manufactures side the major export has always been electrical and electronic goods, and this continued to grow more than other manufactures throughout the 1980s and early 1990s. Within this category, electronic components, which were three-quarters of the total in 1980, have now fallen to under a half, while electrical machinery has risen to more than a half. Electrical appliances have never been more than about 10% of electrical exports. The other important manufactures exports are textiles and clothing and transport equipment. Both rose in share in the late 1980s, transport equipment increasing the most.

Some of the transport exports were for special reasons; for example aircraft (about a third of the 1990 total) were returns after leasing, but the rise also reflects that in car exports. These are going to new markets, but until 1993 entirely to those which share Malaysia's own non-tariff barrier against car imports: right-hand drive, including the UK, Ireland, Singapore, New Zealand, and further afield, Nigeria, Jamaica and Mauritius. From 1994, to meet new Asian and other European markets, left-hand drive models are planned.

At the world level, Malaysia's exports of electronic components are significant (7% of world trade in 1988), but it still remained a major supplier only in some primary goods: palm oil (normally processed), tin, and wood, although these were much less important to the Malaysian economy than petroleum or electrical exports.

By 1991 Malaysia was trading about equally with the industrial and the developing countries, which, so far, means almost exclusively Asia, but this equality marks a change (Table 8.3). The share to the industrial countries had risen from 55% in 1970 (when the economy began its shift into manufactures trade) to about 60% between 1975 and 1980. It then started to fall, to 55% by 1985. The increase in the share to Asia in the 1980s is in line with the change for other Asian countries. Although the absolute level is high, some of this can be explained by the high share with Singapore (about a quarter of Malaysia's total exports, and of its manufactures), much of which eventually goes outside the region. The principal industrial country market for Malaysia's manufactures remains the US, also about a quarter, with the EC taking 18% and Japan only 8–9%. For all goods, however, the shares of these three areas are much more equal; the US takes about 17%, Japan about only slightly less, at 16%, a decline from over 20% in the early 1980s. This shift probably reflects the decline in the share of primary products in

Table 8.1 Malaysia: export structure by principal commodities

Commodity	SITC	1970	1975	1980	1985	1990
Total value ($m)		1,686.6	3,846.6	12,944.7	15,637.9	29,418.7
			percentages			
All food items	0−1−22+4	12.6	23.2	15.0	17.4	11.7
Agricultural raw materials	2 less (22+27+28)	50.0	34.1	30.9	18.3	13.8
Fuels	3	7.3	10.9	24.7	31.5	17.8
Ores and metals	27+28+68	22.6	13.9	10.2	5.3	2.1
Manufactured goods of which:	5 to 8 less 68	6.5	17.3	18.8	27.2	54.2
Chemical products	5	0.7	0.9	0.6	1.1	1.7
Other manufactured goods	(6+8) less 68	4.2	10.2	6.7	7.4	16.4
Machinery and equipment	7	1.6	6.2	11.5	18.7	36.1
Crude petroleum	331	3.9	9.3	23.8	23.1	13.4
Petroleum products	332	3.4	1.5	0.8	2.9	1.5
Textile fibres, yarn and clothing	26+65+84	0.7	2.0	2.9	3.5	5.9
Metals and metal manufactures	67+68+69	20.0	13.7	9.5	5.2	3.0
Machinery						
Non-electrical	71	0.7	2.2	0.8	1.7	4.5
Electrical	72	0.3	3.3	9.9	15.5	26.6
Transport equipment	73	0.6	0.7	0.8	1.5	2.4

Source: UNCTAD, *Handbook 1992*

Table 8.2 Malaysia: principal exports 1970–91 (percentages)

3-digit	SITC category	1970	1975	1980	1985	1990	1991	1993
729	Electrical machinery nes	0.1	0.5	8.4	12.1	15.4	14.6	
724	Telecommunications equip	0.1	0.5	0.8	2.4	8.6	9.7	
714	Office machines	0.0	0.8	0.0	0.2	2.3	4.0	41.7
891	Sound recorders, producers	0.0	0.1	0.1	0.2	2.5	3.3	
722	Elec pwr mach, switchgear	0.1	2.2	0.7	0.9	2.0	2.7	
719	Machines nes non-electric	0.3	0.8	0.5	0.7	1.4	2.0	
861	Instruments, apparatus	0.1	3.5	0.2	0.4	1.0	1.4	
841	Clothing not of fur	0.3	1.1	1.2	2.1	4.5	4.5	
331	Crude petroleum, etc	3.9	9.3	23.8	23.1	13.4	10.8	6.5
332	Petroleum products	3.4	1.5	0.8	2.9	1.5	1.1	
687	Tin	19.5	13.1	8.9	4.4	1.2	0.7	0.5
231	Rubber crude, synthetic	33.4	21.9	16.4	7.6	3.8	2.9	1.8
242	Wood rough	12.5	7.3	9.3	7.4	5.1	4.4	6.3
631	Veneers, plywood etc	1.5	2.0	1.5	0.8	1.3	1.4	
243	Wood shapes	4.0	4.8	4.8	3.0	4.5	3.7	
821	Furniture	0.0	0.1	0.1	0.1	0.6	0.8	
422	Fixed veg oil non-soft	6.0	15.9	10.7	12.2	5.5	5.3	4.9
341	Gas natural and manufctd	0.0	0.0	0.0	5.4	3.4	3.6	2.3

Sources: GATT, 1993 vol. 1; government 1994 budget estimate

Table 8.3 Malaysia: principal markets 1970–91 (percentages)

Partner	1970	1975	1980	1985	1990	1991
US	13.0	16.1	16.3	13.0	16.9	16.9
Japan	18.3	14.5	22.8	23.8	15.8	15.7
EC	16.8	19.5	17.3	14.2	14.4	14.3
UK	6.6	6.0	2.8	2.6	3.9	4.4
Germany	0.0	0.0	3.6	2.6	3.9	3.6
Netherlands	3.2	8.4	6.0	5.9	2.6	2.4
Singapore	21.6	20.3	19.1	19.5	22.8	23.3
South Korea	2.6	1.7	2.0	6.0	4.6	4.4
Hong Kong	1.2	1.1	1.9	1.3	3.2	3.4
Taiwan	1.3	1.4	1.8	2.3	2.2	2.7
China	1.3	1.4	1.7	1.1	2.1	1.9
Thailand	0.9	1.5	1.5	3.4	3.5	3.2

Source: GATT, 1993 vol.1

total Malaysian exports. The EC is only slightly lower. An alternative breakdown, suggested by the government, shows that 58% of its trade is with 'East Asia': ASEAN, Japan, South Korea, China, Taiwan, Hong Kong, and Vietnam.

TRADE CONSTRAINTS IN FORCE

Malaysia receives GSP preferences from most industrial importers, and is a member of the ASEAN and the new AFTA trading areas, but it has no special access programmes to any of the industrial countries. On palm oil, it faces escalation of tariffs in the EC and Japan (from 4% on crude to 12% for processed), and most of its exports of processed oil are to other developing countries. Exporters have attempted to evade the problem by investing in refineries abroad, but this is opposed by the refining industry in Malaysia.

As was seen in Chapter 2, Malaysia has been one of the principal users of GSP, in the EC, US and Japanese schemes, and, except in the Japanese scheme, it has not been particularly badly affected by an overlap between NTBs and GSP preference. It has also been a principal beneficiary of the US outward-processing arrangements.

Table 8.4 shows the principal NTBs it has faced. Overall and in each of the markets, it ties with Colombia in this study for the lowest barriers. It does, however, face high barriers on some of its important individual exports. It faces MFA controls from the US, the EC, Canada and Norway, and except on the last it approached full utilisation of all quotas by 1991 (GATT, 1993, vol 1: 156). The low figures for total controlled trade in these categories suggest that these are the goods which it exports to other markets (shoes, textiles, processed vegetable oils). In recent years, some non-EC European countries (Norway and Sweden) have reduced or removed quotas on some textiles, and exports have been diversified into the EC from the traditional market, the US, but also into Singapore and Taiwan (Malaysia, Bank Negara, 1992). It is the uncontrolled exports and uncontrolled markets which have seen the largest increases (Tables 8.2, 8.3).

One development in which Malaysia was a leader was in countertrade, which it was among the first to introduce, in 1982. By 1983 countertrade was specified as part of public procurement policy. Malaysia was one of the major users identified in Chapter 4. It regarded this trade as a way of reducing the public sector's need to borrow at a time when it was government policy to avoid international borrowing, especially by public enterprises. It was not introduced as a way of encouraging manufactured or new exports. The shares of countertraded goods by market and between primary and manufactured goods were very similar to those of Malaysia's total exports, apart from the predictably higher share for trade with the centrally planned economies. Countertrade was principally used for primary products, which amounted to about 75% of total exports in the mid-1980s. The value (Table 8.5) was on average in the 1980s about 3% of total exports, but at its peak, in 1985, it may have been over 10%. This would have made it temporarily more important than the trade covered by NTBs. It declined quickly after 1985, and the policy was officially scrapped in 1991. (A government study found that most of the profits went to the trading brokers.)

Malaysia is not a major recipient of aid, and therefore (again like Colombia) it is one of the countries for which aid finances only a very small proportion of total imports. Most of its remaining aid flows (Table 8.6) are bilateral and therefore tied, but the values are so small that these ties cannot be considered a significant extra cost to Malaysia. They include some examples of aid/export credit linkages in which Malaysia faced competing packages. The effective extra cost to it of tying may have been further reduced because there was a choice of ties (it may even have resulted in net subsidisation). Normally, most aid is from Japan, and is often in the form of technical assistance.

Malaysia is a major recipient of foreign investment (Table 6.14), and is receiving an increasing share of the total going to Asian countries. It has one of the highest shares for all countries of foreign capital in domestic investment (Table 6.11). It is the highest among the countries studied here; and it has maintained this position more consistently than any other country apart from Singapore and Botswana. Investment data in detail for Malaysia are on an approval, not a realisation, basis, so the series cannot be reconciled directly with those for total flows. But the principal sources in recent years have been Taiwan and Japan, followed by the US (at about a quarter the level of the other two in the period 1986–91, but with a large inflow in 1992), then France, Singapore, and the UK (MIDA data, see Table 8.7). Apart from

Table 8.4 Malaysia: non-tariff barriers (percentage 1986 weights on 1990 data)

SITC	Product area	EC	US	Japan	Total[a]	Total[b]
0 + 1 + 22 + 4	All food items	5	2	32	2	3
0	Food + live animals	9	6	66	7	
22	Oilseeds and nuts	10	100	0	2	0
2 less (22 + 27 + 28)	Agricultural raw materials	0	0	0	0	0
27 + 28 + 67 + 68	Ores and metals	3	11	7	5	1
67	Iron and steel	4	100	0	1	
5	Chemicals	0	0	66	18	
6–8 less (67 + 68)	Manufactures, not chemicals	15	13	2	5	4
65	Textiles, yarn and fabric	100	100	13	19	
84	Clothing	57	64	0	43	
85	Footwear	100	0	0	29	
(0–9) less 3	All items, excluding fuels	7	11	6	4	4
0–9	All items	7	11	4	4	4

Notes:
[a] Totals and subtotals found by applying 1986 importer weights to 1990 totals and subtotals
[b] Totals and subtotals found by applying 1986 importer weights to each commodity, and summing the commodities

Source: Calculated from UNCTAD database

Table 8.5 Malaysian countertrade

	Exports	Imports
Product analysis		
Value ($m)	1714	
Average value	49	
Apparent share of exports	3	
Product group observations (%)		
Agriculture, forestry and food products	52.4	16.4
Ores, minerals and metals	14.0	20.9
Crude oil, gas and related products	6.1	0.0
Vehicles, transport equipment and military equipment	1.8	14.5
Manufacturing/processing equipment and construction projects	2.5	20.0
Miscellaneous manufactured products	23.2	27.3
Services and miscellaneous	0.0	0.9
Total	100.0	100.0
Major product sub-group observations		
Vegetable oils	17.1	
Timber and plywood	11.6	
Rubber	9.8	
Tin	7.9	
Cocoa and products	6.7	
Construction projects		8.2
Railway equipment		5.5
Cereals		4.5
Yearly data – number of deals: total 66		
1980 0		
1981 0		
1982 1		
1983 5		
1984 6		
1985 30		
1986 10		
1987 13		
Shares by market (%):		
Industrial	41	
Other developing	42	
Centrally planned	17	

Source: Jones and Jagoe, 1988

Table 8.6 Malaysia: multilateral and untied aid ($m or per cent)

Malaysia	1970	1975	1980	1985	1990
Ratio of aid to imports (%)	1.91	2.72	1.25	1.86	1.60
Multilateral	4	8	19	12	14
Multi-EC	4	8	19	12	14
Bilateral	23	90	106	203	459
Untied bilateral	7	26	57	70	255
Total untied	11	34	76	82	269
Tied/imports (%)	1.17	1.78	0.55	1.19	0.68

Note: The average tied ratio for all bilateral aid is assumed for all areas

Sources: OECD, *Development Co-operation* and *Geographical Distribution of Financial Flows to Developing Countries*, annual issues

Taiwan, which has become important since 1988, these are the traditional sources. The high share for the US means that (according to US data), Malaysian exports display one of the highest shares of intra-firm and multinational trade among developing countries (Tables 6.5, 6.6, 6.9). In 1986–9 about 20% of Malaysia exports were by US affiliates, about 10% by Japanese, and an estimated further 15% by affiliates of other countries. Singapore was probably an important participant in this. The figures included intra-firm trade with the US of about 5%. A Malaysian estimate for trade with Japan was about 3% as a maximum. Over half of Malaysian electronic exports in the mid-1980s were by US MNCs (Ramstetter, 1991). The falls in the relative importance of the US as a market and of components in total exports probably reduced these numbers (1989 was already below 1986). They remain, however, a major share of Malaysia's exports. What is puzzling is that Malaysian data are unusually sparse on investment flows as well as on intra-firm trade.

EFFECTS OF TRADE CONSTRAINTS

The data on each of the constraints discussed here thus suggest that Malaysia is approaching the level of industrial countries in terms of the nature of the external economic environment which it faces and the potential constraints on its exports. It faces low barriers, receives few preferences, and has substantial investment linkages with the major economies. But this is clearly a false interpretation. The tariffs which its actual and potential exports face, and the escalation in those on commodities, are serious barriers, for example on palm oil. The reason that it faces low NTBs on average is in large part because of the still high share of primary commodities in its trade. (This is true of the other apparently low-barrier country, Colombia, as well.) It faces

Table 8.7   Foreign investment approvals in Malaysia, 1986–92[a]

Industry	Total	Taiwan	Japan	US	France	Singa-pore	UK
				(million Malaysian dollars)			
Food manufacturing	2,059	281	171	159	–	376	174
Beverages and tobacco	63	29	–	3	–	4	2
Textile and textile products	2,162	495	299	87	0.2	289	17
Leather and leather products	62	33	7	–	–	8	0.4
Wood and wood products	2,718	567	551	30	–	320	460
Furniture and fixtures	447	240	54	49	–	63	10
Paper, printing and publishing	975	40	55	125	15	490	41
Chemicals and chemical products	7,114	705	1,871	1,170	18	253	1,954
Petroleum and coal	16,374	1,375	54	3,597	4,054	4	750
Rubber products	1,533	257	95	243	69	135	68
Plastic products	1,387	203	621	35	4	111	30
Non-metallic mineral products	2,782	217	1,001	31	–	138	29
Basic metal products	9,326	4,316	991	49	420	679	84
Fabricated metal products	2,745	1,581	409	31	–	126	29
Machinery manufacturing	1,818	224	684	200	–	136	1
Electrical and electrical products	10,941	2,650	5,045	727	145	702	58
Transport equipment	776	43	343	47	–	76	32
Scientific and measuring equipment	473	28	390	1	–	4	–
Miscellaneous	340	112	51	3	1	81	
Total	64,096	13,395	12,691	6,586	4,726	3,995	3,740

Note: [a] To August 1992

Source: Malaysian Industrial Development Authority, data supplied

average or high levels of barrier on most of the individual commodities included in Table 8.4, but not on petroleum (at least on the definition of NTBs used here), or on most of its primary exports. At the other end of the processing spectrum, it also faces low or no barriers on electrical machinery and electronic components, its developed country-type export. It appears to have specialised in the two extremes at which NTBs are negligible, avoiding the middle ground of competitive low-cost manufactures (although clothing is still significant). The apparent low level of barriers also reflects a deliberate choice of markets: one of Malaysia's principal primary exports (palm oil) faces very high tariffs, but Malaysia avoids exporting it to the industrial countries. The very high shares of its exports undertaken by multinational companies are almost entirely by firms external to Malaysia (unlike the US or Japan where high shares are by their own firms).

Malaysia's principal concerns about trade are also clearly those of a developing country. They relate to tariffs, GSP, and the risk of anti-dumping. It is also worried by the growth in regional preferences in the rest of the world. In terms of products, its major concerns are about its most developing-country type products – agricultural products and textiles and clothing – and they are a mixture of fears of hitting quotas and tariffs and of losing preferences. The existence and threats of interventions are elements in both official and private decisions about most exports and investments, although in many cases they seem to have influenced in what form, or through what marketing arrangement something is exported, or to which market, not whether or not it is produced or traded.

GSP has been particularly important to Malaysia. It is the only important preference which it receives. It now expects to lose it, on the grounds of being relatively advanced, and has already lost it in some unimportant markets (Poland and Bulgaria), and on some products (some rubber products to the US). Research on Malaysia has previously found (Davenport, 1986) and interviews for this study confirmed, that GSP was seen mainly as an attraction for introducing a new product or moving into a new market. This is still important in individual cases, although they are becoming a smaller proportion of total exports.

Neither the government nor individual exporters appeared to experience major difficulties in meeting the GSP local origin requirements, but they were well aware of them and had become expert at handling them. The certificates required for share of local content (different for the US (35%) and the EC (60%), but with special provisions for TV sets for the US) are administered by the Ministry of Trade and Industry, and it and exporters agree that they are issued promptly. Where there are quotas or other ceilings, these are administered by industry associations. The peculiarities of the regulations are accepted as a necessary part of a purely concessional scheme.

Similarly, no concern was expressed in interviews, independently or in answer to direct questions, about standards, of quality, health, or other types, but again this was because exporters had taken, as a matter of course, the appropriate steps to meet them. Individual exporters had followed different routes, normally involving technical advice from the market country, contracted in various forms. They have come to regard meeting them as a normal part of business, and therefore not a 'problem'. As both their major markets, Singapore and Japan, have high quality standards, meeting these has been considered sufficient training for other markets.

The present ASEAN preference scheme is of little importance because tariffs are already low, but the Asian Free Trade Area could be more important. Government officials would expect Malaysia to gain on balance (Malaysia's own tariff rates are lower than those of most other members, Table 2.4), but to lose in high-labour-cost industries. The economies of the region are now considered by AFTA's supporters to be sufficiently mature to face competition, although others are more doubtful about individual industries (and political pressure from firms). Shoes and cars are mentioned as potentially competitive commodities for Malaysia. But AFTA was presented and supported very much as a reaction to other groups, the EC and NAFTA in particular, and to the possible failure of a GATT settlement. There is also the same argument from government officials as is used by official Mexican supporters of NAFTA, and by Malaysians thinking about NAFTA as a threat, that its existence (rather than any identifiable trade effects) will attract foreign investors because of confidence effects. Foreign investors and exporters did not use this argument, and with one exception (in chemicals) they seemed significantly less interested in and informed about AFTA than about all other trading policies or restraints covered in the interviews.

There is concern about exclusion from NAFTA for two reasons. Malaysians expect US investment for re-export to move to Mexico, and they expect to lose potential Malaysian exports of manufactures to Mexico because of US competition. Latin America is an area into which they have been diversifying, so this loss cannot be measured in terms of present exports. In response, they are not withdrawing from the market: they are reducing their costs of trading with Mexico, establishing direct air links, and accelerating trade promotion there and in other Latin American countries, in order to develop links, before the markets are diverted.

Both the government and investors are concerned about potential anti-dumping actions by the US and the EC, although they have not yet found them a serious problem. The response is to devise strategies to make any case difficult and costly to press, for example by exporting differentiated products or from multiple sources.

Some potential NTBs cause Malaysia concern. The two which are exceptions to its usual acceptance of meeting standards as a normal part of exporting are new environmental standards and Japanese obstacles to food. These were clearly considered different in kind. The former, particularly labelling of all exports of a particular good (cf. the Malaysian Government's complaint reported in GATT, 1993, vol.2: 34) is not a type which the government or an exporter can take action to avoid; this absolute disadvantage may be why it is particularly resented. The most important case cited in 1992 would be one on tropical woods (wood and wood products are 10% of Malaysia's exports, and it is a major world supplier). The requirement to label tropical woods for environmental reasons (Austria requires this; the major markets do not, yet) is being strongly opposed, and Malaysia has been among the leaders in opposing environmental conditions imposed on developing countries, in exports or other areas. On food, it was believed that the Japanese obstruction was deliberately intended as a barrier. EC food regulations, sometimes found difficult to meet by other countries in this survey, were not mentioned as a problem, but Malaysian food exporters to the EC are in rather specialised lines.

Threats of NTBs have demonstrably been a deterrent. To export Malaysian cars to European markets other than the UK and Ireland will require substantial investment to shift the driving controls: manufacturers hesitated until 1993 because of the implicit threat of quotas, diversifying first into other right-hand-drive markets. But the role of NTBs is more complicated than this. The car exports might not exist at all if limits on Japanese car exports to the EC had not encouraged Japan to offer Malaysia substantial technical assistance to produce, and encouraged EC importers to seek, a substitute Japanese-without-the-label car. Malaysian producers have developed a banana to compete with Caribbean bananas, but will not put it into production because of the EC quota system to protect Caribbean access. Again, it is not clear whether the Malaysian banana would be competitive in an unrestricted world banana market.

Losing MFA would temporarily damage Malaysian exports, because it is now protecting them against competition from lower-cost suppliers. Moving into more advanced types of textiles requires more training and education. Malaysian manufacturers expect to move out of present clothing and textile products within the ten-year phasing out of the MFA.

On both the GSP and the MFA, the view seems to be that they cannot last and that it is more productive to find strategies to exist without them than to fight for their retention. These include other ways of promoting new exports, both by individual companies and with government assistance. An equivalent small financial preference can be engineered from shipping rates. Malaysia manages these, so that the rates for exports are less than those for imports. This has the advantage of not being a concession given and subject to removal from outside, but the disadvantage (unlike GSP) of not being an approved derogation from international rules.

FOREIGN INVESTMENT

Malaysia is starting to question the value of its very high receipts of foreign investment. In the past, it did not display the normal concern about loss of national control over the economy, partly because there was more interest and resentment over control by different ethnic groups within the country. Throughout the 1970–90 New Economic Policy, there were rules on Malay ownership shares as well as limits on foreign ownership. There was also specific government policy on the different nationalities of foreign investment (with shifts from and to the UK and to and from Japan). This reflected worries about particular countries' dominance in trade, investment, and culture rather than about foreign investment or trade in themselves. There is evidence both for and against a change in this lack of concern, but policy still does not appear to be particularly targeted at trade by the multinationals. The emphasis on export promotion as a tool of development has made high exports by any investor welcome.

The diversification of exports into more types of electrical equipment has been led by Japanese companies. Although these firms have been throughout the 1980s, and remain, unwilling to share ownership, and their activities are much more controlled from outside than other nationalities, they have not faced restrictions for this reason. Foreign ownership restrictions were relaxed in the late 1980s, with 100% foreign ownership now allowed for firms producing 'substantially' for the export market; 50% local ownership is required for those for the local market.

In interviews with foreign investors both in 1984 and in 1992, it was found that most nationalities made some types of decision within Malaysia. Only the most strategic, on the location of production of major company products or on new investments, were made in the home country. In most cases, Malaysian staff could be and were promoted to almost all management posts (to all in US companies). But Japanese companies did and do refer decisions on production and trade to Japan, and continue to find it 'more difficult' to find suitable staff to promote to director level or suitable local partners for joint ventures. But what is considered important in official reports on existing foreign investment and strategies for the future is the number of firms exporting (88% of foreign-controlled firms exported more than 80% of their output in 1987–9, according to a Bank Negara survey). The lack of data on inflows, value added, the real extent of processing, and trade can be considered a sign of lack of concern.

Only one Asian multinational, in a very specialised range of food products, was interviewed but a strong concern was expressed about building networks of relationships with trading partners in other countries which seemed to substitute long-term for intra-company relationships. This attitude corresponds to other general views of how small and medium-sized Asian multinationals operate, and to findings for the clothing industry in the case studies, especially for Mauritius and Bangladesh but also for Colombia, Jamaica and Zimbabwe. It was also true of a new Malaysian firm supplying Japan. If it is typical, it suggests that more Asian participation in Malaysian industry could lead to a fall in apparent intra-firm trade, but its substitution by long-term relationships which have some of the same characteristics of stability. It could, however, like the relationships found in clothing, be more typical of the particular industry than of the nationality of ownership.

Up to now growth, investment and export targets have been more important than national control. So far, the targets of diversification of the economy and of exports have been shared by foreign investors. This is partly because the recent surge of Japanese investment was into a variety of new industries and into at least one major new export market, Japan itself, following the rise in the yen in the mid-1980s.

Malaysia in turn is now promoting its own sales in its neighbours by investing in them. This was initially to preserve sales in protected markets and to encourage exports of machinery. The strategy was based on the view that high imports of equipment were a cost of promoting investment into Malaysia, along with the costs of remittances of profits, and this cost could be offset by reversing the direction. Although this is not a new concern for other countries receiving foreign investment, it has not been stressed by Malaysia in the past. Initially Malaysian investment went to countries importing from it, including Australia, Singapore, and the UK, and included the palm oil refining mentioned above. Since about 1990, however, it has also been seeking low labour costs, with the locations moving to Vietnam and China.

On the other hand, Malaysia itself seems less outstandingly attractive to foreign investors than it was at the beginning of the 1980s. This is partly because of the consequences of growth and high investment – it has lost some of the advantages which it had then of low labour costs and relatively generous provision of infrastructure for the size of the industrial sector – and partly because of the emergence of Vietnam and China, and other Asian countries, as credible competitors. Just as there is a limit to the period in which a country wants and is able to attract official aid, so there is possibly a similar limit to extensive use of foreign investment, at least on the Malaysian scale. But such a change must be kept in proportion. Any fall in demand or supply of foreign investment, or in the quality of infrastructure, would be from such a high level that Malaysia would still remain among the highest in the world. The transport infrastructure about which Malaysian officials and foreign investors now complain still produced the shortest turnaround (order to delivery) time of any of the countries discussed here for the archetypal foreign investor for export (using inputs not themselves supplied by air). A factory producing to Japanese designs, for the Japanese market, from South Korean inputs (on Japanese capital equipment), could offer 3–4 month delivery; the factory, in the country and well outside the designated industrial zones in the region, was, in normal although not in Malaysian terms, near both the port and the airport. This does not match Mauritian shipments by air, but other countries had poorer ports, longer distances, or fewer shipping lines, and poorer internal transport. Even with half its current investment ratios, Malaysia would have one of the highest foreign shares in the world.

LESSONS FROM MALAYSIA

Malaysia's success as an exporter is one of the examples quoted of the unimportance of barriers to trade. Clearly this assertion is not valid. Trade barriers are an important element for both public and private sectors in analysing the possibilities for trade and investment, but the result of that analysis is rarely simply to export less of the controlled commodity. Both government and producers were entirely familiar with the various rules and systems which Malaysia faced, and efficient in dealing with the international systems and with each other. This was partly because they had been doing so for 10–15 years, so that they had experience and confidence. On the rules on foreign investment (on which interviews were conducted in 1984 as well), there was, by 1992, a notable improvement in relations and flexibility, partly because of familiarity, and partly because Malaysia and its companies had become successful enterprises, confident in their ability to make reasonable agreements.

The feared component of any administered system, corruption, was certainly present, but was not seen as being as pervasive as in other countries. On the whole, it was blamed in specific cases, but not for any general inefficiency or added cost. It is noteworthy that countertrade, which had been introduced with a very high degree of political support and promoted as a gesture of Malaysian initiative in trade, was officially abolished after an internal research report, and that it had lost importance very quickly.

Although regional trade and investment were extremely important in practice, only official sources were strongly interested in AFTA as a means of promoting them. Investors and exporters appeared to believe that the present trading arrangements were sufficient, with at best only limited advantages in a regional group.

Many of the expected effects of the individual types of constraint can be seen in Malaysia, but usually only in a modified form because investors have gone beyond the initial reaction. The effects of tariff escalation on primary products are certainly important. It is worth remembering that 'promoting resource-based industries' has been a Malaysian declared objective for at least 20 years, in rubber, tin, palm oil, wood, etc., but there is still little sign of this in the trade data, and there are specific examples of tariff escalation as an obstacle. NTBs have moved exporters into new products and new markets, although diversification has been a Malaysian strategy for production and export for other reasons. Malaysia will adapt to the EC single market and NAFTA by taking more, not fewer, initiatives, in those areas to pre-empt any increase in protection or loss of investment. The data show that it has moved steadily away from the most protected markets.

Malaysia offers an example of a country for which growth, exports, employment, and (at least at some periods) the distribution of income among domestic groups have been the central objectives. How the exports

or investment needed for this were achieved has been of secondary importance. Concerns about constraints met practical solutions as problems to be
overcome, not avoided or negotiated away, and with little attention to
considerations like foreign control. Malaysia would have increased its
exports more rapidly, and probably with a different composition, had it not
been faced with its existing barriers.

9

THAILAND[1]

BACKGROUND

Thailand's present trade structure is much more obviously dependent on external constraints than is that of Malaysia. Thailand has the highest share of its exports covered by NTBs of the countries in this study (except for Mauritius) and relies heavily on GSP. It has shifted away from trade with its Asian neighbours, with which it now has a low share compared with other Asian countries, to more trade with the industrial countries. Thai trade shifted during the 1980s first towards the US, then more to Japan (Table 9.1). Trade with the Asian NICs has changed little, and with other ASEAN countries has fallen slightly. Its dependence on foreign investment began more recently than that of Malaysia, but is now even higher. However, this also remains much more from the industrial countries. Japan is still the most important investor. Although Hong Kong, Singapore and Taiwan normally come next, they are well behind, another contrast to Malaysia (Table 9.13).

In many ways, Thailand is at a turning point for a country facing trade barriers. It has moved sufficiently beyond primary exports for its present trade to be dominated by the protected commodities and markets found in Chapters 2 and 3 to be characteristic of the early stages of processing and light industries. Although it is diversifying into more products, many of these are also protected. But some of these exports appear to be reaching the limits of expansion, while its industrialisation, growth, and trade targets imply continued expansion. It has thus been through many of the stages of changing exports and hitting barriers which still face other countries. Thailand may indicate some of its future problems without yet having put some of them behind it, as has Malaysia.

The Thai economy grew at an average 7.5% during the 1980s, with only two years below 7%, and after three years (1988–90) above 10% is now back at that average. It is, however, still well behind Malaysia, with a per capita income of under $2,000. It is a much larger country with a population of 58 million. Manufacturing grew at 9%, and increased its share of the economy from 21% in 1980 to 26% by 1990, while the share of agriculture halved, to

156

Table 9.1 Thailand: export structure by principal commodities

Commodity	SITC	1977	1975	1980	1985	1990
Total value (US$m)		685.2	2,162.2	6,369.2	7,057.1	23,002.4
				percentages		
All food items	0+1+22+44	52.3	62.7	47.0	46.2	28.8
Agricultural raw materials	2 less (22+27+28)	24.7	12.3	11.2	9.2	5.1
Fuels	3	0.3	0.6	0.1	1.3	0.8
Ores and metals	27+28+68	14.6	7.4	13.6	4.4	1.0
Manufactured goods of which:	5 to 8 less 63	4.7	14.7	25.2	38.1	63.1
Chemical products	5	0.2	0.6	0.7	1.3	1.9
Other manufactured goods	(6+8) less 68	4.4	12.8	18.6	23.0	41.4
Machinery and equipment	7	0.1	1.3	5.9	8.8	19.8
Unallocated		3.3	2.2	2.9	0.8	1.2
Cereals	04	32.4	27.7	21.4	16.9	5.8
Textile fibres, yarn and clothing	26+65+84	7.5	8.1	10.0	14.3	16.7
Metals and metal manufactures	67+63+69	11.8	6.0	12.1	5.0	2.3
Machinery						
Non-electrical	71	–	0.2	0.4	2.5	9.0
Electrical	72	0.1	1.1	5.2	6.1	9.8
Transport equipment	73	–	0.1	0.2	0.2	1.0

Source: UNCTAD, *Handbook* 1992

only 12%. On the trade side, the structural transformation was even more striking (Table 9.1), with the share of agricultural goods falling from more than a half in 1980, to a third, and manufactures rising from a quarter to more than 60%. The change in the 1970s, however, had been even greater. Agriculture was not stagnant in the 1980s, growing at 5%, and this sector clearly remains an important element in the country's exports, while its manufactures' share is slightly below the average for Asia, or indeed all developing countries. It is in primary commodities that Thailand is a major world trader, with 35% of world rice exports, 20% for natural rubber, and shares of 10–15% for some types of fish (UNCTAD, *Handbook*). Total exports have increased from a quarter to 37% of GDP. These trends are expected to continue in the 1990s, at about the same rate as in the 1980s.

By the early 1980s, Thailand's exports were already much more diversified than those of Malaysia, or of most developing countries of its level, and by 1990 this had increased greatly (Table 9.2). The principal export in 1980 was still rice, but its share then fell to only 5% by 1990. Textiles, the traditional manufactures product, took its place at the top. The other principal exports remained primary goods. But below these new primary and manufactured goods were appearing, including fish and fruit, and among manufactures electronics and a broadening range of wood and other consumer products. The fish products, grouped together, have overtaken rice. By the end of the 1980s, the most rapidly growing primary exports were still the new fish and vegetable products, with electrical and electronic leading the manufactures. Clothing remained important, but was growing more slowly and losing share. The striking fact about the 1990 list is how many controlled goods it includes, among both old and new products.

It was therefore partly because of the growing importance of manufactures in trade, but also because of the types of primary and manufactured product in which its trade was concentrated, that barriers and preferences began to be a major consideration for Thai trade. Table 9.3 shows the principal markets in recent years.

TRADE CONSTRAINTS AND PREFERENCES

The share of Thai exports eligible for GSP treatment[2] has risen sharply since the mid-1980s, both for the total and within manufactures (Table 9.4). In 1988, although not before, Thailand was one of the major beneficiaries of the EC scheme (Table 2.7). The recent rise in GSP exports probably reflects the increase in the share of manufactures other than clothing and textiles. However, there appears (Table 9.5) also to have been at least a small shift of industrial products away from the three principal industrial markets. It was agricultural products which went increasingly to the industrial countries, and among these to Japan. The EC, however, remains the principal importer of the GSP-eligible products. It is particularly important for agriculture

Table 9.2 Thailand: principal exports 1970–90 (percentages)

1970		1980		1985		1990	
Rice	17.0	Rice	14.6	Textile products	12.2	Textile products	14.3
Rubber	15.1	Tapioca products	11.2	Rice	11.6	Rice	4.7
Maize	13.3	Rubber	9.3	Tapioca products	7.7	Rubber	4.0
Tin	11.0	Tin	8.5	Rubber	7.0	Tapioca products	3.9
Tapioca products	8.3	Textile products	7.2	Integrated circuits	4.3	Precious stones	3.7
Mung beans	1.7	Maize	5.5	Maize	4.0	Integrated circuits	3.7
Prawns	1.5	Integrated circuits	4.6	Precious stones	3.3	Prawns	3.5
Fluorite	1.5	Precious stones	2.4	Sugar	3.2	Footwear	3.4
Tobacco leaves	1.3	Sugar	2.2	Tin	2.9	Sugar	3.0
Kapok fibre	0.9	Prawns	1.5	Canned fish	2.7	Canned fish	2.7
Precious stones	0.9	Jute products	1.1	Prawns	1.8	Jewellery	2.2
Sorghum	0.7	Mung beans	1.1	Canned pineapple	1.7	Furniture and parts	2.0
Sugar	0.6	Canned pineapple	1.1	Footwear	1.2	Plastic products	1.5
Tungsten	0.6	Tobacco leaves	1.0	Mung beans	1.2	Frozen fowl	1.3
Jute products	0.5	Wood products	1.0	Jewellery	1.1	Canned crustaceans	1.2
Share of top 10	71.7	Share of top 10	67.1	Share of top 10	59.0	Share of top 10	46.9
Share of top 15	75.0	Share of top 15	72.4	Share of top 15	66.0	Share of top 15	55.1
Share of top 20	76.5	Share of top 20	76.1	Share of top 20	70.8	Share of top 20	59.0

Notes: Textile products includes garments; percentages represent shares in total exports

Source: Sibunruang and Brimble, 1992

Table 9.3 Thailand: principal markets 1980–91 (percentages)

Region/country	1980	1985	1990	1991
US	12.64	19.66	22.67	21.27
EC	25.76	19.07	21.56	20.69
Japan	15.09	13.36	17.20	18.06
ASEAN[a]	16.21	14.49	11.37	11.84
Asian NIEs[b]	7.17	7.51	7.83	8.02

Notes:
[a] Singapore, Malaysia, Indonesia, Philippines, Brunei
[b] Hong Kong, S. Korea, Taiwan

Source: Chirathivat, 1992

rather than industry, although the actual share of eligible goods within agricultural exports to the EC fell sharply (Table 9.5) from 69% in 1990 to 65% in 1991. Its principal agricultural export to the EC is tapioca (41% of exports to the EC in 1981, 12% in 1991). In manufactures, textiles and clothing (18%, up from 3%) and electrical appliances (16%) are the most important (Chirathivat, 1993). The US is more important for industrial goods, in spite of the limits on the sectors eligible. The principal exports to the US are shellfish and fish, integrated circuits and other machine parts, some electrical products, and shoes. But the most important GSP products are electronic parts and products, jewellery and toys. GSP has apparently been used principally by large exporters, rather than small or new exporters, suggesting the usual advantages for experienced traders.

Thai officials do not consider that graduation from the GSP for economic reasons is an immediate threat. Thailand was, however, recently (June 1993) threatened by the US with withdrawal because of violations of workers' rights, and undertook legal reforms in response. This was not expected in interviews in Thailand immediately before the 1992 US presidential election, when fears were that the US (under the Republican administration) might use threats to GSP to persuade Thailand to adopt effective patent and copyright enforcement. Both threats indicate the vulnerability of a developing country to external policy under a non-contractual preference scheme. The tariff reductions under the Tokyo GATT Round substantially eroded Thailand's GSP preference margins in the early 1980s, and those to be implemented under the Uruguay Round may virtually eliminate them. For both these reasons, the value of GSP may not be as high as the coverage figures in Table 9.4 might suggest. Its value is also limited because, even with GSP Thailand is still at a disadvantage in both the US and the EC compared with countries receiving more preferential terms. In exports of fresh fruits and vegetables and tobacco to the EC, for example, it is inferior to the ACP countries which enter with no tariff.

Like Malaysia, Thailand is a member of the ASEAN trading group, but

Table 9.4 Thailand: exports eligible for GSP by market and sector (percentages)

	EC			US			Japan			Total		
	Agri-culture	Industry	All	Agri-culture	Industry	All	Agri-culture	Industry	All	Agri-culture	Industry	All
1980										28	72	12
1981										39	61	12
1982										36	64	14
1983										31	69	14
1984										30	70	13
1985										29	71	15
1986	34	66		15	85		21	79		27	73	18
1987	26	74		12	88		14	86		22	78	21
1988	25	75		11	89		11	89		20	80	21
1989	22	78		8	91		9	81		16	84	22
1990	20	80	58	6	94	25	11	89	20	15	85	24
1991	20	80	44	8	92	20	19	81	15	16	84	20

Source: Chirathivat, 1991; Chirathivat, data supplied

Table 9.5 Thailand: relative importance of GSP exports in different markets (percentages)

	Agriculture				Industry				Total			
	EC	US	Japan	Other	EC	US	Japan	Other	EC	US	Japan	Other
1986	64	13	11	12	48	29	17	6	52	25	15	8
1987	66	14	9	11	51	29	14	6	54	26	13	7
1988	65	13	9	13	48	26	19	7	51	23	17	9
1989	63	13	11	13	43	27	23	7	46	25	21	8
1990	69	10	10	11	49	26	15	10	53	24	14	9
1991	65	10	15	10	52	24	13	11	54	22	14	10

Source: Chirathivat, 1991; Chirathivat, data supplied

sees no significant effects from it. It has proposed an exceptionally long list of exceptions to any tariff reductions in an AFTA, and its own tariff rates (Table 2.4) are among the highest in the region, although it has declared an intention to reduce them by 1996. It does not expect any benefits from higher net exports to the region, although, as in Malaysia, some researchers have suggested that a regional group might encourage higher foreign investment.

The potential opportunities from regional trade are seen to come much more from economic changes, especially its neighbours' rising income, than from formal regional pacts. The relevant region is taken to be the Pacific, in which Thailand includes at least Japan, China and Australia, and perhaps the more distant Pacific countries, the US and Canada.

The regional organisations of the rest of the world are seen as a problem mainly because they mark a change in the international system (Chirathivat, 1992) rather than because they impose economic costs. But there have been some adjustments: the response to possible changes in barriers includes investment in clothing production in Mexico to get inside NAFTA and investigation of opportunities in the US, as well as improving the efficiency of Thai production.

Thai calculations suggest that liberalisation of agricultural trade as a result of the Uruguay Round would benefit the value of its exports, on balance, with quantity gains outweighing price losses. This is in line with international estimates, and results from increasing rice exports to Japan. Thailand will move to a more regional orientation, but principally because of faster growth, and therefore increases in trade and intra-area investment, in Asia. In summary, the Thai view is that AFTA and ASEAN need a regional policy because the rest of the world is becoming regionalised, and Thailand needs one because the other Asian countries are embarking on one. EC-1992 and NAFTA have not been analysed for their quantifiable effects on individual exports as carefully as they have in Malaysia.

External constraints on food exports have been a clear problem for Thailand throughout the period being examined. One response was to move into more processing, higher value and more processed foods (the prawns and canned pineapple in Table 9.2), and into other industries notably clothing. Each of these new exports was, in turn, controlled by the importers.

Table 9.6 gives the estimates for the share of Thailand's controlled exports using the same definitions as for the other case-study countries, and Table 9.7 those by Chirathivat (1991). The only important difference is in agricultural exports to Japan (his estimates are much lower because they exclude some informal barriers); the average figure is not seriously affected by this, however, because the actual levels of trade are very low. (Both estimates would be much higher if they measured potential rice exports.) The EC barriers are higher on food and the US on manufactures, suggesting that the benefits from better GSP coverage may be substantially offset by NTBs in each of these flows. This is supported by Table 3.7, which showed that more than half of Thailand's potential exports to the EC are affected by NTBs. For the US, the barriers are highest for primary products.

The principal barriers are on foods, including rice (by Japan) and sugar (quotas in the US and no possibility in the EC under CAP controls); the CAP also restricts rice. Tapioca faces quotas to the EC and Japan. Most other foods have problems in Japan because of health standards. Thai vegetables and fruits face the same problems into the EC as those from Malaysia, including seasonal limits and higher duties and poorer access than competing ACP countries (mainly East African for these products). Frozen fish and chicken face minimum import prices in the EC, and some come up against quotas or health regulations. The Thai allocation of tapioca quotas has been described as 'so complicated that details of this policy could not be provided' (GATT, 1991 vol. 1: 136). It combines allocation and auctions, and is intended in part to reward exporters who seek out other markets outside the quota-constrained importers. Meeting technical standards other than health standards has not been a problem.

On manufactures, it is textiles and clothing and steel into the US which suffer the most serious barriers. Textiles and clothing do not receive GSP treatment from the USA. Thailand has been one of the users of the US outward-processing scheme, although it is much less important than for the Asian or Latin American NICs, or than Malaysia (Table 2.10).

It has also been moving out of textiles and clothing products, at least in US and EC markets. By 1987, most fabric exports were to non-MFA markets (55%). Although the EC and the US were still among its main markets, they had been joined by Singapore, Hong Kong, Japan, and the United Arab Emirates.[3] Table 9.8 shows that the share by value of clothing exports going to MFA-controlled markets had fallen from over 80% in 1977 to just over a half by 1987. But within this, the share by volume had fallen much more severely, to 40%, suggesting that one response to quantitative limits has been to increase the value added of those exports which are sent to the controlled markets, whether by increasing profit margins or by moving to higher-priced clothing. The non-MFA markets include other Asian countries, but also, more recently, Eastern Europe. Thai textiles and clothing exports have moved dramatically from under 0.5% (too low to figure in Table 9.2), to 7% in 1980, to peak in 1985–90 (the actual peak for Thailand was in 1987 at nearly 20%). This phenomenon of very rapid and very temporary growth for this item will be observed in several of the countries studied. In some, like Colombia, the process had already been completed before the 1980s. In Mauritius, Bangladesh, and Jamaica, the rise dates only from the mid-1980s, and in Zimbabwe it is even more recent. Both these characteristics, the changing unit value and the rise, stabilisation, and fall over a time period much too short to be attributable to changing relative

Table 9.6 Thailand: non-tariff barriers (percentage 1986 weights on 1990 data)

SITC	Product area	EC	US	Japan	Total[a]	Total[b]
0+1+22+4	All food items	81	36	63	67	67
0	Food + live animals	84	38	64	69	
2 less (22+27+28)	Agricultural raw materials	18	2	4	75	75
27+28+67+68	Ores and metals	2	53	8	14	18
67	Iron and steel	5	97	0	17	
6–8 less (67+68)	Manufactures, not chemicals	52	27	6	22	23
65	Textiles, yarn and fabric	83	72	53	37	
84	Clothing	94	92	0	35	
85	Footwear	100	0	68	36	
0–9	All items	67	28	35	28	22

Notes:
[a] Totals and subtotals found by applying 1986 importer weights to 1990 totals and subtotals
[b] Totals and subtotals found by applying 1986 importer weights to each commodity, and summing the commodities

Source: Calculated from UNCTAD database

Table 9.7 Thailand's exports under managed trade with three major trading partners (percentages)

Product area	EC	US	Japan	Share of total exports to these areas	Share of total exports
Primary commodities	76	16	26	44	23
Manufactures	45	27	1	29	17
Total	53	25	14	32	18

Source: Chirathivat, 1991

Table 9.8 The volume and value of Thai clothing exports (percentages)

| Year | MFA | | Non-MFA | | Total |
	Share by volume	Share by value	Share by volume	Share by value	$ (m)
1977	82	82	18	18	83
1978	72	76	28	24	131
1979	65	60	35	40	221
1980	58	63	42	37	279
1981	56	63	44	37	358
1982	52	62	48	38	375
1983	54	72	46	28	382
1984	52	78	48	22	514
1985	51	71	49	29	584
1986	41	63	59	37	807
1987	40	55	60	45	1,454

Source: Suphalchalsai , 1990

costs in Thailand or its competitors, strongly suggest that the explanation should be sought in policy rather than economic comparative advantage.

The textile industry was first established on a modern scale in the early 1960s, with considerable support from Japanese investment in joint ventures including some of the major Japanese companies(e.g. Toray, from the Mitsui Group). This was principally to secure access to the protected local market, but it occurred at a time when Japan was a target for the earliest textile agreements (see Chapter 3) and also for bilateral Voluntary Export Restraints (VERs) imposed by the US (Suphalchalsai, 1990). As in other middle-sized countries, including Zimbabwe and Bangladesh, the Thai clothing industry was initially based on local textiles, but the expansion of clothing production for export left domestic textile production behind, in both quantity and quality, and imported textiles are now important. Textile exports under quota are mainly of grey (unfinished and undyed) cloth, suggesting insufficient quality or technical sophistication to bring this industry to the standard needed for Thai clothing exports. Internationally, the textile industry, unlike the clothing industry, became a technologically advanced, capital-intensive one with a strong developed country base during the late 1970s and 1980s. Even the relatively advanced developing countries, therefore, have tended to obtain supplies either from the industrial countries or from the NICs (notably Hong Kong and South Korea) which have become industrial leaders. This, of course, implies potential problems in meeting local-content or value-added rules for any exports seeking to use restricted preference schemes.

In Thailand, there may have been additional obstacles arising from other government protection for machinery and the chemicals needed for finishing and dyeing. As long as quotas limit any expansion, the pressure for ending local obstacles may have been limited. The prospects for reform or ending of the MFA under the Uruguay Round have led to renewed interest in doing this.

Thailand has been within the MFA system from the beginning, but only started to reach its quota limits in the mid-1980s (Suphalchalsai, 1990). The industry thus was initially encouraged by international restrictions, as long as these affected only its competitors – the existing suppliers in Japan and the old NICs; then it was discouraged by barriers directed at it. The pattern of a rise and then steadying of exports fits this exactly.

Quota allocation within Thailand follows the pattern most common among the countries studied here. It is administered by government allocation, with most (in Thailand, 70–80%) allocated to existing exporters, according to their record of past exports. The rest is allocated through trading companies either to established exporters who are expanding or to new exporters. Thailand sets a series of criteria for this allocation, including use of Thai inputs and domestic value added. For a new company, acquiring a share in the residual quota entitles it to apply for its own quota from the principal allocation the following year (Suphalchalsai, 1990; GATT, 1991 vol. 1). As in all countries using quotas to their limits, the actual initial allocation plus those available for new exports sum to about 20% above the limit to allow for inevitable shortfalls, year-end inefficiencies, etc. It is notable that variants of this system are found in almost all MFA countries, in spite of the bias in the literature towards more variable systems (at the extreme, auctions). This suggests that security of market access, a long-term relationship with markets on at least an informal basis, is a desired part of exporting. This system seems suitable to provide a mix of the security which any existing firm needs to seek orders and plan ahead, with some flexibility to ensure that quotas are removed from those who no longer use them and allocated to new suppliers.

In Thailand, quotas cannot be transferred (some illegal selling does occur; one expert estimated the premium at about 20%). Unused portions must be returned to the government or companies will be penalised in the following year. New firms are clearly at some disadvantage relative to old ones, in that they must compete for all their quota, not just for additions. The normal barriers to entry into an industry are thus raised. It is not clear whether this should be regarded as inefficient or as offsetting the artificial incentive to move into an industry in which producers receive some excess profit or rent from possessing a quota. The effect has apparently been to encourage new producers into the non-quota markets (Suphalchalsai,1990), or, presumably, into different industries. Either of these may be an appropriate response to an external constraint.

The question of what can happen next to the industry depends partly on policy, the future of the MFA but also on an economic question, Thai labour costs. Although the speed of the rise of Thai clothing exports and the abruptness of its cessation indicate that policy played a strong part, the pattern is a speeded-up version of normal changes in industrial competitiveness. For successful exporting, the industry requires a degree of labour productivity and efficiency and a regularity of supply which put it beyond the least developed countries, but, under the present technology for clothing, it needs a relative cheapness of labour which makes it unsuitable for the more advanced. Thailand, with Japanese assistance, achieved the first during the 1970s, but has lost the second since the late 1980s. (Other countries in this study, in particular Bangladesh, are among those to whom it has been lost.) Both foreign and Thai investors are now looking to other producers. The current Thai response to the cost changes is to investigate production possibilities in Vietnam and China (and Indonesia, although that is starting to be an established, rather than a new, clothing exporter).

Other manufactured exports have not escaped controls. Electrical exports are beginning to face anti-dumping and countervailing duties. Shoes are still a minor export for Thailand (Table 9.2: 3.4% in 1990); they were only 1.2% in 1985. By 1986, however, they were facing barriers in some markets (Table 9.6). Although footwear started as a Thai industry, by the late 1980s firms from Taiwan and South Korea (both countries which had faced barriers to their own exports) were entering the market, as well as some from the potential market countries, Japan, Australia and the US. Travel goods, which may have been seen as a substitute within leather goods, are now rising rapidly, with a history similar to that for clothing. Toys are appearing, as they already have done in Malaysia, with investment from Hong Kong and Taiwan, where they now face trade restraints. The Thai Trade Ministry, at least, fears constraints on these.

External constraints have thus bounded both primary and manufactures exports for Thailand, and those on manufactures have effectively limited the escape route from those on primary products. The question to be asked about the effect of external constraints on Thai industrialisation and development, therefore, is whether the fact that the extra impulse for the introduction and then the loss of industries, particularly the clothing industry, was given by policy has had permanent effects on how this industrialisation has affected the rest of the economy. Unlike some of the other countries examined here, the presence of the raw materials and the labour force and the example of the nearby NICs strongly suggest that clothing and footwear would have developed as export industries in any case. The need (especially strong for new producers without their own quotas) to look for new markets offsets the incentive given by quotas to old producers to remain with apparently secure markets, so that it is not possible to judge the net direction of effect on the propensity to search for new markets. In Thailand, some of the Japanese investors were leaving sales decisions to Thai joint venture partners by the early 1980s.

The Thai textile industry faces problems under the present system of quotas, government limits on imports of inputs, and technological conditions which now favour more advanced countries. The combination is holding it back. Even if removal of the first constraint were to create local pressure for the removal of the second, and if by 2000 Thailand were moving to a technology and labour-skill level suitable for the new-style textile industry, the industry would still be constrained by current controls. It is certainly potentially so constrained, and the controls are limiting the incentive to progress.

There is a belief among policy-makers that preferences and protection may not last. The threats to GSP have been discussed. Thailand supported the ending of the MFA in the Uruguay GATT Round, on condition that there was a transition period. By the end of the agreed 10 years the economic case for Thailand leaving this export industry will have prevailed.

COUNTERTRADE AND TIED AID

These are no longer important for Thailand. It introduced countertrade in 1985 to promote exports, but not particularly of new products. It was intended for agricultural products, and had become a negligible portion of Thai trade by 1990. Occasional examples can still be found (cement in 1992), but for selling a product in surplus cheaply, rather than for either export promotion or balance-of-payments reasons.

Although aid was still equivalent to 5% of Thai imports as late as 1985 (Table 9.9), it has now fallen to around 2%. Tied aid is unlikely now to be an important constraint on Thailand's international income or payments, but it has been so recently enough for there to be a potential effect on perceptions about the international environment. Concessionary financing was a relatively high and growing part of external public sector financing in the late 1970s and early 1980s (Chunanunthathum, 1991), because of increased

Table 9.9   Thailand: multilateral and untied aid ($m or percentages)

Thailand	1970	1975	1980	1985	1990
Ratio of aid to imports (%)	5.70	2.74	4.54	4.97	2.39
Multilateral	5	16	103	62	70
Multi-EC	5	19	101	49	61
Bilateral	69	74	305	386	732
Untied bilateral	20	21	163	133	406
Total untied	25	40	264	182	467
Tied/imports (%)	3.80	1.52	1.67	3.00	0.99

Note: The average tied ratio for all bilateral aid is assumed for all areas

Source: OECD, *Development Co-operation* and *Geographical Distribution of Financial Flows to Developing Countries*, annual issues

lending by Japan, at more concessionary rates. During this period bilateral aid increased strongly, in amount and as a proportion of the total, with the result that by 1985 the apparent tied aid ratio was returning towards 1970 levels.

The loans went principally to infrastructure development, and helped to offset limited public and private investment in these sectors, the official Thai view being until recently that the country could not afford extensive investment of this type. During the early 1980s when the economy was probably deterred from other types of external financing by a combination of external conditions and official unwillingness to incur debt, the preferences of aid donors probably did constrain imports to a particular pattern, although clearly not on a scale approaching that of the less developed countries in this study. To the extent that aid went to infrastructure projects earlier than the government would otherwise have provided finance for them, it may be that, as in the clothing industry, the constraint merely accelerated a normal process. Some of the aid will have benefited the donor countries and supplying industries, although, like Malaysia, in some cases Thailand was offered a choice of donors and therefore of ties.

Like its still high primary exports, the recent importance of aid is a reminder of how recently Thailand has become an active, rather than a reacting, participant in the international system, and therefore perhaps of how weakly established its responses to incentives or disincentives at the international level may be.

FOREIGN INVESTMENT

Foreign investment accounted for 2% of total investment in 1970 and was still at that level in 1980 (as Table 6.11 shows, its average share rose to 3%,

Table 9.10   Net capital outflow of Thai investors abroad
(equity investment US$m)

Country	1980	1985	1987	1988	1989	1990	1991
Total	3.04	0.85	168.42	24.32	49.98	139.78	174.96
Japan	0.02	0.01	–	0.15	0.05	0.11	2.27
US	0.10	0.63	39.68	1.83	37.90	42.44	47.15
Hong Kong	2.29	–	97.89	0.26	0.59	39.38	52.14
Singapore	0.54	0.01	29.39	1.22	9.41	2.98	34.52
Italy	–	–	–	–	–	–	10.92

Source: Bank of Thailand, data supplied to author, 1992

then fell back to 1.5% in the late 1970s, the years when external assistance briefly revived as a source of finance). It is only since 1985 that Thailand has become one of the major recipients, with the share reaching 8% by 1990. In private investment, the pattern is similar (although the rise can be seen from the mid-1980s), and foreign investment is now about 10% of the total.

Thailand's impressive record in attracting foreign investment cannot be separated from external trade constraints. The Japanese investment in textiles in the 1960s and the Asian in footwear in the 1980s and toys in the 1990s stem in part from barriers to the investors' home country exports. The high figures for intra-company or foreign investors' exports, like those for Malaysia, should be considered, in part at least, as a result of quota constraints rather than an independent element of external dependence.

Thailand's recent emergence as an investor itself is also a response to constraints (Table 9.10). Some is to overcome traditional (or potential) types of import constraints in its market countries (the NAFTA induced examples in Mexico and the US), but other investments are more specifically connected to NTBs on its exports. For instance, it has bought a canned fish company in the US as a way of reducing unjustified use of health constraints. In either case, trade barriers are inducing a diversion of investment and production away from Thailand, although perhaps not of income.

Not all foreign investment is associated with trade constraints. The electric and electronics industry demonstrates that rapid growth can correspond to purely economic forces. The industry came to seek first local markets for electrical goods, then a base for exporting from a producer with lower costs than the home country. It has become a major source of exports, with all electronics products taken together now overtaking textiles and clothing. In 1990, they accounted for 18% of total exports, having risen from trivial levels in 1970 to 1% by 1975; and as late as 1980 and 1985, they were still only 5% and 7%. Components are still the most important part, but, as in Malaysia, final products are beginning to join them (Sibunruang and Brimble, 1992). Tables 6.5 and 6.6 suggest that trade by and within multinationals is an unusually high proportion of Thai trade with the US and (Table 6.9) with the world: in 1977, it accounted for 11% of Thai exports, rising to 16% by 1986, and 27% by 1989. The share of foreign companies in Thai manufactures exports rose from 11% in 1974 to 15% by 1986 (Ramstetter, 1991). In the earlier year, when the textile and clothing industry was new, foreign (mainly Japanese) controlled firms accounted for up to 50% of its exports, but by the mid-1980s this had fallen to 15–20%. Foreign firms were also important in chemicals (about 50% in the 1970s, down to 20% in the mid-1980s), again mainly Japanese, and metals, which were almost entirely foreign in the 1970s (probably European), but also fell sharply in the 1980s. Electrical machinery exports, the new export of the 1980s, remain mainly foreign, but the USA has been most important here. Local firms have not yet developed (Chirathivat, 1992).

Table 9.11 shows how much foreign investment has been tied to exporting. The figures are similar to the estimates for Malaysian foreign firms. Although the US firms have the largest ratios, as expected, all the foreign firms are predominantly in exports, although the Asian less so than the industrial countries and the European and Japanese less than the US. As was suggested in Chapter 6, wholly-owned subsidiaries have a higher propensity to export than joint ventures, but two explanations must be added to the profit incentive suggested there. Although there are no formal requirements enforced on Thai ownership, all investment must be approved, and foreign firms entering the local market will find it easier to get approval if they offer either exports or a Thai partner. They may also find a Thai partner an advantage in local markets.

Both the dependence of some foreign investment on policy-created export opportunities and its extremely rapid recent growth (Table 9.13) suggest that it cannot be considered a stable source of either domestic investment or future export growth. The increase in the 1980s came largely from an increase in the shares of Japan and the Asian countries, and within this Japan remains much more dominant than it is, for example, in Malaysia (Table 9.12). While the former major investor, the US, rose from $90 million to only $240 million, Japan increased from US$56 million to US$1 billion (Table 9.13). Although the direction of its investment was determined by Thailand's economic advantages, and the opportunities particularly in the electronics industries, the amount of total Japanese overseas investment and its timing were the result of the rise in the yen, and the consequent loss of competitiveness of domestically produced products. This cannot be considered a basis for the extrapolation of inflows into the future. The change in Japanese investment between 1990 and 1991 (from 44% to 30%, or in dollar terms from US$1 billion to US$600 million, largely explaining a drop in total foreign investment of US$500 million) illustrates the risk. In 1992, foreign investment remained lower than in 1990 (Table 6.14), and may have fallen again in 1993. Some of the 1991 fall was in traditionally volatile sectors

Table 9.11 Thailand: export shares of major manufacturing firms
by ownership 1990

Country/region	Combined percentage of product exported	Disaggregated percentage of product exported
USA	77	
Joint ventures		72
Subsidiaries		85
Japan	66	
Joint ventures		60
Subsidiaries		90
Europe	62	
Joint ventures		52
Subsidiaries		89
NICs	83	
Joint ventures		77
Subsidiaries		97
ASEAN	52	
Joint ventures		45
Subsidiaries		100
All firms	66	
Thai		63
Joint ventures		69
Subsidiaries		91

Source: Sibunruang and Brimble, 1992

like petroleum, hotels, and commerce, but part was in more directly industrial sectors like electrical appliances.

CONCLUSIONS

Chirathivat (1991) concludes that 'the future performance of exports will strongly depend on the country's ability to adjust the management of trade policy to the changes in the trading system', but that so far Thailand has shown itself less able to adapt to this type of external constraint than to macroeconomic shocks from the international economy (Chirathivat, 1992). This puts the emphasis on the need for an official response to the problem. The growing willingness to protest to industrial countries about their constraints (current problems were listed in GATT, 1991, vol 2: 44–5; these form the basis for request lists sent to the importing governments) and government interest in AFTA follow this path.

The alternative is to rely on an industrial response. The analysis in the first part of this study has suggested that this is more difficult for a country faced

Table 9.12 Thailand: shares of net inflows of foreign direct investment by investing country (percentages)

Country/region	1970–9	1980–2	1983–6	1987–9	1990	1991
APEC member countries	86.22	72.94	79.86	86.38	88.89	87.02
North America	35.72	27.03	30.57	12.65	9.50	11.82
US	35.56	27.25	29.71	12.36	9.35	11.52
Canada	0.16	−0.22	0.86	0.29	0.15	0.30
Japan	29.78	22.89	32.87	44.30	44.50	30.34
Asian NIEs–3	10.32	14.06	11.06	22.70	24.24	28.43
Hong Kong	9.59	13.88	9.68	11.25	12.01	22.50
South Korea	0.35	0.07	0.09	0.70	0.78	0.57
Taiwan	0.38	0.11	1.29	10.74	11.45	5.36
ASEAN	6.38	7.57	4.00	6.04	10.30	12.80
Brunei	0 00	–	0.04	0.00	0.00	0.00
Indonesia	0.10	0.24	0.05	0.05	0.10	0.17
Malaysia	0.61	1.12	0.74	0.11	0.73	0.04
Philippines	0.28	0.00	−0.12	0.00	0.01	0.00
Singapore	5.11	6.21	3.28	5.87	9.45	12.59
Oceania	0.46	1.39	0.93	0.22	0.19	3.55
Australia New Zealand	0.46	1.39	0.93	0.22	0.19	3.55
China	0.00	0.00	0.44	0.48	0.16	0.08
Non-APEC countries	17.34	27.06	20.14	13.62	11.11	12.98
EC and other Europe	15.40	19.16	11.73	8.47	6.86	10.09
Total	100.00	100.00	100.00	100.00	100.00	100.00

Sources Bank of Thailand, data; Chirathivat, 1992

with policy rather than with market constraints from outside. So far, however, Thailand, even more than Malaysia, appears to have relied on it.

The success of Thai exports suggests that the entrepreneurship needed to search for new production and trading opportunities has remained strong on balance, although foreign companies have also played an important role, particularly in the initial years of each export. The very high share of Thai exports remaining in markets covered by either restraints or GSP could suggest that some attraction persists, whether from the MFA experience or other factors, for seeking created, rather than competitive, opportunities. But this could be an over-interpretation of an unavoidable situation. The problem for a country at Thailand's intermediate level of development arises from the interaction of preferences, tariff escalation, and controls, as described in the first part of this study. It is difficult to think of any product which it could export, which is within its technological and endowment

Table 9.13 Net flows of foreign direct investment in Thailand by country (US$ m)

Country	1980	1985	1988	1989	1990	1991
Total	189.40	163.55	1,105.54	1,777.98	2,528.63	2,013.92
US	35.77	87.91	125.91	203.11	240.53	231.95
Japan	44.10	56.48	577.51	729.97	1,091.69	611.09
Hong Kong	54.39	23.90	110.48	222.38	274.67	453.25
Singapore	13.54	−41.31	62.15	106.92	239.82	253.53
Taiwan	0.09	6.28	123.99	196.96	279.85	107.91
UK	4.03	4.48	34.98	8.65	44.19	10.06
W. Germany	12.79	6.12	24.56	31.81	44.95	33.02
France	0.63	5.27	11.12	15.28	26.66	48.84
Netherlands	1.07	−1.55	11.41	63.40	25.40	29.29
EC sub-total	26.10	15.70	88.90	148.60	164.60	155.40
Others	15.37	14.62	81.60	170.06	237.44	200.83

Source: Bank of Thailand, data supplied to author, 1992

possibilities, is competitive, but is not produced in either the industrial countries themselves or one of their more preferred developing areas, and therefore subject to actual or potential barriers. A pessimistic exporter could argue that up to now every export at which Thailand has seemed to be successful has attracted controls, rather than that Thailand has concentrated by choice on such products. The answer to the fundamental question of why Thai exporters have concluded from this that they should try a series of new exports, and then move on to the next, rather than giving up seems to be that successful development requires the desire for growth to be greater than the discouragement from controls while a country is going through this stage. In other words, this reaction is a pre-condition for development.

As in Malaysia, it appears that up to now the need to increase exports has led to an encouragement of any type of investor, including foreign, in order to promote exports. But a recent survey (Sibunruang and Brimble, 1992) suggests that linkages to local industry have not been important, and the share of output exported, like that of foreign firms in exports, is strikingly high. There has, however, been more of a tradition of joint ventures in Thailand, particularly for Japanese investors, than in Malaysia. (In contrast to Malaysia, Japanese investors in Thailand are said by the government to be more willing than US investors to go in for joint ventures.) These also seem, on the basis of a previous survey (Page, 1986), to be more genuinely joint than the sleeping partners often found in Malaysia, so that there is the potential for linkage by experience even if formal industrial linkages are less in evidence.

The worrying phenomenon for Thailand is the speed with which it appears to be moving from its first acquisition of foreign investors to losing them (and Thai investors) to new opportunities. This may be a characteristic of all economic flows – that responses to new incentives are becoming more rapid, a fact which Thailand has to accept as characteristic of developing now rather than twenty years ago. It is a sharp reminder of the risks of relying on foreign investment. The rise in Japanese investment in the late 1980s clearly depended on special Japanese factors (the yen), as much as on any international or Thai opportunities or constraints. The very short-lived period of high investment, however, may make readaptation to its loss easier than in other countries which have relied on inflows over long periods.

NOTES

1 The trade sections of this chapter are substantially based on the data and analysis in Chirathivat, 1991 and 1992. I am grateful to Suthiphand Chirathivat for his generous help in supplying data and advice. An advantage for the researcher of Thailand's present level of exposure to protection is that local studies are excellent.
2 All the GSP data quoted here and in the tables are for products eligible, and make no allowance for under-utilisation.
3 The UAE appears frequently in textiles and clothing trade. There are large quantities of clothing exports recorded as from there (notably Dubai). Some clothing is produced there using migrant labour, but in any market as controlled as that for textiles and clothing, there are suspicions about the accuracy of recording.

10

COLOMBIA

Colombia, with a population of about 33 million and a per capita income of about $1,400, is in broadly the same size and income group as Malaysia and Thailand, both in absolute terms and in relation to its own region. It is the largest member of the Andean group, although small compared with the North American countries, including Mexico, or with Brazil. It is neither among the richest nor the poorest. A difference which may be important, however, is that it has held this position, and income level, for longer. Its period of (relatively) rapid growth was in the 1970s, at an average of about 6% p.a. (a rise, but not a transformation, from 5% in the 1960s), with only 3.4% p.a. in the 1980s and the early 1990s. On the other hand, although its growth slowed, it did not suffer the absolute fall in the 1980s experienced in most other major Latin American countries. It is not a country which has undergone recent major economic changes; its disruptions have been political and social.

TRADE PATTERNS

The trade pattern of Colombia is superficially as conservative[1] as its aggregate economic performance. It remains (Table 10.1) basically an exporter of primary goods, and the rise which did occur in manufactures in the early 1970s was not continued. Although early, contested, estimates for 1992[2] claimed that 'non traditional' exports had finally reached half the total, this included primary goods like metals and 'new' food and flower exports; these goods have been called 'non-traditional' for up to twenty years. This is a very different pattern and attitude from those of most of the other countries examined here, even Zimbabwe.

In terms of the 'vulnerable' primary products identified in Table 5.8, while Colombia's total share has fallen only slightly, and remains by a large margin the highest of the countries considered here (at almost 70%), there have been large changes among them. Although coffee is still important, it is no longer dominant: from half of all (legal) exports in the mid-1980s, it had fallen to a quarter by 1990 and under 20% by 1992. Petroleum and petroleum products

177

Table 10.1 Colombia: export structure by principal commodities

Commodity	SITC	1970	1975	1980	1985	1990
Total value ($m)		727.7	1,464.9	3,945.0	3,551.9	6,765.0
				percentages		
All food items	0+1+22+44	75.0	64.7	71.8	59.3	32.8
Agricultural raw materials	2 less (22+27+28)	6.2	7.0	4.7	5.5	4.3
Fuels	3	10.1	7.2	2.8	16.3	36.9
Manufactured goods of which:	5 to 8 less 68	8.0	20.9	19.6	16.9	25.1
Chemical products	5	1.2	4.0	2.3	3.6	3.4
Other manufactured goods	(6+8) less 68	6.0	14.7	15.0	12.3	20.5
Machinery and equipment	7	0.8	2.2	2.3	1.1	1.3
Crude petroleum	331	8.1	–	–	–	22.8
Petroleum products	332	2.0	7.0	2.6	12.7	6.1
Textile fibres, yarn and clothing	26+65+84	7.2	11.9	8.5	5.3	9.6
Metals and metal manufactures	67+68+69	1.0	1.4	1.1	2.5	3.2
Machinery:						
Non electrical	71	0.5	1.3	1.3	0.6	0.7
Electrical	72	0.1	0.5	0.4	0.3	0.5
Transport equipment	73	0.1	0.5	0.7	0.2	0.1

Source: UNCTAD, *Handbook*, 1992

Table 10.2   Colombia: principal exports 1990–1
(percentages)

Commodity	1990	1991
Coffee	20	18
Petroleum	28	19
Coal	8	8
Ferronickel	2	2
Bananas	4	5
Flowers	3	3
Fish	2	2
Coffee products	1	1
Textiles	1	2
Clothing	7	8
Leather and leather goods	2	2
Shoes	1	1
Paper and paper products	2	2
Chemicals	3	5
Gold	5	5
Emeralds	2	2

Source: ANDI, 1992

are rising. They overtook coffee as the major export by 1990. Coal also became important (Table 10.2). The fall in the value of coffee has reflected the decline in its price, although the volume has also fluctuated. The concentration on a remarkably small number of products remains: Colombia has the least diversified export structure of the countries studied here, and one of the most concentrated for all countries of its middle-income level and economic size. The resulting vulnerability is offset by persistent good luck in finding new large-scale resources: its oil discoveries could now make it the second largest Latin American exporter, with almost $5 billion by the end of the 1990s, a rise of about $3.5 billion, which will be a respectable addition to its present export value of about $7 billion. In international terms, Colombia is now a major supplier of coffee, flowers (second only to the Netherlands, holding more than 10% of the world market), and coal, and is expected to become one of oil.

This persistent cushion of external income from a series of primary goods, which appear almost exogenously, is an essential part of the background to official and industrial attitudes towards exporting and towards conventional prescriptions about appropriate changes in composition and policy stance. Although most of the rest of this chapter will deal with more conventional obstacles, external and internal, to its exports of manufactures, the unusually weak felt need to expand exports means that any obstacle need not be strong to be sufficient. (The nearest parallel among the countries studied here is Bangladesh, with its high inflows of aid.) Colombia does not need more manufactured exports to permit rapid growth (Colombia does not grow rapidly), or to repay debt (Colombia did not incur large debts), or to replace stagnant primary exports (each of Colombia's primary exports may be stagnant, but there has always been a new one), or to supplement inadequate inflows of capital (Colombia's illegal flows come in, instead of going out, with the black market exchange rate at times higher than the official). Although not a very large country, Colombia is of a sufficient size and total income to permit large companies to operate with exports of around 30% of total sales, a common range for the companies interviewed for this study, and this allows each of them, like the government, to take a relatively relaxed or unresponsive view of problems in international markets.

Coal, as a major fuel with a small number of often politically unstable suppliers, is as vulnerable to political pressures and international events as oil. Most of Colombia's coal exports have been to the EC, especially to the UK, where domestic suppliers of coal and other fuels are able to influence decisions about imports. The return of South Africa and Poland as major suppliers could be important influences in the 1990s. By the early 1990s, coal amounted to about 8% of Colombia's total exports, about half the level of coffee.

The only manufactured product with an export share of more than 1–2%, and one which has been in the top five intermittently throughout the last twenty-five years, is clothing. Others in which Colombia is important in some markets are shoes, other leather products, and paper and printing products (in the last, it is one of the major developing country suppliers). For all of these, except some leather products, exports are less important in aggregate, and to most individual companies, than domestic sales. This is an important difference from the primary products, both traditional and non-traditional. (Although there are domestic sales of flowers, the export industry is almost entirely separate.)

Clothing became important in the early 1970s, when Colombia was one of the first countries to do outward processing for the US, but growing costs and the MFA were then blamed for reducing its competitiveness and potential expansion. In the late 1980s and early 1990s, values revived. It had remained an important industry at the national level, so that it was in a position to respond to external forces by contraction or expansion, rather than establishment or disappearance.

Shoes have been exported since the early 1970s, and exports are again an extension of a successful national industry. The main export market is the US (which provides a large volume market both because of its absolute size and because of a relatively high average consumption of shoes). For one major company exports have normally been at least a quarter of output. This fell in the 1990s to under 20%. The industry was faced by increased competition for large orders from other suppliers (notably China), and the need to choose between contracting or moving into a much more diversified market, either the EC or, in the US, into different types of cheaper or more differentiated production. It has chosen to contract. It is perhaps appropriate to extend the term traditional exports to all these long-term exports, primary and manufactured, which have tended to respond to domestic discoveries or external changes in price or demand, rather than taking a more aggressive approach.

The other reasonably important 'minor' exports – other leather goods, flowers, and printed products – have experienced apparently more directed export strategies, although paper and printing also has a major domestic base. Flowers and leather goods are primarily exported to the US (80% for flowers, 70% for leather goods); the printing industry is largely within Latin America, for language reasons, but exports outside that are mainly to the US.[3] Some specialised products (for example, carnations and leather for furniture) go to European markets. Exports to Japan or other Asian markets are negligible.

Total Colombian exports to Japan and the Asian developing countries amounted to only 4% of exports in 1992, almost entirely to Japan. Colombia's exports are mainly to the US (Table 10.3), although there has always also been a high share to the EC. Although Latin America as a whole is more dependent on the industrial countries, with a smaller share to Asia (Table 7.2d), than the average for Asia or for all developing countries, Colombia's share is extremely low. Latin America, however, has been the most slowly growing region, and until recently the most restrictive on imports (Table 2.4), so that Colombia has had less incentive to move into Latin American markets than the Asian countries have had to move into Asian. The 1991 doubling to Venezuela and Ecuador, and the rise of the Latin American share to almost a quarter, were therefore major changes.

COLOMBIAN TRADE POLICY

Colombia's trade policy in the years since 1986 has undergone radical changes. These make it difficult to judge whether recent export changes are more a response to national changes or to other countries' policies. Colombia has cut its own tariffs and other barriers like licences, and also removed the system of import duty rebates and the export subsidies offered to shield exports from these. It established a new ministry of foreign trade, opened more trade promotion offices, restructured its export promotion agency into an export bank, and established an investment promotion office. The policy emphasised removal of regulation as well as of specific barriers. The end-1994 tariff reduction target, of an average level of 15%, was achieved by 1991, and traders agree that there has been a real reduction in regulatory obstacles. But the policy also revived a regional arrangement of the 1970s, the Andean Pact. With Venezuela an accelerated tariff removal was adopted so that virtually all barriers between the two countries have

Table 10.3 Colombia: principal markets 1970–92 (percentages)

Region/country	1970	1975	1980	1985	1990	1991	1992
Industrial countries	80	75	76	79	79	72	73
US	36		40	33	44	39	38
EC	25		31	35	26	25	25
Japan	3		4	4	4	3	3
Developing countries	15	23	21	18	19	27	26
Asia	0	0	0	1	1	1	1
Africa	0	0	2	2	0	0	0
Latin America	11	22	18	14	17	24	23
Venezuela	1	6	7	4	3	6	7
Mexico	0	0	1	0	1	1	1
Chile	1	2	2	1	2	2	2
Ecuador	1	2	2	2	1	2	2

Source: IMF *Direction of Trade Statistics*; ANDI, 1993

been removed. All of this affected the major exporting industries through effects on their home markets as well as by removing barriers in their export markets. In addition, there were effects on the exchange rate, which rose, and many firms had gained more through the subsidy system than they needed as compensation for the costs of importing machinery and materials, so these incentives were also altered.

The reform also generated three types of uncertainty. First, in the domestic market, which is now more uncertain because imports are more available and because, as some producers have complained, the lowering of tariffs proceeded more rapidly than originally announced, thus making them hesitant about trusting future declarations of staged policies (particularly in regional integration). Second, there is uncertainty over whether the reforms imply more or less intervention in trade, as there are now more potentially active institutions, and intervention on exports and investment seems to have replaced previous controls on imports. Third, there is the question of whether the reform will last. Colombia's policies on regulating imports and promoting 'non-traditional' exports have changed regularly over the last twenty years, as has its participation in regional and other trading organisations, depending partly on ideological shifts and partly on balance-of-payments needs.

The effects of both policies and expectations may not be as serious as they would be in other countries because of the small proportion of Colombian exports which are dependent on Colombian policies, and the small share of exports in many firms' sales. In addition, calculations[4] apparently indicate that effective protection remains high, although the system of tariffs has been simplified to two to three rates. These are still sufficient to protect individual manufactured goods, and the difficulties of transport (discussed below as a barrier to exports) also hinder imports.

Colombia had not been as strongly and consistently inward-orientated as some of the Latin American countries, and it already had a strong lobbying presence in the USA. Reducing barriers and extending the focus of policy to the EC and the rest of Latin America were, however, important as a signal of the official change of emphasis.

A comprehensive survey has been undertaken by FEDESARROLLO (1993) of the effects of the liberalisation (Table 10.4), which also included questions about some of the external policy changes. This pointed to some, but small, adverse effects. The survey was mainly of small or medium-sized firms, and not of exporters of the major products or all major exporters of the new products, so that the responses are perhaps most useful as indicating attitudes and potential Colombian trade. Not surprisingly, the survey showed an overwhelmingly favourable response to the removal of import tariffs on inputs and capital goods, the simplification of procedures, and the institutional reform (not shown here). Table 10.4 indicates some of the more controversial aspects, and those dealing specifically with exports.

Only a minority of firms found the removal of controls on competing imports unfavourable, but this was more serious for the larger companies. One explanation offered by Colombian researchers was that the protection had largely offered higher profits, not protection for inefficiency, so that sales were not reduced for companies able to cut their prices to the new import level. This still seems an 'unfavourable' result; it is likely therefore that the alternative explanations, that the liberalisation was not as great, in effective terms, as it appeared, and that the survey was not representative of the largest firms, may be important. But even with these allowances, the reactions are still surprisingly restrained. The loss of the export subsidy was the major blow, to all companies, but particularly to the largest. The more specific areas of liberalisation, of trade with Venezuela and Ecuador, which had already happened, and with Mexico, Chile, and the US, which was under discussion, are also welcomed by most firms, with Mexico considered the least desirable. At the end of 1993 an agreement with Mexico was signed. On almost all questions, the largest firms (and on many, the most important exporters) are the least favourably disposed towards liberalisation.

These results tend to support the view that the major effect of liberalisation has been to reduce the administrative burdens of trading. For small firms or inexperienced exporters, the benefits from reducing these, especially if supplemented by lower-cost imports, outweigh any losses from greater competition in their home markets. For the larger firms, which were experienced in dealing with the forms and in extracting benefits from the compensatory export subsidies, the gains are smaller, and the losses greater.

The principal implication for this study, however, is how unimportant trade barriers (or their removal) appear to be for Colombian firms in any of

Table 10.4 Colombia: effects of internal and external liberalisation, 1993 survey results (percentages)

	All firms	Large	Medium	Small	Type of products				Type of exporter			Cloth-ing	Shoes	Print-ing
					Con-sumer	Primary	Capital	Con-struction	All	Major	Minor			
(observations)	(393)	(58)	(251)	(84)	(174)	(124)	(70)	(21)	(212)	(56)[a]	(156)	(25)	(14)[c]	(13)[c]
Reduction of tariffs on competing														
Favourable	15	19	16	12	18	12	18	14	15	15	16	13	28	23
Unfavourable	40	57	39	34	35	45	46	39	47	47	48	39	21	23
Removal of export subsidy														
Favourable	3	0	5	3	4	2	4	5	1	2	1	4	7	0
Unfavourable	63	76	62	56	63	58	70	65	84	93	81	88	86	75
Expected exports in next 2 years														
Rise in US$ >50%	16	17	8	8	19	15	13	0	23	20	24	16	29	23
20–50%	38	42	37	35	38	37	42	29	52	55	51	48	43	46
<20%	24	25	23	28	21	27	25	38	21	20	22	24	29	8
Fall	6	2	6	11	6	5	10	0	3	5	2	4	0	8
Major obstacles to exports[b]														
High local costs	32	32	34	26	31	40	24	19	38	39	37	52	43	38
Uncertainty about exchange rates	23	34	22	18	24	19	24	10	18	11	20	28	43	8
Lack of markets	19	22	19	16	18	19	19	24	24	23	25	16	21	23
Effects of EC preferences														
Favourable	27	30	25	30	29	28	23	17	29	38	26	48	50	23
Unfavourable	2	0	0	3	1	0	5	0	1	0	2	0	0	0
Effects of Andean preferences by US														
Favourable	44	50	43	46	46	46	38	43	46	51	44	50	50	69
Unfavourable	1	0	1	0	1	0	1	0	0	0	0	0	0	0

Table 10.4 Continued

(observations)	All firms (393)	Large (58)	Medium (251)	Small (84)	Type of products				All (212)	Type of exporter		Cloth-ing (25)	Shoes (14)c	Print-ing (13)c
					Con-sumer (174)	Primary (124)	Capital (70)	Con-struction (21)		Major (56)a	Minor (156)			
Liberalisation of trade with Venezuela														
Favourable	70	71	70	70	63	70	63	71	76	84	74	88	65	77
Unfavourable	10	17	10	7	10	12	9	10	8	5	9	0	0	0
Liberalisation of trade with Ecuador														
Favourable	69	74	69	63	71	71	64	45	74	83	70	84	78	54
Unfavourable	5	12	3	6	5	7	1	10	3	0	4	0	0	0
Would liberalisation of trade with Mexico be:														
Favourable	51	57	48	51	55	47	43	44	55	65	51	70	77	70
Unfavourable	24	32	26	12	19	25	33	25	26	21	27	9	15	20
Would liberalisation of trade with Chile be:														
Favourable	59	63	59	57	59	56	43	40	68	84	63	69	77	70
Unfavourable	4	6	5	5	6	4	5	0	2	0	2	0	0	10
Would liberalisation of trade with USA be:														
Favourable	60	62	61	60	64	57	58	53	64	66	53	76	75	63
Unfavourable	14	27	13	10	12	18	16	12	14	8	17	8	0	18

Note: The gradations in the survey of 'very favourable or unfavourable' are omitted. The difference between the sum of favourable and unfavourable and 100 is 'indifferent'

a Export >30% output;   b Only major responses;   c Not including the largest company in each of these industries

Source: FEDESARROLLO, 1993

the classifications. More support than oppose liberalisation with every country listed. The loss of protection is seen as damaging by only a minority (with the exception of the largest firms). Barriers are not one of the major obstacles mentioned to exports. And (this result is discussed more fully below), improved preferences by the US and EC are found helpful by at most a bare majority in all classifications.

Although opinions expressed by official and academic observers in interviews in Colombia for this study and in other sources revealed considerably greater concern about liberalisation effects, other evidence supports this assessment. There was surprise at how great the benefits of liberalising trade with Venezuela proved to be. The lack of a trade and investment promotion institutional structure, of the extent seen in Malaysia or Thailand, supports this view of trade's place among other priorities. Although the quotas imposed on banana exports to the EC (described in the next section) were a matter of considerable concern, one of the reasons for Colombia's loss of market access was seen as lack of sufficient bargaining effort with the EC. If this is correct, whether it was deliberate or by default, it suggests a relative lack of official concern for access (at least for a 'minor' product).[5]

TRADE CONSTRAINTS AND PREFERENCES

For the dominant primary products in Colombian exports, tariffs are zero or negligible (Tables 2.1 and 2.3). But on coffee products, tariffs would be significant, at around 15%. As Table 10.2 shows, Colombia has scarcely moved into such exports. If Colombia's benefits and potential benefits from preferences are measured against present exports, therefore, they are small, but this cannot be taken as evidence that other preferences would be unimportant. In 1991, a third of the country's exports to the US entered tariff-free under normal, MFN, rates. Although a high proportion of the potential exports under GSP were affected by other barriers (60% in 1989, a third in 1991, Table 3.7), the total which would have been eligible for GSP even without these was only about 10% of all exports to the US. Although Colombia achieved one of the highest utilisation rates of the available GSP access (over 90%), GSP was clearly not important to its aggregate exports to the US. Table 2.7 confirms that it was also not a major user of the EC GSP. This was not (as in other countries) because it was using other schemes: it was also only a minor user (by Latin American standards) of the US outward processing arrangements (Table 2.10).

In 1991, both the US and the EC extended improved GSP access to the Andean countries, equivalent to that granted to low-income countries or, for the EC, to that offered to the ACP countries. This gave Colombia a potential advantage over other Latin American or other middle-income countries, and, temporarily (it was the first country to comply with the full conditions of the offer from the US), over the other Andean countries. As

Table 10.4 shows, these preferences were considered beneficial, but did not attract very great interest, especially the EC scheme, although, in many cases, the tariff reductions from the EC scheme were greater.

The effect of such preferences was inevitably small, given the small share of tariff-paying exports on which it operated, but comments from individual industries or companies provided more specific reasons. The most important difference between the US and EC schemes was that the US scheme was for 10 years, with the possibility of indefinite renewal, while the EC was for four years, with less certainty of renewal (and the issue of banana preferences was repeatedly cited as indicating the risk of EC policy changes). This period was considered too short not only to make new physical investments, but also to justify the cost of finding new markets, and potentially jeopardising old ones (if supplies were not sufficient for both). This was particularly important in industries like clothing and shoes where, although long-term contracts are not normal, repeated contracts with the same purchaser are common (as was found in all the countries with clothing exports), and also in markets for leather goods where specialised knowledge of different tastes is important. The issue of diverting supplies or investing to produce large quantities was particularly important for the large firms characteristic of Colombian exporters which prefer to deal with large orders. In both the EC and US markets, competition from lower-cost producers (the Chinese for shoes, in particular) was seen as a much more important current influence on demand.

There were individual cases of benefits (of particular flowers in which Colombia now enjoys a considerable tariff advantage over competitors, or vegetables, where the return to producers may now be more competitive with that from illegal drugs), and offering an alternative to drugs was of course the objective of the US and EC schemes. The Colombian experience may offer the extreme case of GSP's role as a microeconomic scheme, easing the entry of new firms or into new products, not a macroeconomic contribution to the trade or development of a country.

Colombia was, however, more concerned about the negative effects of losing to more preferred suppliers of bananas than pleased with the benefits from these preferences. This is not surprising, given the higher share of bananas in its exports (Table 10.2). Prior to the European harmonisation for the post-1992 single market, about half Colombia's banana exports had gone to the EC, mainly to Germany, which had neither controls nor tariffs (and the reunification of Germany had boosted these exports). To guarantee the access of bananas from the EC's 'traditional' suppliers among the ACP countries, the general EC tariff (of 25%) was extended to German imports, and an overall quota for imports into the EC was established. This was cited by exporters of all products to the EC as an example of the risks of arbitrary changes, and the vulnerability of preferences and trade in general. As mentioned above, it can also be seen as an example of Colombian lack of attention to trade bargaining.

Following the liberalisation of trade between Colombia and Venezuela at the end of 1990, exports to Venezuela more than doubled in 1991, and rose again in 1992. The increase in exports to Ecuador, where liberalisation was more limited and later, was 70%; there imports rose even more. There were smaller rises to the other Andean countries. In total, the share of these two countries in Colombian exports rose from 4% in 1990 to 9% in 1992 (Table 10.3). This was a significant aggregate contribution to Colombian exports, especially in 1992 when total exports fell slightly.[6]

There are important differences between these increases and those found for trade among the Asian countries. The first is that they are clearly policy-induced. Venezuelan duties on some products exported by Colombia, for example in the printed paper sector, had been over 100%. Their removal inevitably brought a large rise, but on a small base. The relatively slow growth of the Latin American region does not offer the future advantages of Asian growth for Asian exporters. The second is that trade with the other Latin American countries has tended to be seen as a first step for traders, into an 'easier', more familiar market than the industrial countries, especially for manufactures. The principal products in trade with Venezuela or Ecuador are very different from the list in Table 10.2. They include some agricultural primary products, but also chemicals, leather, printed materials, cotton clothing, and small metal goods. (A major shoe company, now exporting predominantly to the US, had first exported twenty years ago to the then-new Andean Pact.) This makes Latin American trade potentially important for its effects on individual industries, but, like preferences, not as a way of engineering a permanent market shift for Colombian trade. If it permits an increase in the share of manufactures in total exports, however, this could contribute to structural change and development (Rodríguez, 1992).

The other Latin American countries with which Colombia is in trade negotiations (Mexico and Chile) take even smaller shares of its exports (Table 10.3). The apparently random network of special arrangements among various sets of Latin American countries and the links of each with the US are seen in Colombia as steps towards a general liberalisation. Mexico offered the fewest direct advantages from access, and high potential risks from its more advanced industry and lower costs, but it would be attractive if a pact were arranged as part of an arrangement to obtain more access to the US.

Table 10.5 and a comparison of it with Table 10.1 show why the average non-tariff barriers faced by Colombia are low even compared with other Latin American countries. It exports mainly primary goods on which the barriers are not high. On those exports for which it does face high barriers – leather, clothing and shoes – it exported mainly to markets outside the industrial countries even before the post-1990 surge to the Andean countries. It thus avoided the markets or the goods which are most controlled. This strategy, however, appears to have become more difficult. As Table 7.1 shows, the weights of its 1986 pattern of trade give a lower average level of control, and using 1990 commodity weights further increases the 1990 average.

On most individual commodities, the EC controls appear more extensive, suggesting that the higher average figure for US controls arises because of the higher share of controlled goods in exports to that market in spite of the barriers. This is supported by interview evidence that US barriers are seen as less serious. One reason is essentially circular: greater familiarity with the US market because it is more important has meant greater ease in dealing with it (this was cited, in particular, in the case of anti-dumping provisions). But in general the regulations were seen as less tight there, both in measurable terms (rules of origin requiring lower local content) and in predictability of administration (although here again, familiarity could be a factor). The EC market was also seen as more fragmented, in both taste and regulatory terms, so that firms which exported in volume and were unwilling to adapt to a differentiated market chose the US.

On health and safety standards, Colombian exporters saw problems in all markets. Recent examples in early 1993 included reaction to the outbreak of cholera; pesticides (the need to deal with concern about both their impact on consumers' health and their effect on Colombian workers); packaging (for the new Japanese market for flowers). The examples did not appear in real terms more serious than those regarded as normal conditions of exporting in the Asian countries studied.

All these barriers (as shown in the survey) were considered unimportant relative to some of the internal Colombian problems. Notable among these were lack of transport facilities (particularly from the largely inland and plateau-based exporters to the ports); the ports themselves (designed for the convenience of coffee exports); the lack of direct maritime access to any markets except the EC or the US; and constraints on electricity after a year (March 1992—March 1993) of rationing by cuts of up to 8 hours per day.

COUNTERTRADE, TIED AID AND FOREIGN INVESTMENT

Countertrade was introduced in Colombia as part of the strategy of promoting non-traditional exports (although it also coincided with a period of balance-of-payments strain, and the initial uncertainty about its implementation may have contributed a useful temporary pause in imports). It was announced as an official requirement for some types of import in late 1983, but only given detailed regulations by mid-1984, then immediately restricted to only a few goods, and finally abolished in 1986. The plan was to require some importers (particularly of foreign industrial inputs) to prove that they

Table 10.5 Colombia: non-tariff barriers (percentage 1986 weights on 1990 data)

SITC	Product area	EC	US	Japan	Total[a]	Total[b]
0+1+22+4	All food items	2	3	6	2	9
0	Food + live animals	2	3	6	2	
031	Fresh fish	8	0	100	6	
051	Fresh fruit and nuts	2	8	99	22	
054	Fresh vegetables	100	1	0	85	
061	Sugar and honey	100	90	45	75	
292	Vegetal materials	99	98	0	91	
2 less (22+27+28)	Agricultural raw materials	67	99	0	68	74
27+28+67+68	Ores and metals	10	0	6	5	6
67	Iron and steel	13	0	0	6	
3	Fuels	12	0	100	2	
5	Chemicals	5	0	0	0	
6–8 less (67+68)	Manufactures, not chemicals	55	30	0	5	6
61	Leather and furs	24	0	0	8	
65	Textiles, yarn and fabric	99	68	83	4	
831	Travel goods	0	1	0	1	
84	Clothing	99	81	0	24	
85	Footwear	100	0	0	27	
(0–9) less 3	All items, excluding fuels	5	18	5	10	15
0–9	All items	6	12	8	8	10

Notes:
[a] Totals and subtotals found by applying 1986 importer weights to 1990 totals and subtotals
[b] Totals and subtotals found by applying 1986 importer weights to each commodity, and summing the commodities

Source: Calculated from UNCTAD database

had exported new products or to new markets as a condition of obtaining foreign exchange. On the available data (Table 10.6), it was significant in aggregate terms only in 1984 and 1985 when it may have affected 5–6% of exports. Lack of information appears to have put severe temporary constraints on some firms' imports in the first half of 1984. The exports involved included textiles and clothing and cars and car parts, indicating some success in promoting manufactures (and coal was a new export at the time). Table 10.6 also shows a higher proportion of deals with industrial countries than in other countries' countertrade data. This could indicate success in finding new markets for manufactures.

Colombia had ceased to be a major recipient of aid by the mid-1970s (Table 10.7), and when the US and the EC wanted to assist it in shifting from drug-based activities they used trade preferences in 1990. On the import side, external intervention does not appear to be an important current influence.

As Table 6.11 showed, foreign direct investment became an important contributor to Colombian investment from the early 1980s (at about 6–7%). Although the data are inconsistent between sources, and details are uncertain for the most recent years, it is clear that this went largely into developing the mining industry, especially coal, in the 1980s (Table 10.8). A similar inflow began in the 1990s for developing the oil reserves. Except for the appearance of Venezuela in 1992–3 (Colombian investors have also moved into Venezuela), the investors remain the traditional ones. Large, well-established Colombian companies which already have a major interest in Latin American markets are rationalising their activities through Andean investments. Thus on capital as on trade, the advantages from external sources accrue principally to the production of primary goods, and therefore they relatively disadvantage manufactures. But the small scale of the advantages, in both cases, is such that it is difficult to see this as a problem for Colombia's national interest.

This concentration of foreign investment in mining means that intra-firm trade is relatively small for Colombian trade with the USA, at about 6% (Table 6.5), and it fell for trade in manufactures in the 1980s (Table 6.6).

As in the Asian countries, there are fears that NAFTA will divert foreign investment into Mexico, but this would probably mainly affect investment in manufacturing, which is small in any case. The opening of the Mexican oil industry to foreign investment is more limited than in other sectors, and the prospects for Colombian oil in the 1990s are sufficiently favourable to attract investment.

In addition to investment inflows, which at $500 million a year are a significant addition to exports of about US$7 billion and imports of about US$5 billion, there are the inflows of profits from drugs. Under the combined influences of a Colombian amnesty and low US interest rates, the inflow in 1992 was estimated at about $3 billion. The effect of these non-trade legal and illegal inflows was to hold the exchange rate at a high level.

191

Table 10.6 Colombian countertrade

	Exports	Import
Product analysis		
Value ($m)	820	
Average value	22	
Apparent share of exports	3	
Product group observations %		
Agriculture, forestry and food products	49.4	7.0
Ores, minerals and metals	16.4	1.8
Crude oil, gas and related products	0.0	5.3
Vehicles, transport equipment and military equipment	8.9	40.3
Manufacturing/processing equipment and construction projects	0.0	21.0
Miscellaneous manufactured products	25.3	22.8
Services and miscellaneous	0.0	1.8
Total	100.0	100.0
Major product sub-group observations		
Coal	12.7	
Clothing and textiles	11.4	
Cotton	8.9	
Road vehicles and parts	8.9	31.6
Tractors		5.3
Crude oil		3.5

Yearly data – number of deals: total 49

1980	2
1981	0
1982	1
1983	0
1984	17
1985	21
1986	4
1987	3

Shares by market %:

Industrial	59
Other developing	27
Centrally planned	14

Source: Jones and Jagoe, 1988

CONCLUSIONS

Colombia is superficially like Malaysia in its specialisation in uncontrolled exports (or markets), but its natural advantages, and unnatural luck in finding a series of new resources, mean that trade policies, its own or those

Table 10.7 Colombia: multilateral and untied aid (US$ m or percentages)

Colombia	1970	1975	1980	1985	1990
Ratio of aid to imports (%)	18.98	5.75	1.93	1.50	1.72
Multilateral	32	24	58	25	9
Multi-EC	30	24	58	24	4
Bilateral	116	62	32	37	86
Untied bilateral	33	18	17	13	48
Total untied	63	42	75	37	52
Tied/imports (%)	11.50	2.97	0.32	0.61	0.79

Note: The average tied ratio for all bilateral aid is assumed for all areas

Sources: OECD, Development Co-operation and Geographical Distribution of Financial Flows to Developing Countries, annual issues

Table 10.8 Colombia: investment inflows by sector and source
(US$ m or percentages)

	1980	1984	1985	1986	1989	1990	1991	1992
Net investment in								
Colombia (IFS)	51	561	1,016	612	547	484	433	740
(Colombia)	104	310	490	441	259	196	197	308
					percentages			
Share by industry								
mining	5	57	90	84	39	45		4
coal						24		2
manufacturing	98	36	5	17	58			
machinery	50	5	4	4	27			
cars						11	27	1
chemicals	26	28	4	2	17		9	10
Share by source								
US	65	69	92	81	61	60	20	30
Japan	1	6	1	1	-3		29	0
EC	11	20	7	16	22			18
Germany	0	2	1	1	0	4		0
UK	3	23	2	8	1	9		6
Switzerland	12	5	0	4	11			4
Latin America	18	0	1	4				14
Venezuela	16	1	0	0				13

Sources: IMF, International Financial Statistics; Colombia, Department of Planning; data supplied

of others, have been less important to it than to most countries, while its size has permitted manufacturing firms to develop within an internal market. Although it has tried or benefited from a series of schemes to promote non-traditional exports, more or less precisely targeted, the effects of these have been largely on particular industries, not on the performance or structure of the economy as a whole. The (understandable) lack of sustained commitment to promoting development through manufactured exports has in itself increased the uncertainty, and therefore reduced the incentives, for exporters or potential exporters. The result has been that Colombian exporters have been more likely to respond to obstacles by stopping exporting, than by taking steps to remove them.

Exporters are ready to respond directly to new opportunities (like the liberalisation of Andean trade). Colombia was among the original countries to do outward processing for the US clothing industry in the early 1970s. It abandoned this when the MFA was imposed, but returned with the new provisions in the late 1980s. Established exporters of other products (shoes, for example) maintain their existing markets in the face of new competition from lower-cost suppliers, but are unwilling to adapt to try to maintain market growth, either by competing directly or by changing the type of production or moving to more difficult markets. The US, as the large, familiar market, is preferred. This traditional preference is reinforced by the real difficulties of exporting manufactures to the EC market. The regional market is likely to be treated more as a broadening of the national market, including some relocation of production, than as a change in trading strategy.

Industries which follow the more ambitious Asian exporter model do exist. Flowers and leather goods seem to be 'resource-based' industries which have gone well beyond their resource by deliberate promotion, on the NIC model. Although both sectors existed as domestic suppliers, the present industries, which are largely for export, are not closely related to the traditional producers and, in the case of leather, are increasingly dependent on imported inputs. As in other leather industries which will be discussed here, for example in Bangladesh, and as in the Thai and Zimbabwe clothing industries, the national input is not of sufficiently high standard to correspond to the quality of the processing industry so that what may have begun as a 'natural resource-based' industry has ceased over time to be one. These industries are thus dependent now on their own efforts and the incentives available in importing countries to be competitive. They have traditional concerns about liberalisation and loss of preferences against their competitors. Both expanded rapidly in the second half of the 1980s (possibly with a fall in 1992 for leather goods), gained from preferences, and are damaged by high exchange rates. There are other, smaller exporting industries with similar conditions and concerns. (The newly expanded banana industry could be seen as similar to flowers.) The difference from similar industries in the other countries studied here lies not in Colombian companies' nature or skills, but in the limited importance of these goods to total exports, to the economy as a whole, and therefore also to policy-makers.

NOTES

1 'Conservative' is the word which every commentator is driven to use about Colombia, about its performance and its policies, whether as praise or criticism. Its growth is steady, but never spectacular. Its policies avoid large jumps. This perception colours Colombians' and foreign observers' reactions to its recent trade liberalisation and its results.
2 The data for the rise in some exports were disputed with manufacturers, in a climate in which the government had an interest in showing the success of its liberalised trading and high exchange-rate policies, and the industries did not.
3 Colombia is a world leader in some specialised highly labour-intensive areas, including pop-up books.
4 Prepared for the government, but unpublished.
5 The semi-official classification of all but the four major exports as 'minor', and of all but coffee as 'non-traditional', may be further evidence of an official attitude which would not be seen in the Asian new NICs.
6 Table 10.3, however, also shows that a similar rise in trade with Latin America occurred between 1970 and 1975, when the Andean Pact was first formed: such increases are not necessarily the beginning of trends or irreversible.

11

ZIMBABWE

Zimbabwe is the first of the two low-income developing countries in this study, and it is also one of the three smallest. Its population is only 9 million, with a per capita income of well under US$1,000 (Table 7.1). It also suffered severe restrictions on its output in 1991–3 because of drought. This directly affected its agricultural production and its manufactured output (because of shortages and formal rationing of electricity). It also had indirect effects on markets, confidence, and policy-making. The resulting 9% fall in GDP in 1992 means that any appraisal of the structure of the economy must use a combination of recent and more normal figures.

Since becoming independent in 1980, Zimbabwe has had a brief period of rapid growth: two years at 12% p.a.; followed by five years of near stagnation to 1986, growing at 2% p.a., then a slow growth of 3.5% up to 1991. With a return of the rains during 1992, this slow progress was expected to resume. Manufacturing output showed a similar pattern through the 1980s, rising at 1% a year in the first half and 4.4% from 1986 to 1991, but falling 9–10% in 1992.

TRADE AND PRODUCTION PATTERNS

Although Zimbabwe is a new country, its industry and its history of manufactures exports are not as new as in the Asian countries (or the other small or poor countries still to be discussed). It had some exports of manufactures as early as the 1950s and 1960s, and many of the companies now becoming prominent are long-established, often family, firms. The pattern is thus more like the Colombian, of existing firms moving into exports from an established base in the home market. Its producers of primary goods also generally have a long history. Exporters are therefore firms which have seen and survived or benefited from a wide range of Zimbabwean and trading partner policies.

With Colombia, Zimbabwe is one of the two countries studied here which are still mainly dependent on primary commodities (about two-thirds of exports, or higher if the semi-processed metals are included as in Table 11.1), but these are much more diversified in Zimbabwe, including both agricultural and metal products. It remains, however, highly dependent on tobacco exports, about a quarter of the total (Table 11.2). Their fluctuations in recent years largely reflect changes in the export price. This rose in 1991, explaining most of the 1991 rise in value and share of total exports, before falling sharply in 1992 and 1993 (by about a half, and then by a further 40%). The influences on the other primary exports have also been market-, rather than policy-, based, with the gold price falling since the early 1980s, and ferro-alloys depressed in the early 1990s by new supplies from Russia.

Although the consequent year-to-year fluctuations are significant, what is remarkable in these tables compared with those for the other countries examined is how little Zimbabwe's export structure has changed since 1970. And the only major change, the decline in ores and metals, was in the 1970s. The share of manufactured exports also fell in the late 1970s, because of the sanctions operated against the illegal Rhodesian Government (Riddell, 1990), but the subsequent recovery has been limited (Tables 11.1, 11.2).

This does not mean, however, that manufactures exports have not been important in changing the structure of the economy, particularly at the end of the 1980s and since 1990. This is obscured in Table 11.2 by the performance of metals (which rose in the mid-1980s, then declined), but the other important manufactured exports show what is happening. Table 11.3 shows that the share of manufactured exports in total output, and for the most important products identified in Table 11.2, was only about 10% as recently as 1986. By 1988, the average share was 15%, and in 1990/1,[1] 18%. The change is particularly large for clothing, where the share has now reached 30%. Although the figures are uncertain because of high inflation and inconsistent years for data, Table 11.3 suggests that most of the recent increase in sales in these industries has come from exports. The rise can be seen in their share in Table 11.2, and these ratios are supported by those found for individual companies and from industrial data. Few firms export more than half their output (Riddell, 1990). The major exporters among the clothing firms had shares of 50% and 70%, but textile firms were much lower (and even those with temporary high exports because of low domestic demand in 1992 had the intention of returning to around 20%); 20% was also normal for shoes, with 30% for the major exporter. Other minor exports, for example of machinery or equipment to the African region, also had figures of at most 20%. (Smaller firms typically did not export.)[2]

Although originally based on local resources, of cotton for textiles, textiles for clothing, and hides for shoes, all these industries have moved increasingly to using foreign inputs, particularly for the export part of their industries (with a few exceptions among companies with integrated processing of several stages). The types or quality or immediate availability of local inputs do not correspond with those required for the types of export demand which they face. This means that in domestic policy and in looking

Table 11.1   Zimbabwe: export structure by principal commodities

Commodity	SITC	1970	1975	1980	1985	1990
Total value (US$m)		844.8	1,259.8	1,053.0	1,019.0	1,419.0
				percentages		
All food items	0+1+22+44	36.2	29.3	36.3	39.0	41.7
Agricultural raw materials	2 less (22+27+28)	9.1	9.3	13.2	11.8	9.5
Fuels	3	1.2	1.5	1.5	1.5	1.4
Ores and metals	27+28+68	26.0	21.8	13.0	13.4	13.9
Manufactured goods of which:	5 to 8 less 68	27.4	37.3	30.9	29.9	29.4
Chemical products	5	1.1	1.0	2.2	2.1	1.9
Other manufactured goods	(6+8) less 68	23.4	34.4	26.9	25.6	25.5
Machinery and equipment	7	2.9	1.9	1.9	2.3	2.0
Unallocated		0.1	0.8	5.0	4.4	4.1
Cereals	04	4.6	1.5	2.7	6.2	n.a.
Crude and manufactured fertilizer	271+56	–	–	0.1	0.2	n.a.
Textile fibres, yarn and clothing	26+65+84	11.5	1.2	12.2	11.8	n.a.
Metals and metal manufactures	67+68+69	27.9	14.7	25.4	26.8	n.a.
Machinery						
Non electrical	71	1.3	–	0.5	0.4	n.a.
Electrical	72	1.0	0.1	0.4	0.4	n.a.
Transport equipment	73	0.6	0.1	0.5	0.8	n.a.

Source: UNCTAD, *Handbook*, 1992

Table 11.2   Zimbabwe: principal exports, 1981–91 (percentages)

Commodities	1981[a]	1986	1988	1990	1991
Tobacco	25	19	17	20	29
Gold		19	13	14	14
Ferro-alloys		10	12	9	8
Nickel		4	10	6	6
Cotton		6	5	5	4
Maize	4	4	4	6	3
Asbestos	9	4	4	3	3
Iron and steel		3	4	3	3
Sugar		3	3	4	3
Beef	1	1	2	0	0
Copper		2	2	2	1
Clothing		1	2	2	3
Textiles	1	2	2	2	3
Others discussed					
Hides		0.3	0.4	0.4	0.4
Shoes		0.3	0.4	0.3	0.5
Flowers		0	0.2	0.3	0.4
Manufactures		28	41	34	33

Note: [a] excluding gold

Source: Zimbabwe, *Quarterly Digest of Statistics*

at their reactions to market countries' policies, they must now be seen as separate industries.

On textiles, the problems are particularly severe, with the stage of finishing and dyeing the one considered most uncompetitive, supporting the usual identification of textiles as less suitable than clothing as an export industry for developing countries.

The direction of Zimbabwe's trade shows a similar overall lack of change (Table 11.4), but with some significant exceptions. It has traditionally had a larger than usual share of trade with its own region (Table 2.5), and this remains true. After independence, there was an adjustment down from the high dependence on South Africa balanced by an increase in trade with the EC. These remain the two principal trading partners, but there has been an important increase in the share of trade with other African countries. Some of this may be in primary goods to meet temporary shortages (food exports in some years, for example), but this is also an area which is important for some of Zimbabwe's manufactured exports.

South Africa has traditionally been an important market for clothing, but the new expansion of exports has been either to the EC or to the US (in most cases, firms seem to have specialised in one or the other, while still maintaining some exports to South Africa). Textile exports expanded initially to the EC, but later also to the US (Riddell, 1990: 42). There has

Table 11.3 Zimbabwe: share of exports in manufactured output 1986–91 ($Zm and percentages)

| | 1986 | | | 1988 | | | 1991 | 1990 | |
	Exports	Sales	Share	Exports	Sales	Share	Exports	Sales	Share
Clothing	23	239	10	48	356	13	141	438	(32)
Footwear	7	114	6	13	172	8	29	194	(15)
Textiles	38	595	6.4	42	903	5	140	1,128	(12)
Total manufactures	614.9	5,874	10.5	1,228.1	8,222	14.9	1,802.4	10,279	(18)

Source: Zimbabwe, *Quarterly Digest of Statistics*

Table 11.4 Zimbabwe: export markets 1981–91 (excluding gold) (percentages)

Region/Country	1981	1986	1988	1991
US	8	6	7	6
Japan	3	5	7	7
EC	31	41	41	40
UK	7	12	11	14
Germany	8	9	9	11
Italy	5	6	7	4
Belgium	4	3	2	4
South Africa	22	12	10	10
SADCC and PTA	14	12	16	18
Botswana	3	4	6	6
Malawi	2	1	3	3
Mozambique	1	3	3	3
Zambia	4	3	4	4
China	3	3	2	6
Eastern Europe	1	2	2	1

Sources: Zimbabwe, *Quarterly Digest of Statistics*; IMF, *Direction of Trade*; Riddell, 1990

been some increase to the other African countries. Shoes and also some equipment, like agricultural tools, tend to be exported to other African countries (with some shoe exporters now moving into the EC as well). For clothing and shoe exporters, the principal difference which dictates their choice between the US and EC markets is the same as that cited by Colombian exporters: the size of the US market and therefore of US orders. The EC market is smaller and still diverse. The role of constraints and preferences needs to be seen in the context of this economic difference.

One completely new type of export is represented by flowers (see Table 11.2). Specialised, especially high value, vegetables and fruits are similar in the conditions which they face and in their history,[3] and in total amount to about the same value as flowers. These are industries entirely for export, which were established in the mid-1980s. In land and ownership, they represent a diversification by tobacco (and to a lesser extent sugar) farmers, and thus by experienced exporters into new products, not existing producers into exports. The exports go to the EC.

ZIMBABWE'S TRADE POLICY

Throughout most of the period since independence, the Zimbabwe economy has been highly regulated internally, with controls on both exporters and importers. The period of sanctions had seen very close cooperation of the government with private industry (at a time when their political interests were the same), followed by equally strong intervention by the new government in the 1980s, but with different objectives and less support from the private sector. Foreign-exchange controls, import licences, and domestic price fixing for the major export commodities were used. It is against this background that exporters' and official reactions to conditions in external markets must be assessed.

Since 1990, Zimbabwe has greatly altered the conditions for exporters, partly directly by removing some of the foreign-exchange controls and also the subsidies, but also by liberalising the import regime. As most exporters of manufactures are principally producers for the home market and all depend on imported inputs, they have, like the Colombians, faced potentially offsetting changes. The objectives of the economic programme explicitly included stimulating exports of manufactures, to increase income and to aid development (Robinson, 1993). It included a phased increase in the amount of export revenue which could be retained by companies to finance their own imports (or, eventually, transferred to other companies), from 7% in the first half of 1991 to 35% by 1993, a gradual freeing of imports from restrictions, accompanied by higher tariffs for those on the unrestricted list, and financial liberalisation which resulted in higher interest rates, including on credits needed by exporters. There was also a large devaluation, followed by a year of exchange-rate stability (during which inflation eroded the devaluation) and a further devaluation at the beginning of 1993.

The effects on individual exporters varied with the extent to which they had been able to obtain imports under the previous restrictions. Some large firms therefore found that the higher tariffs on derestricted imports and the higher interest rates offset any gains from freer imports. This failure to benefit large exporters by removing restrictions parallels that in Colombia, and suggests that programmes of 'liberalisation' may have very different effects on large and small producers. The total effect also depended on the extent to which producers' own output faced greater competition in the Zimbabwean market (or was expected to do so at later stages). Because of the pressures on exports from the drought and power shortages and from poor economic performance in South Africa and the EC, and because of the lack of full data for 1992, it is too early to assess the results, in particular whether exporters are more or less responsive to external policies. The interviews with exporters in Zimbabwe took place in early 1993 when further changes had been announced. Some of these were major, including further increases in import duties when the initial liberalisation had led to higher than expected imports (Robinson, 1993), and increases in the foreign-exchange retention, from 35% to 50% for 1993. The changes as originally announced, and the modifications which followed, created some uncertainty, but on the whole appeared to be favourably received by producers.

A study carried out when the reform was under consideration (Robinson, 1993) had suggested that the major advantage to be expected was removal of administrative delays and interference, and more generally reduction in detailed control of the economy. At this time, some industries were identified as less or more vulnerable to imports, and therefore suitable for early or later freeing from restrictions. Further analysis of these industries after the liberalisation found that it was individual companies' characteristics, for example, more or less recent investment and exposure to debt, or ability to respond to markets abroad, that helped to explain their actual performance. Given Zimbabwe's background of premature diversification because of sanctions, the effectiveness of a liberalisation policy should be expected to be seen more in reducing or eliminating inefficient suppliers than promoting new ones. But exporters in Zimbabwe have a history of adapting to a variety of conditions. It is therefore perhaps not surprising that the companies themselves expected to perform better than an appraisal of their current products' current competitiveness might suggest, either by moving to new products or by improving efficiency. Under these conditions, an appraisal of the suitability of individual products, rather than firms, for liberalisation may be misdirected. Even firms which expected to be, and were, damaged by the early liberalisation of competing imports remained in 'little doubt about [their] underlying long-term comparative advantage' (Robinson, 1993).

The unexpected support for liberalisation, even when their current products were immediately damaged, and the optimism of managers, which was found in both the Colombian survey and the Zimbabwe interviews by Robinson in 1990–1 and for this study, suggest that under some conditions liberalisation is preferred even to favourable intervention. Of the products examined in detail here, clothing and textiles remained under import control, but with the expectation of decontrol, while shoes were put on open licence. Although the shoe producers suffered immediate loss, their assumption was that removal of protection would have had to come eventually. Combined with the advantages of less intervention, the costs were considered worth paying. While industries preferred to retain protection for themselves, the clothing industry naturally objected to it for textiles, and would have accepted simultaneous decontrol. Even textiles were optimistic about their ability to survive in some products in some markets, given planned investments. The attitude towards domestic policy which these interviews suggest is thus that, while favourable treatment is welcome, it is not regarded as an essential element in companies' success, and the inconvenience of regulation and the vulnerability inherent in depending on it greatly reduce its value.

TARIFFS, PREFERENCES AND NTBs

The typical African pattern (see Tables 2.4 and 2.8) is to face low tariffs on exports to the industrial countries, because of negligible duties on primary goods and preferences on most manufactures, and relatively high tariffs in the regional market. African countries also (if they receive Lomé access to the EC) face low NTBs into their principal industrial country market. This helps to explain the low share of regional trade in their exports. Zimbabwe differs from this in some respects. The tariffs and barriers which it faces in the US and the EC are significant on some primary products, while it has special arrangements with its major African trading partners which improve its access to them. Even at the aggregate level, the tariffs which it faces in industrial markets appear in Table 2.8 as above-average, while Table 11.5 shows that the low NTBs which it faces overall (if the EC figures for manufactures are ignored because of ACP privileges) hide some high ones.

The principal export, tobacco, does not face high tariffs, but does face high, variable, and potentially rising excise duties in most markets. The effect of the EC Single Market, for example, has been an upward harmonisation of duties. In Japan, it faces a state monopoly purchaser. In 1993, the USA introduced high local-content rules on US cigarettes. It is therefore a commodity in which external policy decisions are very important (and in recent periods have been damaging).

Tariffs are not high for most of Zimbabwe's metal exports, and preferences have given it a useful advantage in industrial country markets over the other major suppliers, including South Africa and Russia, although not all the ferro-alloys obtain GSP treatment from the US (one was added in 1993).

Zimbabwe does receive the usual ACP preferences in entering the EC, and GSP for the US and Japan, but its exports make it vulnerable to other controls. Its major manufactured export to the US is clothing which does not receive GSP treatment. This explains the high tariffs it encounters there. Although it does not face tariffs or controls on clothing or textiles into the EC, giving it a strong advantage over non-ACP developing countries, in order to obtain this access it must meet the rules of origin. Given the type of simple clothing which it produces, this normally means using either EC cloth or cloth which has gone through all stages from finishing upward in Zimbabwe. Companies claim that importers prefer clothing with such a certificate of origin even if the price is higher than the price plus duty chargeable if using imported cloth. In contrast, for the US market, where there is no duty advantage to local origin, they use imported cloth. This has resulted in specialisation of companies in one or other of the two markets, reinforcing the differences imposed by the US–EC contrast in degree of diversity and size of market. Zimbabwe's freedom from quotas appears to be a major advantage in both markets (a clear piece of evidence given by one textile exporter was that orders tended to be higher at the end of the year, as importers found other countries' quotas exhausted). Textile exports to the US began to exceed those to the EC in the late 1980s (Riddell, 1990: 45).

The initiative for moving into these markets appears to have come more from importers seeking new supplies or from the recession in the Zimbabwean (or other African) markets than from Zimbabwean exporters

Table 11.5 Zimbabwe: non-tariff barriers (percentages 1986 weights on 1990 data)

SITC	Commodity	EC	US	Japan	Total[a]	Total[b]
0+1+22+4	All food items	20	39	50	12	13
0	Food + live animals	58	64	9	26	
051	Fresh fruit and nuts	97	100	0	82	
061	Sugar and honey	100	100	0	67	
121	Tobacco	0	0	100	1	
22	Oilseeds	100	100	0	99	
2 less (22+27+28)	Agricultural raw materials	3	0	0	2	2
27+28+67+68	Ores and metals	30	0	0	22	16
67	Iron and steel	54	0	0	29	
68	Non-ferrous	8	0	0	8	
6–8 less (67+68)	Manufactures, not chemicals	17	0	0	10	10
65	Textiles, yarn and fabric	22	0	0	10	
84	Clothing	50	0	0	33	
0–9	All items	20	10	2	11	11

Notes:
[a] Totals and subtotals found by applying 1986 importer weights to 1990 totals and subtotals
[b] Totals and subtotals found by applying 1986 importer weights to each commodity, and summing the commodities

Source: Calculated from UNCTAD database

seeking to exploit the preferences or expand their sales. It was only more recently that some altered their production to promote such exports. Europe remains the industrial market of choice partly because of these privileges but also because the companies have European ties (and existing contacts) (Riddell, 1990).

Although, as a small country, Zimbabwe would be expected to be vulnerable to the difficulties created by the rules of origin of preference schemes, these have not yet proved a major barrier to using preferences because Zimbabwe has tended to fill gaps (small orders, end-of-year non-quota supplies, etc.) rather than attempting to secure and maintain a major role as a low-cost supplier. But it also has the advantage over other small countries of its initially integrated industrialisation because of sanctions. If it becomes more specialised through either macroeconomic policy (the adjustment policies) or the nature of the industrialisation process (the recent moves by clothing and shoes to external suppliers), rules of origin could become more of an obstacle.

Its traditional food exports, beef and sugar, have preferential, but quota-limited, access to the EC market (on these, the barriers shown in Table 11.5 are real). Until recently this gave sufficient access for the Zimbabwean level of production (in part because of special use of others' unmet beef quotas and transitional extra quotas on sugar for Portugal), and in 1991–2 drought conditions meant that it could not meet its own quotas. Under normal growing conditions and current trends, these will shortly become barriers. The US also controls sugar imports.

The horticultural industry benefits greatly from freedom from the controls and high tariffs on non-ACP exporters (tariffs would be 15–20% for flowers and fruits and vegetables), although there are some seasonal barriers into the EC. As in textiles and clothing, the initiative on new products in the mid-1980s appears to have come from buyers seeking a new source and unrestricted suppliers, but a Zimbabwean industry, with its own initiatives and plans to diversify to defend itself from any losses of preferences, has emerged. (It is attempting to diversify the type of flower.)

Shoes do gain on tariffs under GSP and Lomé (but in the EC only against a low MFN tariff of 5%), and in the EC from immunity to the threat of the controls which have been imposed on some non-ACP suppliers. The gain would be greater into the US or Japanese markets, with their higher tariffs (Table 2.3), but the manufacturers involved in exporting (one is a foreign company) both have European links, and prefer that market. These companies also make, from the opposite perspective, the point made in Colombia that the EC is more interested in small runs, and is therefore suitable for a small supplier. The choice, however, does suggest that preferences are seen more as support than as a reason for actively choosing among markets. All three major industrial markets show higher tariffs for more processed over less processed leather products. Consistent with this, Zimbabwe's exports began in the early 1980s with hides and wet-blue leather (Riddell, 1990). Shoe exports were initially only by a foreign investor to the immediate region (treated almost as an extension of the local market). Shoe exports have now also begun to Europe and by producers who originally considered the quality and other barriers insuperable. This trade remains difficult, and hide and leather exports remain important.

In Africa, Zimbabwe has special arrangements with South Africa and Botswana, and in the early 1990s was negotiating access with other countries, including Malawi, and it has been the most enthusiastic member of the PTA. The obstacles to regional trade have thus been lowered. With South Africa, the agreement dates from 1964, and was originally negotiated to avoid other countries' sanctions on Zimbabwe. Its agricultural products enter South Africa without duty, and there are preferential rates for its manufactures. When these were suspended for clothing in 1992, this was seen as a major blow to the industry, and was taken seriously by the government as damaging to the country. It took action to persuade South Africa to remove the temporary duty and attempted to accelerate renegotiating the original agreement.

Other African countries are seen more as an extension of the local market than as 'exports' with different products and conditions of marketing. This makes such trade more like the regional trade found among Latin American countries than that among Asian. Zimbabwe is the most advanced country in the PTA in manufactures production and trade, and exports clothing and some finished machinery, particularly agricultural, as well as metals and chemicals, a pattern very different from the aggregates seen in Table 11.1. The exemption from some administrative requirements is seen (as in its Lomé trade with the EC) as being an advantage additional to the tariff preferences. It is competing less with other PTA countries (or local suppliers) than with external suppliers, including South Africa. If South Africa is admitted to these arrangements, Zimbabwe will lose its preference over what is probably its most important potential competitor. Both industry and government again regard such a loss of preference as perhaps having a cost, but as not seriously damaging or to be opposed. This is in part because of confidence in Zimbabwe's competitiveness (evidence on South African labour costs and high level of protection would support this, Page and Stevens, 1992), but like the lack of strong opposition to other losses of preference, the attitude appears also to be based on the assumption that the loss is inevitable and therefore any cost must simply be accepted as normal adjustment to new conditions. Some suppliers are starting to see favourable results from import liberalisation in other African countries (and the high levels of tariffs and foreign-exchange controls in many of these suggest important potential advantages) so that the share of regional exports may continue to rise.

Any interest by the government or by Zimbabwean industry in preferential access is new. Until the late 1980s, and even the first consideration of liberalisation in 1990–1, there was little awareness of external barriers or preferences. The history of sanctions preventing trade, followed by the explosive growth of domestic demand in the early 1980s, had discouraged interest in exporting. The new exports, however, notably clothing and horticultural goods, are goods which face high MFN duties. Tariffs and changes in them are therefore important. Zimbabwe thus began to take an interest in existing and new bilateral agreements, and also in multilateral negotiations. It is expected to gain overall from the Uruguay Round because of eventual diversification into new markets, particularly in Asia (its trade there is already higher than the average for African countries, Table 11.4), although both the government and individual exporters expect that the GATT settlement will mean loss of preferences on present exports and markets because of the general reduction in tariffs and NTBs on clothing and horticultural products. This loss, however, did not create as much concern or pressure against a settlement as might have been expected. Both in 1990 (Riddell, 1990: 45) and 1993, there was a clear assumption among exporters and officials that any Lomé or general privileges were temporary.

The imposition of sanctions on Rhodesia from 1965 to 1980 was a major influence on how the economy developed, creating a diversified, largely autarkic system. The types of barriers faced since have not had such fundamental effects. Domestic demand and other, non-trade, economic policies have been much stronger influences on companies, but also there is a general distrust of depending on policy. Zimbabwe has not actively moved into sectors because of external trade barriers or preferences. The shift into higher and different exports which occurred hesitantly from about 1986–7 and strongly from 1990 across a variety of sectors, cannot be linked to any external change. It has, however, been influenced by external policies in the direction of trade or the type of product within sectors. It has traded much more with its region than have those African countries which lack its special access arrangements or which have a set of exports facing less protection in external markets. Agricultural producers, in particular the tobacco exporters, have moved out of a product facing increasingly negative intervention in market countries, as well as local controls, into products which receive particularly favourable preference arrangements. Most manufactures producers have looked principally to the EC and African markets, in which they have preferences, although some have benefited from demand in the US. This stems from Zimbabwe's advantage over other suppliers of freedom from quotas. As in Colombia, therefore, external preferences appear to have influenced aspects of Zimbabwe's industrialisation, but not its fundamental directions.

STANDARDS AND REGULATIONS

More Zimbabwean exporters than Malaysian or Thai complain about NTBs in the form of special labelling or inspection requirements, etc., in the industrial country markets, but as in Colombia this appears to reflect lack of experience and perhaps also the smaller importance of exports in total sales rather than higher barriers. The companies which export often enough or in sufficient quantity to become familiar with these requirements do not find them difficult to meet. (One agricultural equipment exporter was facing pre-shipment inspection on its inputs, because of Zimbabwean regulations, and on most of its exports, because its other African markets required it, and did not find either a problem, but less experienced Zimbabwean producers or officials complained.) The labelling requirements for clothing and textiles which were quoted as problems were not different from those faced by other suppliers. For small producers, with largely domestic sales, such requirements clearly represent an additional deterrent to starting to export or to diversifying to new export markets. It is possible that such factors help to explain why, once exports did start to increase (i.e. once the barrier had been overcome), further increases in share came rapidly. They can also explain the concentration of trading on experienced traders, even if they move into different products.

The problems of Zimbabwe's productive and trading infrastructure were seen as barriers to both imports and exports, and they were clearly worse than in the Asian countries, although the contrast with Colombia was not so great. In the immediate period of study, 1992–3, the rationing of electricity was a major obstacle to production. Transport was a problem, with any surface transport to non-African markets needing to go through countries which had been either unstable or unfriendly during most of the 1980s (South Africa, Mozambique), and with only limited air links. The improvement in both of these which had already occurred or could be expected with some confidence in the 1990s may have helped to encourage exports. The greater frequency and reliability of flights was particularly important to all the new exports (clothing as well as horticultural exports used them). The use of air freight remains a limit on which products and markets can be seriously considered.

COUNTERTRADE, TIED AID, AND FOREIGN INVESTORS

In the mid-1980s, Zimbabwe saw countertrade as a way of increasing national and government control of trade, and also of permitting trade with countries which also faced foreign-exchange controls and which were therefore more likely to favour obviously balanced trade. As indicated in Chapter 4, it was an obvious choice for a controlled economy and an inexperienced exporter. But Zimbabwe also had a higher than usual share of its counter-

Table 11.6 Zimbabwe countertrade

	Exports	Imports
Product analysis		
Value ($m)	133	
Average value	5	
Apparent share of exports	3	
Product group observations (%)		
Agriculture, forestry and food products	56.1	13.3
Ores, minerals and metals	31.5	4.8
Crude oil, gas and related products	0.0	0.0
Vehicles, transport equipment and military equipment	1.8	19.0
Manufacturing/processing equipment and construction projects	0.0	15.2
Miscellaneous manufactured products	8.8	46.7
Services and miscellaneous	1.8	1.0
Total	100	100
Major product sub-group observations		
Tobacco	36.8	
Cereals	10.5	4.8
Road vehicles and parts		10.5
Iron and steel		2.8
Yearly data – number of deals: total 53		
1980 0		
1981 1		
1982 0		
1983 2		
1984 7		
1985 11		
1986 15		
1987 5		
Shares by market (%)		
Industrial	23	
Other developing	39	
Centrally planned	38	

Source: Jones and Jagoe, 1988

trade deals with the centrally planned economies (Table 11.6), about 40%, compared with the average for African countries of under 30%. Zimbabwe data (quoted in Riddell, 1992) suggest that the total value in the 1980s was much greater than indicated in Table 11.6, because it reached its peak relatively late, with 13% of exports in 1987, although it then declined rapidly to 7% in 1988.

By 1991, when the programme to reduce foreign-exchange controls and encourage exports was under way, the government was discouraging it (and requiring a cash share of at least 50% in any deal). Initially, the new export

Table 11.7　Zimbabwe multilateral and untied aid ($m or percentages)

Zimbabwe	1980	1985	1990
Ratio of aid to imports (%)	11.33	22.99	16.01
Multi	47	26	36
Multi-EC	37	22	24
Bilateral	112	214	296
Untied bilateral	60	74	164
Total untied	97	96	188
Tied/imports (%)	4.63	13.69	7.15

Note: The average tied ratio for all bilateral aid is assumed for all areas

Sources: OECD, *Development Co-operation* and *Geographical Distribution of Financial Flows to Developing Countries*, annual issues

retention scheme did require exporters to use any retentions for their own imports, which could be considered a variant of countertrade, but the imports then themselves became transferable.

Countertrade was not used to promote the new exports: tobacco (on both Table 11.6 and Zimbabwe data) was the most important export involved, with cereals and ferro-chrome the other important products. It may have had an effect on the direction of Zimbabwe's trade, and in giving the country some experience in bargaining rather than passively accepting international orders. But as tobacco is a readily marketable commodity it is unlikely that countertrade had a strong effect in changing the composition of Zimbabwe's trade, either exports or imports.

As one of the poorest countries in this study, Zimbabwe remains one of those with a high share of its imports financed by aid (Table 11.7). Tied aid, with its specific difficulties, has probably been reduced in recent years. Its problems were identified as higher prices (particularly on some primary commodities) and difficulties in replacing or repairing existing machinery (if the available line of credit was from a different donor). There were also general delays and administrative difficulties in obtaining finance. As donors have increasingly put money into the funding of open licence imports rather than particular projects, and some have also reduced national tying, both types of problem have been reduced. The principal regular donors, other than the multilateral organisations, have been Germany, Sweden, Norway, the Netherlands, Japan and the UK. As Japanese aid is untied (available for imports from the OECD or any developing country), this does not explain Zimbabwe's high trade with Japan.

Tied aid has also affected Zimbabwe's exports. Some of its food and agricultural and transport equipment exports are financed by other countries' income from aid. Exporters have found this a problem in meeting some quality standards, and also in variability. Withdrawal of aid (for example, for political reasons from Malawi and Kenya) had an immediate effect on orders to Zimbabwe in 1991–2.

Probably more important in external effects on trade than these direction-of-trade effects has been the leverage which the high share of aid in total national resources has given to multinational institutions' consistent pressure towards greater freeing of imports and more incentives for exporters. This move to emphasising a particular set of policies for the external sector was a major shift in the international environment of aid recipients in the 1980s. Unlike the other countries considered so far, Zimbabwe was (and remains) dependent on this flow. The 1990 change in development strategy may therefore be considered a response to external controls, as the earlier one, in 1964, was the result of sanctions.

But as with multilateral policies which promote individual sectors, the effect of institutions' policies on trading partners or competitors which were also recipients needs to be considered. Trade with other African countries has become easier as they have reduced controls on foreign exchange or imports. This reduces the incentive to switch to industrial country markets, and thus discourages Zimbabwe and other countries exporting to aid-dependent markets from following the NIC pattern of trade.

A final major effect of the combination of tied aid, pressure from donors, and the impact of both on trading partners, is to reinforce the perception that most trade is heavily influenced by external, and politically variable, policies.

Foreign investment has not been a major source of funds for Zimbabwe during this period, and in general foreign-owned firms have not been important in the new exports, at least outside Africa. Some existing foreign investors, however, with a Zimbabwean market, were among the early exporters to other African countries (in shoes, textiles and agricultural implements). In other industries, like clothing, where personal contacts and continuing relationships are important, some of the companies have, or started with, immigrant owners. The foreign role, however, was not a direct influence on exports in the sense used in analysing intra-firm trade or the investment-for-export industries of Malaysia and Thailand (although some of the foreign investors appear to have entered Zimbabwe with the intention of using it as a base for producing for the region). Instead, some of the new products have been financed by successful exporters from the old industries.

CONCLUSIONS

For Zimbabwe, in spite of its low share of controlled exports on some of the standard measures used here, a high proportion of its trade, both imports and exports, must be perceived by officials and producers as subject to direct external official intervention. Its major export, tobacco, faces excise duties and changing health controls. Its other traditional exports, maize, sugar, and beef, are subject to the usual interventions in the agricultural market. Its new exports, (clothing, textiles, shoes, horticultural products) face quotas in some markets or benefit from exemption from the quotas on other exports. Even the relatively uncontrolled, and low-tariff, metals have benefited from preferences favouring Zimbabwe over South Africa. It has received, by inheritance or gift, not negotiation, special preferences in both its regional and its industrial country markets, limited by the various rules-of-origin conditions influencing how goods are produced. Its relations with its own donors and its location among other aid recipients have given aid finance a role in restricting choice of products or trading partners similar to that which may result from direct investment in the more advanced countries (but with a higher level of policy, rather than economic, orientation, as discussed in Chapters 6–7), while its own international economic policy has been effectively determined first by sanctions, then by the policies of its aid donors.

From the point of view of producers and exporters, all this 'politicisation', with the vulnerability to changes in policy adding to any problems of the controls themselves, is doubled by the parallel set of national controls. The latter, at least until the 1990s, were more like foreign controls than interventions in Malaysia or Thailand would be because of the lack of sympathy and the limited contact between industry and government. (This last characteristic was also found in Colombia.)

It is possible, although difficult to prove, that the negative view of intervention by their own governments as inevitably arbitrary, delaying and inefficient, if not actively unfavourable, is one reason for Colombian and Zimbabwean lack of interest in pursuing or relying on even beneficial foreign preferences. The increase in exports and the relative welcome for the export and import liberalising programme in Zimbabwe came when a new, less mutually antagonistic, generation of officials and managers emerged in official agencies, industrial organisations, and companies to replace the immediate post-independence ones. The discontinuity should not, however, be exaggerated. The same companies and organisations remain important. The distrust is clearly of controls and preferences as a system, not of individuals.

The combination of the pre-independence government's need to control the economy in the face of sanctions and the lack of foreign finance for new enterprise has encouraged large, often conglomerate, companies. Although not well-placed to respond instantly to new opportunities (in the ways which will be seen by new companies in Mauritius and Jamaica), they are (and believe they are) capable of eventually meeting any changes in Zimbabwean or external policy. This again may contribute to an apparent indifference to policies.

Although Zimbabwe has a much smaller domestic market than Colombia, and potentially more need to trade, at its present level of development it can still also make some choices in whether to export. This is particularly true with the cushion of the regional market. But this attitude, and the relative backwardness of that regional market, mean that, as in Latin America, the regional market is playing a very different role, as an easier market than the 'real' international one, from that which the Asian has for Malaysia or Thailand. There, it is an advanced market, and only 'easy' because it is growing and changing rapidly, and therefore open to new, not to traditional, exports. The African region is therefore not the same stimulus to manufacturing and development, even if it does permit individual industries to expand.

The strong influences from domestic policy and from the aggregate external intervention of first sanctions and then donors have meant that the effects of particular, sectoral controls at the international level have been less important for the pattern of Zimbabwe's development. Exporters' response in adapting products or markets shows that, once they are aware of the opportunities or problems, and if they have sufficient incentive to enter new markets, they can respond.

NOTES

1 Sales figures are not available beyond 1990; detailed export data are not available in 1990 so 1991 data are used.
2 Ndlela and Robinson (1992) estimated clothing exports at about 22% of production.
3 The data for their exports from the industry and from the official sources shown in the table are very different in value (the industry suggests that they are now 2% of total exports), but the pattern of increase is the same.

12

MAURITIUS

AN ECONOMY CREATED BY TRADE POLICY

In contrast to the four countries discussed so far, where trade restrictions were either an element in formulating trade strategies or a recently perceived obstacle, in Mauritius and Jamaica they are a dominant feature of discussion and strategy for exporters and officials, and in Bangladesh, for exporters. The contrast in awareness of current issues and negotiations and information about the country's own position is striking. Of the three, the Mauritian economy and its development are the most completely tied to the past and present trade policies of the major industrial countries.

This overall position needs to be understood as background to the detailed discussion. It emerges clearly from Table 7.1. that Mauritius has the lowest share of trade with other developing countries and the highest share controlled by NTBs. Although it is formally exempt from some of the NTBs with the EC because of its inclusion among the ACP countries, this trade has, as will be seen, itself developed precisely because of the exemption (and it has not in fact always been exempt). Its principal primary export is sugar, one of the most controlled goods in world trade. On the capital side, it has a relatively high share of foreign investment in the economy (with a strong influence on trade), and a still high share in aid compared with the other relatively advanced countries.

Its traditional and its present major exports were both started by outside interests in the context of strong trade preferences, although they may now have acquired domestic economic roots. Sugar was brought to Mauritius by British policy, to supply India under a regime of colonial preference. The clothing industry was originally brought by Japanese and Hong Kong investors to supply markets which quotas had closed to their own exports. The growing service export, tourism, is influenced by the fact that its neighbour, Réunion, is legally part of a member country of the EC (with consequences for regulation of the air industry).

But there is, on the other side, a long tradition of local entrepreneurship in association with foreign investors and of local attempts to modify or exploit the preferences and controls. The sugar plantations and some of the clothing factories eventually became locally owned. The Chamber of Commerce dates from 1850. Mauritius is the only ACP country with its own private sector representative office in Brussels. These phenomena were responses to domination by external policy, but they must now be considered as possible counterweights to it.

OUTPUT AND TRADE

Until 1990 Mauritius was regarded as a clear success in economic development, but the combination of slowing growth and risks to its current major products now makes it necessary to question whether it in fact established a foundation and a path for sustained development. Between 1975 and 1990, it became a middle-income country (on the level of Malaysia or Thailand), in spite of the handicap of small size (a population of little over a million) and geographical isolation from both the industrial countries and the Asian NICs, and also from Africa, of which it is conventionally treated as a part. The mixed location is paralleled by a split population, European, Indian, Chinese, and African, with some similarities to Malaysia in terms of professional differentiation among these. In a much smaller group, the possible problems caused by the resulting reduced labour mobility may be greater. The population growth rate has fallen to under 1%. The level of education is high. Mauritius has experienced periods of strong growth, up to 8% in the period 1985–7, and structural transformation, with manufacturing rising from 16% of GDP in 1982 (the same level it had reached in 1970) to the present level of about a quarter.

But these changes were largely complete by 1988–9, just when the country began to be perceived as a success and potential example for others. Since 1988, the share of manufacturing has scarcely changed; the growth rate has fallen to 5–6% for GDP, and 6–7% for manufacturing; and the target for the 1992–4 Plan is 6% for total output, and 8–8.5% for industrial output (McQueen, 1990; MEDIA, n.d.; MEDP, 1993). These rates are accepted as appropriate (the Asian pattern of more rapid growth and change is explicitly rejected by policy-makers). The slowdown since 1988, however, was not a smooth transition to a different path. As the analysis of individual firms and exports will indicate, there were closures and cuts in output and employment. There was an abrupt switch from importing labour or setting up subsidiaries in foreign countries to meet demand to using these subsidiaries to compete with alternative and cheaper sources. The acceptance of slower growth is combined with a belief that even the new target requires that new products or markets be found. The Plan (MEDP, 1993, vol. 1: 137) accepts that 'The manufacturing sector has reached a turning point as new constraints have emerged'.

As indicated by the low share of manufacturing in output until the 1970s, most manufacturing industries and most companies are at most 20 years old, with a substantial number dating from the early or mid-1980s. Prior to that time there had been only a minor amount of first-stage import substitution in light industry, constrained by the size of the market. In the early 1970s, several foreign investors brought in clothing production, and in the period after 1982 these and additional foreign investors rapidly built it up. The number rose from fifteen in place before 1977 to over 100 by 1990, with the largest increase in 1986–8, immediately before the production plateau (Fowdar, 1992). This rapid creation of a substantial clothing production and exporting sector was not in itself unusual, although some external analysts presented it as evidence of Mauritius' success: the same process was seen for clothing in Thailand and for other exports in Malaysia, and will be seen, at precisely the same period, in Jamaica and Bangladesh. Where Mauritius is, up to now, unusual in this group is in the equally rapid withdrawal: more than half these new foreign entrants closed in the following three years (along with a large number of Mauritian producers), either completely or by moving to other production sites (MEDIA, 1988 compared with MEDIA 1992; Fowdar, 1992). A few electrical and electronics firms in Malaysia followed a similar pattern of opening in 1982–3 and closing by 1984–5 when there was a severe fall in demand for electronic parts for computers, but this was a smaller proportion of the Malaysian economy and of foreign investors.

Like the Asian countries, Mauritius saw a rapid rise in exports of manufactures until 1990 (with real rises of 30–40% a year in 1986–8, slowing to around 10%, McQueen 1990: 15). The value-added component of these exports was only 4.5% of GDP in 1982, but had risen to 13% by 1987–8. This was the peak, and by 1992 it had declined slightly to 12% (MIIT, 1993). The pattern for clothing's share in total manufacturing was similar, rising from 30% to a peak of 55%, and falling back marginally after 1989. In 1991 and 1992, the rises in export value of 6% and 8% suggest little change in volume. Initially, the stagnation of clothing exports was blamed on a variety of special factors: the recession, the effect of warmer winters on demand for woollen knitwear, fashion changes, but firms are now looking at more fundamental explanations; the emergence of new suppliers (notably China and other Asian countries) and rising Mauritian prices. The Plan expects a rise of 10% p.a. in value, and thus a recovery, although not to the Asian NIC level. Under present policies, sugar exports will change little in price or volume, but in the medium term the GATT agricultural settlement will reduce the guaranteed price. Mauritius has normally had a current deficit, covered by inflows of private and official capital. If any one of the growth exports, foreign investment, or aid slows, some form of adjustment will be necessary.

Tables 12.1 and 12.2 show the shift from virtually complete dependence on agricultural exports (almost entirely sugar) in 1970 to manufactures (still mainly clothing). As recently as 1984 sugar was still 50% of the total; it is now under 30%, while clothing has passed 50%. Much of the manufactured export sector is based on imported raw materials, but even if only the value added is included, clothing is now at least as important as sugar. Although dependent now on two exports rather than one, Mauritius' concentration remains high. The other goods which are mentioned as present or potential exports are very minor, and did not grow to replace clothing as that reached its plateau.

Mauritius is now a significant supplier at world level of clothing as well as sugar, the third supplier of woollen garments (McQueen, 1990), with over half the EC market in some garments, and the only significant ACP supplier of clothing to the EC. The EC is its principal market, for both manufactures and sugar (Table 12.3). For sugar, the UK has been its major market, taking over 80% of its exports, throughout this period (the quota system is discussed below), with the USA the only other important market in value terms. This explains the high share for the UK in Mauritius' total exports. For manufactures, however, the EC declined temporarily in favour of the USA during the peak period of exporting; it revived subsequently. The section on NTBs will discuss their contribution to this pattern, but the fall in the share to the USA came at the time of a fall in the utilisation rate of quotas, not a tightening.

Over the period as a whole, France has remained the most important market, while there appears to have been over the 1980s a shift from the UK to the USA. France has been the principal market for woollen products, while the USA and the UK both take cotton products, and in general those which compete mainly on price. The division between the EC and US markets appears within Mauritius in the form of companies specialised almost entirely in one market or the other, and therefore in wool or cotton. This makes the effective vulnerability of each sector even greater. The rise then decline in the US market thus explains what might seem a disproportionate response to the rise and fall in exports in the 1980s in terms of company openings and closures. On the whole, it is the firms which are mainly foreign-owned which have concentrated on the US market (particularly those which arrived in the early 1980s), while the Mauritian and some of the older foreign firms were focused on the EC.

TARIFFS, PREFERENCES, AND BARRIERS

Most of Mauritius' agricultural trade takes place in a controlled market; its few non-sugar exports enter the EC on preferential terms. All its manufactured exports are on preferential or controlled terms. (The Chamber of Commerce, 1993: 36, estimates 97% of the total was on such terms in 1991.) Its dependence on sugar, its small share of trade with developing countries outside its region, and its membership of the PTA make the preferential share high even by developing country standards. The official policy since

Table 12.1 Mauritius: export structure by principal commodities

Commodity	SITC/CTCI	1970	1975	1980	1985	1990
Total value (US$m)		67.5	294.6	420.3	434.6	1,180.5
				percentages		
All food items	0+1+22+44	93.1	88.4	72.5	49.8	31.1
Manufactured goods of which:	5 to 8 less 68	1.8	11.5	27.4	49.7	68.1
Other manufactured goods	(6+8) less 68	1.6	7.7	24.0	48.6	65.1
Machinery and equipment	7	0.1	3.5	2.8	1.2	2.7

Source: UNCTAD, *Handbook*, 1992

Table 12.2 Mauritius: principal exports 1976–91 (percentages)

Product	1976	1980	1984	1985	1988	1990	1991
Sugar	72	66	50	44	34	30	29
Clothing			31	39	49	51	52
Textiles			2	1	1	3	3
Watches and clocks			2	2	4	3	3
Jewellery			3	3	3	3	3
Fish			2	2	1	1	2
Toys			1	1	1	1	1

Sources: MEDIA, 1988, 1992, Bank of Mauritius, 1993

independence (in 1968) has been to join trading (and other regional) groups, and press for preferences. Official statements and observations in interviews stress the importance of formal and informal contacts and agreements, and the expectation that these will imply a commitment to continuing support. A similar attitude is found in the reliance on foreign investors (or in their absence, on agents) as the entry point into export markets. This is an attitude seen in some individual cases or industries in the other countries studied (particularly, as noted before, in clothing) but it is pervasive in Mauritius. Although a former British colony, it sought and obtained the same associate status as the original ex-French colonies with the EC from 1972, using its francophone and African organisation contacts. It is a member of the PTA (which takes effectively all its developing country trade) and there is now an Indian Ocean Commission (with Réunion, Madagascar, the Comoros and Seychelles).[1]

The sugar exports to both the USA and the EC take place with quotas and guaranteed prices above the world market price (by margins of up to 200%). The EC quota at 487,200 tonnes (from a production fluctuating around 600,000 tonnes) now normally takes about 80% of exports, with the USA very much smaller at 15,000 tonnes. The National Development Plan emphasises the need to maintain production (the 1991–2 figures were affected by drought) in order to continue filling, and therefore receiving, the quotas, and Mauritius hopes also to obtain additional quotas taken from other producers. Until the recent rise in clothing exports, sugar was its basic source of export revenue and also of investment funding for other sectors. Sugar producers have provided the Mauritian partners for some of the clothing joint ventures, and are also important in the hotel industry for the new tourist industry. There have also been limited moves into specialty sugars and sugar products, but these are small in value terms.

As an exporter of clothing, Mauritius faces particularly high tariffs in the US market (Table 2.8). US tariffs on woollen clothing are even higher than on cotton (Table 2.3: up to 30–40%, compared with 20%), and clothing and

Table 12.3 Mauritius: export markets 1980–91 (percentages)

Region/country	1980	1983	1984	1986	1987	1988	1989	1990	1991
EPZ exports									
US	12	14	24	27	25	21	21	18	17
EC	84	80	69	68	71	75	74	76	77
France	25	32	27	33	36	34	30	33	29
UK	25	17	16	10	11	13	15	17	17
Germany	14	12	12	13	14	15	13	13	16
Total exports									
US				16	15	13	14	13	12
EC				75	77	77	75	80	80
France				24	26	25	20	23	20
UK				37	35	36	36	36	36
Germany				7	8	10	9	9	11
South Africa				0	0.5	0.5	0.5	0.5	0.4
Malagasy Republic				0	0	0.2	0.3	0.7	0.6

Sources: McQueen, 1990; Bank of Mauritius, 1993; IMF, *Direction of Trade Statistics*

textiles are excluded from the US GSP. In the EC market, Mauritius pays no tariffs, giving it a preference of about 10–14% on clothing there, and is entitled to even higher rates of preference on goods like flowers or fish (17–24%) (McQueen, 1990: 25). Its exemption from quotas under the MFA in the EC (and until the early 1980s also in the US) is, however, much more important to exporters than the price advantage (Fowdar, 1992; McQueen, 1990; and interviews for this book all support this view). It is this which gives Mauritius its advantage over other developing countries which (under GSP) share the tariff preference in the EC and the lack of it in the US. Preferences cannot, however, explain its better performance than other ACP countries. Table 12.4 shows the importance of quotas on all its exports in all markets.

The EC exemptions are guaranteed for the duration of each Lomé agreement, and implicitly beyond, and are regarded in Mauritius as permanent.[2] The US free access proved to be temporary, with quotas imposed from 1984 and reaching their current coverage (of more than 30 principal cotton clothing and some textile exports) by 1988. Although this is similar to Colombia's position, with a fairly certain guarantee of preference to the US and a shorter-term, more uncertain arrangement with the EC, the reactions of Colombia and Mauritius have been very different. In 1989–90, most of Mauritius' US quotas were fully utilised, because its exports had increased rapidly even in response to a temporary opportunity. Quotas were therefore an important constraint on exports. It was then that the inflow of investment and build-up of production for export to the US diminished, and the shift in the share of exports to the EC could be observed.

Since 1990, however, and particularly in 1991–2, the utilisation rate of US quotas has fallen to such a point that the method of allocation has been relaxed on some products. The normal method had been to give 90% to existing exporters, provided that they had used at least 90% of their allocation in the preceding year. If they had not, they received a correspondingly reduced allocation, and those who had used less than half were not entitled to any of the allocation. The remaining 10% plus reallocations were available to new exporters on the basis of the orders they received. (No direct transfer of quotas was permitted.) The system appears to have worked effectively for the (very short) period during which quotas were in force and fully utilised. The government had and made available full information on its own allocations, Mauritian utilisation, and (to indicate opportunities and growing markets) products in which other exporting countries were approaching full utilisation of their quotas. There was thus an active policy of exploiting opportunities both from the Mauritian quotas and from those imposed on others.

For those goods which are now substantially below quota, there is no initial allocation, and quotas are freely available unless the monitoring system indicates during the year that they may be filled. The continuing fall

Table 12.4 Mauritius: non-tariff barriers (percentages 1986 weights on 1990 data)

SITC	Product area	EC	US	Total[a]	Total[b]
0+1+22+4	All food items	93	78	91	91
0	Food + live animals	93	79	66	
061	Sugar and honey	100	65	96	
2 less (22 + 27 + 28)	Agricultural raw materials	83	0	83	83
27+28+67+68	Ores and metals	1	2	1	6
6–8 less (67 + 68)	Manufactures, not chemicals	50	19	44	38
65	Textiles, yarn and fabrics	21	0	9	
84	Clothing	50	19	42	
0–9	All items	71	26	63	58

Notes:
[a] Totals and subtotals found by applying 1986 importer weights to 1990 totals and subtotals
[b] Totals and subtotals found by applying 1986 importer weights to each commodity, and summing the commodities

Source: Calculated from UNCTAD database

in exports to the US and the departure of firms trading with that market suggest that, as some of the exporters reported, a change in competitiveness is important.

The EC freedom from quotas did not mean that the industry to supply the EC market developed as it would have done had it been to an unrestricted market. The question of whether it would have existed at all in the absence of EC restrictions on other suppliers is considered below, along with the same question for that supplying the US. Even as an EC clothing supplier, however, Mauritius was affected. The rules of origin, restricting the non-ACP and non-EC content, are particularly serious for a small country and for new industries. They effectively mean that no stage later than wool tops can come from outside the EC or ACP. The exporters of woollen garments have now reached a point where they can provide sufficient demand to justify setting up an integrated industry to supply them, with finishing and dyeing done within the country. Initially wool fabric was imported from the EC. When high costs made this uncompetitive, it was imported from Hong Kong, and the Lomé advantage was lost. For cotton, only clothes requiring considerable labour, not the simpler garments which are exported to the US, can meet the criteria. These provisions, combined with the US tariffs on woollens, are probably sufficient to explain the split by fibre and by market in the Mauritian industry. The experience with EC requirements means that it was the existing firms that built up exports to this market. The external firms came in explicitly because their quotas in the US market had been exhausted in other countries, and therefore to use Mauritius' freedom from quotas there. They had no incentive to learn and institute the procedures for exporting to the EC.

Other new or small industries face similar choices. The leather goods are based on using EC leather. Again, the industry view is that the preferences are essential. Here, the existence of contacts from previous joint ventures, in other goods, gave the initial stimulus to at least one of the leather products exporters. Thus, as in other countries, it is experienced local exporters, rather than producers of an existing similar product for the local market, who have joined foreign investors in finding new exports.

The present *de facto* freedom from quota in the US clothing market does not imply the end of the influence of US quotas. But it does mean that we can start to ask what the permanent effect of temporary preferences can be. It was the production to exploit Mauritius' exemption which increased employment and therefore wage costs to the point of uncompetitiveness. (The process is now being observed at an earlier stage in Bangladesh.) The question now is whether the experience, training, markets, and investment can be preserved and used to build further development, when the clothing industry leaves for a lower-cost supplier. This would be a variant of the traditional argument for preferences as a time-limited stimulus to an infant industry. It is particularly important for a small country like Mauritius where protection in the domestic market is not a feasible alternative to preference in an external market. In its simplest form, the test of success would be whether a clothing industry can survive even without the relative protection given by exemption from quotas or by more generous quotas (McQueen, 1990: 22). This goal does not seem to have been achieved, at least for the entire created industry. One foreign investor is moving into more expensive, less price-sensitive production, but some of the foreign investors which came in to use the exemption from quotas are leaving, to shift to cheaper countries: Bangladesh (although that may now have passed its peak), Jamaica, which has special conditions of access to both the EC and the USA, China and Vietnam are the most often mentioned. Some Mauritian firms are following their example, and transferring their simpler processes to Madagascar.

The fears about loss of preference suggest that the path of seeking and using preferences runs the same risk as more traditional forms of protection: of becoming a crutch for an infant industry instead of a stimulus. In particular, in 1993 the government showed concern about the outcome of the GATT Uruguay Round for sugar and for clothing, and more generally on MFN tariff levels in the markets where Mauritius receives GSP or Lomé terms. The economy's extreme dependence on preferences at every point in its foreign trade means that the government is probably justified in expecting at least a static loss from any settlement that liberalises trade or prices. The reduction in MFN tariffs reduced the Lomé advantage Mauritius has in the EC and its GSP advantage in the US, and new members of GATT (especially China) would mean that more countries enjoy MFN treatment.

On sugar, Mauritius expected the agricultural settlement to lower its guaranteed high price by 20% (with little change in volume, or even a possible fall); this would reduce total export revenue by 5–6%, and have a severe impact on government revenue as well as export income. As a food importer, it will also lose from the rise in other food prices. On clothing, the phasing out of the MFA will eventually eliminate its principal advantage in the EC market. An estimate has been quoted (MIIT, 1993, March) that EC imports of clothing from developing countries will more than double once the MFA is removed. Mauritius expects to lose substantially to other producers. The evidence that it is losing the US market must support this. It has lost its exports to Sweden since that country left the MFA, and has never exported to Japan.

That the clothing industry moved from minor importance to peak to decline in under 10 years might indicate that the ten-year MFA transition period will be sufficient for Mauritius to find and introduce a substitute. But the fundamental question is whether it has, or has derived from its past success and preferences, some advantage which will provide a substitute for that given by preferential access. Up to now, its comparative advantage in obtaining and exploiting preferences is the one on which all its previous successes (even in the minor exports) have been based. It is one which is now certain to be diminished, if not removed.

Most other trade initiatives of which it is not a member also cause Mauritius concern (and are followed closely). The EC–Eastern Europe arrangements could affect its relative position in the EC market, and in manufactures there is considerable potential competition: in clothing, simple scientific instruments and watch parts, and leather goods. NAFTA (and, although less important, the Caribbean and Andean arrangements of both the US and the EC) could lead to competition on clothing, and from Mexico potentially on sugar. The exception is the EC Single European Market initiative because Mauritius thinks (with justification) that it will be sufficiently alert to benefit, rather than lose, from common standards, harmonisation, etc., so that it expects its European-owned companies and its manufactured exports to the EC to gain.

The climate of uncertainty about the permanence of all existing present preferences means that all new trading opportunities and advantages from current quota- and tariff-free entry are seen as strictly temporary: the need to move on is accepted. The most interesting point, however, is that there is official awareness of all of these agreements and negotiations, and an informed view, which has clearly been widely circulated and discussed within and outside the government.[3]

A broader interpretation of the argument that preferences (or protection) give a permanent advantage would be that the workers and management of the companies had acquired skills, capital, or contacts which would be transferrable to other types of production and export. This has happened with sugar in the past, and there appears to have been a policy favouring it. It is now argued that the export income and profits from clothing should be used by the companies or their owners to finance the next products, and that the sugar industry, which has already financed clothing (and more recently hotels and other tourist services) should repeat this process. But this suggests only a passive role for the existing industries, in financing future development. It does not indicate what will determine the next export or promote it. In fact the role of one export industry in creating the next has been more active. One reason for the form which the export processing 'zone' took (of a concept, not a geographical area, see next section) was that it would permit more contact between it and local industry.[4] The small, closely-knit society of Mauritius should provide opportunity for transfers of knowledge as well as finance and experienced exporters.

From a company point of view, the same evidence which suggested that a clothing industry will not survive can support this broader interpretation of the long-term impact of preferences. The companies which are now investing in clothing factories abroad may have found a sustainable path. From a national point of view, the evidence is less clear. The data in Table 12.2 do not suggest any examples of new exports, and none was found which appeared to have the potential to reach the scale of sugar or clothing. Examination of how clothing and other foreign-owned firms have operated suggests some difficulties. In the Asian-owned clothing firms, and also in joint ventures in less traditional products like toys and leather goods, there seemed to be a rigid division between the local factory, which was expected simply to receive orders, execute them, and get them to the port or airport, and the foreign partner which took full responsibility for sales and marketing and also for strategic decisions like changes in basic product lines or relocation to other countries. In terms of the foreign-owned factories found in other countries, this is an extreme form of the Japanese style of multinational, rather than the more locally independent European or US style. For industries which see themselves as temporary, established to exploit a temporary policy or market, and then to move on, it is not unusual. (Similar firms were found in Bangladesh in clothing.) For those with longer traditions and for joint ventures, it seems unusual. Examples were found even among European immigrants who had originally arrived with external contacts and among Mauritian managers with wide international experience and in the same ethnic group as their foreign partner (the Chinese clothing firms), so it clearly does not imply a hesitancy to deal with unfamiliar foreign customs (in either sense of the word). It is consistent with the preference- and contact-seeking approach to trade policy. Whatever the explanation, it makes it less likely than in other countries with no such tradition that a new company will be able to acquire all the skills needed to develop as a substitute for the existing industries.

MAURITIAN TRADE POLICY

Mauritius imposed high average tariffs, and various additional payments and controls on imports, until the early 1980s. In 1980, its average tariff was 55%, more like the Latin American level than the other sub-Saharan African countries (Table 2.4), and the effective rate may have been substantially higher (McQueen, 1990: 71). Its external preference-seeking can therefore be seen as part of a general protective strategy. Since 1982, and more vigorously since 1986, it has liberalised its trade policy and devalued its currency. The EPZ firms, however, already enjoyed exemption from duties, and were mainly producing for export, so the effect on them may not have been important.

There were other policies directed at exports which need further examination to judge whether they supplement foreign preferences in explaining the Mauritian performance. The Export Processing Zone was created in 1970, among the first for developing countries. This was at the same time as Mauritius was seeking preferences from the EC. This suggests a coherent trade strategy. Although originally envisaged as a normal EPZ, a geographical zone, the zone was established instead as a set of regulations, privileges, and infrastructural services available in any location. This was a practical solution in view of the fact that there was no region which needed special development, and only a very small area or population into or from which unregulated transfers could be made. What is not clear is why the differentiation from the rest of a small island was made at all, or has persisted for more than 20 years. It appears (and this is certainly true of the more recent proposal for a 'free port') that it was thought to be more attractive to foreign investment because of the implied special treatment. Foreign investment did arrive, but this was not until 10–15 years later (Tables 6.11 and 6.14 indicate that it was in the mid-1980s that Mauritius began attracting a high level of investment.)

There is an efficient export promotion agency, MEDIA, but again this was established only in 1985, after the surge in exports had begun. It provides extensive services,[5] but some of the best date from 1988, after the peak in export growth.

By 1993, a further agency had been established to help existing exporters to restructure (the EPZ Development Authority): it is too early to know what its effect will be. It was set up to improve skills, quality, production times, etc. The current strategy thus appears to emphasise consolidation and improvement rather than a repetition of the rapid establishment of new exports.

The decline in Mauritius' current principal export and the risk that the preferences on which it has based its export strategy will be reduced or eliminated have brought two types of policy reaction, and some very different changes among exporting companies. Unlike Malaysia or Thailand (or Jamaica), there does not appear to be a general perception among exporters and officials that all preferences are going to disappear, and therefore that countries should concentrate on finding new advantages. The response among the more traditional official organisations to fears of policy changes is to lobby to preserve existing preferences or to seek new ones, on the grounds that the EC 'has a duty to Mauritius' because of past preferences, either to continue these preferences or to help it to adjust. This is a view more often heard from unsuccessful or non-adapting exporters, such as the traditional banana suppliers to the EC than from successful countries like Mauritius. It is argued that Mauritius should seek relationships with the newly preferred groups, including NAFTA. Another strand of official opinion is in favour of finding general ways of assisting production: the efficiency objectives of the EPZ Development Authority are in this line, along with other ways of improving competitiveness with other clothing producers. This approach accepts the argument that it is higher costs and poor delivery times which have cost Mauritius the US market. The problem with these policies is that they are available to all countries.

The final response of official and private policy is diversification into new products. Those suggested among goods are all familiar from other countries, and some have been repeatedly promoted without success in Mauritius: electronics products were first suggested in the 1970s, revived in the 1980s, and are still on the list. Watches and watch parts have been among the minor exports since the early 1970s, but have never advanced further; a few individual firms have been successful for special reasons, and are likely to remain so. Flowers and other horticultural products at present gain from tariff preferences but given the limited area (and erratic weather) Mauritius is unlikely to be able to compete on a large scale with the African mainland. Printing is one industry exploiting a specific advantage (the multilingual and well-educated society).

There are also some suggestions for services, including tourism (which is growing, but with the problem of distance and cost), or the offshore financial sector and free port proposals. The latter were based on a suggestion that Mauritius should offer its trade services to less developed African countries; they have now probably been overtaken by the expected reintegration of South Africa following its reforms; it has obvious advantages of location, size and existing services.

None of these possibilities can be dismissed as impracticable, but for each the problem remains of how to introduce it in a small economy without the initial assistance offered by either preferences or protection. It is this which makes the dependence of Mauritius on preferences such a worrying basis for future development.

AID AND INVESTMENT

As Table 12.5 shows, Mauritius' dependence on aid has fallen surprisingly little following its development, with no change since 1980. Then it was under pressure from the international financial institutions to adjust its policies. The dependence no longer seems to create the same type of pressures, however. One reason may be the substantial increase in inflows of foreign investment, which rose from 1% of total investment in the 1970s to 4% by the end of the 1980s. This was almost entirely the result of investment in clothing in the EPZ (Table 12.6). In 1990, investment in textiles and clothing fell by more than 30%, and collapsed to only a fifth of the 1989 figure by 1991 (Fowdar, 1992: 85). The National Development Plan expects investment to continue to rise, but with the EPZ taking a declining portion.

Foreign investment came originally in the 1970s because Mauritius was then one of the cheap labour countries, attracting Asian as well as European clothing producers even before quotas became an issue. It then expanded, particularly from Hong Kong in the early 1980s, to take advantage of the lack of quotas, and also because Hong Kong was becoming uncertain about its own long-term status. The European companies arrived in the 1970s because of the ACP advantages to clothing and the minor industries.

Table 12.5 Mauritius: multilateral and untied aid ($m or percentages)

Mauritius	1970	1975	1980	1985	1990
Ratio of aid to imports (%)	8.00	7.88	5.42	5.18	5.50
Multilateral	1	14	8	5	12
Multi-EC	1	12	7	3	4
Bilateral	5	15	25	22	76
Untied bilateral	1	4	13	8	42
Total untied	2	16	20	11	46
Tied/imports (%)	4.77	2.95	2.07	3.15	2.65

Note: The average tied ratio for all bilateral aid is assumed for all areas

Sources: OECD, *Development Co-operation* and *Geographical Distribution of Financial Flows to Developing Countries*, annual issues

Table 12.6 Mauritius: sources and allocation of foreign investment 1985–90

Shares by country – in EPZ	1985	1986	1987	1988	1989	1990	1985–90
China	0	0	0	9	2	5	3
Hong Kong	80	33	5	51	6	20	27
Taiwan	0	2	7	1	4	23	8
Singapore	1	0	0	0	2	0	1
France	9	6	4	6	11	21	11
Germany	0	5	0	1	17	1	5
UK	2	4	3	5	10	0	5
US	3	1	8	0	0	0	2
Switzerland	0	0	0	0	1	7	2
EPZ share in total		74	86	74	56		
Textiles and clothing share in EPZ		88	89	90	87	65	
Textiles and clothing share in total		65	77	67	48		
Investment in EPZ (MRs million)	114	73	189	236	298	270	1,180

Source: Fowdar, 1992; MIIT, 1991; MEDIA, 1988,1992

The question is why such investment came to Mauritius rather than the other countries in this class. One answer is that some of the firms were going to the others as well, suggesting that spreading future exports among a variety of countries in order to postpone any one of them becoming subject to quotas was part of the strategy. Mauritius, because of its past history and population composition, has a variety of links with Europe, India, and China, giving it an advantage in attracting interest from each of these areas over less familiar countries. This is a potential factor at the margin in investment decisions. Relative to other Lomé countries, it had a better trained labour force, better transport links, and a stable government. It was promoting foreign investment in the early 1970s because of high unemployment and the lack of prospects for its traditional export, sugar, and it set up a package of assistance, including the EPZ and the usual tax holidays, like those of the South East-Asian countries, and before others of the subsequent generation of NICs.

What is clear from Table 6.11, however, is that while all these general efforts and advantages did lead to an inflow which gave Mauritius an advantage over other African countries, the very high level of inflows came only at a period when it was exploiting preference advantages. The need for the future is to find a permanent substitute for these.

CONCLUSIONS

Among the quotations heading chapters in MIIT (1991) (from authors ranging from Albert Camus to Adam Smith) is (anonymously) 'There are those who make things happen, those who watch things happen, and those who wonder how things happened' (p. 53). In trade success, Malaysia and Thailand clearly fall in the first class, and Colombia and Zimbabwe in the second. Mauritius appears still to be in the third. This is interesting for a researcher, but is becoming a luxury for a country whose past basis for development may be disappearing. It cannot afford the luxury of the second class because of its size, and it is not clear how it will move into the first.

Its past successes have all been led by foreign investors, although Mauritian partners have shown an unusual ability to follow, for example by taking over initially foreign joint ventures. The conventional explanations (for example, McQueen, 1990: 35–6; MIIT, 1991: 131) include preferences, favourable treatment for foreign investment and exports, and the large, cheap, and well-trained labour supply; perhaps also its diversity of background and languages, and world growth in the 1980s. Political stability and good infrastructure are clearly helpful. But the timing of its success, the financing of that success (both the foreign and the domestic from the sugar sector), and the form and direction which it took all suggest that preferences were the basic element in explaining its extent and nature. McQueen, (1990: 35) suggests that 'Preferences cannot be a sufficient condition for export

231

growth'. This may be true in the long run, but for a period of five years they may have been.

Mauritian belief in the importance of accidental 'links' remains. But these are always put forward in company histories of their own success. The Zimbabwean who knew a supermarket manager who wanted vegetables; the Malaysian who knows a Japanese economist who could advise on setting up a toy factory; the Mauritian with a training in both watch-making and economic planning: all these exist, and explain the form or the timing of a particular export. But in other circumstances of comparative advantage or preference, the same entrepreneurial Zimbabwean, Malaysian, or Mauritian would have exploited one of his other links. And other countries have similar stories, and less successful economies.

One clearly important link for Mauritius is with the Chinese countries with their pivotal role in the international clothing trade. Mauritius is likely to continue to benefit from this. Within Mauritius, the links (through family holdings) among the different industries, starting with sugar, are a strength in financing new industries. Like official assistance, the role of such relationships is general and permissive, rather than a guarantee of development. It is also not unusual (tobacco plays a similar financing and export-seeking role in Zimbabwe), and may be characteristic of small countries and early stages of development. The Japanese *zaibatsu* and Korean *chaebols* suggest that these relationships may have a role in larger economies as well. It risks being a conservative factor if the groups want to protect existing interests, although this is probably a less damaging pressure than sectorally concentrated economic interests. It is interesting that this cross-industry pattern has been so common in Mauritius.

It may be that the ethnic division between many of the economic sectors and the government (like that in Malaysia) plays a role in keeping a strong pressure for economic success as a substitute for political power. The statements accepting that growth slower than in Asia is desirable tend to come more from official than industrial sources.

Against this agnostic view of the prospects for Mauritius must be set many examples of individual companies that are adapting, but not necessarily within Mauritius. Moving to new countries is a strategy followed by both foreign and Mauritian clothing producers. The prolonged period of reasonable growth and political stability means that Mauritius does now have (for its size) numerous relatively old companies (20 years), which have shown their ability to adapt to different external and internal conditions. In a small country, a series of even random small advantages for individual industries can be sufficient to provide the type of conservative but sustained growth which rather larger shocks have given the Colombian economy. The risk is that the probability of participating in whatever the next success may be is necessarily smaller for a small country with fewer existing industries. From this perspective, maximising contacts may have a rational basis as a strategy.

One corollary of such an interpretation of Mauritius' past success and future prospects, however, is that it is a very risky, not a safe, model for other African countries. Another is that success came from a succession of good or lucky microeconomic choices, not macroeconomic policies.

The new strategies (and the new Plan) offer a continuation of the general economic policies. They assume foreign investment, but do not offer a replacement for preferences. It is not yet certain whether preference-based economic growth has given Mauritius the basis for making a transition to 'those who make things happen'.

One industrial lesson from Mauritius' experience must be emphasised before we go on to Jamaica and Bangladesh: its clothing exports went from under 10% of the total production in 1976 to over 50% ten years later, and were falling by 1992. (More dramatically: from being too small to face quotas in 1980, to full utilisation of binding quotas by 1989, to being too uncompetitive to fill them by 1991.) The nature of the clothing industry (initial capital investment requires buying a few sewing machines and putting them in a rented building; initial training requires a few weeks) is such that it became under the MFA quota system the archetypal mobile industry. It cannot be regarded as based on comparative advantage (except that all developing countries have cheaper labour than at least one industrial country), or as a sustainable way of entering into stable international trade. Success in it may bear no relation to the potential for success in more permanent development.

NOTES

1 One official suggested that this owes its existence more to the hope of benefiting from the EC propensity to support regional groups than to any strong mutual interests, although the potential for a wider Indian Ocean grouping seemed at least a possible excuse. This would represent an extreme form of preference seeking.
2 In spite of Lomé, France and the UK imposed VERs on Mauritius clothing exports from 1977 to 1981, thus apparently indicating that the Lomé guarantee is not completely reliable. This did not appear to have affected expectations in the 1980s when exports again rose with official encouragement. The episode appears even to be half forgotten: some officials claimed that there had 'never' been controls, and all were apparently vague about the details. This is in marked contrast to the reactions of Bangladesh to the 1985 clothing quotas or Colombia to the banana quotas. It confirms the much stronger confidence in the permanence of preferential relationships in Mauritius, but it does not go further towards an explanation.
3 The claim by one MEDIA official that the provisions of Lomé IV are part of the school curriculum seems very credible.
4 It may also have been useful in ensuring that workers as well as managers were tied by family to those in other sectors.
5 One is an impressively informative directory of exporters which contributed substantially to the research for this chapter. MEDIA officials also offered exceptionally well-informed advice and generous assistance with the appointments which formed the background for much of the chapter.

13

JAMAICA

A SMALL COUNTRY WITH PREFERENCES AND AID

To the world, Jamaica is another small country, although its population of over 2 million is twice that of Mauritius. Within its immediate region, however, the Caribbean islands excluding Cuba, it is among the larger islands. It is similar in per capita income to Colombia, in the low- to middle-income group. Nevertheless, it still receives very high inflows of aid and donor intervention: 15% of its imports are covered, similar to the share for Zimbabwe, which has only half its income per capita, and much higher than Colombia's 2%, and from the 1980s its policies were under the supervision of a series of IMF and World Bank programmes. Its international position is thus a mixture: a small and dependent country with a high level of income, a strong regional position, and an unusually extensive participation in international policy-making.

The economy grew rapidly in the 1960s, at 6% p.a. over the decade to 1972. Since then, output has been falling or stagnant; the level in 1986 was almost 20% below the peak. There has been some slow growth since then, but in 1991 and 1992 estimates were back to 0.5%. Manufacturing rose slightly faster after the mid-1980s, although still only at about 3% a year, with falls in 1991 and 1992.

Export volume fell even more sharply from the mid-1970s to the mid-1980s (in 1985 it was less than half the 1973 figure), but then started to rise, and by the early 1990s had recovered most of the fall. Although there was some recovery in the volume of the traditional primary and semi-processed exports, bauxite and alumina, sugar, and bananas, there was little in their prices. The important change in both exports and output was in clothing, with output growing at 10% p.a. (JAMPRO, 1992), led by a strong increase in clothing exports. Prior to 1982, the clothing sector had been mainly for domestic consumption, with a few exports, about evenly divided between the USA and the neighbouring Caribbean islands, accounting for less than 1% of total exports.

The Caribbean countries are unusual in being among the most preferred

234

exporters under both the US and the EC trade regimes. Jamaica receives quotas on sugar from both sides, the most favourable level of tariff preferences, and special entry privileges for some goods into each (clothing to the US and bananas and rum to the EC). It thus faces a complex set of quotas and preferences on its trade. On many goods, it has the opportunity to choose which preference to use; this provides a useful test of which preferences are preferred.

The structure of Jamaica's exports has changed significantly in the last 15 years, and this is potentially decisive for its development because exports have a high share in its economy. This is the subject of the analysis of the rest of this chapter. But two aspects of the structure of Jamaica's external sector and its economy modify and limit any conclusions, and must therefore be noted here. Exports of services, in particular the income from tourism and cruise ships, make up about 40% of total exports of goods and services, well above the importance of the principal goods (about a quarter for bauxite and alumina together). This share has been high since 1983, although there has been no shift upwards (Table 13.4). Although there is some foreign investment in this sector, services are much more under local control and without external constraints than the principal goods exports. The sector also has a lower import content and a more direct impact on the rest of the economy.

The other structural characteristic which affects the impact of any changes in exports is that many of the individual exports to be examined here (and also the tourism sector) are produced by companies or linked groups of companies which operate in a wide range of sectors; they are often family-based. A change in the structure of exports need not, therefore, necessarily imply a change in the structure of exporters. Thus, as in Mauritius most obviously, but also in other countries in this study, what appear to be costs to a sector may not be as severe when considered at a company level. This is the opposite of the usual assumption made in international trade analysis and it is crucial to an evaluation of adjustment effects and potential.

PATTERN OF TRADE[1]

Although less dominant than at the beginning of the 1980s, bauxite and alumina still provide more than half of Jamaica's goods exports (Tables 13.1 and 13.2). This is the only export in which it is a major world producer (providing about 4–5% of world exports). Its other traditional exports, sugar and bananas, are not now a very high share of the total. Although bananas have doubled from their exceptionally low levels in the early 1980s to a volume of about 75,000 tonnes a year, this is still only half their 1960s level. These two food exports, however, are important because both are almost entirely determined, and therefore in the short term guaranteed, by quota allocations to the EC (Tables 13.3 and 13.4). The change has come in clothing exports. Nevertheless, even if these are valued at the full export

Table 13.1 Jamaica: export structure by principal commodities

Commodity	SITC	1982	1985	1990
Total value ($m)[a]		767	568	1,158
			percentages	
All food items	0+1+22+44	17	25	20
Fuels	3	3	5	1
Ores and metals	27+28+68	68	51	64
Manufactured goods[a] of which:	5 to 8 less 68	12	19	15
Chemical products	5	3	3	2
Machinery and transport	7	3	6	3
Other manufactured goods[a]	(6+8) less 68	6	10	10
Textile fibres, yarn and clothing[b]	26+65+84	2	10	21

Notes:
[a] Includes only value added for 807 clothing
[b] Total value

Sources: Bank of Jamaica, 1992; JAMPRO, 1993

value, as in the data for the other countries, Jamaica has the lowest share for manufactures, while if only the value added is included for those which are produced under the US outward-processing arrangements, the total share for manufactures has risen only slightly.

The rise in the value and the share of clothing exports took place in a period of only four years, from 1984 to 1987; the rise in value in that period was from US$ 30 million to $183 million, while the share in exports increased from 2% to 23%. Prior to this, clothing had not even been the most important good produced in the export free zones (Table 13.2) or the largest manufactured export (chemicals, largely to other Caribbean countries, were higher).

In total, the geographical distribution of Jamaica's trade (Table 13.3) shows a shift from the US and its Caribbean and Latin American neighbours to the EC, and thus overall a shift to more trade with the industrial countries than with developing countries. After Mauritius, it has the second lowest share to other developing countries among the seven countries examined in this book. These low shares for the smallest countries, which might seem those for which joint production or cooperation with developing neighbours would be most indicated, may be partly because both are islands (there is no cost incentive for border trade), but it is also because the local region available to them would also be small, and slow growing. Africa and the Caribbean or Latin America are considerably less attractive than the local region of the Asian countries. To this explanation must be added the role of preferences, discussed in the next section.

The composition of Jamaica's exports varies widely in different markets.

Table 13.2 Jamaica: principal exports (percentages)

Product	1982	1983	1984	1985	1986	1987	1988	1989	1990	1991
Bauxite and alumina	68	62	64	51	47	42	58	53	56	52
Chemicals	3	3	3	3	3	3	2	2	2	2
Clothing	2	2	4	10	16	23	22	22	21	24
Sugar	7	8	9	9	10	9	9	6	7	7
Bananas	1	1	0	1	1	2	2	2	3	4
Coffee								1	1	1
Rum	1	1	1	2	2	1	1	1	1	1
Yams								1	1	1
'Traditional'ᵃ	76	72	73	60	58	54	58	61	66	63
'Non-traditional'	24	28	27	40	42	46	42	39	34	37
Free zone	3	3	7	19	25	28	31	33	41	44
Clothing	40	50	85	64	72	82	91	86	85	85
(US$ m)										
Total Bankᵇ	767	636	702	568	591	709	883	1,000	1,158	1,145
Total JAMPRO	751	679	697	570	634	793	987	1,102	1,300	1,259

Notes:
ᵃ Bauxite, alumina, sugar, bananas
ᵇ Includes only valued added for '807' exports to USA

Sources: Bank of Jamaica, 1992; JAMPRO, 1992; JAMPRO, 1993 data supplied; Jamaican Exporters' Association, 1992

Table 13.3 Jamaica: principal markets, total and for principal exports, 1981–91 (percentages)

	1981	1982	1983	1984	1985	1986	1987	1988	1989	1990	1991	1992
Total												
US		34	34	51	33	34	37	36	26	29	30	43
EC		1	22	16	20	27	29	29	30	29	32	24
UK		18	20	14	17	19	17	18	16	15	16	15
Canada		12	13	15	16	16	14	15	14	11	10	10
CARICOM		10	12	8	7	7	6	7	7	6	2	8
Latin America		5	3	2	1	1	1	0	2	2	6	
Norway		8	9	4	2	3	3	1	4	11	8	7
Sugar												
UK		94	81	70	80	89	95	92	91	91	90	
US		6	19	30	20	11	5	8	9	9	10	
Bananas–UK										100		
Chemicals–CARICOM		86	82	88	67	63	62	67	67	72	64	
Clothing												
US		67	62	87	98	95	97	93	92	88	85	
EC		0	0	0	1	4	2	5	6	9	13	
France		0	0	0	1	0	0	2	2	4	4	
Italy		0	0	0	0	0	1	0	1	2	3	
Germany		0	0	0	0	0	0	1	0	1	2	
UK		0	0	0	0	0	0	0	0	0	1	
Canada		0	0	1	1	1	1	1	1	1	1	
CARICOM		32	33	9	2	1	1	1	1	1	1	
'Traditional'[a]												
US	54											
EC	20											
CARICOM	0											
'Non-traditional'												
US	21											
EC	18											
CARICOM	43											

Note: [a] Bauxite, alumina, sugar, bananas

Sources: Bank of Jamaica, 1992; King, 1993; JAMPRO, 1993 data supplied; Stevens, 1990; IMF *Direction of Trade Statistics*

Table 13.4 Jamaica: summary of preferences and controls 1982–91 (shares of total exports)

	1982	1983	1984	1985	1986	1987	1988	1989	1990	1991
Exports excluding bauxite/alumina	32	38	36	49	53	58	42	47	44	48
Quota	8	9	11	14	17	20	20	15	18	19
Sugar	7	8	9	9	10	9	9	6	7	7
Bananas	1	1	0	1	1	2	2	2	3	4
Non 807 Clothing to USA	0	0	2	4	6	9	9	7	8	8
Preferences[a]	20	20	17	22	29	32	32	38	33	36
807	2	1	2	5	9	13	12	13	11	13
Exports to EC, not sugar or bananas										
CBI	15	15	9	12	15	15	16	20	17	19
CARIBCAN									0.2	1.0
CARICOM									4	4
GSP on non-traditional									0.2	0.2
Preferences and quotas	28	29	28	36	46	52	52	53	51	55
For reference: CARICOM total	10	12	8	7	7	6	7	7	6	6
Travel and port income/total goods and services	31	37	38	42	37	36	33	36	40	41

Notes:
[a] Including estimate for CBI, CARIBCAN, CARICOM, GSP for 1982–[b]
[b] Includes some exports of alumina for which preferences are not important. This explains why preferences and quotas sum to slightly more than non-bauxite trade

Sources: Bank of Jamaica, 1992; JAMPRO, 1993

Although primary goods are most important in all, the share of manufactures, mainly clothing, is much higher to the US (about a third by the
early 1990s), although bauxite and alumina exports are still the most important. Sugar and bananas are still important for the EC, so that the shift to the
EC as a principal market is more than explained by the growing share of
traditional products going there (Table 13.3). Within the EC, however, the
UK, where sugar and bananas still account for two-thirds of its imports
from Jamaica, has lost its dominant position as principal importer. The
increase in the US role in non-traditional exports also accounts for the
decline in the Caribbean's share in the total, as such exports account for
almost all its imports from Jamaica.

Bauxite and alumina go almost entirely to the industrial countries, notably
the US, Canada, and Norway, but there were also exports in the late 1980s
to the USSR. This contract with the Ukraine collapsed after 1990, while
Russia sold an increased volume on to international markets in 1991 and
1992 (both these changes help to explain the poor performance of Jamaican
exports after 1990).

Prior to the surge in the mid-1980s, clothing exports had been roughly
equally divided between the US and the Caribbean countries (Stevens, 1990),
and initially (1985–7) the new clothing exports went entirely to the US. It
was only in 1988 that the share of the EC (France and Italy) began to rise,
but then the increase was rapid.

CARICOM remained the only important market for other manufactured
exports. Chemicals were the most important, but there were also exports of
furniture. There have been some exports of furniture to the US, but efforts
to export it to the EC have not been successful (because of problems of style
and quality, as well as costs of transport).

In summary, the only important change in the composition of Jamaica's
exports in the 1980s was the increase in clothing exports first to the US
(in 1984–7) and then, on a much smaller scale, to the EC (1988–91). Other
manufactures continue to be restricted mainly to the local and immediate
regional market within which Jamaica appears large and advanced. The
traditional primary goods continue to go to their traditional markets, under
traditional arrangements. The policy questions are therefore: what the role
of external policy was in determining this change and preventing others, and
how important the external structure has been to development.

JAMAICA'S TRADE POLICY

Jamaica followed a policy of development through import substitution in
the 1970s, but the stagnation of domestic demand (and political difficulties)
offered little incentive for local or foreign production for the local market.
Reductions in import controls began from the late 1970s (accompanied by
devaluation in 1978). There was a further devaluation in 1983–4, and tariffs

were cut from 1987, but average tariffs were still 50% by the end of 1989. The policy changes became more fundamental after 1989, with further large devaluations, and a reduction in tariffs to an average of 20% by the end of 1991, with most below 10% by 1992 (Bernal, 1992a). The acceleration was particularly obvious in that year, with a new payments arrangement within CARICOM in June being overtaken by relaxation of all exchange controls in September.

Export firms had been able to claim exemption from import duty since 1956, and free zones had existed. Stronger promotion of exports began in the early 1980s, encouraged (if not forced) by World Bank intervention; this targeted the clothing sector as a way of increasing exports outside the region. In 1988, three existing agencies were brought together to form an export promotion agency (JAMPRO). This policy was already being changed by 1993, with restrictions on JAMPRO's activities, and there was a revision in the rules for free zones.

Neither the reductions in import barriers nor the measures to encourage exports appear to correspond to the periods of increase or change in direction of exports, except for the mid-1980s devaluation which was at about the time of the first increase in clothing exports. Nor did the increase in exports come at the time of very depressed domestic demand (the 1970s).

TARIFFS, PREFERENCES AND CONTROLS

Neither tariffs nor preferences are significant for the ores which are Jamaica's principal exports. There is some escalation for more processed forms, but it is low, and as the power requirements for aluminium make local processing impossible, escalation is not the relevant constraint. Other goods do face high or escalating tariffs in some markets, but neither these nor the tariff preferences to which Jamaica is entitled to mitigate them are significant for its most important exports. Less than 15% of its exports to the US benefit from the Caribbean preferences, while about 40%, mainly ores, enter duty-free under MFN provisions, leaving 45–50% under MFN tariffs. To the EC, all its exports (except sugar which has special arrangements) are duty-free, but for the primary exports which are the principal ones in this market, the preference is not a significant amount, and for clothing it is the benefit of exemption from quota which is the more important advantage.

All its exports other than bauxite and alumina face a range of quotas, high or escalating tariffs, NTBs, and preferences in all its markets. Table 13.4 summarises the identifiable flows.[2]

Table 13.5 confirms that the low total controls from NTBs are the result of the share of ores; controls on the other categories are high. Sugar is subject to quota in the UK and US markets, but with a guaranteed price well above the world level (double for the US in 1993). Jamaica, like Mauritius, expects that the agricultural settlement in the GATT Uruguay Round will lower its export price significantly, by between a sixth and a fifth. Jamaica's exports are entirely of raw sugar, with no efforts to move into more specialty or refined products, as in Mauritius. According to the industry, this is because of the requirements of the EC importer who has sole rights to the contract. Other markets have not been developed because the prices in the US and the UK markets are so favourable, while the quota prevents any further increase to these markets (although Jamaica has received temporary advantages when other countries have been unable to fill their quotas to the EC).

For bananas, Jamaica benefits under the special access arrangements to the EC for Caribbean producers, and does not compete with other producers in non-EC markets. Under the ACP arrangements before 1993, Jamaican bananas had duty-free access and a guaranteed market in the UK. Under the new arrangement for the Single European Market, non-ACP producers are restricted to a quota for the whole of the Community, which can be increased only if the ACP and EC suppliers cannot meet the demand, and the non-ACP exporters now pay a 20% duty in all markets (previously Germany, the largest, was tariff-free). In bananas, as in sugar, producers and policy-makers consider that the quota and preference arrangements are at risk of change. They are therefore less committed to maintaining this preference, and certainly less likely to allow output to respond strongly to it, than countries where such exports are more important. Even after the recovery in the 1980s, bananas are not as important to Jamaica as they are to other, Eastern Caribbean, countries. The large changes, down and up, in the last 15 years suggest that Jamaica could adapt again. On the other hand, the success in lobbying to maintain the preference in the early 1990s may have encouraged the recovery in Jamaican banana exports in recent years, and the fact that the ACP concessions were strengthened could have led to a greater belief in the efficacy of lobbying. This makes the current pessimism about preferences more surprising.

Coffee is almost entirely exported as unroasted beans, and on long-term contract to importers who demand this. As noted with respect to Colombia, there are strong disincentives from tariff escalation in some markets to moving into processing. Nevertheless, contrary to the experience of sugar and bananas, some firms are moving into processing, into new or specialty products, and into new markets. In spite of the preferences available under Lomé, the first moves have been into the US. The companies' explanations were that this market is nearer or more familiar. This is true, but again it suggests an underlying hesitation to build on preferences.

There is a contrast in the reactions of the three food exports to the controls which they face. The two with guaranteed access have concentrated on the guaranteed market, with apparently no changes or adaptation. Together they account for the 10% of Jamaican trade dependent on quota

Table 13.5 Jamaica: non-tariff barriers (percentage 1986 weights on 1990 data)

SITC	Product area	EC	USA	Total[a]	Total[b]
0+1+22+4	All food items	66	12	54	55
0	Food + live animals	74	21	66	
051	Fresh fruit and nuts	21	6	14	
054	Fresh vegetables	100	0	92	
061	Sugar and honey	100	100	83	
22	Oil seeds	12	0	11	
2 less (22+27+28)	Agricultural raw materials	39	0	0	0
27+28+67+68	Ores and metals	5	0	0	0
67	Iron and steel	100	0	100	
6–8 less (67+68)	Manufactures, not chemicals	48	86	80	40
65	Textiles, yarn & fabrics	100	71	84	
84	Clothing	100	88	74	
0–9	All items	37	40	23	17

Notes:
[a] Totals and sub-totals found by applying 1986 importer weights to 1990 totals and sub-totals
[b] Totals and sub-totals found by applying 1986 importer weights to each commodity, and summing the commodities

Source: Calculated from UNCTAD database

arrangements set in the EC and the US. The changes in sugar products in Mauritius suggest that, contrary to the Jamaican producers' arguments, this reaction is not owing to inherent characteristics of the industry. In Jamaica, however, there may be political or employment objectives which make the sugar industry uninterested in adapting. The banana trade, in contrast, is effectively in the hands of trading and importing companies, so that it may be appropriate to consider its reactions later in the context of the role of foreign investment. Jamaican coffee firms have moved, on a limited scale, into new products, but not in the directions which might be predicted by tariff escalation or preferences.

In clothing, a major new export needs to be explained. Table 13.6 shows that the increase in exports in 1984 was marked by a clear shift in the nature of the industry. It had been principally Jamaican and principally for the local market. In 1983–4 US firms came in, and took over half (up from 20%) of Jamaican trade with the US. The shift to an export-oriented industry, away from local or mixed, is also shown by the increase in the importance of companies operating in the Free Zones. The change occurred both in outward processing, the traditional mode of export to the US, and in CMT (cut, make and trim) which grew rapidly to 40% of exports to the US. As clothing exports were excluded from preferences under the Caribbean Basin Initiative (CBI) as well as under GSP, the advantage which Jamaica offered to external companies over other potential suppliers was its initial freedom from quotas in the US market. The existence of established Jamaican firms, and their ability to turn to exports, and the timing of the devaluations and import liberalisation which could have prompted them to seek export markets are also mentioned by the Jamaican government report on the industry as important influences in Jamaica's success (JAMPRO, 1992). But the data in Table 13.6 make it clear that it was US firms which led the increase in 1983–4.

Jamaican firms remained significant in '807' trade, where the Jamaican input (estimated at around 20% by value by producers and officials) is confined to processing materials, with all operations up to cutting and all marketing in the hands of the foreign firm. In the CMT trade, first US, then, only a year later in 1985, Asian firms took the major share. Although Asian firms remain of negligible importance in the '807' trade (which is designed for US firms supplying the US market), they had become the principal exporters by 1987, the end of the period of expansion to the US. The number of firms continued to increase, from both the US and Asia, in the late 1980s (Table 13.7). In 1986, only two years after the growth started, Jamaica received its first quotas to the US, under MFA IV, but only for CMT. Under the 1986 agreement, the CBI countries enjoyed effectively unlimited quotas for the non-US component of '807' trade. In 1988 and 1990, Jamaica was able to negotiate improved access to the US market, and avoid threatened reductions. It also helped to achieve a modification of the

Table 13.6 Jamaica: characteristics of clothing exports (percentages)

Clothing	1982	1984	1985	1986	1988	1989	1990	1991
Where produced								
Free Zone	11	37	48	48	53	49	55	59
Customs territory	89	63	52	52	47	51	45	41
Share of Free Zone								
In exports to US	14	38	47	47	50	46	51	53
In exports to EC	0	0	100	100	100	100	100	98
In exports to								
CARICOM	0	0	0	0	0	0	0	0.04
Share of '807'								
In total exports	67	50	55	57	52	58	52	53
In exports to US	86	58	56	60	56	64	58	63
Producing company								
Jamaican	80	46	32	28	32	31	25	21
US	20	53	34	34	31	36	37	39
Asian	0	1	30	32	38	33	39	41
Shares in '807' exports								
Jamaican companies	80	87	52	48	50	45	40	34
US companies	20	13	45	33	50	55	60	65
Asian companies	0	0	0	0	0.3	0.3	0.3	1
Shares in CMT exports								
Jamaican companies	80	7	8	2	11	11	9	6
US companies	20	93	20	9	10	11	12	9
Asian companies	0	1	68	75	79	80	80	86

Note: CMT: cut, make and trim: the alternative to '807' which is only sewing ready cut material

Source: JAMPRO, 1993 data supplied

terms of the initial US offer on textiles to the Uruguay Round. (By imposing an overall limit on supplies from all sources to the US, that offer would have removed the CBI preference.) But by 1988, quota utilisation was already falling, and by 1991, it was only 29% (JAMPRO, 1992), with only two products with high utilisation. This was attributed to low demand in the US (although it seems to have preceded the decline in utilisation in Mauritius and Bangladesh), and marked the end of expansion to that market. In 1993, there was a revival in US demand for clothing from Jamaica and other Caribbean countries.

When binding, the quotas are allocated to encourage geographical diversification of the exporting firms: only 60% was based on their past performance, with 30% based on regional criteria and 10% for new firms or firms moving into new products. In the 1990s, quotas were given preferentially to firms which were also exporting to the EC, in order to encourage

Table 13.7 Jamaica: clothing producers
(numbers of companies)

Countries of origin	1987[a]	1992
US	13	23
807	9	17
CMT	3	2
Both	1	4
Hong Kong	5	14
807	0	0
CMT	5	13
Both	0	1
S Korea	2	8
807	0	0
CMT	2	7
Both	0	1
India CMT	1	1
Canada CMT	0	1
Total foreign producers		
807	21	47
CMT	11	24
Both	1	6
Jamaican companies	13	
807	8	
CMT	0	
Both	5	

Note: [a] Only major exporters

Sources: JAMPRO, 1993 data supplied; Stevens, 1990

diversification into a quota-free market. As quotas were in effect and binding for such a short period, no arrangements emerged for transferring them or for ensuring that they were used in full.

The increase in exports to the EC in 1988 thus did correspond to government policy, but, as use of quotas for this purpose came later and at the same time that quotas ceased to be binding into the US, it is not clear how important the policy may have been in explaining exports to the EC. In principle, access to the EC had always been more favourable than to the US because it was duty- and tariff-free. In addition, the ACP arrangements are by treaty and thus implicitly more permanent, while the quotas and the CBI arrangements are unilateral concessions.

The obstacle to trade with the EC was the rules of origin. The distance of Jamaica from Europe made importing EC or other ACP cloth impractical, while labour and transport costs were too high to make using Asian cloth and paying duty feasible in competition with Asian suppiers. The exports to the EC began with one Asian firm providing knitted garments (thus meeting the rules of origin by adding sufficient value in Jamaica), and by 1992 were still principally knitted goods.

There were other institutional problems. As Table 13.6 shows, the companies with experience in CMT exports were principally Asian companies. These had gone to Jamaica explicitly to take advantage of unfilled quotas in the US, and (as in Mauritius) were not interested in the smaller and different EC market. The Jamaican companies were in '807' trade, and did not have experience in selling or designing and making clothing. Even the established Jamaican firms which had begun with production for the local market did not have experience in export markets outside the Caribbean and the US, and as long as the US market was available had no incentive to acquire it. If the most pessimistic views of the dependency of outward-processing[3] were correct, then Jamaican firms would not be capable even of moving into CMT processing. These factors explain why the initial impulse went into the US market, led by US and Asian firms. There was by the 1990s a move into CMT for the US market by Jamaican firms. Some of those interviewed had looked also at the EC market when US demand ceased to be buoyant, but they have not entered it. This suggests (and those interviewed argued this strongly) that the EC market, even with its ACP preferences, was less attractive than even a stagnant US market for Jamaican producers, but the move into CMT for the US also suggests that '807' production is not as much of a dead end as the pessimists argue.

The argument that '807' operations result in unsuitable or insufficient training in exporting skills is also weakened (as was found in Zimbabwe and will be seen also in Bangladesh) because some of the managers in the firms, even in the family firms, come from other industries, and some had been trained abroad. Both JAMPRO and donors have supplemented this by technical training. In other export products as well, the successful managers do not necessarily come from a background within the sector. This evidence suggests that to assume a direct link between the experience of a sector and the skills of its managers is invalid. A more indirect argument against such reasoning is that firms which can learn the production (and quota manipulation) techniques as quickly as clothing firms have done are likely to be able to learn marketing or design. And it appears to be the already established Jamaican firms, with a history of success in the local and Caribbean market, which were most successful at '807' exports. New firms initially entered, but were more likely to find themselves unable to meet the commitments. This suggests that the skills of '807' and other clothing production are related and transferable.

The principal reason that there was an increase in exports of clothing to the US and not in other goods or to other markets seems to be that the trade flow was created by US and Asian exporters using Jamaica to exploit new demand in the US and to replace lost market possibilities for quota-constrained Asian exporters, rather than because of any action by Jamaicans, official or in the industry. Until the early 1990s, the market for its mineral exports and the quotas for its principal agricultural exports, and then the inflow of investment for clothing exports, meant little pressure to find new exports or markets. That many managers and companies have not developed the skills to do so is more likely to be a result of this situation than of the nature of the clothing trade. This lack of need could also help to explain the lack of awareness, which some government officials criticised, of the possibilities from EC preferences, but it is probably true that the discouragement felt by those who have examined the rules of origin, and found them difficult to meet, cannot have encouraged others to spend time searching for opportunities. Stories (with variants suggesting that they have reached the status of 'urban myths') of other manufacturers who have tried to export, but found themselves held back by exporting the 'wrong type of biscuit' because of the type of baking or the sugar content, and complaints about inability to discover which countries' cloth would meet the 'local content' rules, confirm an impression that regulations on exports to the EC have acquired a reputation of being too complicated or too arbitrary. Even the exporters who do enter the EC market do so after success in the US, because this is regarded as an easier first step. The low exports to the EC can thus be attributed to the combination of better opportunities elsewhere and the EC obstacles.

Most other preferences which exist are not important in practice. As indicated earlier, the principal advantage of the CBI for Jamaica comes from the effectively quota-free entry of '807' goods, not the other tariff concessions. In Canada, Jamaica also receives preferences but, with textiles, clothing, shoes, and other leather goods excluded, this is of limited importance (Table 13.4).

The exception is CARICOM. The high MFN tariffs of the other Caribbean countries (especially until the liberalisation of the last few years) have made Jamaica's preferred access there more important, and may help to explain Jamaica's willingness to maintain a joint position with them on lobbying positions with the EC, for example on bananas, and with the US, on NAFTA, even when its interests are not identical with theirs. A common external tariff was introduced in 1993, although restricted only to the more advanced members (with confusion even within the government over how many countries this meant and when it would be implemented). Both government and manufacturers consider the CARICOM preference necessary to compete with non-CARICOM imports in the other countries.

CARICOM acquired new importance in negotiating with other blocs first with the EC, in protecting sugar, bananas, and rum during the Single European Market negotiations, and then in the Uruguay Round, to preserve CBI privileges. Potentially it could be important with some of the Latin American regional groups, although Jamaica has arranged a special bilateral preference with Venezuela. It is NAFTA, however, which has provided the principal recent stimulus, directly because the US, Canada, and Mexico have insisted on bargaining with CARICOM collectively and not individually, but also because Jamaica, which sees NAFTA as a major threat to its position in the US market, mobilised CARICOM together with all other possible allies to try to obtain modifications. The negotiation with NAFTA, the need to protect some commodities in the SEM exercise, and some elements of the Uruguay Round together made Jamaica very aware of how vulnerable its preferential access to industrial country markets was to changes in arrangements between the US or the EC and other suppliers, in which it has no formal voice, and in products in which (it believes) it would not be able to compete without preference.

Pre-NAFTA, Jamaica estimated that 10% of its exports to the US had a tariff preference over Mexico (Bernal, 1992b). NAFTA will end this, and eventually (by the end of the 15-year transition), give Mexico an advantage on all goods on which Jamaica pays duty or has quotas (in other words, the 60% which are not duty-free). The lobbying objective was to get equal access to the USA, and to get this guaranteed by treaty, not concession – effectively Jamaican entry into NAFTA. This was not achieved. The most seriously affected good will probably be clothing. The final NAFTA terms incorporated temporary constraints on Mexican sugar (Mexico is not, but it could become, a major sugar exporter). Some foreign investment, it is claimed, had already been diverted to Mexico by 1993, and Mexico has now revised its legislation to offer all investors the concessions NAFTA requires for US investors. This could divert more.

Jamaican entry into NAFTA, however, would not only be probably unacceptable to the three present members. It would conflict with Jamaica's position as a member of the ACP (which does not permit members to make arrangements with other countries unilaterally), and with CARICOM (if the other countries were not admitted, and some would not want to be). It would potentially restrict future Jamaican policy because of the accompanying agreements on investment, intellectual property, etc.

The problems Jamaica saw from the Uruguay Round were also from loss of preference. The agricultural settlement will reduce the price received for its sugar exports under quota. Its preserved access for bananas might be lost or modified under tighter interpretation of MFN rules. Increases, and eventual removal, of the MFA quotas for the Asian countries on clothing will remove their interest in using Jamaica as a base, although some Jamaican producers think that '807' exports for US firms could continue. This would, however, mean, at highest, keeping half its present clothing exports, and even for these would probably only ensure the present level, not their present share in markets. Some producers hoped for more (because wages would rise in what now seem like potential Asian competitors), but the Mauritian and Bangladeshi view that new Asian competitors could offer

249

more and cheaper labour than any of the 1980s exporters seems better informed. Jamaica's income level (and activities like tourism which potentially compete for labour), and its size and distance from sources of cloth, do not give it an economic advantage in clothing.

If, as argued above, all Jamaica's major goods exports except ores depend either on quotas or preferences, it is inevitable that any reduction in tariffs or barriers in world markets or improved preferences for other countries must damage its current exports. All of the increase in its exports and the changes in its industrial structure appear to have been driven by preferences. This makes the preoccupation of policy-makers with preserving and expanding preferences understandable (the new five-year agreement with Venezuela entered into force as late as January 1993). But in fact the most serious damage to its exports did not come from policies. In the late 1980s the fall in exports to the US was because of a decline in demand for clothing. In 1990–2, there was the collapse in exports of bauxite to the Ukraine, followed by serious competition on the international market from a new supplier, Russia, leading to a sharp fall in the price. The price and demand fluctuations in the mid-1980s had also been significant influences on its ore exports. On exports of services, it was hurricanes which had been most damaging. At the same time, some of the companies interviewed showed optimism in being able to adapt to the removal of preferences, and those in services had clearly moved away from vulnerability to external policy, which largely ignored them. Thus, the preservation of preferences may reflect the concerns of policy-makers more than the actual interests and priorities of producers.

OTHER RESTRICTIONS AND INFLUENCES ON TRADE

Jamaica, like Colombia, faces the problem of being a drugs exporter. This raises the costs of trading because goods are subject to more stringent inspection (and sometimes damage or delay) and shipping costs are higher because of the precautions taken with containers and the risk premium incurred by shippers (who are liable under both US and EC legislation). This alters the balance for all exporters, but may be particularly serious for new exporters, who face the same high costs on a lower volume (and possibly more suspicion). It may help to explain continuing reliance on traditional exporters and exports.

Jamaica introduced countertrade for intra-Caribbean trade in 1982, but it was at most a quarter of that trade (equivalent to 2% of total trade), and it was a reaction to the area's general exchange controls rather than a policy instrument. It was replaced by other payments mechanisms, and did not influence the direction of trade.

Jamaica's major aid donors are the US, Japan, Canada, and the Netherlands (Table 5.7), with Japan accounting for most of the recent increase in bilateral assistance. For this reason, the data in Table 13.8 may

Table 13.8 Jamaica: multilateral and untied aid (US$m or percentages)

Jamaica	1970	1975	1980	1985	1990
Ratio of aid to imports (%)	2.11	4.75	11.96	15.21	14.69
Multilateral	6	7	32	11	21
Multi-EC	6	7	28	8	14
Bilateral	13	18	84	158	252
Untied bilateral	4	5	45	55	140
Total untied	10	12	73	63	154
Tied/imports (%)	0.25	3.64	5.30	9.59	6.41

Note: The average tied ratio for all bilateral aid is assumed for all areas

Sources: OECD, *Development Co-operation* and *Geographical Distribution of Financial Flows to Developing Countries*, annual issues

overestimate the impact of tying. Although the role of the international institutions is now greatly reduced from the interventions of the 1980s, in 1992 the Bank of Jamaica's *Annual Report* still emphasised that 'economic activities during 1991 continued to be influenced by IMF programmes' (p. 6), and the IMF standby was renewed in 1991: the new programme included the exchange-control change. The influence on trade is more indirect through the continuing importance of official flows as a major source of import finance. (Official export credits are also higher than average, Table 5.5.)

Foreign investment is an important source of domestic capital formation (Table 6.11), with a share of 6.6% in the period 1986–91. According to the US estimates in Table 6.5, a third of its exports to the US are intra-firm, accounting for 20% of its total exports. But the role of foreign investors is considerably greater than this. The discussion of exports has shown how important foreign firms have been in the new exports of clothing. Clothing exports under '807' are directed by the US importer which supplies the material and takes the output, while those under CMT are over 90% by foreign companies. Most of the ore production, and therefore exports to other countries, is in the hands of foreign investors, although there is one Jamaican (government-owned) company. The banana trade is controlled by the trading and importing companies; they also have an official role in administering the quota system ruling in the EC under the 1993 SEM system. The sugar exports to the EC and most of the coffee exports are effectively administered by the importing companies.

The main source of foreign capital in both ores and clothing, and therefore in total, is the US (no official data for investment by origin are available), probably followed by Hong Kong and Korea because of their role in clothing. Canadian and UK companies are important because of their roles in aluminium and in sugar and bananas, respectively.

The result of this combination of external quotas and preferences, foreign firms, and aid and policy influence by the international financial institutions, is that Jamaican exports, and therefore Jamaican production, and also a high share of imports, are almost entirely determined from outside the country. As long as ores remain important, much of this is related to market conditions rather than preferences or other policies. There are Jamaican companies planning, producing and exporting their own products to markets which they have developed, but these are not characteristic of Jamaican trade. If Table 13.4 were recast to estimate trade largely determined by foreign firms, this would include most of bauxite and ores, all clothing, sugar and bananas (a minimum of 80%), before allowing for any foreign share in other goods.

CONCLUSIONS

In the past, the apparent result for Jamaica of this pervasive dependence was an acceptance of its position as a recipient of preferences, and a concentration of policy on attempting to maintain or improve these. In the early 1990s, this changed to a belief that preferences were going, and that Jamaica ought to adapt to a more market-determined future. It is not clear that government actions have yet changed. Some officials argue the proposition of the end of preferences convincingly as a general rule because of the decline in the general level of preferences discussed above or because small countries will lack leverage in the absence of the strategic importance given by previous security considerations (Bernal, 1991), or because the Caribbean is becoming less central to the EC's interests (because of the growth in German influence following reunification). There is, however, no indication of what the alternative for Jamaica ought to be, or of an appropriate industrial policy to exploit the new conditions.

Jamaica faced the simultaneous appearance of threats to its position from the Uruguay Round, EC 1992, and NAFTA. The immediate reaction has been confused. Although the trade negotiation focused attention on its vulnerability to foreign trade concessions, it also emphasised the short-term need to intervene actively in negotiating and lobbying to prevent loss of preferences, and Jamaica has, it could be argued, been exceptionally successful in this. Efforts continued to find new preferences – with Venezuela, in an expanded NAFTA, in the all encompassing Enterprise for the Americas Initiative (Jamaica has accepted the investment and debt provisions for this). It did achieve security for its traditional exports in the EC, it modified the US and EC positions in the Uruguay Round, and it made some gains in modifying NAFTA. This apparent high return to lobbying must offer an attractive incentive to continue to use these skills. One official argued that an advantage of the present quota system was precisely that they could increase their quotas by persuading the US (as they have done in the past).

But it is not only the international economy which appears politicised from a Jamaican official perspective. There is a corresponding attitude to the domestic economy. Sugar is seen as a political problem. More generally, the role of trade unions in the political system affects attitudes to what can be done in labour markets. The problem of drugs is not an exogenous one: it damages exports because Jamaica is unable to restrict it domestically.

While there are companies which have moved into non-preferred markets or exports, and there is now an important class of 'non-traditional exporters', they account for only a small share of goods traded and they did not emerge because of the success of any government policy. They began to adapt before there was any change in government policy. One problem, which may be called the Colombian variant of the Dutch Disease, is that while primary or preference exports remain successful, and as long as there are always some unexploited preferences to turn to, there is no need to look further. This is rational behaviour from the point of view of short-term interests, but it does not constitute a pattern for development and has clearly not given Jamaica even the moderate growth rates which have made this solution tolerable for Colombia. Jamaica also lacks the local market which allows firms to live with a low export ratio for their manufactures and the government to live with vulnerability to external controls or prices on primary exports.

The development strategy of some of the new exporters is based on moving first from one protected market to another one (a clothing firm moving from import substitution to CARICOM, to '807', to CMT exports, and only then into new markets, and even into non-clothing exports). There are now diversified firms in a variety of industries, including the growing tourism sector. To the extent that preferences have involved local firms in trade, using policies as the stimulus rather than more 'real' signals, this may be effective, and a few such firms now seem able to adapt to new, non-preference, conditions. But the foreign firms which were only involved in export, not in the local market as well (as they have been in Malaysia and Thailand), are likely to adapt by moving to another country.

It is difficult to know whether the traditional industries which have not yet had to adapt can do so: the contrast between the responses of the sugar industry in Jamaica and Mauritius is not encouraging. The contrast between some successful companies' attitude of looking for marketing rather than preference-based advantages (thus the fact that the US offered familiarity and nearness helped outweigh the EC's greater preferences for CMT clothing and for some minor exports) and the official choice of preference-seeking and preference-maintaining efforts is very striking, and does not suggest a firm base for cooperation between public and private sectors. It is not yet clear in Jamaica whether a long history of preference and quota-driven growth can provide a base for sustainable development.

NOTES

1 The usual first table of each country chapter, showing the shares of export sectors in a standard format and SITC classification, is not taken from UNCTAD in this chapter because the table there follows SITC Rev.1 and classifies alumina as a chemical (aluminium oxide) rather than Rev.2 which classifies it with bauxite as a mineral ore.

2 The difficulty of obtaining full direction of trade by commodity data and the difference in Jamaican sources in valuation of clothing exports make the figures subject to some uncertainty.

3 'The criticism most often levelled at outward-processing is that it creates a dependent industry in the host that becomes familiar with only part of the production process (assembly and sewing), gaining little experience of design, cutting, marketing.' Stevens, 1990: 17.

14

BANGLADESH

BACKGROUND

With a population of over 100 million and a per capita income of $250, Bangladesh is the largest and poorest country covered in this study. Like most of the largest developing countries it has a relatively high share of manufactures in its exports (Table 14.1), although until recently these have been lightly processed forms of its principal export crop, jute. The high share of manufactures means that it is not vulnerable to any of the controls on primary exports, but its shift into clothing exports in the 1980s (Table 14.2) has meant that barriers on clothing exports, its own and those of its competitors, have become a crucial influence on its exports. Because of its size, it is less vulnerable to trade, and therefore potentially to external policy, than the other countries, while its poverty means that exports are less important relative to other types of external influence. Many of the most important trade effects of the external sector come from its dependence on aid to finance more than half its imports.

The economy grew at about 5% p.a. from 1975 to 1980, slowing to just under 4% in the first half of the 1980s and slightly over 4% in the second. With population growth now estimated as about 2.2% p.a., this indicates a slowly rising level of income (Bangladeshi estimates tend to underestimate the growth rate and the change between the early and the later years). Growth had reached 5.8% in the fiscal year 1989/90[1] but fell back to around 4% in the following two years. This fall was partly because of the impact of the Gulf War on Bangladeshi export markets and on its migrant workers in that area, and of the floods in April 1991, but the latter are estimated to have cost only about 0.6% of GDP, a much smaller impact than that of the drought on Zimbabwe. Exports grew more slowly than imports in the 1970s (5% compared with 6%), but accelerated in the 1980s. They grew at 4% p.a. in the first half, but more than 10% in the second, while imports slowed to under 2% in the first half, recovering to just under 6% in the second.

Manufacturing is still only 10% of the country's GDP. It fell after independence in 1971, to slightly below 10% by 1980. Since then, data are

255

Table 14.1 Bangladesh: export structure by principal commodities

Commodity	SITC	1970	1975	1980	1985	1990
Total value ($m)		302.9	740.4	973.7	1,305.0	1,512.0
				percentages		
All food items	0+1+22+44	9.8	12.5	17.9	15.0	12.5
Agricultural raw materials	2 less (22+27+28)	26.4	18.7	13.3	7.7	7.9
Manufactured goods of which:	5 to 8 less 68	63.6	67.6	65.8	75.2	75.5
Chemical products	5	0.1	1.4	0.2	0.3	0.7
Other manufactured goods	(6+8) less 68	63.4	65.0	64.1	73.7	74.3
Crude and manufactured fertiliser	271+56	–	0.5	–	n.a.	1.0
Textile fibres, yarn and clothing	26+65+84	73.2	74.5	67.5	n.a.	66.0

Source: UNCTAD, *Handbook of International Trade and Development Statistics*, 1992

Table 14.2 Bangladesh: principal exports 1972–92 (percentages, fiscal years)

Products	1972/3	1977/8	1982/3	1983/4	1984/5	1985/6	1986/7	1987/8	1988/9	1989/90	1990/1	1991/2
Jute products	90	70	63	53	58	51	38	31	29	30	23	18[a]
Ready-made garments	0	0.01	1.6	4	12	16	28	34	35	40	43	51[a]
Hosiery	0	0	0	0	0	0	0	0	0	1	8	
Household linen	0	0	0.1	0	0	0.1	0.1	0.1	0.2	0.3	1	
Leather	5	9	8	10	7	7	12	11	11	12	8	
Leather shoes	0	0	0	0	0	0	0	0	0	0	0.2	
Tea	3	9	7	8	6	4	3	3	3	3	3	2
Frozen shrimp	–	4	9	8	8	11	10	9	11	8	7	5
Fruit, vegetables	0.2	0.8	1	1	1	3	2	2	1	1	0.5	
Naphtha and furnace oil	0	2	4	3	2	2	1	1	1	1	2	
Fertiliser (chemical)	0	0	2	1	0.5	0.3	0.4	2	4	1	2	
Pharmaceuticals	0	0	0.1	0	0	0	0	0	0	0.1	0.5	
Total (US$ million)	357	494	687	811	934	819	1,077	1,231	1,292	1,524	1,718	2,098[b]

Notes: [a] Estimate; [b] 1992

Source: Bangladesh, Export Promotion Bureau 1992a, 1992b and data supplied; IMF, Direction of Trade Statistics

contradictory, but the most reliable appear to indicate a small rise to about 12% (Bakht, 1992).[2] The sector's share of employment is similar. Agriculture and, more recently, services are the major sectors of the economy. The principal industries are jute processing, followed by cotton textiles, then chemical fertilisers and petroleum refining. All these involve large firms, with typically over 500 employees, while for industry as a whole, the average on published figures (which may be underestimates: see below) is only 50. The principal export industries, even including jute manufactures, along with clothing, leather, processed fish, and packaged tea, make up only 17% of the sector, and 12% of employment (Bakht, 1992).

Industry is thus clearly still small, and mainly import-substituting, rather than for export. Because of the absolute size of the country and its manufacturing sector, even direct first-round effects of the expansion of clothing production for export have had little perceptible effect on the total volume of manufacturing (clothing production was estimated at 1% of the manufacturing sector in 1990: Bhuyan and Rashid, 1992). The export industries that do exist are almost without exception purely for export, not extensions of domestic industries as they are in Colombia or even Thailand, the other 'large' countries in this sample. As will be seen in the discussion of individual products, the apparently related commodities (leather and leather goods, textiles and clothing) are effectively independent sectors. There is a small regional market for pharmaceuticals (although all the major countries have their own industries) and for some oil products. Exports are therefore clearly not next stages, in any industrial sense, of a development process, suggesting that an alternative development explanation, or domestic or international policy, must be the cause.

PATTERNS OF TRADE

Until the early 1980s, jute and jute products were Bangladesh's dominant export, although shrimp, leather and tea were becoming important. The following decade brought a complete transformation, with jute products falling from over 60% to under 20% in the nine years after 1982/3 and clothing rising from under 2% to over 50% (Table 14.2). Of the 1970s exports only leather maintained its share, and the least processed form of that (wet blue) was banned from export in 1991.

Although its exports are a small part of its own economy, its size means that Bangladesh remains the major world supplier of jute (73% of total trade in 1990). The fall in exports is the result of other materials becoming substitutes in packaging and carpet, not alternative suppliers. Bangladesh is a significant supplier of shrimp and of clothing, at global level and in the US and EC markets. In 1992, it was the largest external supplier of T shirts and other shirts to the EC and the seventh largest to the US (BGMEA). This is the opposite of the normal position of the smaller countries in this study, where exports are important to them but small relative to their markets, and has important implications for the role of trade policy.

Bangladesh has a much broader spread of markets than most of the countries examined here (Table 14.3), and this is true also for individual commodities (Table 14.4). Its share of trade with other Asian countries is high, compared with the non-Asian countries (Table 2.5), but is well below that of Thailand or Malaysia. As in Thailand, the share has been falling in recent years. Bangladesh also had a high share of trade with other non-industrial countries, particularly in the Middle East, but also in Africa and the former centrally planned economies. Within Asia, its trade has gone both to the other countries of South Asia and to East Asia. All these developing country markets declined in the late 1980s or early 1990s, with particularly strong falls for the Middle East. There low oil revenues and war reduced demand in its major trading partner, Iran. After 1989, the USSR and Eastern European market declined. The main growth in exports after 1985 was to the industrial countries. The share of exports to the EC and the US doubled between 1985 and 1991; there was no increase in those to Japan. Bangladesh thus appears to have shifted on to the early path of the successful East and South-East Asian countries.

The change corresponds to their history in terms of the products to each market as well (Table 14.4). Although some jute products had gone to the industrial countries, most had gone to the other Asian countries, the Middle East, and some specialised markets (e.g. Australia, to pack wool). Tea had been exported to the Middle East and the USSR, and the few chemical exports went to immediate neighbours. In contrast, the new exports, first shrimp, then clothing, went to the more advanced markets. For Bangladesh, as for Africa and Latin America now and the Asian countries in the 1970s, the regional market is for traditional goods. By 1990, Australia was still taking mainly jute (84% of Bangladesh exports to it in 1990/1); China imported jute and leather; jute was the principal export to India (70%); Pakistan, Iran and Iraq took jute and tea. The Eastern European countries bought jute, with the USSR also taking tea and leather.

The EC had always been an important market because of a few countries' imports of jute, notably Belgium, but the clothing exports went into different markets, into Germany, the UK and France. Prior to this, in the 1970s, the increase in leather exports had gone to Italy. The first major exports of clothing and, before that, shrimp were to the US and Canada (and Japan for shrimp). The progression from traditional goods to new ones thus seems unrelated to exploiting either existing markets or existing products.

CHARACTERISTICS OF THE NEW EXPORTERS

In both clothing and leather, Bangladesh specialises in high-volume runs of simple, low-cost items, probably, of the countries examined here, most

Table 14.3   Bangladesh: principal markets, countries and regions (1972–92) (percentages)

Region/country	1972	1977	1982	1983	1984	1985	1986	1987	1986/7	1987/8	1988/9	1989/90	1990/1	1992
EC	28	22	16	20	25	17	21	23	26	29	30	32	39	36
Germany	3	2	2	2	2	2	3	4	4	5	5	6	10	8
UK	13	8	5	6	7	5	5	5	6	6	6	6	8	7
Italy	2	4	3	4	7	4	5	8	9	9	8	9	7	7
France	2	2	1	1	1	0	1	1	1	2	3	4	5	5
Belgium	6	3	3	5	5	4	4	3	4	3	4	4	5	3
US	17	14	10	14	14	18	24	30	30	29	27	29	30	36
Japan	4	3	6	7	7	7	8	6	6	5	4	4	2	2
Asia, developing	8	15	27	17	19	15	13	12	11	11	14	10	11	10
Singapore	3	2	11	2	4	3	2	4	3	3	4	3	3	2
China	0	3	3	3	1	1	3	2	2	2	2	1	2	1
India	0	0	3	1	3	3	1	1	1	1	1	1	2	0
Pakistan	0	7	5	7	7	4	4	3	3	3	2	2	2	1
Middle East	2	5	10	17	15	15	10	7	8	7	5	7	4	5
Iran	0	0	2	9	8	8	4	2	4	2	1	3	2	1
Africa	14	13	10	6	5	11	8	6	7	6	7	4	4	2
Eastern Europe and the USSR	12	9	9	10	6	5	6	5	5	5	6	7	3	1
USSR	5	5	5	6	3	3	3	4	3	3	3	4	1	1
Brazil	0	0	0	0	0	0	1	1	1	1	1	1	1	1
Australia	3	3	3	2	2	1	2	2	2	1	1	1	1	1
Canada	2	2	1	1	2	1	2	2	1	2	1	1	2	1

Sources: 1986/7–1990/1: Export Promotion Bureau, 1992b, 1972–1986, 1992; IMF, *Direction of Trade Statistics*

comparable to the Jamaican industry but even larger and cheaper. The factories visited expected fewer skills from their labour force, in terms of being able to switch even among products on the same machines, than in the other countries in this study; this was confirmed by the industry organisations and Bangladeshi researchers. The first export factories were established with South Korean advice in the late 1970s and early 1980s (Spinanger, 1987), with exports beginning in 1981, and the main rise starting from 1984 (Table 14.2). The Koreans were joined by Hong Kong and Indian companies. Some were trading companies; others were producers with factories producing similar products in their own and other countries. Throughout, the factories have been in local ownership but, until some recent exceptions, the foreign purchasing of inputs and sales have been entirely in the hands of foreign companies, with the Bangladeshi firm limited to CMT (cut, make, trim) operations. The source of the materials as well as the fabric and design were entirely externally specified. The cost of the materials was estimated by industry sources and individual firms at about 80% of output value. These are almost entirely imported, giving a Bangladeshi valued added of 20% (consistent with estimates for Jamaica). As indicated below in the discussion of the role of preferences, some producers are now considering the potential advantages of increasing the use of local fabric, and some firms for the US market buy local accessories. The advantages offered by Bangladesh were cheap labour and, initially, no quotas to any market.

The move of the clothing industry to Bangladesh coincided with similar moves into Mauritius and Jamaica, and from the same East Asian countries. Table 14.4a shows that the principal market initially was the US, with the EC starting to become important after 1987, and then increasing rapidly in importance. There are indications, including the source of accessories and the amount of training normal for workers (weeks for the US market; months for the EC), that the EC market was seen here, as in other countries,

Table 14.4a Bangladesh: markets for principal commodities (percentages). Clothing

Fiscal year	US	EC	Germany	UK	France
1977/78	100	0	0	0	0
1982/83	43				
1983/84	58				
1984/85	81	11	5	2	3
1985/86	81	8	4	2	1
1986/87	78	14	7	1	1
1987/88	63	20	10	4	4
1988/89	58	34	9	2	6
1989/90	56	35	9	7	8
1990/91	51	42	13	8	7

Table 14.4b   Bangladesh: markets for principal commodities
(percentages). Other exports

Commodity	1989/90	1990/91
Jute manufactures		
US	12	14
EC	18	24
Belgium	9	11
Australia	7	9
Middle East	21	17
Tea		
USSR and Eastern Europe	31	24
Middle East	21	29
Asia	32	27
UK and Germany	9	7
Chemical fertiliser		
Asia	100	100
Pharmaceuticals		
Asia	79	89
Middle East	21	0
Japan	0	8
Leather		
EC	64	53
Italy	53	35
Brazil	11	12
Asia	6	16
China	2	7
Japan	7	7
Shoes		
EC	0	92
Shrimp		
US	41	33
Japan	22	14
EC	34	52
Belgium	11	17
Household linen		
EC	19	75
Belgium	10	50
US	79	18
Hosiery		
EC	81	70
Germany	30	24
US	14	26

Sources: Export Promotion Bureau, 1992b; Jackson, 1992; Eversley, 1991

to require a greater range and higher quality of goods. As in other countries, this would explain the apparent division of suppliers.

The local firms were initially, and on the data appear still to be, small factories (50–100 machines is the most common size, BGMEA), each with individual contacts with one or a limited number of agents, and each tied to supplying the agents' markets in either the US or the EC. Some firms, however, now in fact control a number of apparently separate factories, with some directed at the US market and others towards the EC. Other firms specialise entirely in one or the other, but some of these when interviewed were considering the alternative, or other markets. The specialisation and the dependence on individual relationships with external agents are not as universal as they may appear, although there are firms and factories where they occur. This accords with the experience of locally owned firms found in other countries.

There was some evidence that, more than in the other countries, the importing countries preferred to deal through an agent, located in Hong Kong or other East Asian country, suggesting that Bangladesh was regarded as a direct substitute or extension of the clothing industry in these countries rather than an independent supplier with its own characteristics. This was initially an advantage for the firms in becoming established, but was an obstacle to moving beyond this, with neither the US and EC purchasers nor the Bangladeshi exporters familiar with each other or the procedures for trading between them, and no reputation for Bangladesh as an exporter.

There is a large textile production industry in Bangladesh, but its fabrics, both the grey cloth and the dyeing and finishing stages, are considered by the clothing producers to be of too low quality for clothing for export. The establishment of the clothing industry for export, therefore, had no relationship to this. Some clothing producers are now trying to improve the quality of local fabric supplies because of fears for the supply of imported fabric and for the market for clothing with a low local content when the MFA is changed. The textile industry, unlike the clothing, has considerable public sector involvement and for that reason and because of its size potentially more political constraints.

The leather sector has some similar characteristics, including the apparent divide between the raw material and processing. The locally produced hides include one very high quality type of goat, which is sent abroad for processing for products which meet fashion and quality standards, and low quality cattle, not suitable for leather goods for export. Local finishing and dyeing are of low quality. The leather goods industry is therefore attempting to develop as a sector based on processing imported materials for low rather than high fashion items for re-export, similar to the clothing sector. The export data suggest that it has been much less successful. The following sections suggest that the difficulties imposed by local conditions are sufficient to outweigh the cheap labour advantages which Bangladesh can offer in both leather and clothing processing, in the absence of the quota influences which have assisted its clothing industry.

TARIFFS AND PREFERENCES AND NTBs

Bangladesh is not a member of any industrial country preference scheme. It is entitled to GSP treatment, but this does not apply to most of its exports of clothing, because clothing is not included in the US GSP scheme and Bangladesh does not meet minimum local content requirements on most products for the EC. (There is some export of yarn from India for knitting into fabric for clothing exports to the EC, and about 5% of clothing exports use local fabric.) This puts Bangladesh at a cost disadvantage (the relevant tariff on most of its products is about 15% to the EC) relative to suppliers with ACP or other privileges which would be difficult to recover at any labour cost as labour accounts for only about 10% of the final price. The need to import fabric with high shipping costs puts it at a further disadvantage relative to any competing country with access to local fabric. This would include China, India, and Pakistan among those who supply it now with fabric and orders, although not Hong Kong and Korea. It is clearly quotas on the competition which give Bangladesh its only advantage as an exporter. GSP does cover jute, although any competitive advantage there must be measured against suppliers of synthetics, not alternative jute suppliers. It also covers its other new exports: leather goods, fruits and vegetables.

In its official statement on trade policy to the GATT when its policy was reviewed (GATT, 1992), Bangladesh cited tariff escalation as a problem, but this does not seem to apply to any of its exports, and the segmentation between stages of its important export industries suggests that it would be a misleading concept even if it did. In most cases, it is not facing the choice of exporting at successive stages of processing of the same product. The leather which it exports is not an input into the type of leather goods which it produces.

Officials and some exporters, in interviews in late 1992, expected the US to suspend Bangladesh's GSP status because of complaints about the employment of children, even though the complaints were about clothing in which Bangladesh does not get GSP access from the US. No change had been made by the end of 1993.

Bangladesh is a member of the GSTP (Global System of Trade Preferences) among developing countries: this applies to tea, jute, and leather, but not clothing or its other new exports. It is also a member of various regional groups, including the South Asian Association for Regional Cooperation and the Asian Free Trade Association, neither of which has implemented any trade policies.

It faces unusually high non-tariff barriers (Table 14.5) for an Asian country, especially given its relatively low share of trade with industrial countries. This is because of the high share of its exports of clothing products. It also faces high barriers to exports of shrimp. Although by including the EC quotas on clothing imposed in 1985–6, and subsequently removed, Table 14.5 overstates the nominal present position, bilateral agreements are in force which would permit them to be reimposed, and both the government and exporters see this as a real and imminent threat. The history of the imposition of controls indicates why.

When the clothing industry was introduced into Bangladesh, not only did it have no MFA controls, but no country classified, as it is, as 'least developed' was subject to the MFA (Bangladesh remains the only least developed couuntry under the MFA). These countries were singled out as deserving special preferences and exemptions from controls. In 1985, when it had become a significant, but not a major exporter of clothing (Table 14.2), first the UK and France, then the US, followed by Canada, imposed quotas on some types of shirts. There had been 'rumblings' (Spinanger, 1987) at the end of 1984, but the exporters had not expected a sudden change in policy, Shipments already on the way were stopped, and about two-thirds of factories had to close, temporarily or permanently (Jackson, 1992). Although the EC quotas were removed in 1986, and the US quotas eventually allowed for relatively high growth rates (10%) and left some goods uncontrolled, the exporters continue to feel vulnerable to a repetition.

At the time, the Bangladeshi share of the market was extremely small, and the reaction of sympathetic outside observers (see, for example, Spinanger, 1987) was that the recent spurt of growth could not be extrapolated to an expectation that the US market would be overwhelmed by Bangladeshi products. Although the subsequent history of Bangladeshi exports suggests that the potential for further growth was extremely high, it was not perceptible in the figures of exports to the UK and France by 1985 (Table 14.4a). It is probably more important that this was the time of the general shift of the quota-controlled Asian countries into other countries, several of which were starting to be significant suppliers at the same time (including several in this study). A warning shock was probably one of the intentions of the quotas. It is the impact on Bangladeshi attitudes, the creation of a constant fear of new controls, that is more unusual, and in need of explanation, than the fact of the quota imposition.

In 1990, the USA took anti-dumping and countervailing action against one product which was already controlled by quota. This again increased exporters' caution about relying on quota-controlled markets.

Although the EC had been the first to impose quotas, it did remove them. The US has kept them. By 1992, a third (28 out of 84) of Bangladeshi products exported to the US were under quota, accounting for 70% by value. At least half of these were effectively at full quota utilisation (BGMEA), and this was already true by 1990/1 (GATT, 1992 vol.1: 226).

Table 14.5 Bangladesh: non-tariff barriers (percentage 1986 weights on 1990 data)

SITC	Product area	EC	US	Japan	Total[a]	Total[b]
0+1+22+4	All food items	73	0	100	61	61
0	Food + live animals	74	0	100	61	
031	Fresh fish	89	0	100	58	
036	Shell fish	70	0	100	50	
2 less (22+27+28)	Agricultural raw materials	4	6	14	5	0
27+28+67+68	Ores and metals	0	0	0	0	0
6–8 less (67+68)	Manufactures, not chemicals	21	40	63	23	31
61	Leather and furs	0	0	16	0	
65	Textiles, yarn and fabric	100	0	80	6	
84	Clothing	51	57	0	44	
85	Footwear	100	0	0	66	
0–9	All items	34	35	86	26	

Notes:
[a] Totals and subtotals found by applying 1986 importer weights to 1990 totals and subtotals
[b] Totals and subtotals found by applying 1986 importer weights to each commodity, and summing the commodities

Source: Calculated from UNCTAD database

The US had remained the market of choice, even with quotas. This was particularly true for existing suppliers. These companies and their agents were familiar with the US market. It was only when new firms and new Asian agents looking for cheaper as well as EC-quota-free sources came into the industry after 1985 that exports to the EC started to build up, becoming significant only in 1987/8. But this contrast between 'new' and 'old' firms should not be exaggerated in an industry where an old firm means (at earliest) established in 1982–4, i.e. one still managed by its, probably young, founder.

The quotas are allocated using criteria set by the government but administered by the industry association, the Bangladesh Garment Manufacturers and Exporters Association (BGMEA). The end-1992 system was similar to that in other exporting countries, with about 20% overallocation, and 90% reserved for existing suppliers. There was an allowance of 10% for users of local fabric, but this was not fully used. The government attempted to introduce a change to increase this reservation for local fabric (to 15%) and to increase the discretion in awards on the basis of past performance, but this was opposed (successfully) partly because of the local content rule, but also because of distrust of the government's use of discretion. Given the way in which the industry operates, with production only on the basis of advance orders, and long lead times (to obtain imported inputs), any uncertainty would carry a high risk, but the potential for government corruption was also an argument. The quotas are transferrable, either through sale or through sub-contracting orders to other factories.

Companies shifting to non-quota markets thus have two gains in terms of reducing vulnerability to policy: to domestic quota allocation and to foreign quotas. But the latter may not be seen as significant. The 1985 actions by importers clearly indicated that quotas could be imposed by any importer at any time. And, at the time of interview, most officials and exporters expected EC quotas to be re-imposed in 1993, because of high exports, or adjustments to the Single European Market, or clear indications from EC officials that Bangladesh was suspected of being a source of illegally re-exported goods from quota-controlled countries. This parallels the GSP fears quoted earlier, and earlier reports and statements on trade showed that such fears were not unique to end-1992.

Expectations for the Uruguay Round of GATT were mixed. Bangladesh gained from lower tariffs on tea, vegetables, and leather, but thought that the GSP scheme would not be improved to make up for developing countries' loss of relative preference. It expected to lose share in clothing as the MFA was phased out, for two reasons. Those countries which had used Bangladesh to supplement their own production, effectively as a location for outward processing to get into markets in which they faced quotas, no longer need to do so. They will choose to produce at home instead. This applies particularly to India and Pakistan. In addition, as most of the fabric used comes from countries which could process it themselves, even if the Bangladeshi firms had the low costs and marketing contacts to maintain market share, Bangladeshi firms will be unable to obtain the supplies. Hong Kong and Korea do not have their own fabric, but they obtain fabric from China, which could also prefer to make its own clothing for export. On costs, Bangladesh feared competition from lower-cost suppliers like Vietnam.

The reaction was not to attempt to protect its preferences (as in Mauritius and, to a lesser extent, Jamaica), but to try to increase use of local textiles which would remove its GSP and its shipping cost disadvantages as well as ensuring supply (and reducing delays in meeting orders). It is notable that, in spite of the evidence from their own experience of how quickly an industry can be established (or, in the case of jute, lost), government and industrial decision-makers were assuming that the basis for adjustment should be to start from the now mature clothing industry rather than looking for other types of advantage derived either from Bangladesh's low processing costs or from exploiting preferences. While, as in other countries, the managers had been able to acquire more of the skills of marketing, purchasing and design than are expected in the more pessimistic assessments of operating a CMT industry, they do not seem to have acquired that of identifying a new industry, or recognising the need to do so. The difference from the post-MFA expectations of Jamaica or Mauritius cannot be attributed (as some Bangladesh policy-makers do) to the inexperience in exporting because, as an export industry, Bangladeshi clothing is the same age, although the firms themselves are newer.

There are some phytosanitary problems with exports, with the oil used to soften jute or the hygiene in shrimp processing, but these are not important, and are unlikely to have long-term effects.

BANGLADESHI POLICY

This has had serious effects on the ability to respond to market opportunities, and probably also on the attitudes to preferences and barriers in other countries. Since independence, government intervention has been extensive in terms of the industries covered and the detail and quantity of administrative intervention. This may explain why industries build their operations around an expectation of delays and changes in policies. The declared strategy of the 1970s was of import substitution in industry, with government intervention in key sectors, including jute and other textile manufacturing. In 1982, 1986, and 1991, relaxations of industrial and import control policies were made. There was also intervention to promote new exports starting from the establishment of the Export Promotion Board in 1978 and an export zone in 1984.

There is not, however, a strategy either for helping the industries designated for the 'Crash programme' or for helping new exports, so that the systems have tended to favour existing, traditional exports or those established because of the external influences described above. This makes moving out of established industries more difficult than adjusting within them. This is reinforced by administrative requirements.

Although formal licensing of imports has been reduced, especially for exporters, and the 1991 reforms were considered to have been significant, the procedures that remain still favour established firms operating to fixed orders or long-term contracts. An exporter with a 'passbook' listing the imports which he has shown that he needs, and with an order and letter of credit from his importer, can obtain the imports (duty-free if they go into his bonded warehouse or an export processing zone) and credit for working capital to permit him to fulfil the order. The principal practical constraint is delay. He cannot order the materials or keep stocks until he gets the order. The importer must be willing to use the system and make arrangements for an exceptionally long credit and order period. Given the use of imported fabric or leather, combined with Bangladesh's location off the main shipping routes, the time from order to delivery is estimated fairly consistently as a minimum of six months, and up to seven or eight, including shipping of the material, and possibly sending of samples at the beginning, a long production period of one to two, or even three, months, as well as shipping the final product. Other difficulties include: the inflexibility in imports (if a new type of order requires a new import or if prices change, the pass book must be amended); the inflexibility in procedure: no possibility of production before an order, or for a new exporter to establish himself with small, short-term orders (as in those countries where the earliest exports were sometimes to meet end-year demand for goods where other suppliers had used up their quotas).

This is a system which makes only large orders really practical. It is reinforced by the preference, because of poor training of workers and the inexperience and lack of training of managers, for long production runs. Companies quoted delays of several days for switching between products in the clothing industry, substantially higher than in the other countries where it was measured in hours. As long standard runs mean supplying the quota-controlled products and the US market, the regulatory structure makes switching out of these difficult. Bangladesh import tariffs are high, except for exporters' exemptions (the reductions of the 1980s brought them down on average only from 200% to 100%, and then to 70%, with various taxes on top), and working capital is difficult to obtain, so there is no alternative to following this procedure. There were provisions for duty refund, but these were too cumbersome to be practical (Bhuyan and Rashid, 1992; interview notes). Many of the special assistance measures for exports, bonded warehouses, for example, are available only to named commodities (clothing, leather, some textiles) (Bhuyan and Rashid, 1993), again discouraging new exports.

Because the working capital supplied was against the total export order, such arrangements do not encourage switching to lower exports, with higher local value added, although the delays in acquiring imports do give encouragement in this direction.

COUNTERTRADE, AID AND INFRASTRUCTURE

Until 1989, Bangladesh had countertrade agreements with the East European countries and the USSR. (Individual deals normally made by the public sector industries were also possible.) Table 14.6 shows the share of imports financed by it. As the value of imports is more than twice that of exports, this means that it reached a peak of about 14–15% of exports (Table 7.1), one of the highest shares, but only because of its high share to the centrally planned economies, not as a tool of export policy. It was seen as a way of promoting total exports by increasing trade with the planned economies, not of increasing the share of new exports. The principal commodity exported to the USSR under it was tea. The other important products were jute, hides, and leather, although other products were eligible (GATT, 1992, vol. 1: 132). It is not used now because trade with the USSR has been put on a currency basis (Export Promotion Bureau).

Foreign investment into Bangladesh has been insignificant, and what has occurred has gone into non-traded sectors, including finance and commerce. The roles which it has played in the other countries studied have been filled in a variety of ways. In terms of initiating industries and finding markets, it has been replaced by the agents and trading companies in the CMT arrange-

Table 14.6 Bangladesh: how imports are financed 1972–91 (percentages)

Fiscal years	Aid flows	Countertrade	Exports	Migrants, etc.
1972/3	55	5	37	3
1977/8	56	4	39	1
1979/80	50	3	32	15
1982/3	56	3	30	11
1983/4	48	3	34	15
1984/5	43	3	35	19
1985/6	39	5	35	21
1986/7	48	4	41	7
1987/8	44	4	41	11
1988/9	34	5	38	23
1989/90	32	3	41	24
1991/92	27	4	48	21

Sources: GATT, 1992 vol.1: 76, vol.2: 76; Bhuyan and Rashid, 1992: 96

Table 14.7 Bangladesh: multilateral and untied aid (US$m or percentages)

Bangladesh	1975	1980	1985	1990
Ratio of aid to imports (%)	72.37	48.56	40.81	58.37
Multilateral	253	362	499	1,008
Multi-EC	192	329	492	949
Bilateral	704	850	622	1,103
Untied bilateral	200	455	215	612
Total untied	392	784	707	1,561
Tied/imports (%)	42.6	18.39	15.31	14.98

Note: The average tied ratio for all bilateral aid is assumed for all areas

Sources: OECD, *Development Co-operation* and *Geographical Distribution of Financial Flows to Developing Countries*, annual issues

ments found in the clothing industry. Their activities include an element of technology transfer, through the designs provided. The amount of help has varied, with less for those companies producing standardised products for the US market and more for the slightly higher value-added products for the EC market. It has been limited, however, to what was needed by second tier managers. Managers of Bangladeshi firms were operating effectively as factory managers for a foreign firm. In other industries, including leather, technology and design have been bought in. In terms of external finance, it is aid which has replaced foreign investment.

The value of aid is equivalent to more than half Bangladesh's imports, much the highest of any country included here (Tables 14.6 and 14.7), and higher than the country's total value of exports. It directly finances almost a third of imports. In the 1970s its predominance as a source of finance was even greater. In 1990, it was equivalent to more than 10% of GDP (Table 5.2), down from 15% in the early 1980s. It is equally divided between multilateral and bilateral, with the main bilateral sources now being the EC and Japan (Table 5.7). Although the US inflow is less than either of these, Bangladesh still receives more US aid than any other country of those studied.

There are no direct Bangladeshi data on the amount of aid which is tied by country (Sobhan, 1990),[3] but most of the US and EC aid is believed to be tied, while Middle East, including Saudi Arabian, aid is not tied (*ibid.*). Aid from Japan is restricted to developing or OECD countries, although it tends to be used with Japanese suppliers. Two surveys are available of the cost in terms of price differentials of tied aid. GATT (1992, vol.1: 133) quotes figures for cotton imports from Sudan in 1986, giving a premium of 34% over the cash price for aid-financed purchases, and almost 90% for barter. Sobhan (1990: 129) did a more extensive survey, although again restricted to commodities and imports by the public sector corporations, for purchases between 1977 and 1984. This found that the premium for purchases made with untied aid was about 7%, for tied 28%, with none of the observations giving a tied figure below the cash price or the untied price. These results imply, first, that the value of tied aid should be reduced by about 30%, with a corresponding deflation in the value of imports (the 1990 figures in Table 14.7 would then be 56% for the ratio of aid to imports and 11% for tied aid to imports). This does not greatly alter the picture of significant dependence on official flows. What is more important is that these results, and the fact that even the untied aid is tied by project or type of use, suggest strong restraints on Bangladesh's own choice of imports or industrial strategy.

Some specific constraints have been identified. In the 1970s, about half the US programme was made up of food aid under PL 480 (Sobhan, 1990: 147). This remains an important constraint on the composition of imports. There is a high use of foreign consultants, with a corresponding emphasis on foreign sources of expertise and supplies for projects (*ibid.*; local evidence). There appears to be a reinforcing effect, with donors complaining, with justification, about the competence of government officials, and potentially competent officials choosing not to remain in a government where all the important strategic decisions are made by the donors. While this is an often argued risk of aid programmes, the scale of the aid contribution and therefore of the policy intervention in Bangladesh is significantly different from that in the other countries, so that a Bangladeshi perception of helplessness, even if exaggerated, is probably inevitable and justifiable.

Given the share of aid in both imports and national income, the sectoral priorities of the donors strongly influence policy. These have emphasised construction and agricultural development. Donor statements offer little evidence of support for industrialisation (and repeated opposition to the import-substitution policy in the last 10 years). In particular, there is no evidence of any awareness of the possibilities of a clothing-led export boom until well after it had happened. The emphasis seems to remain on agriculture and infrastructure. This is a significant contrast to the industrial and exporting role of foreign capital in the countries where foreign investors were active.

While other countries in the group have been able to 'use' donors more effectively, they have not faced the complete dependence found in Bangladesh. Some of the others have experienced parallel difficulties in influencing foreign investors' role in investment or trade, so here aid seems to show similar characteristics to investment, but the scale of aid in Bangladesh greatly exceeds that of foreign investment in any of the countries considered here. As Table 14.6 shows, a central fact about the nature and form of external influence on Bangladesh is that aid flows, even taking only their most direct effect on trade, were greater than exports until 1988/9, and in total value they continue to exceed exports. Or, in terms of Table 7.1, trade controlled by countertrade, aid, and NTBs comes to a total of between

90 and 95 % of the value of exports, or about half the value of imports. Combined with the local controls on all imports and, through controls over the imported materials, probably on 70% of exports, it would be difficult to expect a Bangladeshi exporter to consider trading a purely market and price-led activity.

Table 14.6 also shows that migrant remittances have been up to half as important as exports in financing imports. This must reinforce the dependence on aid in reducing the likelihood that the government will perceive exports as a policy priority.

CONCLUSIONS

Bangladesh acquired a major new export in the 1980s almost entirely because of other countries' trade policy. It was started and largely managed by companies seeking a non-quota-controlled alternative to their existing factories. The 'almost' is because Bangladesh was chosen. This suggests that it had some identifiable advantages over other possible new production locations. These did not stem from any special access of its own (unlike Mauritius and Jamaica, for example, which had Lomé and CBI privileges). They are likely to have been its low labour costs (and large labour supplies). The experience of other industries, however, notably leather and leather goods, does not suggest that Bangladesh could have attracted clothing without the MFA spur. But the question for the future is whether the cost advantage, plus the fact that it does now have a clothing industry with, therefore, some capital, worker training, and managerial experience, and potentially linkages to other sectors, will be sufficient to maintain an industry without the policy advantages; in particular, with the reforms which will follow under the Uruguay Round settlement. The capital and worker experience are probably not significant: both can be acquired in other countries at low cost and within at most a few months (as they were in Bangladesh). The type of subcontracting operation which has characterised the clothing sector in Bangladesh is an extreme form of that normally considered not to have long-term effects on the industrial structure either in terms of linkages to the rest of the economy or through management skills because of the minimal local input to both. Thus Bangladesh offers a severe test of the permanent effects of a temporary preference.

There are additional obstacles. The type of orders which the structure of the Bangladeshi industry and policy administration make it most able to deal with – large and slow – are the type which other countries find are becoming less important. As the quota system ends, the present fabric supplies will be greatly reduced. Therefore it is not sufficient for the industry simply to be able to continue: it needs to be able to adapt, either by changing its structure and markets or by means of firms moving into different sectors (as has happened in the most advanced countries, Malaysia and Thailand, and in

273

Mauritius and Jamaica) or into supplying local demand (the Colombian, and in the past the Zimbabwean, solution).

New firms have been established, with less dependence on agents, and the existing firms have moved away from such dependence and into new markets. Both at a firm level and on the aggregate trade figures, the industry has adapted. The current strategies, however, of looking for backward linkages rather than for new export or local production possibilities are not those which have proved successful in other countries, and the economic difficulties of making a highly technology- and capital-intensive industry like textile finishing competitive in a country with Bangladesh' resources (and without support from the major suppliers of capital, the aid donors) remain as large as they were before clothing appeared in 1982.

There are new managers, in (at present small) new industries: in specialised pharmaceuticals, leather, possibly in some services. But the local constraints on building up a new industry, and the scale required to make an impact on the manufacturing sector of a country with the population of Bangladesh (100 times that of Mauritius), will make it difficult to achieve even one repetition of the clothing example, much less a sustained process of replication, not just substitution for the sales that may be lost when quotas go. While the impact of clothing exports on the individuals in the industry and on total exports is clear, the lack of perceptible impact in either raising total manufacturing output or changing the generally dismissive attitude to exports in particular and Bangladesh's ability to perform satisfactorily in general[4] suggests that even an equal impact to that of clothing will be seriously insufficient.

The unimportance of exports relative to other external income encourages the attitude on the part of officials and donors that clothing exports are a pleasant, but unexpected and unrepeatable, benefit to some sectors of the economy (creating some employment, raising the status of women, replacing the stagnating jute exports), but not really a serious policy variable. Industrial policy and discussion of export promotion remain abstract and centred around the effects of Bangladeshi policy intervention (whether in accordance with or against the objectives of the donors), not the policies of other countries. The small scale of exports and of the manufacturing sector makes this attitude understandable, but if industrialisation and meeting international competition are important elements of development, it is questionable from a strategic point of view.

The external dominance of Bangladesh's economy obviously comes more from aid than from trade. But both influences have led to a view of trade, imports and exports, as largely outside national or economic control. The distrust of external policies (and the pessimism about changes in them which was evident in expectations for the Uruguay Round, GSP, EC quotas, etc.) may, as in Zimbabwe, also be related to a more general disbelief in continuity of policy at home. This was explicitly given as a reason for not expanding or seeking new opportunities by several managers interviewed, and was evident in the more general use of explanations like lack of political stability or labour unrest for poor performance.

But the Bangladeshi pessimism should not cloud analysis. Bangladesh is, like Zimbabwe, one of the youngest countries, without, until within the working life of current managers, the opportunity to take policy decisions, public or private. The ability to create, even with external assistance, an export which has grown to 50% of total exports in under a decade, including achieving a recovery within months from the impact of the 1985–6 quotas, suggests some ability to take advantage of new conditions. That its managers had not yet in 1992 found a suitable strategy to adapt to a change in the MFA which was not certain until December 1993 and which will take up to 10 years – equivalent to the entire period since clothing was established as an export industry in Bangladesh – is not evidence that they cannot do so.

In a poor country, with limited savings, rationing these by cumbersome procedures and to established exporters has disadvantages, but the alternative would not be unlimited finance at reasonable cost, but either high interest rates (with consequences for cash flows and the viability of any production) or more arbitrary allocation. It is clear from the reaction to the proposed discretionary quota scheme in clothing that discretion would not be welcome to industry. An alternative scheme might be more suitable for new producers, or for rapid response, but it is possible that other constraints, such as lack of training and transport infrastructure, would still impede the type of industry found in Mauritius or Jamaica, or even Colombia and Zimbabwe. Relying effectively on importers for working capital, combined with the freedom to use migrants' funds, may be an effective way of using the only sources of foreign exchange (and the main sources of savings) available, other than aid flows which are directed by foreign decisions into non-industrial uses.

A lesson for the structure of industry, which has already been mentioned in connection with other countries, is the inappropriateness of judging the boundaries of an 'industry' in terms of apparent relations among products. The leather and clothing industries of Bangladesh are not, for economic purposes, related to the hide and textile sectors.

NOTES

1 11 July to 30 June.
2 Data on growth and composition of GDP are unusually variable in published analyses of the economy, reflecting considerable distrust of the official sources and attempts to find alternative methods of estimation. Bakht and Bhattacharya, 1991 gives a fall in the 1980s to 9%.
3 For Table 14.7, as in the corresponding tables in other chapters, the average for all OECD aid flows is used.

4 Sobhan (1990: 177) quotes Just Faaland, the World Bank's representative in the early 1970s: 'The opportunity for the aid-givers to impose their views on Bangladesh was made all too clear when it became the accepted view that Bangladesh simply could not manage her economy without the assurance that large amounts of aid would be forthcoming'.

15

DEVELOPMENT UNDER
A CONSTRAINED TRADING
SYSTEM

External constraints or other policies cover almost all the trade of the seven countries examined here, and each faces the indirect consequences of constraints and preferences on the exports of other countries. In terms of measurable controls on individual commodities, Bangladesh is probably the worst affected, although closely followed by Mauritius and Jamaica. But the analysis of how the trading structure has evolved even in an apparently less controlled country like Malaysia shows that the actual impact of controls goes beyond the direct effects to the role of the external sector, and attitudes to it, in each country. The results for individual countries thus confirm those found in Chapter 7.

TRADE IS POLICY-DRIVEN

All the countries take as a basic assumption of their own approaches to trade that the international system is policy-driven, although within this they vary in their confidence in their own ability to be successful through economic efficiency, and the more active traders also recognise differences among products or markets, and have targeted their own trade accordingly. The nearest to being an exception to this mode of thought is perhaps Colombia, if only because the external sector is simply of less concern to its industry and policy-makers. But even there the recent impact of regional changes has made a substantial impression. The spectacular and clearly MFA-driven performance of clothing in four of the countries during the period examined is only the most obvious evidence which they could cite.

The presence or absence of barriers informs all Malaysia's trading decisions, and the role of preferences is similar in Mauritius. Both also show a strong cooperation between industry and official policy. In terms of specific effects, there seems to be good evidence that the high tariffs on more processed goods have deterred Malaysia from following its intention of a 'resource-based' export policy, although the effect appears to have been to move it towards other types of processing, i.e. into new products, rather than to hold it back from manufacturing, as a simple view of tariff escalation might imply. The objective of the strong Malaysian emphasis on trade has been principally to promote all exports and investment, not any particular type, and it is clear that barriers have held this back.

Thailand has left more initiative to industries to respond, in both local production and export promotion. At present, its exports appear to be more concentrated in protected goods than Malaysia's, but this could be the result of its stage of development.

Mauritius has also had a high share of exports in protected industries, but in the case of the new exports this has been because of a choice to exploit particular goods in which it has a preference (or does not have a quota). This may have left it in a vulnerable position as preferences decline. Jamaica is a much more subdued example of the same strategy. Preference-driven exports are a smaller share of the total, and official promotion has been less systematic.

Colombia and Zimbabwe have taken less active roles in looking for preferences. This is true of both government and industry. Traders are very conscious of barriers and controls, but as rather vague obstacles, rather than well-known constraints to be avoided or exploited. Bangladesh's clothing industry and some of its other new industries are similar to those in the other countries in making use of the advantages available to them under the international system, but the way in which the industries were established and the export industries themselves seem more detached from the rest of the economy and from other government policy than in other countries.

The evidence is that the countries have responded to the changes identified in the amount and distribution of protection since the mid-1970s. It was then that barriers rose in the industrial countries and the relative restriction continued to increase in the 1980s because of falls in some developing country barriers. The rise particularly affected the middle ground of commodities, reinforcing the pattern found here that it is neither primary nor high technology goods which face the highest barriers. The particular countries examined have faced increasing protection because they have been moving into the most protected area, the early and middle stages of processing. On the industrial side, those countries with developing country markets available and opening to them (Malaysia, to a smaller degree Thailand and Zimbabwe; in the 1990s, Colombia) increased their exports to their own region or to Asia.

In the 1970s, when the successful NICs of East Asia were developing, one important element of their strategy was to move into the fastest growing or more advanced markets, first the OPEC countries, then the industrial countries. In the late 1980s and 1990s, the same strategy could explain why the Asian NICs, and Malaysia, moved into their own regional market. All possible influences favoured Asia for Malaysia: it became the fastest growing area, able to absorb the same type of manufactures already exported to the industrial countries, as well as offering lower barriers. The other Asian countries in this study, Thailand and Bangladesh, were still at the stage of moving out of the traditional commodity or light manufactures goods which had given them high initial shares to Asia, and therefore in aggregate they were moving away from Asia. Similarly, Zimbabwe was still moving into industrial markets and the goods appropriate to them. The moves of Colombia from the EC towards the US and more recently Venezuela are attributable to lower barriers, as have been the changes in Jamaica's trade, reinforced by the fact that, while the EC offered more favourable access to its traditional exports, the US does to its newer ones. Mauritius shows no major changes.

It must be emphasised that the actual choice of market depends on the opportunities available to different countries in different regions, as well as international comparison of barriers or growth. Mauritius is the extreme example, effectively lacking a local region. Latin America and Africa still offer an important market only for relatively basic goods, and one which is smaller and growing more slowly than Asia. Although some effects from low or changed protection were perceptible globally in individual products, even in these experience varied widely.

The other virtually universal shift of the more advanced Asian developing countries during their peak development years was into exports of machinery or transport equipment, the point at which, as shown in Chapters 2 and 3, the level of tariffs and non-tariff barriers starts to fall as processing increases, instead of rising. Only Malaysia and Thailand have reached this stage, so for the rest minimising barriers has meant moving into goods in which either they face less protection than other countries or which are less protected than their other exports. This can mean primary goods or simple manufactures different from those which they already produce. Thus their new exports are on the whole still goods which face barriers or preferences in at least some markets.

In general, and particularly in the case of the most commonly found new industry, clothing, the move has been into a good in which they face less protection than other countries, not one on which they face less protection than on their existing exports. Thailand, Colombia and Zimbabwe have all diversified into primary goods other than their traditional exports: the now almost traditional fish, exotic fruit and vegetables, and flowers. Malaysia and Colombia have done well on their traditional primary exports. That four of a group of countries selected to represent industrialising countries have chosen to increase their primary exports as well as promoting manufactures, is at least suggestive evidence to support the bias against the early stages of manufacturing found in the structure of tariffs and NTBs. There are few major examples of increased processing of countries' own natural resources, aside from first-stage preserving of some of the fish and fruit.

In the countries where clothing or footwear have been introduced as major export activities, processing industries for local cloth or hides either do not exist or are not used. In Bangladesh, Mauritius, and Jamaica, the clothing-for-export industry has no link with the domestic textile industry (although Bangladesh is now trying to integrate backwards), while Zimbabwe has found it necessary to move away from local fabrics to make its clothing competitive. The countries with footwear or other leather product industries, Colombia, Zimbabwe, and Bangladesh, initially used local hides, but these are not of a suitable quality or type, and leather is therefore imported. The evidence suggests that tariff escalation was not the problem; the more important influences were the nature of the industry (in both, the stages of finishing and dyeing, unlike clothing or shoes, are capital- and technology-intensive) and the influence of the quota or preference regimes which affected the local industry or its competitors in other developing countries.

FOREIGN INFLUENCE ON NATIONAL RESPONSES

The important question remains of how far the response to the external situation has been by local initiative and how far by foreign purchasers or investors. Where there were domestic industries of a reasonable size and maturity – Colombia, definitely; Zimbabwe, perhaps – the response has been made, and successfully, by the local producer. In other cases, exporters already operating in other industries have been able to make the move – owners of the traditional crop in Zimbabwe, Mauritius, and, in a few cases, Jamaica. These three countries, two small and one subjected to a period of involuntary autarky under sanctions, are perhaps special cases in having relatively large diversified enterprises or holding companies across a range of economic activities at an early stage in their economic development.

In general, export innovation has involved some active external intervention, whether by foreign investment, notably in Malaysia and Thailand and initially in Mauritius, or foreign subcontracting of various forms, as in Mauritius, Jamaica and Bangladesh in clothing. In Malaysia, national government intervention also played an important role.

Local firms have had or are starting to have a more independent role, even where the initial foreign role was dominant, for example large Mauritian clothing companies and some of the Jamaican. It is still unclear, however, even in these cases, how far the countries would be able to manage a response to a new opportunity or obstacle on their own. The appearance of some local companies or managers with initial experience deriving from association with a foreign company but willing to attempt their own exporting, suggests that a 'sufficient' foreign presence and example may trigger a local response, but it is not clear what is the minimum level or duration. The share of foreign investors in even Malaysia's investment and trade is still high.

POLICY AS A REACTION TO POLICY

As well as responding in economic terms to the barriers, all of those countries for which exports are an important part of their economic strategy have also responded politically, by seeking to maintain or increase the trading preferences available to them. The higher concern with the trade policy of the industrial countries dates from 1974; it rose sharply in the late 1970s and in the 1980s; as protection rose in the industrial countries, active policy lobbying increased. Although Malaysia and Thailand are now active in promoting foreign investment, both have been and remain major and well-informed users of the only preference available to them, the GSP. The most active lobbyists have been Jamaica[1] (especially in the USA recently, but traditionally and for its traditional products in the EC) and Mauritius. Bangladesh took some part in clothing pressure groups during the Uruguay Round, and there was lobbying on its behalf when quotas were imposed in 1985, but it could not be said to have taken a continuing independent initiative on this. Colombia and Zimbabwe have been (until recently) less interested. The lobbying has in general been to preserve preferences (including preventing new quotas for others) rather than for either increased preferences or freer trade in general, and therefore reflects a basically conservative[2] approach to trade policy on the part of the developing country governments, as of course it is in the industrial countries imposing the protection. In the documented cases of Colombia and Jamaica in the USA (UNECLAC, 1990), lobbying was to promote coffee and tourism respectively, not new exports, and more recently (Bernal, 1991, 1992 on NAFTA for Jamaica) to protest against preferences for others.

The greater than average politicisation of trade in the 1980s may prove to have been a temporary phase, triggered by the recession in the industrial countries, and the consequent growth in the barriers, reinforced by the emphasis on the part of some researchers and international institutions on the role not just of trade but of trade policy in the success of the NICs. It reached a peak in the late 1980s and early 1990s with the US shift to unilateral intervention, the EC self-preoccupation in the steps towards the Single European Market, and the final years of Japanese acquiescence in external pressure on its trade. The end of at least the second and third of these came in 1993. The Uruguay Round settlement brought a possibility of reducing the first, and of resuming the pre-1974 progress towards a more regulated and more liberal international trade regime. Industrial countries may draw back from detailed intervention, and the understanding of why developing countries succeed has moved away from emphasis on their trade policy to other sectors and other types of intervention.

Some of the reasons for different approaches to trade policy emerge clearly from the country studies and this summary. The importance of international trade to a country's economy, whether because of its physical size or the nature of other external influences, is clearly fundamental. Colombia can take a casual view of trade policy because it has a substantial domestic market and many of its companies are large and well-established. Exports are typically 20% of their total sales, and the country as a whole has had good fortune in discovering new exports through natural resources. Zimbabwe, because of its period of isolation, is relatively self-sufficient for its size, but is much smaller, in population and income, and neither its economy nor its companies are as well established. It has followed a similar pattern of neglecting exports, but is now shifting to more deliberate export promotion as this approach becomes clearly insufficient for sustained rapid growth. Thailand, although large enough to follow a slow strategy like Colombia, has moved into exports much earlier, in order to permit more rapid growth, perhaps spurred by the example of its neighbours.

Malaysia, which is extremely aware of its relatively small size (by Asian standards), Mauritius, and Jamaica have little choice but to take an active interest in exports.

Bangladesh is large, but poor and with very young firms. The reason for its policy-makers' lack of interest in exports (and the rather less committed approach by many of its manufacturers) is more likely to lie in the small role of exports relative to aid or migrants' earnings in its external economy. They are not quantitatively the major part of its external strategy as they are in all the other countries. (The lack of interest on the part of its aid donors, particularly the international institutions which have stressed the role of exports in the NICs, is more puzzling.) Although Bangladesh is an extreme example, a high level of dependence on other types of external income is not unusual for a developing country at an early stage of its development. Aid dependence, however, can also reinforce a country's perception of trade as basically policy-determined, especially because so many of its imports are influenced by policy as well: in type, direction, or price.

Dependence on aid, rather than exports, may have other effects on reactions to barriers to trade, and to processing in particular. In Bangladesh, and to a lesser extent in Zimbabwe, the bias of aid donors has been towards infrastructure and agriculture. As long as this characterises a major source of investment finance, it reinforces any bias of the trading system against industrialisation. This is in sharp contrast to the type of foreign intervention and financing through foreign investment in manufactures found in Malaysia, Thailand, or Mauritius.

In Zimbabwe and in Bangladesh most notably, and perhaps also in Colombia, it is clear that industrial decision-makers have not had the same degree of cooperation with their own government, and trust in the basic benevolence and consistency of policy, as those in the NICs have had. Among the countries considered here, certainly Malaysia and Mauritius, probably Thailand, have had this trust. Jamaica seems intermediate. This can affect reactions to other countries' policies in two ways. Exporters do not expect the same degree of government intervention on their behalf in response to foreign policies, and they are less likely to have confidence in the preferences of other governments if they judge these in the light of their local experience. They are therefore less likely to build their own production around available preferences and quotas. Mauritians and Malaysians, in contrast, may have much greater confidence in the willingness and ability of their governments to institute effective policies and to influence those of others and also in the reliability of others' preferences. The interaction of countries' own characteristics with the preferences which they face provides convincing explanations for their attitudes to and use of preferences.

Mauritius is small. Its industries trust their own government. It has access to strong preferences, and, in the early 1980s, it faced few quotas. It is not surprising therefore that it has followed a highly preference- and quota-based trade strategy. It was able to exploit its advantages because it had some established exporters of its own (although these were not active in the right products) and an impulse from foreign investors and contractors in clothing, and in some of its minor exports. Its location and its policy on education and training provided the infrastructure pre-conditions.

Jamaica is similar, with a less close relationship between industry and government but with even greater preferences, and more access to foreign contracting and investment because it has the option of using the various US schemes as well as all the EC ones available to Mauritius. Its traditional exports, however, remain more important to it than they are to Mauritius, which slightly reduces its interest in trade policy. Its trade infrastructure is also poorer. It is less active and less committed to seeking trade preferences, but still probably comes second only to Mauritius.

Malaysia is not so small, but feels itself to be. There is trust now (not in earlier years) between industry and government, but it never had as ready access to preferences. It is now, however, moving beyond the relevant high tariff-facing stage of industry.

Thailand uses preferences more, and takes more interest in them, because its exports are different in composition. But its lack of access to any special preferences and the lack of a tradition of active government assistance have kept this usage well below the Mauritian level.

Zimbabwe is developing a closer relationship between industry and government, and sees more need to promote trade, as it becomes less satisfied with its rate of development. It is moving into more interest in and more reliance on trade policies, both its own and foreign ones.

Colombia is large. Its government has political and military worries which are more important than trade. Its industries have more important domestic markets. It is only recently that it has received important special preferences, both regional and to the US and the EC, and there is no tradition of relying on them. New exporters are responding as exporters do in the smaller countries, but neither trade nor trade policy is as crucial to Colombia's development as they are to the other countries.

For Bangladesh, poor markets should mean attention to exports. But lack of relationships between exporters and the government and the existence of much larger external links in the forms of aid and migrants' remittances mean that efforts are diverted away from trade policy to seeking other external support.

TRADE STRUCTURE AND HOW IT CHANGES

The evidence here also suggests some conclusions about the nature of the role of external trade in developing countries. The most obvious is how quickly trade composition and also foreign investment can change. To characterise countries as, for example, 'clothing exporters' or dependent on foreign investment or aid lacks any long-term meaning. The figures for the way clothing exports can change bear repeating. For Thailand, from zero in the 1970s to 7% of exports in 1980, peaking at 12–14% before 1990 and hitting quotas; now in decline, almost before academic analyses made on the way up can conclude that they were not constrained by quota. For Mauritius, from under 10% in 1976 to over 50% and subject to a quota in 1986; to full utilisation of quotas in the late 1980s, and decline by 1992. For Jamaica, 2% in 1980, 10% in 1985, 23% in 1987, probably flat since then. The largest relative to exports, although the least relative to manufacturing in the economy as a whole, is Bangladesh: zero in 1977, over 10% in 1984, 50% in 1991/2, with the first signs of under-utilisation of quotas by 1992/3. Figures for the growth of total manufactured exports are often as striking (as they were for the four Asian NICs from 1970 to 1980).

The results highlight long-term relationships in trade, but they are found in different forms in different industries, and show themselves in a variety of ways in trade or investment data. This suggests that, rather than looking specifically at characteristics either of countries and trade or of multinational firms, it may be more useful to look at characteristics of particular industries, and how the advantages of long-term relationships and the need for long-term familiarity with markets and between purchasers and suppliers are achieved using a variety of different legal arrangements. Foreign investment for export is one way of achieving this, and has been important (in these countries) in machinery and also in some basic primary goods.

In clothing, the long-term relationships are more likely to be informal networks between some traders or producers and final markets. The figures quoted above for individual countries' exports show how these operate in the face of the imposition of quotas. The evidence across all these countries is that, whether through investment or other forms of purchasing or subcontracting, Asian companies have had a major role. Thus, although the clothing industry appears to be one not dominated by large firms, the role of existing firms in the supply chain may make local producers as dependent on decisions by foreign firms as if they were subsidiaries of multinationals. (There are similar network patterns, often with an ethnic element, in the industry within and among industrial countries.)

Tension in trade and trade policy can arise when the importance of long-term relationships and stability of supply and marketing conflicts with the wishes and ability of some countries or suppliers to develop extremely rapidly. The reaction of the industrial countries in the 1970s, of seeking to slow adaptation by putting country and product quotas on to developing country exports, while failing to recognise that imports were more tied to supplying companies than to the supplying countries, helped to produce the type of artificial spread of production seen in clothing in the 1980s.

The longer-term effects of the protection are also less obvious than looking only at effects on clothing production and trade and static competitiveness might imply. Just as not having or losing preferences can be interpreted as being as damaging as facing trade discrimination (the arguments which appeared during the Uruguay Round for compensating developing countries for any loss in the margin of preference given by GSP or Lomé when MFN tariffs were reduced), it is clear that not having quotas acted as a preference for the countries discussed here whose clothing industries date from the early 1980s. But, as with industries created by import substitution through protection, while clothing might not have been the most suitable export at that time for all of them, and some might never have moved into it without quotas on other countries and the intervention of foreign investors or agents, this does not mean that the industry or its influence will disappear if the quotas are now removed. The discussion in Chapter 14 of the long-term effects on Bangladesh, apparently the least trade-affected economy, suggested that temporary exemption from quotas was one way of injecting the foreign interest and experience which is desirable, if not essential, to stimulate new exporters.

Whether a quota or preference or other external intervention produces a sustainable development must depend on three elements: the size of the action; the share of exports in the economy; and the readiness of the economy to respond: its infrastructure, training, and existing firms. Malaysia and Thailand received weak preferences, but had high exports and good conditions for industrialisation and export. Mauritius and Jamaica were high scorers on size of preference and share of exports, and now probably are on ability to respond, but they may still need continuing favourable external shocks. Zimbabwe still relies mainly on the first, the level of preference, but it is doing better on responsiveness. Colombia has had sufficiently large benefits from natural external shocks, including the discovery of new resources, not to need as large a policy stimulus, and it scores well on broadly defined infrastructure. Bangladesh has a low share of exports and poor infrastructure, so the risk of now losing its favoured quota status is the most serious.

THE COSTS OF INDIRECT PROTECTION

Preferences (including the implicit preference of not being subject to quota) serve in principle the same purpose as national protection to promote import substitution. They stimulate initial production and offset some of the economic or institutional barriers to entry for a new producer. They are a way of implementing a policy of encouraging a specific sector or activity, in particular, industrialisation, which is considered to have an importance in development strategy beyond simply contributing to growth in national output. In a country with a small domestic market (whether because of absolute size or poverty), preference for an export may be more effective than protection for import substitutes.

There are significant differences between the two policies. The most obvious is that preferences are chosen by the market country, not the developing country, and substitute locations when quotas are imposed either by purchasers in the market country or by producers in the quota-controlled countries. Secondly, the costs of protection are allocated differently. Initially, preferences place the cost of helping the industry in the preferred country partly on industry in the market country and partly on industry in competing and non-preferred countries, with some benefits to purchasers in the market country. Exemption from quotas puts the costs principally on the quota-controlled countries, and also on the market country's purchasers.

Protection puts the cost on purchasers in the developing country, with some impact on the former exporting country. In most cases, therefore, it could be argued that national protection is the most costly, but is potentially most effective for the developing country (as it can choose the sector to protect). Taking advantage of others' quotas is the lowest-cost tool, but is least under the exporting country's own discretion.

WHAT IS A PRODUCT

Looking at products in terms of conventionally defined related industries is not helpful. On the one hand, processing of one product may be more closely related to processing another than either is to its apparent raw material or to other stages of processing in terms of the type of labour and capital input and experience needed. As noted above, clothing and footwear were more likely to be found with each other than with cotton or animal production or with fabric or leather producing and finishing. This suggests that, while the fact that tariffs are higher on processed than on primary goods clearly has a potential distorting effect on trade, the concept of 'tariff escalation' – computing the tariff specifically on the processing of a com-

286

modity by comparing one level with the next – may often tell little about the real cost of protection because it does not measure the alternative opportunities for a country producing at the lower stage. Moving from stage one (for example, growing and spinning cotton) to stage two (finishing and dyeing) may not be an option because stage two is technology- or capital-intensive, while stage three (making clothing) may be a reasonable option whether or not a country has its own cotton or its own textiles. Marketing and design may be further separable activities. On the other hand, this conclusion suggests that rules of origin imposing a high 'local content' requirement as a condition for preference may be more onerous and distorting for all countries, not just small ones, than they have been judged. It suggests that there is no economic logic to treating a purely processing or assembly industry as artificial, or as constituting *prima facie* evidence of exploiting a preference loophole.

On the other hand, firms may be not 'clothing producers' but trading conglomerates, producing sugar, clothing, and tourist facilities (and employing potentially the same workers or their family members in all of these). For this reason, individual producers may be less, not more, vulnerable than sectors, to economic or policy changes. Policy-makers may therefore be less subject to sectoral vested interests of the conventional type than much economic policy discussion assumes.

Looking at products also obscures the role of exchange of technology, especially the technology of being a manager and exporter or of being a semi-skilled worker, among firms. In many of the countries studied, the background of the local clothing or other new managers was not in anything related to their current product, but rather in either general engineering training or training in a company in another country. These managers could have responded equally to any other industry for which there were the special conditions enjoyed by clothing in the 1980s, and they (or their juniors) could do so to other conditions in the absence of clothing. The question in some of the countries is whether, given the size of the country and its short history of industry and exporting, there are now enough of these companies and managers to replace a loss of the foreign interest created by external policies, especially in the absence of an effective substitute from government policy, and, in Bangladesh, the presence of implicit discouragement on the part of the major providers of finance.

THE RESULTS OF OFFICIAL AND PRIVATE EXTERNAL POLICIES

In the countries studied here, the operation of external controls on them and on their competitors has, as expected, had long-term effects on their productive structure and on their potential for future development and structural change. The bias towards primary production and against manufactures of the tariff system, preferences and trading blocs, the operation of quotas, and the preferences of aid donors, have all deterred movement into manufactures and stimulated moves into new primary exports instead. Some countries have benefited from preferences or from absence of quotas; they have had short-term gains in the value of exports and potentially long-term gains in experience of producing for export. In all cases, however, these gains have been simultaneously offset by other barriers, by the risk of entering a quota-controlled industry, possibly by diversion of resources into preference-seeking or quota-avoiding,[3] and, often very quickly, by quotas on their own exports. It is difficult, in the absence of any uncontrolled countries or world system to supply a realistic alternative, to compute a balance of costs and benefits, but it is clear that there has been at world level a loss of efficiency in redistributing production to less suitable (and, usually, to too many) suppliers. The clothing industry is the most common example found here.

If the period of preference (whether direct or by means of not having quotas) has brought in the foreign influence needed to stimulate exports, or has stimulated existing domestic firms into exporting on a sufficient scale relative to domestic demand or other foreign influences, then it may have altered the economy permanently towards exports, provided that the other conditions in the domestic and external economy permit this: infrastructure, physical and training; level of barriers on the intermediate stage of production where these countries are likely to find themselves. If the foreign impulse or the resulting national one can last long enough to move the country's trading sector beyond this into the declining barrier stage occupied by the industrial countries and perhaps the NICs, this may be considered to be sustainable development. Malaysia is approaching this stage.

Preferences, quotas, and protection are not the only way of obtaining this stimulus. Countries with strong natural advantages – natural resources or exceptionally cheap labour – may attract foreign investment without them, and some investors, like Hong Kong, would certainly have moved out of their own country into some alternative supplier at some point. But the countries with preferences clearly had an advantage in attracting this, and the threat and later the reality of the spread of quotas probably led to a much more scattered pattern of clothing production. Not all those who were moved into clothing would have had the opportunity, but some of them might have had greater and more influential flows of foreign investment.

The source of capital is not directly relevant to the subject of this book, but it brings us back to the question of the difference between public and private external constraints on trade. The lower-income countries face mainly the first, but (through companies' responses to quotas) also some of the second. The higher-income have more of the second, but still face preferences and quotas. But superimposed on this normal pattern, the growth in protection in the 1970s and 1980s meant that all countries faced more official controls, quotas, complicated levels of preference, and varying preference areas, than in the past, while the decline of foreign investment during the 1980s made aid flows more important in relative terms in all developing countries than they had been in the 1960s or 1970s.

Both public and private interventions respond to decisions taken outside a developing country and (except for the largest countries) in ways which it cannot influence. In that, both are constraints on its trade. The public interventions, however, are intended (however misguided they may seem in some cases) to protect some combination of the national and the private interest in the developed country, and in some cases the donor's view of the interests of the recipient. They may therefore be relatively unsusceptible to economic arguments or actions by the developing country, but they may be vulnerable to political intervention by it or to negotiation. The private interventions will be in the private interests of a company in the developed country, and therefore at least potentially susceptible to economic intervention by private or government interests in the developing country. This means that the nature of the response which is encouraged in the developing country is different. Whether a particular developing country prefers one or the other will depend therefore not only on the nature or value of a particular intervention, but also on whether the country wishes to take an interventionist approach to development and on whether private interests there have a tradition of seeking or trusting official intervention. Both choices, to seek preferences or investors, have been found in the case studies; both have potential for success. The preference for one or the other may also, of course, differ between official and private interests in the developing country.

Government intervention may be more rigid, and long-lasting, in part because it may be perceived as an official guarantee (the Multi-Fibre Arrangement; regulation of agriculture in the industrial countries), which a government has a duty to maintain. The private control of a market may be easier for a new entrant from a developing country to break into (or at least no more difficult than for a new entrant from a developed country): the appearance of local competition for electronics companies in Malaysia and Thailand, in some cases using people trained in the multinationals. That this can happen is the argument basic to the technology-transfer case for foreign investment.

If there is an important difference in the implications for development between official and private constraints in international markets, then the implications of imposing more official regional trading groups differ from the simple regionally-biased response to regional growth which has appeared in the past. This interpretation also implies important differences between the 'globalisation' of production based only on the activities of multinational companies and deliberate attempts at opening markets to imports or foreign investment on the part of governments or official international agencies. Official promotion of a country's trade or investment through national subsidies or policy pressure on market countries is as market-distorting as official restraints on trade. This is seen here in the effects of quotas on non-quota third countries. It is also as much a 'politicising' of trade and production signals to private firms, and to public perceptions in developing countries of how the international system works.

In the 1990s, if the trends towards declining intervention in trade and increasing foreign investment, and also the falling rates of growth of official assistance, all continue, then there may be a return to more importance for private rather than official external intervention. This does not mean that, in terms of products or trade flows covered, the scope of all external control will necessarily be different, especially if proper allowance is made for the role of other long-term trade relationships, in addition to those through foreign investment, as barriers to entry. It does not alter the realities of the economic weakness of small or poor countries or those still outside the existing networks. Potentially, however, it reduces the bargaining strength of those countries with special political or other claims on industrial countries, relative to the economic strength of high-income or rapidly growing countries. It can, therefore, offer developing countries more potential to influence their trading performance through economic changes in their own countries and their own policies.

NOTES

1 UNECLAC (1990) documents this for lobbying by foreign governments in the US, with Colombia and Jamaica among the leading countries.
2 In the Corden sense of a conservative welfare function.
3 It is not necessary to accept the argument that preference-seeking creates a long-term culture of dependency to note that the need for any exporter to keep and consult full documentation on a complicated preference or quota scheme has the immediate effect of diverting some efforts from other ways of improving efficiency of sales or output.

GENERAL BIBLIOGRAPHY

Anderson, K. and Blackhurst, R. (eds) (1993) *Regional Integration and the Global Trading System*, Harvester Wheatsheaf, Hemel Hempstead.

Balasubramanyam, V.N. and Greenaway, D. (1992) 'Regionalism and FDI: The Case of East Asian Investment in Europe', paper presented at Annual Conference of International Economics Study Group, University of Nottingham, September.

Baldwin, R.E. (1989) *Measuring Non-Tariff Trade Policies*, National Bureau of Economic Research, Working Paper No. 2978, NBER, Cambridge MA.

Bank for International Settlements (1993) *63rd Annual Report*, BIS, Basle.

Banks, G. (1983) 'The Economics and Politics of Countertrade', *The World Economy*, 6 (2).

Barbone, Luca (1988) 'Import Barriers: An Analysis of Time-Series Cross-Section Data', OECD *Economic Studies*, 11/Autumn, OECD, Paris.

Beetz, C. and Van Ryckeghem, W. (1993) 'Trade and Investment Flows Between Europe and Latin America and the Caribbean', Intra-American Development Bank. Background paper for seminar on Latin America's competitive position in the enlarged European Market, Hamburg, March.

Chirathivat, S. (1992) 'External Economic Influences, Regional Cooperation and the Role of Thailand as a Newly-Industrialising Country', paper presented at the Conference *The Making of a Fifth Tiger? Thailand's Industrialisation and Its Consequences*, Australian National University, 7–9 December.

Clark, D.P. (1991) *Incidence of Non-Tariff Measures on Imports of GSP-Covered Products*, UNCTAD, Geneva.

Davenport, M. and Page, S. (1991) *Europe 1992 and the Developing World*, ODI, London.

de Rosa, Dean A. (1986) 'Trade and Protection in the Asian Developing Region', *Asian Development Review*, Asian Development Bank, Manila.

Erzan, R. and Svedberg, P. (1989) *Protection Facing Exports from Sub-Saharan Africa in the EC, Japan, and the United States*, The World Bank, International Economics Department, WPS 320, Washington DC.

Finger, J.M. and Olechowski, A. (1987) *The Uruguay Round: A Handbook on the Multilateral Trade Negotiations*, The World Bank, Washington DC.

GATT (1991) *Trade Policy Review, The European Communities*, vols 1 and 2, GATT, Geneva.

GATT (1992) *Trade Policy Review, The United States*, vols 1 and 2, GATT, Geneva, April.

GATT (1993) *An Analysis of the Proposed Uruguay Round Agreement, with Particular Emphasis on Aspects of Interest to Developing Economies*, GATT Secretariat, Geneva, November.

Hammond, G.T. (1990) *Countertrade, Offsets and Barter in International Political Economy*, Pinter Publishers, London.

Havrylyshyn, O. (1988) *Trade Control Measures and Developing Country Trade. An analysis using the UNCTAD Trade Information System (TIS) Data Base.* Trade Information System on Barriers to Trade Among Developing Countries, UNCTAD/UNDP Study, Geneva.

Healey, D. (1991) *Japanese Capital Exports and Asian Economic Development*, OECD, Development Centre Studies, Paris.

Helleiner, G.K. and Lavergne, R. (1979) 'Intra-Firm Trade and Industrial Exports to the United States', *Oxford Bulletin of Economics and Statistics*, XLI (4) November.

Hveem, H. (1989) *Countertrade: The Global Perspective*, Oslo Countertrade Project Report No, 1. Program for International Development Research, University of Oslo.

IDE (Institute of Developing Economies) (1990) *Trade Policies Towards Developing Countries*, IDE, Tokyo.

Inter-American Development Bank (1993) *Economic and Social Progress in Latin America*, IDB, Washington DC.

IMF, *International Financial Statistics*, Monthly and Yearbooks, IMF, Washington DC.

IMF, *Exchange Arrangements and Exchange Restrictions*, Annual Report, IMF, Washington DC.

IMF, *Direction of Trade Statistics*, Yearbooks, IMF, Washington DC.

IMF, *Balance of Payments Statistics*, Yearbooks, IMF, Washington DC.

IRELA (1993) *El Mercado Unico Europeo y su Impacto en América Latina*, Instituto de Relaciones Europeo-Latinoamericanas, Madrid.

International Trade Centre UNCTAD/GATT (1988) *Countertrade Information Resource File*, ITC, Geneva, April.

Jones, C.D. (1983) *Visible Imports Subject to Restraint*, Government Economic Service Working Paper No.62, Department of Trade and Industry, London.

Jones, S.F. (1984) *North/South Counter-trade Barter and Reciprocal Trade with Developing Countries*, The Economist Intelligence Unit, London.

Jones, S.F. and Jagoe, A. (1988) *Third World Countertrade*, International Marketing and Research Produce Studies, Newbury.

Kostecki, M. (1987) 'Should One Countertrade?', GATT paper, GATT, Geneva.

Kuwayama, M. (1992) *New Forms of Investment (NFI) in Latin America–United States Trade Relations*, Economic Commission for Latin America and the Caribbean-ECLAC, Working Paper No.7, United Nations, Santiago, September.

Laird, S. and Yeats, A. (1990) *Quantitative Methods for Trade-Barrier Analysis*, Macmillan, Basingstoke and London.

Lipsey, R.E. (1991) 'Foreign Direct Investment in the United States and US Trade', *Annals of the American Academy of Political and Social Science*, 516, July.

Little, J.S. (1987) 'Intra-Firm Trade: An Update', *New England Economic Review*, May/June.

Oman, C. (1994) *Globalisation and Regionalisation: the Challenge for Developing Countries*, OECD, Paris.

Organization of American States (1992) *CECON News*, Washington DC, October.

OECD, *Geographical Distribution of Financial Flows to Developing Countries*, OECD, Paris. Various issues.

OECD *Development Co-operation*, OECD Report, Paris. Various issues.

Page, S. (1979) 'The Management of International Trade', in R. Major (ed.), *Britain's Trade and Exchange Rate Policy*, Heinemann, London.

Page, S. (1981) 'The Revival of Protectionism and its Consequences for Europe', *Journal of Common Market Studies*, September.

Page, S. (1986) *Relocating Manufacturing in Developing Countries: Opportunities for UK Companies*, National Economic Development Office, Economic Working Paper 25, NEDO, London.

Page, S. (1987) 'The Rise in Protection since 1974', *Oxford Review of Economic Policy* 3 (1), Spring.

Page, S. (1989) *Trade, Finance and Developing Countries: Strategies and Constraints in the 1990s*, ODI in association with Harvester Wheatsheaf, London and Hemel Hempstead.

Page, S. (1991) 'Europe 1992: Views of Developing Countries', *Economic Journal* 101, November.

Page, S. (1992) *Some Implications of Europe 1992 for Developing Countries*, OECD Development Centre, Technical Papers No.60, OECD, Paris.

Page, S. with Davenport, M. and Hewitt, A. (1991) *The GATT Uruguay Round: Effects on Developing Countries*, ODI, London.

Ramstetter, E.D. (ed.) (1991) *Direct Foreign Investment in Asia's Developing Economies and Structural Change in the Asia Pacific Region*, Westview Press, Boulder CO.

Ramstetter, E.D. (1992) 'Prospects for Foreign Firms in Developing Economies of the Asian and Pacific Region', ADB Development Round Table on Foreign Investment in the Asian and Pacific Region, Kansai University, Japan.

Ray, E.J. (1981) 'Determinants of Tariff and Non-tariff Trade Restrictions in the US', *Journal of Political Economy* 89, 105–21.

Riedel, J. (1991) 'Intra-Asian Trade and Foreign Direct Investment', *Asian Development Review*, 9(1).

Rugman, A.M. and Eden, L. (eds) (1985) *Multinationals and Transfer Pricing*, Croom Helm, London.

Rutter, J. (1991) *Trends in International Direct Investment*, US Department of Commerce, International Trade Administration, TIA Staff Paper Series, Staff Paper No. 91–5. USDC, Washington DC.

Safadi, R and Yeats, A. (1993) *Asian Trade Barriers Against Primary and Processed Commodities*, The World Bank, Policy Research Working Papers WPS 1174, World Bank, Washington DC.

Stewart, F. and Singh, Harsha.V. (1988) 'Do Third World Countries Benefit from Countertrade?' in Sidney Dell (ed.), *Policies for Development: Essays in Honour of Gamani Corea*, Macmillan, Basingtoke and London.

Tambunlertchai, S. (1993) 'Foreign Trade and Investment Nexus in Asia and the Pacific', paper submitted to the International Trade and Tourism Division, ESCAP, January.

Taniuchi, M. (1992) *Foreign Direct Investment in the Asia Pacific Region – Its Recent Dynamic Development and Major Issues*, Paper No.15, Japan Center for Economic Research, Tokyo.

Tran van Tho (1989) *Direct Foreign Investment*, Japan Centre for Economic Research, Tokyo.

Turner, P. (1990) *Foreign Direct Investment in the Developing World: The Experience of the 1980s*, Bank for International Settlements, Basle.

UK Department of Trade and Industry (1990) *Security Export Control*, British Overseas Trade Board, London.

UK Department of Trade and Industry Database on Countertrade Deals.

United Nations (1992) *World Economic Survey*, New York.

United Nations Statistical Office *Monthly Bulletin of Statistics*, United Nations, New York. Various issues.

UNCTAD, *Database on Trade Measures*, UNCTAD, Geneva.

UNCTAD *Handbook of International Trade and Development Statistics*, UNCTAD, Geneva. Various issues.

UNCTAD (1983) *Protectionism, Trade Relations and Structural Adjustment*, Report by the UNCTAD Secretariat, Geneva.

UNCTAD (1986) *Problems of Protectionism and Structural Adjustment*, Introduction and Part I: Restrictions on trade and structural adjustment. Report by the UNCTAD Secretariat, Geneva.

UNCTAD (1988) *Protectionism and Structural Adjustment*, Statistical and Information Index, TD/B/1160/Add.1, UNCTAD, Geneva.

UNCTAD (1993a) *Trade and Development Report*, UNCTAD, Geneva.

UNCTAD (1993b) *World Investment Report: Transnational Corporations and Integrated International Production*, United Nations, New York.

United Nations Centre on Transnational Corporations (1988) *Transnational Corporations in World Development – Trends and Prospects*, United Nations, New York.

United Nations Centre on Transnational Corporations (1991) *World Investment Report 1991, The Triad in Foreign Direct Investment*, United Nations, New York.

United Nations Centre on Transnational Corporations (1992a) *World Investment Directory 1992, Volume 1, Asia and the Pacific*, United Nations, New York.

United Nations Centre on Transnational Corporations (1992c) *The Determinants of Foreign Direct Investment, A Survey of the Evidence*, United Nations, New York.

United Nations ECLAC (1990) *Latin American and Caribbean Lobbying for International Trade in Washington, D.C.* LC/G.1632, United Nations, Santiago.

United Nations Transnational Corporations and Management Division (1992b) *World Investment Report 1992. Transnational Corporations as Engines of Growth*, United Nations, New York.

van den Bulcke, D. (1985) *Intrafirm Trade of Multinational Enterprises: Characteristics and Implications for Developing Countries*.

Wagner, N. (1989) *ASEAN and the EC – European Investment in ASEAN*, Institute of Southeast Asian Studies, ASEAN Economic Research Unit, Singapore.

Walter, I. (1971) 'Non-tariff Barriers and the Export Performance of Developing Economies', *American Economic Association Papers and Proceedings*, 61 May.

Walter, I. (1972) 'Non-tariff protection among industrial countries, some preliminary empirical evidence', *Economia Internazionale* 55, May.

COUNTRY BIBLIOGRAPHY

MALAYSIA

Davenport, M. (1986) *Trade Policy, Protectionism and the Third World*, Croom Helm, Beckenham.

GATT (1993) *Trade Policy Review, Malaysia*, vols 1 and 2. GATT, Geneva.

Japan External Trade Organisation (JETRO) (1992) *Japanese Related Companies in Malaysia*, Kuala Lumpur, March.

Mahathir, M. (1992) 'Malaysia: The Way Forward', *Malaysian Management Review* 27(3) September.

Malaysia, Bank Negara Malaysia, *Annual Report*. Various issues.

MIDA (Malaysian Industrial Development Authority) (1990) *Annual Report*.

THAILAND

Chirathivat, S. (1991) 'Managing Thai Trade Policy to Better Access Developed Countries' Markets', *ASEAN Economic Bulletin* 8(1).

Chirathivat, S. (1992) 'External Economic Influences, Regional Cooperation and the Role of Thailand as a Newly-Industrialising Country', paper presented at the Conference *The Making of a Fifth Tiger? Thailand's Industrialisation and Its Consequences*, Australian National University, 7–9 December.

Chirathivat, S. (1992 3), data supplied to author.

Chirathivat, S. (1993) 'The New Global Context of EC–Thailand's Trade and Investment Relations', paper presented at the Conference *Thailand and the European Community: New Dimensions of Interdependence*, Chulalongkorn University, Bangkok.

Chunanunthathum, S. (1991) *The External Financing of Thailand's Imports*. Technical Papers: Special series on mixed credits, OECD Development Centre, Institute for International Economic Cooperation and Development (ICEPS), Paris.

GATT (1991) *Trade Policy Review – Thailand*, vols 1 and 2. GATT, Geneva.

Hill, H. and Suphachalsai, S. (1992) 'The Myth of Export Pessimism (even) under the MFA: Evidence from Indonesia and Thailand', *Weltwirtschaftliches Archiv* 128 (2).

Sibunruang, A. and Brimble, P. (1992) *Export Oriented Industrial Collaboration: A Case Study of Thailand*, prepared for the United Nations Centre on Transnational Corporations, Bangkok.

Suphalchalsai, S. (1990) 'Export Growth of Thai Clothing and Textiles', *The World Economy* 13(1) March.

Thailand, Bank of Thailand (1992), data supplied to author.

Thailand, Office of the Board of Investment (1992) *Key Investment Indicators of Thailand*, September.

COLOMBIA

ANDI (1992) *Revista ANDI 118*, September/October.
ANDI (1993) *Revista ANDI 120*, January/February.
Angel Arango, Carlos A. (1993) 'Los Avances en Materia de Integración', Bogotá, March.
Colombia (1992) *Anuario de Comercio Exterior 1990*, Columbia Departmento Administrativo National de Estadística, Bogota.
Colombia, Department of Planning, data supplied.
FEDESARROLLO (Fundación para la Educación Superior y el Desarrollo) (1993) *Resultados del modulo especial sobre la apertura economica*.
GATT (1990) *Trade Policy Review – Colombia*, GATT, Geneva.
Ocampo, José Antonio (1992) 'Colombia y la integración con México', *Coyuntura Económica* XXII (4) December.
Restrepo Palacios, Jorge (1992) 'Política Económica: Aproximación a un Análisis de la Politica de Apertura Económica', *Revista ANDI 118*, September/October.
Rodríguez, R. Luis Hernando (1992) 'Apertura Comercial y Crecimiento Económica', *Desarrollo y Sociedad* No. 30, September.

ZIMBABWE

Ndlela, Daniel B. and Robinson, Peter (1992) 'New Technologies and Export Orientation: A Study of African Manufactured Exports. The Zimbabwe Case Study', prepared for UN University – Institute for New Technologies.
Page, Sheila and Stevens, Christopher (1992) *Trading with South Africa: the Policy Options for the EC*, ODI Special Report, London.
Riddell, Roger C. (1990) ACP *Export Diversification: The Case of Zimbabwe*, ODI Working Paper 38, London.
Riddell, Roger C. (1992) *Zimbabwe: At the Heart of a Growing Region*, London, Economist Intelligence Unit Special Report No. M205, London.
Robinson, Peter (1993) 'Will Zimbabwean Industry Survive ESAP?', paper prepared for the Institute of Bankers of Zimbabwe.
Zimbabwe, Central Statistical Office, *Statistical Yearbook*.
Zimbabwe, Central Statistical Office, *Quarterly Digest of Statistics*.
ZimTrade (1992) *Export Directory of Zimbabwe 1992/3*, Harare.

MAURITIUS

Floyd, Katherine (1992) 'Export and Develop? Export Processing Zones as a strategy for development – the case of Mauritius', Part II Dissertation, Sidney Sussex College, Cambridge.
Fowdar, Narud (1992) 'Foreign Investment in the Mauritian Textiles and Clothing Industry', *Textile Outlook International*, November.
McQueen, Matthew (1990) *ACP Export Diversification: The Case of Mauritius*, ODI Working Paper 41, London.
Mauritius, Bank of Mauritius (1993) *Annual Report 1992*.
Mauritius, Chamber of Commerce and Industry (1992), *Annual Report 1991*.
Mauritius, Mauritius Export Development and Investment Authority (MEDIA) (no date) *Data for Investors*.

Mauritius, Mauritius Export Development and Investment Authority (MEDIA) (1988) *Mauritius Export Directory 1988–1989.*

Mauritius, Mauritius Export Development and Investment Authority (MEDIA) (1992) *Mauritius Export Directory 1992–1993.*

Mauritius, Ministry of Economic Planning and Development (MEPD) (1993) *National Development Plan 1992–1994*, 2 vols.

Mauritius, Ministry of Industry and Industrial Technology (MIIT) (1991) *Mauritius at Crossroads. The Industrial Challenges Ahead.*

Mauritius, Ministry of Industry and Industrial Technology (MIIT) (1992) *Industry Focus* No 1. November.

Mauritius, Ministry of Industry and Industrial Technology (MIIT) (1993) *Industry Focus* No. 4 and No. 5, March and April.

JAMAICA

Bank of Jamaica (1992) *Balance of Payments of Jamaica 1991.*

Bernal, Richard L. (1991) 'A Caribbean Perspective of the Enterprise for the Americas Initiative'. Paper presented at Seminar on the Caribbean and The Enterprise for the Americas Initiative, Kingston.

Bernal, Richard L. (1992a) 'The Implications of the NAFTA for Jamaica and the CBI Region: a Policy Proposal'. Statement before House Ways and Means Subcommittee on Trade, North American Free Trade Agreement Hearing, Washington DC.

Bernal, Richard L. (1992b) 'The Impact of NAFTA on the Economic Development of the Caribbean and US/Caribbean Trade'. Statement at the Hearing before the House Committee on Small Business, Washington DC.

Jamaica, JAMPRO (1992) *The Jamaican Textile and Apparel Industry.*

Jamaica, JAMPRO (1993), data supplied.

Jamaica, Jamaican Exporters' Association (1992) *The Jamaican Exporter.*

King, Peter (1993) 'Jamaica's External Economic Relations: CARICOM, NAFTA, GATT and the EEC'. Address given at 'The Jamaican Economy in a Changing World. The Way Forward: 1993/94 and Beyond', Headley Brown and Company, Seminar.

Stevens, C. (1990) *ACP Export Diversification: Jamaica, Kenya and Ethiopia*, ODI Working Paper No. 40, London.

BANGLADESH

Anderson, K.H, Hossain, N. and Sahota, G.S. (1991) 'The Effect of Labor Laws and Labor Practices on Employment and Industrialization in Bangladesh', *The Bangladesh Development Studies*, XIX(1and 2), 131–56.

Bakht, Z. (1992) *Bangladesh Industrial Sector Study*, a report prepared for the Asian Development Bank, January.

Bakht, Z. and Bhattacharya, D. (1991) 'Investment, Employment and Value Added in Bangladesh Manufacturing Sector in 1980s: Evidence and Estimate', The Bangladesh Development Studies, XIX (1 and 2) 1–50.

BGMEA Bangladesh Garment Manufacturers and Exporters Association, data supplied.

Bangladesh, Export Promotion Bureau (1991) *Annual Report 1990–91.*

Bangladesh, Export Promotion Bureau (1992a) *Export from Bangladesh 1972–73 to 1990–91.*

Bangladesh, Export Promotion Bureau (1992b) *Bangladesh Export Statistics 1990–91.*

Bhuyan, A.R. (1991) 'Expanding Cooperation in SAARC: Opportunities and Prospects in Some Neglected Areas', *Social Science Review* 8(1 and 2).

Bhuyan, A.R. and Rashid, M.A. (1992) *Trade Regimes and Industrial Growth: A Case Study of Bangladesh*, International Center for Economic Growth and Bureau of Economic Research, Dhaka University, Dhaka.

Bhuyan, A.R. and Rashid, M.A. (1993) *Trade Regimes and Industrial Growth: A Case Study of Bangladesh*, International Center for Economic Growth, San Francisco CA.

Eversley, J. (ed.) (1991) *The Multi-Fibre Arrangement and Developing Countries: Including a case-study on Bangladesh*, a discussion paper from the International Organization of Consumer Unions, April.

GATT (1992) *Trade Policy Review – Bangladesh*, vols 1 and 2, Geneva.

Hoffman, K. (1991) 'Transfer of Technology for Entrepreneurial Development in Bangladesh', in Proceedings of the GOB/ESCAP/UNCTC/UNIDO Workshop, held in Dhaka, Bangladesh, 4–8 March 1990, UNESCAP, Bangkok.

Jackson, B. (1992) *Threadbare. How the Rich Stitch up the World's Rag Trade*, World Development Movement, London.

Rahman, Sultan Hafeez (1992) 'Structural Adjustment and Macroeconomic Performance in Bangladesh in the 1980s', *The Bangladesh Development Studies* XX (2 and 3).

Rahman, Sultan Hafeez (1992) *Trade Policies and Industrialisation in Bangladesh: An Assessment*, (draft), March.

Rahman, Sultan Hafeez (1992) *Macroeconomic Performance, Stabilization and Adjustment: The Experience of Bangladesh in the 1980s*, BIDS Working Paper, March.

Sobhan, R. (ed.) (1990) *From Aid Dependence to Self-Reliance. Development Options for Bangladesh*, The University Press, Dhaka.

Sobhan, R (1991) 'An Industrial Strategy for Industrial Policy: Redirecting the Industrial Development of Bangladesh in the 1990s, *The Bangladesh Development Studies* XIX (1 and 2), March.

Spinanger, D. (1987) 'Will the Multi-fibre Arrangement Keep Bangladesh Humble?', *The World Economy*, 10 (1), March.

UNESCAP (1991) *Asia–Pacific TNC Review*, United Nations, ESCAP/UNCTC Publication Series A. No.8, New York.

INDEX